Praise for *The Bengalis*

'A fascinating, charming book that will give you insight into why we are the way we are, an enigmatic people.'—Pritish Nandy

'Replete with both serious, well-researched information and interspersed with wry, tongue-in-cheek commentary, Bengalis and "not-Bengalis" alike should congratulate the author for undertaking such a monumental task of defining an entire community.'—*The Statesman*

'Written with verve, energy, and polish, and drawing on considerable resources, both anecdotal and archival, Chakravarti's book takes its place beside other contemporary attempts at 'collective' portraiture, such as Jeremy Paxman's *The English* and John Hooper's *The Italians*.'—*The Hindu*

'*The Bengalis* is by far the best non-fiction book from India I have read this year!'—*Hindustan Times*

'*The Bengalis* is an important work, melding scholarship and reportage-fed analysis with style...the book will be read, defended and torn apart for years to come. For non-Bengalis, well, there's no better way of finding out what the "others" are all about.'—*OPEN*

'Chakravarti has written an excellent tome on the Bengalis...a unique genre: one that is both historically serious and culturally situated while being incredibly observant of our mores, language and myriad idiosyncrasies and being outrageously funny to boot.'—*Indian Express*

'I was deeply disappointed with this book. I was hoping to point out all the things the author had missed... but he seems to have covered everything... Chakravarti passes a difficult test with flying colours.'—*Swarajya*

'[A] compact and brilliant work...dazzling virtuosity... The clipped descriptions of Noakhali and Naxalbari are worthy of Hemingway.'—*The Tribune*

'*The Bengalis* is an astonishingly good book, written by an author at the height of his powers.'—*The Pioneer*

'Chakravarti has written a charming and serious book, which is fun to read...[His] wicked sense of humour makes this book a great read.'—*Business Standard*

'Wit and elegance are perfectly matched along with research to make this offering a real page-turner.'—*IANS*

'Chakravarti somewhat dons the hat of a later Wittgenstein...[he] dwells deep into various facets of what has gone to make up the Bengali identity over the recent centuries, not just through a nostalgic lens, but has been equally critical of Bengal society.'—*Deccan Chronicle*

'[A] remarkable feat.'—*Scroll.in*

'It's hard to enumerate all the salient features that mark a Bengali—love for Tagore, PhDs, football, nicknames, argument, and addas don't even start to cover it. [Chakravarti] makes a valiant stab at it in *The Bengalis*, his lively account of their history, politics, ethnic identity, warts and all.'—*Times of India*

'[A] definitive book on the Bengali community. It is no easy feat to put together an entire community within a book's pages but [Sudeep] does it with a lot of finesse...'—*New Asian Writing*

'Extensively researched, deeply felt and engagingly narrated, *The Bengalis* is a compelling read... The book will strike a chord with every Bengali. And perhaps some not-Bengalis too.'—*The Asian Age*

'Whether you are Bengali or not-Bengali, go ahead and read the book, if not for anything but for the sheer beauty of being allowed to understand (no, you don't have to necessarily empathise; Chakravarti himself doesn't seek it), indeed comprehend, a community that "lives under a vast sky".'—*kitaab.org*

'Chakravarti, whose ambition is daring, provides a roving writer's haptic sense of place and time...embraces the encyclopaedic mode, sauntering effortlessly between the past and present of his subject... Hence, his Bengal, rendered in prose that is often biting, is all-encompassing: two Bengals and the broader Bengali presence... I would especially recommend Chakravarti.'—*Biblio*

Books by Sudeep Chakravarti

NON-FICTION

The Bengalis: A Portrait of a Community (2017)

Clear. Hold. Build: Hard Lessons of Business and Human Rights in India (2014)

Highway 39: Journeys Through a Fractured Land (2012)

Red Sun: Travels in Naxalite Country (2008)

FICTION

The Baptism of Tony Calangute (2018)

The Avenue of Kings (2010)

Tin Fish (2005)

PLASSEY

THE BATTLE THAT CHANGED
THE COURSE OF INDIAN HISTORY

SUDEEP CHAKRAVARTI

ALEPH

ALEPH BOOK COMPANY
An independent publishing firm
promoted by Rupa Publications India

First published in India in 2020
by Aleph Book Company
7/16 Ansari Road, Daryaganj
New Delhi 110 002

ISBN: 978-81-943657-2-3

3 5 7 9 10 8 6 4

Printed at Parksons Graphics Pvt. Ltd, Mumbai

domina in caelis

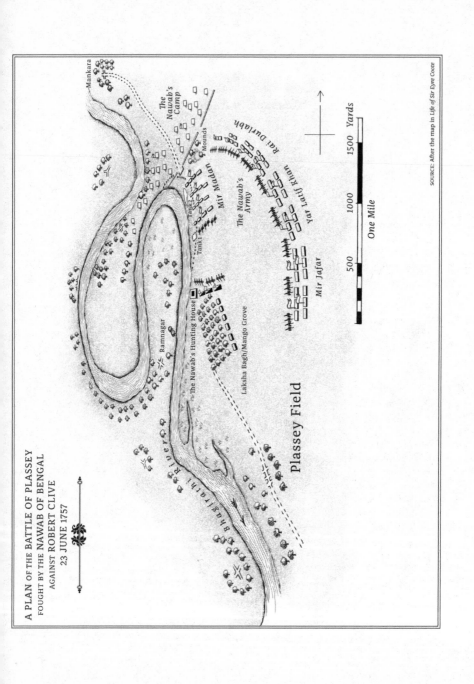

A PLAN OF THE BATTLE OF PLASSEY
FOUGHT BY THE NAWAB OF BENGAL
AGAINST ROBERT CLIVE
23 JUNE 1757

Mankara

The Nawab's Camp

Mounds

Mir Madan

Rai Durlabh

Tanks

Tanks

The Nawab's Army

Yar Latif Khan

Ramnagar

Mir Jafar

The Nawab's Hunting House

Laktsha Bagh/Mango Grove

Plassey Field

Bhagirathi River

500 1000 1500 Yards

One Mile

SOURCE: After the map in *Life of Sir Eyre Coote*

CONTENTS

CAST OF KEY CHARACTERS

Siraj-ud-daulah: Nawab of Bengal (April 1756–June 1757); Subahdar of Bengal, Bihar, and Orissa.

Alivardi Khan: Nawab of Bengal (1740–1756); Subahdar of Bengal, Bihar and Orissa. Siraj's maternal grandfather. Designated Siraj his heir. Alivardi's death triggered a chain of events culminating in Plassey.

Sharf-un-Nisa: Alivardi's wife, Siraj's grandmother.

Amina Begum: Alivardi's daughter, Siraj's mother.

Mir Madan: A commander in Siraj's army, and a loyalist. Played a pivotal role at Plassey. His death changed the complexion and, possibly, outcome of the battle.

Mohanlal: Siraj's confidante, diwan, and a commander at Plassey.

Lutf-un-Nisa: Siraj's principal wife.

Mirza Mahdi: Siraj's younger brother. Later given the title of Ikram-ud-daulah.

Jean Law: Chief of the French Company's trading post at Qasimbazar. Watts's rival. Conduit for Siraj's outreach to the French government in Pondicherry.

Renault de St Germain: Governor of the French settlement of Chandannagar (sometimes spelt Chandernagore), north of Calcutta along the Hugli River.

Jacques Ignace Courtin: French factory chief in Dhaka.

Robert Clive: Lieutenant Colonel in the East India Company's army that defeated Siraj-ud-daulah's forces at Plassey. Later Lord Clive, Baron Plassey. Negotiated from the Mughal emperor the formal grant of the diwani, or revenue administration of Bengal, for the Company. Plassey co-conspirator.

Mir Jafar: A general in the armies of both Alivardi and Siraj. Censured by Alivardi, and demoted by Siraj from the rank of paymaster general of the Bengal army. Plassey co-conspirator. Nawab of Bengal (July 1757–October 1760, and July 1763–February 1765).

Ghaseti Begum: Alivardi's daughter. Aunt and nemesis to Siraj. Conspired against Siraj after the death of her adopted son, Ikram-ud-daulah—Siraj's younger brother. Resident of the fabled Motijheel Palace.

'Jagat Seth' Madhab Rai: Head of an immensely powerful Murshidabad-based banking family, which also controlled Bengal's mint and managed the subah's revenues. Accorded the title 'banker to the world' by the Mughal emperor. Plassey co-conspirator.

'Maharaja' Swaroop Chand: Madhab Rai's cousin and partner in the family firm.

Rai Durlabh Ram: Influential Murshidabad courtier and commander. Plassey co-conspirator.

Mir Daud: Brother of Mir Jafar. Faujdar of Rajmahal. Arrested a fleeing Siraj.

Mir Miran: Mir Jafar's eldest son. Ordered Siraj's execution, and that of several of his family and retainers.

Charles Watson: Admiral in the Royal Navy. Commander of the joint Company & Crown force that took back Calcutta from Siraj's control in January 1757, and subsequently attacked the French settlement at Chandannagar.

William Watts: Chief of the Company trading post at Qasimbazar. Clive's eyes and ears at the Court of Murshidabad during the move northward from Calcutta to Plassey. Company resident at Murshidabad after Plassey. Co-conspirator.

Roger Drake: President in Council for the Company at Fort William, Calcutta.

John Zephaniah Holwell: Company surgeon. Inadvertent warrior during Siraj's siege of Calcutta and influential raconteur of the subsequent incident at the 'Black Hole'.

Major Eyre Coote: Officer of His Majesty's 39th Regiment of Foot. Participated in battles from the re-taking of Calcutta and the conquest of Chandannagar, Katwa, and Plassey. Voted for an immediate attack on Siraj at a pre-Plassey council of war convened by Clive, going against his commander's vote. Clive subsequently changed his mind and opted to attack immediately. Maintained a valuable journal of the campaign. Was later appointed commander-in-chief of British troops in India.

Major James Killpatrick: Officer of the Madras European Regiment. Engaged in battles from the re-taking of Calcutta and the conquest of Chandannagar, to Plassey. Voted against an immediate attack on Siraj, following Clive's cue, at the pre-Plassey council of war. In accounts of the time his name is sometimes spelled Kilpatrick.

Raja Nabakrishna: Munshi—clerk—to Clive, and later, Warren Hastings. Stood by Company employees during their exile from Calcutta after Siraj overran the settlement in June 1756. Accused of enriching himself with Plassey spoils.

Any work that sources material from various periods, languages and inflexions has to deal with matters of composite presentation. As with several other works of similar genre, this work too seeks to retain the original flavour of documents, books, and observations and, at the same time, attempts to convey the narrative to the specialist and general reader alike. This approach is impelled by, among other things, source material (books, essays, articles, and records of the British East India Company, for instance) in both archaic and modern English, material in archaic and modern Bengali, English phonetics applied to Indic and West Asian languages, and Indic phonetics applied to European languages.

For names of places this work employs Anglicized versions, such as Calcutta, as opposed to the more Bengali Kolkata of the present day (the city having officially jettisoned 'Calcutta'). Similarly, Madras instead of Chennai, and Mysore instead of Mysuru. While quoting from archival sources I have remained faithful to spellings of groups (Morattoes: Marathas), individuals (Jaffier Cawn: or Jafar Ali Khan Nasiri, which is how Murshid Quli Khan is sometimes referred to), places (Cossimbazar in documents, otherwise Qasimbazar), objects (chaubuc: chabuk: whip) and activities or expressions (expence: expense). Such phonetics and spellings are explained where necessary.

Sometimes places are spelt differently in the same document, such as 'Bengalla' and 'Bengala', for Bengal. At times, documents refer to the 'nabob' as well as the 'nobab'—the same as nawab. There's Hugli and Hooghly, used both for the river and the trading settlement which gave the name to a length of the river, otherwise the Bhagirathi—a distributary of the Ganga. In Western texts and records, Plassey is sometimes referred to as Plassy, Placy, Placis, and Palassy—but usually not Polāshi, the way Bengalis say it. Bahadur, or brave, is sometimes spelled 'bahadre' in Company records. As with punctuations and the archaic construction of sentences, these quirks are left undisturbed for authenticity when quoting archival sources, as are spellings and other grammatical usage in such sources.

The British East India Company is variously referred to as 'Company', 'the Company', and 'John Company', as distinct from the mercantile entities of other European nations—which are specifically identified with their names and nationalities. 'Plassey' is used in this work as much as the name of a place and location of the battle as, sometimes, the chain of events that led to it. 'Clive & Co.' is used for the potent combination of the British East India Company and one of its celebrated employees and militarists, Robert Clive.

There is the occasional use of Bengali—Bānglā—phonetics in this book, which seemed to me natural, as after all the theatre of Plassey and its immediate aftermath was set in Bengal, but mostly on account of this work referencing several sources in Bengali. For readers who are unfamiliar with the language and yet wish to pronounce it in a way that does not require them to use the expertise of the linguist and scholar (Bengali in Roman script is a complicated matter), some established norms have been modified after consulting linguists and scholars.

This has meant avoiding transliteration and what is called the International Phonetic Alphabet, and staying closer to transcription. The arrangement is not perfect, but is intended to reach an audience beyond that of the linguist, scholar, and reader of Bengali. To reduce confusion, it is applied mostly to a few vowels. An example: if Bānglā were to be written as Bangla, then those familiar with pronunciation in English but unfamiliar with the language of the Bengalis may pronounce it as Bang (as in 'hang') la. The emphasis on ā removes both that possibility and the need to write it as the more cumbersome Baangla.

For 'aw' as in 'thaw' the capital or lower-case 'o' is employed, distinct from the 'o' as in 'go'—which is shown in this book as 'ō'. For the 'ay' sound 'é' is applied. 'U' and 'i' are left alone. So 'u' is used both for the softer and extended 'oo' that Bengali has. For the soft and extended 'ee' (as one would the 'i' in 'indicate' and the extended 'ee' sound in 'unleash'.), 'i' is used. I was advised that the use of diacritics in 'u' and 'i' would complicate matters—best to keep things as simple as possible, but for a few extended 'ee' sounds for which 'i' is entirely inadequate.

Unless specified, translations and interpretations from Bengali to English are mine.

WHO? WHAT? WHERE? WHY? HOW?

'...the low falsehoods this dispute has brought to the fore'

Plassey, if you are British, or if you are much of the world, as once the British imagined they were. Palasi, if you are Indian. And, if you are Bengali, Polāshi, the place of flowering polāsh trees, flame of the forest.

Beyond different pronunciations, it's a place of history, deceit, victory, defeat, even a lament—a Rashomon of collective and selective memories.

Some say India was won, or lost, at Plassey, when forces of the British East India Company led by Lieutenant Colonel Robert Clive defeated the compromised forces of the young nawab Siraj-ud-daulah. Others claim an extension of the stumbling, fracturing Mughal India, bereft of any mooring after the death of Emperor Aurangzeb in 1707, lost to aggressive British mercantilism married to geopolitics. Siraj-ud-daulah, the subahdar or governor of the Mughal subah or province of Bengal, Bihar, and Orissa, was defeated as much or more by a grand conspiracy between the ambitious and rancorous his courtiers and generals, a deeply resentful aunt, a vastly influential Bengal banker, and the Company, as the rout at Plassey. Siraj's defeat established the Company as a regional power in India. The British already had an impressive foothold in Calcutta, and were well-placed, as events would demonstrate, to leverage that into great strides for control of eastern India.

Whatever the nuances, in a hundred years from a memorable victory in a brief battle on 23 June 1757, fought by a mango orchard—today a four-hour train ride north of Calcutta-now-Kolkata—the British went from being a significant European power in the Indian subcontinent to the only real power. The equally ambitious French company, the briefly soaring Dutch enterprise, and the freely marauding Marathas, who emerged as a significant political force in the subcontinent in the late seventeenth century with their tearaway chieftain Shivaji, were left in the wake of the surging British East India Company and the British government. It's significant that Siraj's taking of Calcutta from the Company on 20 June 1756 (the much-debated Black Hole incident ensued that night, during which several dozen Britons and a few Europeans and Eurasians were kept in a small cell in Fort William, leading to numerous deaths), the subsequent Company and Crown fightback from December 1756, the retaking of Calcutta by Clive & Co. in January 1757, the British attack on the French settlement at Chandannagar (or Chandernagore) upriver from Calcutta that March, and the Battle of Plassey were undertaken without so much as a by-your-leave from the Mughal court. A court to which both Siraj and the Company owed, at least on paper, their position and privileges.

Delhi was its own diminishing island of the Mughals' faded glory and fading symbolism, a pay-per-farman operation that was empire only in name. In 1765, a scant eight years after Plassey, Clive & Co. would pressure the titular Mughal emperor Shah Alam II to grant the Company the 'dewanny'—diwani, or the right to collect revenue—of Bengal, Bihar, and Orissa. It was an unparalleled achievement that truly marked the arrival of the Company (and Crown) as a political force in the subcontinent and in Asia. In 1803, a mere forty-six years after Plassey, 'John Company', as it was commonly known, had grown enough in territory and heft to capture the Mughal capital of Delhi as a consequence of what is known as the Second Anglo-Maratha War. The Company would from then on control much of 'India' in letter and spirit and, with the knowledge and assistance of the British government, would be the protector of the Mughal court and its puppet emperors. Farcical Mughal rule would finally end a hundred years after Plassey in 1857 after the 'sepoy' revolt—or India's first war of independence, depending on politics and perception—led to the transference of administrative power in India from the Company to the British Crown.

Victory at Plassey also helped transform John Company into the greatest mercantile and military force of the era, helped to create the British empire in India and Asia, support its African colonies, and partially offset the loss of America as a colony. It began a run of geopolitical and geoeconomic dazzle before the destitution of Empire nearly two hundred years later. The process begun at Plassey would fuel much of Britain's industrial revolution and its many wars in the name of civilization. Indian men and women, Indian materiel, and Indian money would significantly underwrite both World Wars. 'In Corsica the young Napoleon Bonaparte dreamed of going to India and returning home a nabob,' writes Piers Brendon in his *The Decline and Fall of the British Empire*, quoting Bertrand Russell, 'Bismarck in youth had much the same idea until he thought, "after all, what harm have the Indians done me?"'

And, of course, it transformed Clive from a mere lieutenant colonel in the service of the Company into Lord Clive, Baron Plassey—a peer of the British realm, demigod to some, demon to others.

It appeared from such depiction that Clive had lived up to all the restlessness and energy he had displayed as a child in Hope Hall, an estate in Manchester, where he was placed in the care of his maternal uncle by marriage, Daniel Bayley.

The Family of Bayley of Manchester and Hope by Ernest Axon mentions that Bayley wrote of his concerns to Clive's parents, Rebecca and Richard:

> I hope I have made a little further conquest over Bob, and that he regards me, in some degree as well as his Aunt May. He has just had a suit of new clothes, and promises by his reformation to deserve them. I am satisfied that his fighting (to which he is out of measure addicted) gives his temper a fierceness and imperiousness, and he flies out upon trifling occasion; for this reason I do what I can to suppress the hero, that I may help forward the valuable qualities of meekness, benevolence, and patience. I assure you, sir, it is a matter of concern to us, as it is of importance to himself, that he may be a good and virtuous man, to which no care of ours shall be wanting.

Clive's overall Yin and Yang character development didn't quite work out that way. 'Plassy showed,' writes Axon, 'that the worthy uncle was unable to "suppress the hero" in his young charge'.

Plassey and its aftermath would enrich Clive, his Company, his land, and a great many Britons, besides, among other things, speeding up a transformation in India of landlords and zamindars into pliant rajas and maharajas, and flower the romance of 'Raj' exotica that lives on in breathless British novels and films, and continues the stereotype of India in popular Western imagination.

This much is fâit accompli.

But presentation and interpretation are dynamic activities. More than 250 years after Plassey, and nearing a hundred years since India and Pakistan led an insistent parade of departures from colonial capture, 'Plassey' still excites discussion and debate as living history. And that is the purpose of this book: to add to the existing body of work related to Plassey, offer more crossover-understanding, if you will, of the crucial run-up to a watershed event, the event itself, its immediate aftermath and how Plassey is conveyed to this day as moral prop and propaganda. Sometimes, the barriers of politics, identity, language, access to information, selective use of such information, and a remarkable need for justification have prevented greater understanding and appreciation of this root event of subcontinental history.

In order to do that I have attempted to reach diverse sources and interpretations, largely from the subcontinent and Europe. These span contemporary records of the Company to histories and chronicles written by Company employees of that era; chronicles and histories originally written in Persian and French which come to us translated; colonial-era works ranging from records to biographies— some of these are hagiographies—and histories written by both Indians and Europeans; and twentieth- and twenty-first-century observations, histories, research papers, biographies, essays, articles, even depictions of Plassey (here and elsewhere in the book I often use Plassey as a composite to convey the entirety of the process and dramatis personae, not just the location of the battle) in film, theatre, and popular fiction. There is also a treasure trove of active popular imagination that is to be found in and around Plassey, including Bengal's capital at the time, Murshidabad, today a place of ruins, museums, and dramatic memories.

One important strand of information was sourced from the Bengali, a source that has been largely untapped by historians and chroniclers of Plassey in English. While Bengali chroniclers, historians, and commentators often reference sources in English, several not-Bengali Indians and Westerners either do not, or cannot, reference sources in Bengali. The work of Bangladeshi scholars and writers, of a milieu where the rewriting of history, including the Plassey narrative, has remained predominant since the country's independence from Pakistan in 1971, is linguistically and culturally even more distant from such recognition.

◆

Versions are important, as they shape perceptions—some are designed to shape perceptions—even as multi-disciplinary historians and chroniclers continue to engage in the forensics of truth and probability.

Like Clive, Siraj too is painted at the very least in binaries. This nawab, who attacked the Company city of Calcutta when he was twenty-three, and was killed in the aftermath of Plassey at twenty-four, is often portrayed as a villain whose behaviour and very presence demanded his overthrowing. A spoilt brat who led an extended debauch that partly ended with the undertaking, at his grandfather's deathbed, that he would give up alcohol. The nawab who victimized the Company. The demon who threw women and men alike into the Black Hole of Calcutta. An unacceptable risk to Bengal's power structure and the Company's agenda. Equally, Siraj is portrayed as a martyr in several textbook histories of the subcontinent. For some he was the last 'free' nawab of Bengal wronged by greedy, vile traitors and greedy, vile British.

Similarly, the battle at Plassey is regarded by many as a mere skirmish, the battle won before it even began, relatively insignificant in the grand schema of global and local churn.

Others view it as among the most significant battles, even if short-lived, to have been fought in the modern era. Or, at any rate, a series of events that added up to a grand historical denouement. The British force's quick advance up the Hugli–Bhagirathi, and the speed of events from the taking of the fort at Katwa, the march north to Plassey, the Bengal army's rout, and the subsequent disintegration of Siraj's command and control, a combination of blitzkrieg and conspiracy that has remained a thing of wonder nearly three centuries later.

Still others (including, as we shall see, a nervous, even frantic, Clive) viewed it as a battle that could have gone either way.

So, can the Battle of Plassey be reduced to a matter of rain and renegades, as some chroniclers suggest? Rain drenched the Bengal army's gunpowder. Clive's army had their stock protected. The Bengal army was largely devoid of its troops through the on-field inaction of the Plassey conspirators. Clive & Co. had this non-performing asset on their side. While there's truth to this, to telescope the sprawling Byzantine history and mechanics of Plassey into these two factors may be too simplistic.

◆

It isn't as if people haven't tried justifying British colonial steps in India, and it isn't as if people haven't responded. If I may illustrate with a few examples here (several more appear in appropriate contexts throughout the book).

Take George Bruce Malleson's *The Decisive Battles of India from 1746 to 1849*, which is considered required reading for Plassey.

Malleson, an officer and civil servant in India who transitioned from Company to Crown after 1857, offered a paean to the British treatment of its colonial subjects in India as compared to the injustices Russian despots practised on their subjects:

> Not in this way did the British behave towards the races of India.
> In all their onward progresses they had the assent and support
> of the populations who desired to maintain law and order. The
> decadence of the Mughal rule was proceeding rapidly when
> Clive first landed in Bengal. Then the buffalo was to the man
> who held the bludgeon. These pages show how, under English
> rule, the buffalo is the property of the man, woman or child
> who has the legal right to possess it. We have shed no blood
> except on the battle-field, and the blood we have shed there
> has been the blood of the oppressors of the people.

While it isn't difficult to disprove this astonishing declaration in these relatively unblinkered post-colonial times, aided by greater access to information and saturation-research, Indian historians and chroniclers active in the late-Raj era of the twentieth century did so too. But they, and their colleagues who followed, both in India and overseas, also readily grasp at a certificate to Siraj that Malleson provides in the same work:

Whatever may have been his faults, Siraju'd-daulah had neither betrayed his master nor sold his country. Nay more, no unbiased Englishman, sitting in judgement on the events which passed in the interval between the 9th February and the 23rd June [1757], can deny that the name of Siraju'd-daulah stands higher in the scale of honour than does the name of Clive. He was the only one of the principal actors in that tragic drama who did not attempt to deceive!

Nobel laureate for literature Rabindranath Tagore actually referenced this assertion of Malleson in a critique of a book, *Sirajuddaula*, by the historian Akshaykumar Maitreya in 1897. Both the book and the critique were in Bengali. Maitreya's tone is often sarcastic when remarking on the post-Plassey era ('Ekhon āmrā shōbbhō hōiāchhi'—we are now civilized—when discussing life in rural Bengal, for instance), and his work was arguably the first that offered a structured defence of 'the unfortunate Sirajuddaula, riven by calumny and perennially held by history as guilty'. This quote from a translation of Tagore's critique by the scholar Rosinka Chaudhuri concludes the comment: 'Sirajuddaula may not have been a person of the highest character and greatness, but his bravery and simplicity...and humility...sparkles in the low falsehoods this dispute has brought to the fore. That is why Malleson highlighted it...'

Tagore conceded that Maitreya had gone somewhat overboard in his defence of Siraj. 'In only one department has he [Maitreya] broken the laws of history. Although he has not tried to conceal any of the flaws in Siraj's character, nevertheless, he has taken his side with a shade too much of enthusiasm. Instead of presenting his material calmly with the sole aid of historical witness, he has revealed his own opinion at the same time with a little too much impatience and ardour. Fighting a rigid and hostile prejudice and facing blind and unfair opinion at every step, he naturally becomes extremely agitated. But the peace that resides in truth has been destroyed in the process, and the reader has occasionally been a little troubled by the thought, quite without foundation, of favouritism.'

But Tagore also had a word in his critique, written in 1898, on an Anglo-Indian paper being livid about the book: '...as long as we are weak and the English strong, our criticism of the English is nearly harmless to them, their criticism of us is deadly. Our newspapers may only cause a bit of ear ache to them and their memsahibs, but their newspapers spray bullets into our heart...'

◆

Cherry-picking Plassey as a justification for empire or, depending on the point of view, the beginning of a rapacious project, has for several hundred years added layers to the already complex event. It can be exasperating, but it's also exciting—and underscores Plassey's importance as the pivot it was.

For some historians, the assertion that Company-folk were merely merchants was quickly proven to be specious in the run-up to Plassey, let alone the aftermath of Plassey. The Company and the Crown behaved like a joint entity, much as their counterparts did—France, for example. Calcutta was leased to the Company, but the British government took as much interest in its well-being as the Company. During times of tension and war between Britain and France, British and French mercantile interests in India, including the enclaves and towns where the trading companies were headquartered and maintained operations, were very much considered to be in the national interest of both countries—as documents show. British naval vessels on call to protect John Company's interests in India sailed under the country's flag, were underwritten by the Company, and both Company employees and Crown forces shared in the spoils of war.

Some British- and Raj-friendly historians and chroniclers have taken great pains to point out the brutality and single-minded pursuit of power practised by Muslim princes, generals, and pretenders across the subcontinent. In that world usurpers routinely topple a dynasty, often one that fed, watered, and enriched them, to establish their own 'royal' line. In the chronological context of Plassey, it was as true of Mughal suzerains as of their lieges in Bengal, the nawabs, especially with Murshid Quli Khan, who for all practical purposes broke away from Delhi in 1717, and evidently applied a barbaric hand to overhaul administration and cement his authority.

Such tellers detail how Aurangzeb became Emperor Alamgir by militarily beating off fraternal challenges twice over, from his brother Dara Shukoh—the favourite son of their father, Emperor Shah Jahan. The Venetian traveller and sometime Mughal courtier, Niccolao Manucci, writes in his *Storia do Mogor*, a chronicle of the Mughals from the mid-seventeenth century to 1708 (the year after Aurangzeb's death), about how Dara Shukoh was killed and brought to the emperor to gloat over. Upon his death, Aurangzeb's son Shah Alam, the prince Muazzam, defeated his challenger-brother Azam Shah, and took the throne as Bahadur Shah (or Shah Alam I).

It was only natural, proffered this school of thought, that Alivardi Khan would, without compunction, depose Sarfaraz Khan, the grandson of his benefactor, Murshid Quli. That coup in 1740 ended the three-ruler Nasiri dynasty that began with Murshid Quli (from his formal name, Jaffar Khan Bahadur Nasiri) and began the two-ruler Afshar dynasty: beginning with Alivardi and ending with his grandson Siraj. That natural order of things continued with the compact of Siraj's enemies that culminated in Plassey. In the aftermath, Mir Jafar became the first nawab of the Najafi dynasty. In the eyes of chroniclers of this school, Plassey wasn't a traitors' parade, merely business as usual.

Some British and pro-British writers and historians in particular seem obsessed about justifying the moral underpinning of the rapidly evolving Company and Crown project in India and elsewhere. Even someone like the well-regarded chronicler John Keay, generally lauded for restraint, spends some energy doing so in his fine general study, *India: A History*.

> Although the drama and scandals of 'the Famous Two Hundred Days' are often characterised as a 'revolution', no one could seriously contend that the Company had not observed the conventions of power-seeking under the later Mughal empire... Nor is it evident that most power-brokers in Bengal opposed their new superior. In fact many argued strongly in favour of British intervention. Foreign rule in India was seldom regarded as objectionable per se.

The Cambridge historian Christopher Bayly was firm in his assertion that without support from Bengal's aristocracy, as distinct from the general population, Plassey could not have come about. As he notes in his book, *Indian Society and the Making of the British Empire*:

Indian capital represented by the [banking house of the] Jagat Seths and Omichand [the merchant Umachand, sometimes also referred to as Amir Chand] connections, along with the zamindars of west Bengal and dissident military entrepreneurs, had provided the support and the occasion for the British coup in Bengal.

True. So is the earnest justification.

Relatively easier to disagree with in that respect is the work of, say, an unabashed fan of empire like the writer Nirad C. Chaudhuri, who presented Siraj's immorality on historical hearsay, alongside a moral whitewash of Clive & Co. in his *Clive of India*, an engaging biography of the stupendously successful general-merchant. Chaudhuri attempted to prove that the battle was between venality and decadence—in Bengal and India—versus a sort of Puritanical application of aggressive mercantile endeavour married to a loyalty to king and country—British—and reiterated that the outcome of the conflict got Siraj exactly what he deserved. He quotes the third-generation-dynastic-decay maxim propagated by Ibn Khaldun, the fourteeth to fifteenth-century CE Arab historian, to suggest it was inevitable.

Plassey is a Petri dish of sophistry and uncomfortable views. Sometimes, from surprising sources.

An influential Bengali voice weighed in on the matter of Siraj and Plassey in the mid-nineteenth century. Ishwar Chandra 'Vidyasagar' remains a legendary figure in Bengal for his pioneering work as a scholar, grammarian, educationist, and social reformer in the period sometimes called the Bengal Renaissance. In 1848, he published a popular and influential two-part history of Bengal in Bengali, *Bānglār Itihāsh*, based on the writer and historian John Clark Marshman's work, *Outline of the History of Bengal Compiled for the Use of Youths of India*. Ishwar Chandra's book included material which he thought relevant, ignored large sections that didn't fit his narrative, and offered layers of commentary that enhanced Marshman's already pro-British, pro-Company telling with occasional viciousness. In his Preface Ishwar Chandra describes Siraj, with whose reign the second volume begins, as 'ōti durāchār' or a person of extremely poor character and behaviour. William Cavendish-Bentinck, appointed governor general of the Bengal Presidency in 1828, and later designated the first governor general of India, the period of whose time in office till 1835 concludes the book, is in comparison referred to as 'Chirōshorōniyō Lārd William Bentinck'—or Lord William Bentick, who shall forever be remembered. (Ishwar Chandra's social reforms and, indeed, the Bengal Renaissance, were underwritten by policies and practices of the Company's Bengal Presidency headquartered in Calcutta.)

A description follows of Siraj's character immediately upon his accession to Bengal's masnad—an ornate, raised and cushioned platform usually of marble or other fine stone that functioned as the throne—in April 1756. The description is without any corroboration, and of immense import for both cultural memory and regional historiography, coming as it does from a person as venerated in Bengali society as Ishwar Chandra. I offer a translation of his high-Bengali into less formal English:

> Several immature, excitable people of poor character and poor habits became his favourites and confidantes. Every day they would advise him to pursue unfair and cruel practices. The result of such advice was evident: it could be said that during his reign nobody's property, nor the honour of a lady was safe.

Every step followed the get-rid-of-the-Nawab-whom-nobody-could-stand narrative. In Bengali 'Black Hole' is generally referred to as ondhōkup—literally, blind well. Here there is a subtle shift from a 'Bengal' enterprise to a 'Muslim' enterprise: 'At the height of summer the Mussalmans threw into that tiny room all the European prisoners.' Clive and British admiral Charles Watson's retaking of the British concession of Calcutta is described in complimentary terms: '...the English regained Calcutta but this was done without the loss of a single life' on the side of the British. (Historians like Jadunath Sarkar, whose work I refer to later, rubbished the established narrative of the Black Hole, ascribing it to the fevered imagination of those like John Zephaniah Holwell, a Company surgeon and defender of Calcutta whose version of the incident as eyewitness is widely quoted as both proof and calumny.)

◆

The need to establish national identity and an acceptable national history and narrative has led to the adding of more layers to Plassey in Bangladesh. Its capital Dhaka was once Jahangirnagar, the capital of Bengal named after the Mughal emperor who permitted the Company to trade in India. In 1704, Murshid Quli relocated the administrative centre to the small town of Makhsudabad and named it after himself. In Bangladesh, Siraj remains a symbol for the reclamation of national spirit and pride.

Willem van Schendel in his *A History of Bangladesh* puts forward the Bangladeshi perspective to Plassey—and, as I have written in *The Bengalis: A Portrait of a Community*, it is pertinent as that country today forms by far the greater part of Bengal in general and deltaic Bengal in particular. This perspective is markedly different from Indian nationalist writing, which focuses on the imposition of colonialism as a direct result of Plassey and an anti-colonial struggle to remove 'this blot on the national escutcheon', as he dramatically puts it.

Van Schendel points out that other foreign rulers had preceded the British: the Mughal empire, 'centred in far-off Delhi had taken control in 1612 after many battles with local opponents'. Indeed, such rule preceded Mughal domination by several hundred years, as an ingress of Afghan and Turkic invaders replaced Bengal's local kings and dynasties from the thirteenth century onwards. So, Van Schendel correctly maintains, in Bengal inhabitants had 'long been accustomed to a mulcting administration dominated by foreign officials'. While that would hold true for all Bengal, including the present-day Indian state of West Bengal, for Bangladeshi historians, colonial rule didn't end in 1947, as it did in India and Pakistan when they gained independence from Britain. In Bangladesh, Pakistan is also considered a colonial power, as it imposed a language, laws, administration—and, ultimately, ignored a popular electoral victory in East Pakistan nee East Bengal, that led to horrific repression, genocide, war, and the birth of Bangladesh in 1971. 'What ended at the battle of Polashi, then,' writes Van Schendel, 'was not indigenous rule in the Bengal Delta but the ancien régime of the Mughal state.'

It has not prevented a dramatization of Siraj and events around Plassey in Bangladesh, and the claiming of Siraj as Bengal and Bangladesh's own. A three-hour long biopic released in 1989, *Nobāb Shirājuddoulā*, opens with a Company official on horseback harassing a group of farmers and boatmen loading a boat by a riverside. When one of them objects and talks back, he is mercilessly whipped by the Company man, played by a local actor. The flailing whip is suddenly grabbed by a handsome, moustachioed man on horseback. He is dressed in flowing black robes. His mien is fierce. A black turban on his head sports the five-pointed star of Islam.

The Company man is outraged. 'You fool!' he screams, and threatens the Bengali 'black man' with his life, speaking a mix of accented and broken Bengali and Urdu ('Bangāli kālā ādmi, hāmi tōmār jān liyé lébé!').

'Chōp-rāō béādōb!' Siraj thunders, asking the 'uncivilized' man to shut up, employing the common Bengali usage of the Urdu chup rahō, béādab. The assembly is awestruck. Siraj then thunders off on his horse across rice fields as the opening credits roll. He thereafter reaffirms an oath to not let the Company build fortifications or increase its forces. It all ends in lengthy tragedy. Mir Jafar is portrayed as the worst of the villains.

Based on a screenplay by Khan Ataur Rahman, the melodramatic movie reminiscent of the 1960s and 1970s approach in Bollywood freely acknowledges as sources a mix of historians and writers from Bengal (here I mean: Bengali homelands situated in India and East Pakistan—eventually, Bangladesh). Among them, Maitreya, the historian Ramesh Chandra Majumdar, the prolific littérateur Sikandar Abu Zafar, who wrote a play about Siraj in 1965, and Sachindranath Sengupta, a theatre-legend who also wrote a play on Siraj.

A tear-jerker and a transparent Bengali—Bangladeshi—pride-and-heritage project that shows the country's flag in the beginning, the movie effortlessly transforms Siraj from the last 'free' nawab of Bengal to a Bengali nawab, which is far from being the same thing. Similar sentiments are attached to the work of some writers just mentioned, and certainly a more recent work. The Bangladeshi scholar and historian Abul Kalam Mohammed Zakaria published his monumental *Nobāb Shirāj-ud-Daulā* in 2015. The work in Bengali is an earnest if emotionally wrought thesis to right a wronged Siraj. Hotōbhāgā Shirāj, unfortunate Siraj, is a frequent exclamation in the book.

In the occidental arc, the writer of racy historical fiction Alex Rutherford, known for his travellers'-favourite series of novels on the Mughals, has also weighed in on Plassey. His focus is on Clive, whom he appears to correctly describe in his book, *Fortune's Soldier*. Rutherford tells his tale through the eyes of a fictional friend of Clive's, and a colleague from Clive's early years in India. The plot and characters are formulaic, on the lines of fantastic tales attempted by some British writers of heat-and-dust Raj fiction, as it were, with obligatory incomprehensible names such as the 'vizier' of Siraj, Naraigan Singh; and the near-obligatory John Masters-like description of the attraction between Clive's fictional friend Nicholas Ballantyne and a nautch girl.

Rutherford paints Siraj in an even-handed manner. Clive comes off as greedy and ambitious, a man who is portrayed as trying to deal with his own personal demons as much as he deals with matters on the Company's behalf. In one instance, he even speaks of investing his money to trigger a war so he can step in as both kingmaker and peacemaker, and, in the process, harvest more riches. Nicholas is the conflicted but ultimately upright and honourable Company man, the moral compass for imminent empire as he retires to a suitably exotic address, New Glenmire, The Himalayas; while Clive embraces a life, first as a nabob in India and then as a grandee in Britain, of immense wealth, fame, and infamy.

The sentiment isn't far from some of the work by Rudyard Kipling, like his poem *The White Man's Burden* or in particular these lines from a poem in the book, *Stalky & Co.*:

Some beneath the further stars
Bear the greater burden;
Set to serve the lands they rule,

(Save he serve no man may rule)
Serve and love the lands they rule;
Seeking praise nor guerdon.

There won't be an end to benevolent-empire tales, the same as there won't be a drying up of malevolent-empire tales from the South Asian perspective in which Plassey remains one of the major underpinnings.

◆

There are also histories of the period from what is sometimes called a Marxist perspective or, more recently, simply known as people's history, which also includes subaltern history, as distinct from a history written from a colonial perspective, or nationalist history, or a top-down history, as it were. These essentially turn occasional causality by the elite into widespread effect for common citizenry and the country—or territory.

The historian Irfan Habib makes the purpose of a people's history quite clear in his preface to Amar Farooqui's *The Establishment of British Rule, 1757-1813*, part of an easy-to-access series titled 'A People's History of India': '...And if many events are viewed here from the point of view of the subjugated people, this is, indeed, what should be the case in a people's history.' Farooqui is a little more aggressive, criticizing the 'tendency' in some 'recent writings' to 'pass by the intensely violent character of the Company's intrusion'. He adds: 'There is also a tendency to see the British regime as merely a successor to the earlier states in India, a view particularly favoured by C. A. Bayly and others.' He sets out to provide a balance—in his opinion a necessary view of the neglected and superseded 'other': the catchword of subaltern historians, sociologists, left-leaning intellectuals, and a growing tribe of seminarists in the subcontinent. In this case the 'other' being people of much of the subcontinent.

'A People's History of India' is intended to guide readers to a particular avenue of logic, such as questioning the credibility of Holwell's description of the Black Hole—done decades earlier by Jadunath Sarkar and others, but Sarkar's Bengali-nationalist stance is not always positively referenced by later, or 'liberal' historians. It attempts to expose the orientalist approach to gathering 'colonial knowledge' suited to governing a growing empire, and unsurprisingly refers to the post-colonialism don Edward Wadie Said and his 1978 work, *Orientalism,* to link the eponymous theme to the 'colonial project'.

In a note in his own book in the series, *Indian Economy under Early British Rule, 1757-1857*, Habib lucidly explains the shifts in the debate on economic and political history of the eighteenth century. 'By a conventional view among historians, the Eighteenth century used to be divided into two parts. There was, first, an "anarchical period which intervened between the death of Aurangzeb (1707) and the establishment of the British supremacy", a period in which, according to an extreme judgement, "nearly all the notable men (of India) led vicious lives, stained by gross sensuality, ruthless cruelty and insatiable greed".' Here Habib quotes the Raj-era Indologist Vincent Arthur Smith. In contrast, he explains, Indian nationalist historians viewed this period of economic and political 'decay' as one that opened the doors to a 'national catastrophe'—colonization. Others viewed the period as a time that 'further underlined the enormous civilizational gulf between "the native" and the British rulers.' Plassey provided the marker.

There was an attempt to diminish this marker's significance from the 1960s on, Habib claims, a 'trend' that travelled from Western to Indian scholars. 'Among the first salvoes was the one fired by [Professor] Holden Furber (1969), who argued that, despite some disputes between them, the original European intrusion resulted in the creation of a network of mutual cooperation between European merchants and their Indian and other Asian counterparts.' More scholars followed. The next substantive step came in 1983, Habib continues, when Bayly—a bit of a punching bag in the series—in his *Rulers, Townsmen and Bazaars: North Indian Society in the Age of British Expansion 1770-1870*, extended the 'concept of partnership' beyond Plassey. '"British conquest often meant no more than the slow drift to the East India Company of (Indian) soldiers, merchants and administrators,"' Habib quotes Bayly. 'Indeed, even colonialism could be perceived as a joint enterprise', Habib notes, pointing to a sub-chapter entitled 'The indigenous origins of the "colonial economy"'.

He further illustrates this school of thought by referring to the second volume of *The Cambridge Economic History of India*, in which Kirti Narayan Chaudhuri—Nirad Chaudhuri's younger son—'minimized the effects of the British conquest on the Indian economy, arguing that "Indian trade still continued to flow along traditional channels" in the period following the "revolution of 1757", i.e. Plassey'. Habib also holds up the views of American historian Burton Stein, specifically his assertion that the colonial regime was in essence 'a continuation of prior indigenous regimes of the subcontinent'.

'This has led to some strange revisions of previously accepted judgements,' Habib observes, including, '...methods of tax gathering as revenue farming practiced by both the late Mughal administration and the East India Company in Bengal, denounced almost universally by contemporary writers, wins much commendation from Bayly, and following him, [the historian] Muzaffar Alam, who acclaim it as a measure that won over local "corporate groups" to the side of the administration. To some Indian historians it has appeared a satisfying thought that the British should have considered some Indian administrative institutions worth following.'

◆

It may seem that in the academic and ideological scrum offering different views about the stunning aftermath of Plassey, the events and people surrounding Plassey itself are placed in an increasingly diffused background. Even so, all these and several other works help to illustrate the import of Plassey beyond the central story of a young nawab who stood in the way of a company's business plan, a plan that turned into a corporate coup to beat all other corporate coups.

Despite the numerous published interpretations of Plassey and its aftermath, the questions continue to thrive. Was it really a battle or was it won before it began, as some historians surmise? What were the politics of the time that spurred Plassey—from a ravaged Mughal empire to the insecurities of the Seven Years War between two of the principal actors, Britain and France? What were the attractions of the plains and rivers of Bengal, the lifeline of trade and commerce that for centuries brought the produce of Bengal, the richest province of several Indian empires, to the homes and balance sheets of Europe? Was the incident of the Black Hole of Calcutta, that was used by some to morally underpin the British expedition to Plassey, real, exaggerated or fictional? How is that incident and Plassey carried forward to this day, as the present remembers the past in various versions of living history?

Clive is portrayed by some as almost a yogi on the eve of battle, engaged in deep contemplation, a philosopher-warrior who battled his options and demons for the winner-takes-all gambit that Plassey became. Clive at Plassey-on-the-Bhagirathi was painted in glorious hues. Grand motives were imputed to him. But was he just a desperately hopeful man whose future—as much as the future of the Company, which had bases elsewhere in India, and the Western hemisphere—hinged on a battle that, even with all the chess pieces in place, could have gone either way? For Clive, hero of the Carnatic and Calcutta, it was the ultimate throw of the dice. As we shall see, even with the assorted machinations in play there could be no guarantee of victory until victory arrived.

Was Siraj, who is usually portrayed by some British and British-loyalist historians, chroniclers and commentators as a nervous wreck, a boy-man desperate to cling to a ruinous rule, simply out of his depth? How close was he to escaping his fate?

And who were the dramatis personae of Plassey beyond Siraj and Clive, the two main faces of the face off? What are the stories behind the stories of the spurned general, the ambitious aunt, the rude and covetous cousin, the stone-cold and insulted banker? What of British merchants who saw war as just another day at the office? After all, as Syed Ghulam Hussain Khan Tabatabayi, author of the *Siyar-ul-Mutaqherin*, a Persian chronicle published in 1781 and which translates as 'A Review of Modern Times', or 'The Manner of the Moderns', eloquently writes of the Company as well as the Crown:

> This nation, which has not its equal in prowess, and courage, and strength of mind, but which is as covetous as any other; (and indeed where is the man, who in the pride of conscious power and victory, has not an avidity for conquests, especially if the means be ready, and already provided at his hand?)

The plot of Plassey presents an arresting cast of characters who fused ambition, treachery, greed, profit, politics, and geopolitics. It was a reality show that helped to reorder the world, a game of thrones and vast treasures. Plassey was—is—a lot more than a battle that ended just a few hours after it began. I hope this work adds layers as well as peels away layers.

S. C.
Calvim, Goa
October 2019

BOOK I

THE BACKGROUND

1

BUSINESS AND POLITICS: THE LAY OF THE LAND

'And that we keep an Extraordinary lookout...'

The eighteenth century, when the nawabs of Bengal and John Company came into their own, was a time of considerable political churn, strategies, and tactical moves in the subcontinent.

It all played out with the Mughal empire in fracture.

As with many empires, at one time it seemed inconceivable that the Mughals could ever decline even though the complex dynamics of a complex subcontinent has always made rule implicitly vulnerable to hubris. The empire was established by the Turkic warlord Zahir-ud-din Muhammad 'Babur' in 1526, after defeating the Afghan-origin Lodi dynast of Delhi and holding off a serious challenge a year later from Rajputs led by Maharana Sangram Singh of Mewar. Babur's son and successor Humayun assumed the throne in 1530, but had a rocky run from 1540. He experienced a fifteen-year exile after being defeated and displaced by Sur rulers of Afghan origin. The first of that dynasty was Sher Shah Suri, whose impact on administration and communication was no less than that of any Mughal. Among other things, he refurbished and extended the ancient route between eastern India and Afghanistan, what came to be called the Grand Trunk Road in British colonial times. Few gave the Mughals, who traced direct lines from Genghis Khan and Timur (or Tamerlane) a chance until Humayun reclaimed his throne in 1555 from a crumbling Sur empire, for a short-lived second reign that lasted a year.

His son Akbar oversaw a period of great expansion of the empire, and when the reins of empire passed to his son Jahangir in 1605, the Mughals were firmly established in form and function, with a definite imperial framework and cultural imprimatur. His son Shah Jahan, whose legacy as the builder of Taj Mahal often overshadows his legacy of empire, followed in 1628. The reins eventually passed to his son Aurangzeb in 1658 after a bitter fratricidal war of sucession. The irony is that, while the Mughal empire under Aurangzeb witnessed its greatest reach, from Afghanistan in the northwest to Bengal in the east, and nearly all of peninsular India to the south, there was already the birth of great resistance, such as from the Marathas—as we shall soon see.

The meltdown was spectacular. There would be six Mughal emperors between 1707, the year Aurangzeb died, and the accession of Muhammad Shah in 1719. Cracks in the empire had already begun to show during Aurangzeb's forty-nine-year reign but they began to widen after his death.

Aurangzeb's son, Azam Shah, ruled for a year before being killed in battle by his half-brother, who assumed the throne as Bahadur Shah—Bahadur Shah I—in 1707. His reign lasted just shy of four years before Jahandar Shah, his son, took the throne for less than a year after deafeating his brother Azim-us-Shan in a war of succession. In 1713, Farrukhsiyar, Azim-us-Shan's son, who would grant the Company an all-important farman, became emperor for six years after defeating Jahandar Shah, widely regarded as a debauch, in battle. Farrukhsiyar granted the embassy led by John Surman what the Company had pursued through the reign of several Mughal emperors: a farman, royal grant, that, besides a slew of other privileges and guarantees, permitted the Company the right to trade in the subah of Bengal, Bihar, and Orissa without any duties. This duty-free privilege, which came at the relative bargain of 3,000 rupees a year, would be used and misused—a fact acknowledged by the Company's own records. And, several decades later, light a fuse for young Siraj-ud-daulah.

In the seven months between February and September 1719, from the time Farrukhsiyar was deposed to the time Muhammad Shah was declared emperor, two emperors, Rafi ud-Darajat and Rafi-ud-Daulah (also known as Shah Jahan II), had come and gone.

It would be all downhill from there for the dynasty. The later Mughals '...sauntered away life in secluded places,' we read the disdainful yet generally apt reference in Raj-proponent Thomas Babington Macaulay's *Critical and Historical Essays*, 'chewing bang [or bhang, cannabis], fondling concubines, and listening to buffoons'.

This decay of imperial authority, what Irfan Habib calls 'internal decay', had set in during the later years of Aurangzeb's reign, and was 'increasingly shaken by a number of uprisings (of Jats, Sikhs, Satnamis and, above all, the Marathas)...the strength or success of which has been attributed partly to agrarian causes, as peasant distress and resurgence of the zamindar class'. Among other things, Habib notes, the centralized imperial network 'collapsed'. The uprising produced new 'states', like the Maratha dominions, the Jat 'kingdom' and Sikh 'chieftaincies'.

By the 1730s, the successor states of the Mughals were in control of nearly all of central, peninsular, and northern India, breaking away on account of 'internal revolts in Oudh [Awadh], Mysore and elsewhere,' as Piers Brendon puts it in his *The Decline and Fall of the British Empire*. These were in a state of flux with some of these battling each other to gain or retain territory and influence. The Marathas controlled a vast band from Gujarat to Orissa, in a west-to-east run of chieftains: the Gaikwads, Peshwas, Scindias, Holkars, and Bhonsles. Hyderabad, to the southeast of the Deccan plateau, was its own behemoth. The rest of the south was carved up between the Northern Circars, the Carnatic, the kingdom of Mysore, and Travancore which was outside the Mughal pale. Bihar was controlled by the autonomous Bengal province, with the third element, Orissa (hence the title: subahdar or governor of Bengal, Bihar, and Orissa), increasingly under Maratha attack. Northern India was carved up among the Rajput states, Kashmir, the Jats to the south of Delhi, the Rohilla kingdom of the Pathans to the east of Delhi. Awadh, further east, brought up the border with Bihar.

Brendon writes:

> Foreign invaders also took their toll. Delhi was sacked by the Persians in 1739 [led by Nadir Shah] and by the Afghans in 1756 [led by Ahmad Shah Abdali, also known as Ahmad Shah Durrani, who had been part of Nadir Shah's foray] the former carrying off the Peacock Throne and the Koh-i-noor Diamond ('Mountain of Light') as well as booty worth a billion rupees, the latter carrying out rape and massacre on an inconceivable scale.

Nadir Shah encouraged rape and massacre on a vast scale too, but perhaps for the British, the Koh-i-Noor, which is now part of Britain's crown jewels, remains of some import.

The British East India Company, which is discussed in some detail in the next chapter, warily watched the developments from the time of Aurangzeb's fading reign. 'Considering the great Confusions and Troubles that may arise in Bengal during the Inter Regnum, Agreed that we Order all our Officers of this Garrison to be constantly in a Readiness...' goes a resolution by the Calcutta Council from those years. 'And that Ammunition be put into the proper places, that are for that purpose on all Bastions, And that we keep an Extraordinary lookout, And that the Gunner mount the Mortars, And some great Guns be placed on the Curtains [walls of Fort William in Calcutta], Also that the Buxie [at this time, an European civil officer in charge of payments] lay in good Store of all sorts of grain and Provisions.'

The Council felt they would then be adequately defensible against marauders especially with troops at hand. 'As for the soldiers we have now about 200 besides Officers, amongst which are about 140 stout Europeans, which with the Company's Servants and Freemen of this Place And the Gunroome Crew, We think will on any Occasion be sufficient to Defend this Garrison.' That sense of security would prevail until the 1750s.

Of the subcontinental tearaways, the Marathas were arguably the most potent force, taking on the Mughals during the early years of Aurangzeb's reign, when the rot within the empire hadn't yet reached its tipping point. Led by Shivaji, the Marathas deeply embarrassed Aurangzeb. As Keay puts it, 'Shivaji's "dignity" was now eclipsing that of the empire.'

'Breaking out of the hills in 1664 [Aurangzeb had by then been emperor for six years] Shivaji personally led his forces north into Gujarat and headed for the great port of Surat,' Keay observes in *India*. There they ran riot for forty days. 'Only the well-defended English "factory" (a fortified warehouse-cum-counting house-cum-hostel) was spared.' It was an example of an off-again-on-again détente between Maratha forces and the Company that would be evident even in the days Robert Clive marched towards Plassey.

The Marathas had a key advantage, as several historians and chroniclers have noted. Keay writes that Shivaji's forces, spearheaded by excellent cavalry moved speedily and with minimal logistics. '... Maratha horse, could travel light and live off the countryside, and was thus infinitely more elusive and wide-ranging than its heavy Mughal counterpart...'

Although Shivaji and the Marathas did suffer significant reverses, during the reign of Aurangzeb, the Marathas came to control a swathe of the Deccan along the Western Ghats, from roughly north of Pune to the south, extending to Raigarh, Satara, and Vijayadurg, and just shy of Portuguese-controlled Goa. Another patch they ruled lay west of Madras, roughly an oval from a little to the north of Vellore to a little south of Jinji. They raided territories nearly at will. Within four decades of Aurangzeb's death in 1707, they had galloped across much of central and eastern India, holding territories to ransom or simply taking over.

The Marathas were of great importance in the context of Bengal. Following a claim of raising revenue—the chauth, or one-fourth of total revenue—in several Mughal provinces as granted during the reign of Mughal emperor Rafi ud-Darajat in the chaotic days of 1719, they would disrupt Bengal, ransack its villages and towns for a decade till 1751 until Alivardi Khan signed a treaty and agreed to pay chauth. Alivardi was also compelled at that time to finally cede control of Orissa, a territory he had repeatedly fought to retain, to the Marathas, thereby retaining the title of subahdar of Bengal, Bihar, and Orissa only in name. (It appears that several of Bengal's generals didn't want to be at risk from the Marathas either. Company Consultations in Calcutta on 29 May 1749 note that Mir Jafar—who once fled a battle against the Marathas—and Rai Durlabh, both future Plassey generals for Siraj, were not keen to be appointed governors of Orissa: 'News of the Nabob [Alivardi] arriving at Cuttack, the Mahrattas fled, the Nabob offered the Nabobship to Dalobram and M. Jaffier, who both refused. The Mahrattas are expected to return next year...')

The Bargi, or Bōrgi, as they were known in Bengal weakened the region's economy, bled its treasury—as well as the population, by several hundreds of thousands—and turned its rulers paranoid. There is a folk rhyme still recalled in parts of Bengal, sometimes as a chilling lullaby. The first words vary in rendition but generally it goes like this:

Khōkā ghumālō pārā jurālō, Bōrgi élō déshé,
Bulbuli-té dhān khéyéchhé, khājnā débō kishé?

As the child sleeps and the neighbourhood quietens, the
Bōrgi have arrived,
The songbird has eaten the paddy, how will I now pay the
tax?

The Company wasn't happy either, even though it would repeatedly
deal with the Marathas to both safeguard its interests and diminish
that of its opponents. That the Company and the British remained
wary of the Marathas is evidenced most tellingly by the 'Mahratta
Ditch' which marked the northern and eastern boundaries of the
relative cocoon of Calcutta in pre-Plassey days, excavated as a defence
against the raiders whom few seemed to be able to counter. (In
Bagbazar in north Kolkata there is to this day a Maratha Ditch Lane.)
To the west, the Hugli formed a riverine barrier, to the south lay
more excavations as an extension of the ditch, and habitations of
locals—as we shall see such concentrations bore the brunt of any
battle. The land beyond, as the Reverend James Long tells us in
Selections from Unpublished Records of Government (1748-1767), was
called 'the continent'. It is scarcely credible when compared to the
teeming, heaving metropolis that Calcutta—Kolkata—is today, or
the thriving Company capital it had become by the mid-nineteenth
century when *Records* was published, to consider a time 'when there
was no Chowringi, and its plain was a tiger jungle...'

Indeed, among the first times we learn of Plassey—as Placy—in
Company records, is in February 1748 when, on the 25th of that
month, the Bengal Public Consultations presided over by the President
in Council noted a letter written by the Council at Qasimbazar, the
European trading hub to the south of Murshidabad along the Hugli–
Bhagirathi, six days earlier. In it an 'Ensign English' is berated for not
waiting at 'Placy' in the face of a Maratha incursion, which would
have permitted the sending of ammunition and reinforcements to
guard the Company's goods in transit—and the Marathas could have
been scared away by approaching forces of the nawab.

Ensign English paid a price for it. As Long adds in an explanation
to the records of March 1748:

> In a letter to Kasimbazar the Council stigmatise the conduct
> of Ensign English as cowardly for allowing the Mahrattas to

seize the Kasimbazar fleet and plunder the goods of which he was in charge; he was subsequently imprisoned, tried by Court Martial and cashiered.

There were several recorded effects of Maratha harassment. Company Consultations at Fort William on 9 December 1751 note:

> A letter from Kassimbazar states The dearness of raw silk and silk piece goods for some years past, they find, is owing to the Mahrattas constantly entering Bengal, plundering and burning the people's houses, and destroying the chief Aurangs [in Bengali, ārong, places of manufacture and storage—depots; also, market] from whence the workmen have fled to distant parts, and not to any malpractice in the gentlemen there.

A similar message was despatched to the Court of Directors in London in January 1752.

Other despatches and consultations mention the inability of Company factors to purchase any 'ready money goods' from weavers in Orissa as the Maratha raids ensured the 'greatest part of them have been obliged to abscond'. The Marathas didn't leave anything, even a wrecked Company sloop. The ship and its crew were plundered.

Although the Marathas were the most worrisome, there were other irritants for European traders, ranging from wayward Pathan mercenaries to government officials who worked to extract what they could from merchants of all nations.

Company Consultations in March 1748 note, 'The Gentlemen at Patna write that the Pattans [Pathans] had plundered the Dutch Factory at Futtua of white cloth and other goods to the amount of 65,000 Rupees.' Local officials managed to bring some order in the town, and reopen shops and houses, but the country 'round about' was in 'the utmost confusion'. From April that year there is a record of 'English' consignments being harassed, in this case, by the zamindar of Palta—now a suburb of Barrackpore, north of Calcutta—who ignored even the order of the faujdar, a military officer, of the prosperous trading settlement of Hugli, upriver from Calcutta: 'The Zemindar near Pulta having stopped several boats with English Dusticks and taken money from them and disregarding the Phousdars of Houghley's orders to clear them.'

Not that the benevolence of the commander of Hugli, who also acted as landlord on the behalf of the nawab of Bengal, was altruistic. He was part of a wheel lubricated by what the Chinese term fragrant grease. In May 1748, the Consultations observed: 'The Hugly Phausdar demanding the usual annual present due in November last amounting to Current Rupees two thousand seven hundred and fifty (2,750)—Agreed that the President do pay the same out of the cash.' Hugli's faujdar was pushing his luck several years later. The Consultations for 30 April 1753 record the agreement 'that the President do pay the same out of the cash' the demands for 'ground rent' for four months from January that year, as made by the 'the Hooghly Phousdar' for 'Sootaloota' [Sutanuti] at 325 rupees and 'Govindpore' [Gobindapur] in Calcutta at 33 rupees'. Although the Company had formally leased the areas the faujdar had still to be kept on their side.

◆

Bengal was drawn into the general churn even as European trading companies competing for the riches of India settled in for what they hoped was the long haul, jostling for every advantage from the Mughal emperor and local governors and rulers as well as over each other. Part of the churn is evident from the shifting of Bengal's administrative bases during the later Mughal empire.

The initial base was Rajmahal, which we shall revisit later in the narrative—it played a colourful part in the Plassey endgame. It is today a small town by the widening Ganga in the borderlands of Bengal and Jharkhand, not far from the Farakka Barrage that now dams the river before it flows into Bangladesh. In 1610, Islam Khan, the Mughal viceroy of Bengal, shifted the capital from Rajmahal, at the time also known as Akbarnagar (after the third Mughal emperor) to Dhaka. It was then known as Jahangirnagar, after Jahangir, one of Akbar's sons who became emperor after him.

The translator of Ghulam Husain Salim's *Riyazu-s-Salatin* (The Garden of Kings), Maulavi Abdus Salam, explains this transfer. It occurred primarily on account of the Mughal—and Muslim—dominions having by then moved considerably eastward. 'Rajmahal ceased to occupy a central position,' he writes. There were other factors, such as Magh or Mog raiders from Arakan pushing into Bengal, besides direct control of the Chittagong region by the Arakan kings (they controlled Chittagong for more than a hundred years until the 1660s). 'To effectually guard against the latter, a powerful fleet was constructed and maintained at Dacca,' Abdus Salam explains, and on the nearby river Padma, or Poddā in Bengali which, at that point in its journey to the Bay, includes the main streams of the Ganga and the Brahmaputra; and the Meghna, further to the southeast. Besides, Salam notes, 'colonies of Musalman feudal barons...were planted throughout Eastern Bengal, especially at places of strategic importance, in order to hold in check all disloyal Afghan elements, and to prevent their intriguing with the Magh raiders'.

Dhaka remained the capital of Bengal through this time for nearly a hundred years except for about sixteen years, when the Mughal prince Shah Shuja shifted the viceregal capital back to Rajmahal. Shah Shuja, a son of Shah Jahan, the emperor who followed after Jahangir, was governor for two decades until 1659. That year he tried to take on his brother, the newly-minted Mughal emperor Aurangzeb, in a battle at Khajuha, in present-day Uttar Pradesh. He lost and had to retreat all the way back to Dhaka and subsequently to the Mughal-enemy territory of Arakan, where he would be executed on a charge of conspiring against the local ruler.

Soon after there arrived in Bengal another colourful character, the governor Mirza Abu Talib, better known by his title Shaista (or Shayesta) Khan, during the early years of his nephew Aurangzeb's rule, when the empire and its governor flexed their muscles in the east. In some ways it could be termed a relatively calm posting for the fierce Shaista, who had a taste of Maratha nerve a year before his posting to Bengal in 1664. Shivaji and a band of his soldiers disguised as a groom's party had ambushed Shaista in Pune, then under Mughal control, and confronted him in a palace where it is believed Shivaji spent a part of his childhood. Shaista had three fingers sliced off as he made his escape. (Shivaji devotees celebrated the 350th anniversary of that episode in 2013.)

Except for a gap of nine years when he was posted to the Deccan, Shaista Khan was governor of Bengal until 1688. During his tenure the Portuguese were ejected from their stronghold in Hugli, and the Arakanese from Chittagong. This playboy subahdar was Clive-like in his taste for wealth and ostentation; the man also leveraged trade monopolies for his own gain even as he aided his emperor, Aurangzeb. At one point he even chased Company traders from their base in Hugli after the Company declared hostilities against Shaista and, by extension, the Mughal empire, after a dispute over customs duties.

There's a back story. During the last six years of Shaista's governorship the trade of the Company was 'seriously hampered,' writes the British-Indian civil servant Lewis Sydney Stewart O'Malley in *Murshidabad*, by 'heavy imposts' levied by him. Several Indian historians write of disputes over customs duties. It blew up in 1686, writes O'Malley, 'when the Company's cargo boats were held up under an embargo and its sale of silver prohibited. Job Charnock [the Company chief in Qasimbazar] was ordered to pay Rs 43,000 in settlement of a claim made by some native merchants, and, according to [the military historian and Company chronicler Robert] Orme, was scourged by the Nawab's orders'. The Qasimbazar factory was besieged by Shaista's troops, in particular to prevent Charnock escaping, but in April 1686 he managed to slip through the 'cordon' (much as his successor William Watts would, seventy years later, to escape Siraj's cordon), and made it downriver to the settlement at Hugli. 'After this, the Cossimbazar factory, in common with the other English factories in Bengal, was condemned to confiscation by Shaista Khan,' writes O'Malley.

Besides being run out of Hugli, a naval blockade and bombardment of Chittagong in retaliation, to expel the Mughals who were believed to be weak at this port settlement on the northeastern arc of the Bay of Bengal, and establish a fortified trading post there, went disastrously. A truce, in great part effected by harassing Mughal shipping and ports elsewhere along the Indian coast, and the Mughals' need for trade and seaborne transportation finally settled matters around, and after, Shaista's departure from Bengal.

◆

We'll take a closer look at the looming British threat to the various rulers of the subcontinent, and Bengal in particular a little later.

Here it is enough to say that the British had begun to push their boundaries right from the time of Thomas Roe, ambassador from the Court of St James to the court of the Mughal emperor Jahangir from 1615 to 1618. Being the ambassador didn't prevent him from harassing Mughal shipping to the benefit of the Company and Crown to override the dictum '..."Let this be received as a rule, that if you will profit, seek it at sea and in quiett trade,"' as Keay notes. '... Roe's idea of "quiett trade" included a gratuitous attack on Mughal shipping once every four years—as he explained, "we must chasten these people"...' But he did suggest, and Company directors agreed with him, observes Keay, of the need to generally avoid conflict, and not burden British inroads into India with 'garrisons and wars'. It was a question of economics 'as a guarantee of favourable trading conditions an imperial farman looked to provide the perfect, because inexpensive, alternative.'

Of course, it didn't quite turn out that way. Fortifications had followed factories. Company and Crown would be cemented in the subcontinent on account of skirmishes and wars. Roe's exhortations would appear tame when compared to that of Gerald Aungier, who became President at Surat and Governor of Bombay in 1669. We read in Sukumar Bhattacharya's *The East India Company and the Economy of Bengal: From 1704 to 1740* that Aungier wrote a 'lengthy' despatch to the directors in London in 1677, recommending 'a severe and vigorous [policy to ensure the stability of the trade]'. Aungier, who appears to have had the mien of a musketeer rather than a merchant, added: 'Justice and necessity of your estate now require that in violent distempers, violent cures are only successful; that the times now require you to manage your general commerce with your sword in your hands.' A diet of Aungier with a supplement of Roe would become the preferred Company way.

The episode with Shaista Khan would be only the first of several run-ins the Company would have with the nawabs of Bengal that, of course, peaked with Plassey. The opposite is as significant: Friction between Company and the governors of Bengal had existed several decades before Alivardi and Siraj sat on the masnad. Grandfather and grandson hardly set the precedent, whatever apologia for Clive & Co. may claim. It dilutes the exclusivity of the storyline of Siraj-harassed-the-Company, a major paper trigger for Plassey.

It is also interesting to note that, even as the Company in Bengal attempted to move on from its ill-advised and outright belligerence against Shaista to a relatively more pacific route under subsequent subahdars, it would plan to take defensive precautions in its bases, in particular Fort William in Calcutta. This was not to pre-empt hostilities with the French, the danger that would consume them in the 1740s and, again, in the later years of Alivardi's reign and the ultimate flashpoint during that of Siraj, but against general chaos in the country that became evident several decades earlier.

The Company would return to the north soon after the end of Shaista's governorship in 1688, and establish its famous base in Calcutta. But for some years, everyone of consequence in Bengal would have to contend with Shaista, who even spawned a common phrase in Bengali for defeating someone, or dominating a situation: shāyéstā korā.

◆

After Shaista's departure from Bengal to Delhi during the latter half of Aurangzeb's reign, the churning resumed in Bengal, the political equations now also irrevocably tied to trade equations and ambitions of transnational companies. They would soon encounter the next significant governor of Bengal, Murshid Quli Khan.

Like much of Bengal, the British too learnt that the nawabs of Bengal, beginning with Murshid Quli, had begun to chart their own course as increasingly autonomous rulers. From the time Murshid Quli was minted as subahdar of Bengal, Orissa, and Bihar in 1717 (the same year the Company implemented its free-trade farman that was granted in the last days of 1716) he began what would be for the next several decades a breaking away from Delhi's command and control structure. The authority of the Mughal emperors and their empire would remain on paper but it was largely worth whatever the viceroy-nawabs of Bengal, like their colleagues in the Deccan, determined it would be.

2

BENGAL: IN FOR A POUND (AND FRANCS, ESCUDOS, GUILDERS, AND KRONERS)

'No part of India possessed such natural advantages...for commerce'

European traders knew of the environs of Makhsudabad long before it became Murshidabad—the viceregal capital of the Mughal empire in the east, for all purposes the capital of its own kingdom under Murshid Quli Khan.

According to the *Riyaz*, a merchant, Makhsus Khan, built a serai or guest house there. The place eventually came to be known as Makhsusabad, and the 'houses of a few shop-keepers were placed there'. 'Abad'—village or habitation—has its roots in Persian: literally, a cultivated place, it began to gain prominence as a trading centre from the early 1600s on. That was several decades before Calcutta, a few days' ride downriver along the Bhagirathi–Hugli, came about in 1690.

Makhsusabad evidently swapped a consonant and became Makhsudabad. The area also made a mark with its products, even though Bengal had already exhibited the wonder of muslin, or malmal, as the historian Irfan Habib reminds us, alongside calico and chintz, or chhint in northern India, and 'silks with warp and weft pre-dyed (patola) and gold brocade (zarbaft) of Gujarat; and hand-painted chintz...of Machilipatnam...', the coastal town in Andhra Pradesh where the Company established its first factory in 1611.

O'Malley writes that the area's quality silk 'attracted the attention' of two English agents '...who were sent from Agra to Patna in 1619 to set up a trading station there'. The following year they recorded an investment of 500 rupees to purchase samples of silk. In William Foster's *The English Factories in India 1618-21*, we read a letter dated 12 July 1620, by one of the agents Robert Hughes addressed to the Company's president and council in Surat—the factory there was established in 1613. Hughes writes of 'Serbandy silke, the best of

Mucksoude and Sideabaude'—Makhsudabad and Saidabad—'from whence these sortes are wound of'.

In a series of volumes, Foster records the thoughts and correspondence of Company agents and factories through much of the seventeenth century, and his work is a trove of early Company interactions as its representatives steadily made their way east—and became increasingly appreciative of the wares of Bengal. After leaving Agra, Hughes and his colleague first encountered the governor of 'Puttana' [Patna], 'Muckrob Con' [Muqarrab Khan, governor of Bihar at the time] who was keen to trade with the English for some 'cloth and hydes...also tapestrye, clothe of tishoo, velvetts, embrodares, fethers, or anye other rich commodities to bee gotten...', and even made a gesture to make them feel at home ('hath given order to serche out for a house for mee').

The two English merchants had already sent what samples of 'rawe silke of Bengalla' they could to Agra, and also promised to send 'some quiltes of Sutgonge [Satgaon near Hugli], wrought with yellowe silke', and seemed to be enamoured of the 'doupattas of Malda', and so taken with 'tusser stufes of Bengala' (tussar silk, and fabric of part-silk and part-cotton—'cotten') they purchased four hundred rupees worth.

As a keen merchant, Hughes also collected intelligence about the competition. He noticed that some 'Portingalls'—Portuguese— were in town, and that some more had left for their bases in Bengal ('latlye gon for theire portes in Bengala'). He asked about them: '...into whose trafiqe I have made enquirye, and gather that theye usialye bringe vendadable here all sortes of spices and silke stufes of Chyna' and some jewellery. In turn they purchased carpets from 'Junapoore' (Jaunpur), 'ambertye' (amber), fine and thin cotton cloth and silk. He notes that 'Mogoles', merchants from Upper India or Persia, were already 'here like bees'.

There is some speculation as to which year, 1658 or 1659, the Company factory in Qasimbazar, a future centre of intrigue and powerplay just south of Makhsudabad, opened for business. O'Malley writes of a letter of the Court of Directors in London to the Company's agent at Hugli, dated 27 February 1658 [he erroneously wrote it as 1758], mentioning Hugli, a few bends up the eponymous river from the future Calcutta, Balasore on the coast of Orissa, Patna, and Qasimbazar as 'the four factories which we determine shall be settled in the Bay of Bengal'. O'Malley speculates that the use of the future tense 'makes it uncertain' whether the Qasimbazar factory started in 1658, and offers the engineer-orientalist Henry Yule's opinion that it is 'doubtful' whether it was 'regularly occupied' before 1659.

At any rate, Qasimbazar—Cossimbazar in most British references—was among the first places in Bengal marked for a Company factory, subordinate to the agency at Hugli. Job Charnock, who is credited by the British for establishing the Company seat at Calcutta, was a junior member among the four representatives at the Qasimbazar factory at an annual salary of £20 (the relative income value of about £85,000 in 2018); his chief, John Kenn, was paid twice that. We learn that Charnock thereafter had a stint in Patna, but returned in 1680 as chief at Qasimbazar, where he formally remained chief until 1686, all through the trade-related tussle with Shaista Khan. Qasimbazar would remain prominent in the Company's scheme of things for more than a hundred years, well after Plassey.

The United Company of Merchants of England Trading to the East Indies, or, in common usage the Honourable East India Company, with its crafty divine indemnity—Deo ducente nil nocet, proclaimed the Company's motto: When (or Where) god leads, nothing can harm—was certainly proactive in the Bengal trade. But John Company, as it became colloquially known, was far from the only transnational interest fishing in Bengal.

Qasimbazar was very important for the French East Indies enterprises too, from the earliest days of the British there. O'Malley refers to the diary of Streynsham Master, the Company's president in council at Madras: during his visit to Bengal in 1676 he wrote of a plot of land allotted to the French. (This was three years after the French established a settlement in Chandannagar, or Chandernagore, just south of Hugli along the western bank of the Bhagirathi–Hugli. The site of the French factory in Qasimbazar would colloquially be known as Farashdanga, French bank, or French land, same as the settlement at Chandannagar.) There was an Armenian settlement in nearby Saidabad. The Dutch were also nearby, with a 'thriving factory' at Kalikapur.

'The object of all was the silk trade, the importance of which may be gathered from the accounts given by both [the seventeenth-century French physician and traveller, François] Bernier and [French traveller and merchant Jean-Baptiste] Tavernier,' writes O'Malley. 'The former says that "the Dutch have sometimes seven or eight hundred natives employed in their factory at Cossimbazar, where, in like manner, the English and other merchants employ a proportionate number." The latter says that Cossimbazar annually exported about 22,000 bales of silk [of 100 pounds each, or a little above 45 kilograms]. "The Dutch generally took, either for Japan or for Holland, 6,000 to 7,000 bales, and they would have liked to get more, but the merchants of Tartary and of the whole Mughal Empire opposed their doing so, for these merchants took as much as the Dutch, and the balance remained for the people of the country for the manufacture of their own stuffs".'

The Dutch had first come ashore at Chinsurah, the location of one of its key factories established in 1656. Chinsurah was sandwiched between the British base in Hugli and the French settlement in Chandannagar. With the formal permission of Mughal emperors and local clearance, equally formal, from rulers of Bengal, the Portuguese had marked their presence within twenty-five years of Afonso de Albuquerque conquering Goa in 1510. For several decades, they indulged in trade and pillage from the mouth of the Hugli in the Bay of Bengal all the way east across Bengal's vast estuaries to Chittagong until they ran into Shaista Khan. The Danes were relatively late to the Bengal matrix. After a failed attempt, they would be finally established at Srirampur—Serampore—in 1755. It would be the southernmost of the European outposts on the Bhagirathi–Hugli, and the closest to Calcutta, by then already a place of great consequence, where palaces, 'nabob'-worthy pleasures and pestilence coexisted. It was just a year before Siraj became nawab. Two years before the battle at Plassey.

◆

The British were perhaps the most persistent in the pursuit of commerce in these parts. The Company concentrated on special products, silk for instance, Murshidabad's 'principal non-agricultural industry'. O'Malley writes that during the reign of Alivardi, between 1740 and 1756, 'raw silk to the value of [rupees] 87½ lakhs [8.75 million] was annually entered in the Custom House books at Murshidabad'. The business was already thriving several decades earlier. In 1670, a factor 'well skilled in silk' was assigned to Qasimbazar from Britain to increase both quality and trade in this 'general market' for silk in Bengal. 'And in 1681, when the Chief was Job Charnock...out of £230,000 sent out by the East India Company as "investment" to Bengal, £140,000 was assigned to Cossimbazar. From this time forward the Company made unremitting efforts to foster sericulture and extend the trade in silk'—here he refers to *Silk in India*, an 1872 study by J. Geoghegan, an undersecretary with the colonial government of India. The effort would work so well that 'by 1776 "Bengal silk drove all competitors, except Italian and China silks, out of the English market"'.

'The wealth of Murshidabad,' O'Malley writes, 'made it a prize worth winning...'

Bengal too. Moroccan traveller Abu Abdullah Muhammad Ibn Abdullah al-Lawati al-Tanji Ibn Battuta, who travelled to India in fourteenth century CE, had set the benchmark for the attractions of Bengal, despite its sapping humidity, trying climate and tropical infestations, when he described the land as '...a hell full of good things'.

Trade would blossom in the years before and, certainly, after Plassey. Major James Rennell in his *Memoir of a Map of Hindoostan*, published three decades after Plassey, mentioned that the river-borne trade of Bengal kept in constant employment 30,000 boatmen. But this was questioned by John Murray in his 1820 work, *Geographical, Statistical, and Historical Description of Hindostan*, that 'probably some mistake must have occurred in the calculation' made just four decades earlier, 'as there are certainly at present much nearer ten times that number'.

There were testimonials of another kind, perhaps more influential in the context of Britain's empire project. Thomas Babington Macaulay, the intellectual architect of some of the most influential initiatives in British India, who said that the 'English language might be well and thoroughly taught' to the 'native' to provide a subservient human resource pool for the Raj, was as effusive in his praise of Bengal as he was withering in his criticism of its people. In an essay on Bengal's corporate conqueror Clive for the *Edinburgh Review* in 1840, Macaulay, usually given to flair over information, wrote an excellent raison d'être for the Company's initial focus on Bengal, and for Clive's persistence:

> Of the provinces which had been subject to the house of Tamerlane, the wealthiest was Bengal. No part of India possessed such natural advantages, both for agriculture and for commerce. The Ganges, rushing through a hundred channels to the sea, has formed a vast plain of rich mould which, even under the tropical sky, rivals the verdure of an English April. The rice fields yield an increase such as is elsewhere unknown. Spices, sugar, vegetable oils, are produced with marvellous exuberance. The rivers afford an inexhaustible supply of fish. The desolate islands along the seacoast, overgrown by noxious vegetation, and swarming with deer and tigers, supply the cultivated districts with abundance of salt. The great stream which fertilises the soil is, at the same time, the chief highway of Eastern commerce. On its banks, and on those of its tributary waters, are the wealthiest marts, the most splendid capitals, and the most sacred shrines of India. The tyranny of man had for ages struggled in vain against the overflowing bounty of nature. In spite of the Mussulman despot, and of the Mahratta freebooter, Bengal was known through the East as the garden of Eden, as the rich kingdom. Its population multiplied exceedingly. Distant provinces were nourished from the overflowing of its granaries; and the noble ladies of London and Paris were clothed in the delicate produce of its looms.

Even as trade expanded, and the wares of Bengal became increasingly popular and coveted back home, there was the occasional example of sending coal to Newcastle, as it were.

Indian Civil Service officer and orientalist Henry Beveridge in his *Old Places in the Murshidabad District*, relates with ghoulish understatement a story taken from a Company-man's diary:

> In 1678, a lady with charming ignorance of Anglo-Indian requirements, sends her brother-in-law at Cossimbazar a box

containing a cravat and cuffs and ribbon of the newest mode and a border of lace for his night cap... Alas, he was dead before the box left England.

♦

There is a legend about Murshid Quli that he was born a Hindu in the Deccan. Several historians and chroniclers refer to it—Jadunath Sarkar is a proponent of this, basing his assertion on a medieval Persian text, *Ma'sir al-Umara*. Certainly, most depictions of Murshid Quli in the profile-driven style of the time have him as somewhat blunt-nosed and chubby, not the typical hawk-nosed and lean-of-body attributes as visualized in portraits of nobles, generals, and nawabs with genes from the regions of the Hindukush and Karakoram, and further west in Persia. (Sarkar, who co-edited the landmark *History of Bengal*, was an expert in medieval Indian texts and history. He authored a formidable four-volume history, *The Fall of the Mughal Empire*, besides histories of the Maratha chieftain Shivaji, and of the kingdom of Jaipur. These took him first to the study of Arabic, Persian, Marathi, Rajasthani, French, and Portuguese.)

When he was ten years old, the eventual nawab Murshid Quli was sold to a Persian offical. He was converted to Islam, and renamed Mohammad Hadi, and travelled to Persia with his master and mentor. The young Hadi returned some years later to work with a diwan—revenue administrator—in central India, and through diligent application eventually came to the notice of Aurangzeb. The *Riyaz* mentions that the emperor sent him to the subah of Bengal as its diwan, and with a title, Kartalab Khan—the seeker of challenges—to go with his formal name at this time, Jafar Khan Nasiri.

This much named and titled man arrived in Jahangirnagar–Dhaka to find as his superior, the prince Azim-us-Shan, appointed viceroy of Bengal, Bihar, and Orissa by his grandfather Aurangzeb. Kartalab Khan, generally held as a person of some integrity, encountered the prince's politics, part of which was massive corruption to build a nest egg to tide over the post-Aurangzeb chaos. It was already clear chaos would arrive, with numerous claimants to the throne in Delhi. Azim-us-Shan wished to be one.

Kartalab Khan outed the prince to his grandfather the emperor, along with a complaint that his life was in danger at the hands of this prince—some texts mention an assassination attempt. The wary and shrewd diwan shifted to Makhsudabad in 1704 (some accounts have it as 1702 or 1703) to distance himself from the prince, whom Aurangzeb eventually shifted to Patna, the administrative and commercial capital of Bihar in 1707, the year he died.

The *Riyaz* gently mentions what transpired between Kartalab Khan and the ambitious prince:

> ...finding that he could not pull on with the Prince, put forward the pretext that the mahals of Bengal were at a long distance from that place, separated himself from association with the Prince, and established himself at Makhsusabad, and placed there the Amlas of Zemindars, and Qanungos and other officials employed in connection with the Revenue Administration of Crownlands. And at Dughariah, which was quite a wilderness, he erected a palace, established the Board of Revenue (Dewankhanah) and the Court of Exchequer, and made collections of the Imperial revenue.

As we have seen, chaos duly followed Aurangzeb's death. Kartalab Khan kept his head down and carried on as diwan and, later, governor of Orissa, meanwhile building an unlikely but valuable acquaintance with a son of Azim-us-Shan, the eventual emperor, Farrukhsiyar. This young prince had moved from Jahangirnagar–Dhaka to spend several years in Makhsudabad, where the diplomatic Kartalab Khan maintained perfect civility with him. When Aurangzeb's successor, Bahadur Shah I, died in 1712, Azim-us-Shan made a play for emperor. He lost, and was killed in March that year. Jahandar Shah became emperor for just under a year, losing his life to a powerplay by Farrukhsiyar. That prince then became emperor, in early 1713.

Kartalab Khan, Bengal and the Company's future would in some ways be tied to this emperor. In 1717, Farrukhsiyar formalized the appointment of Kartalab Khan—now the nawab Murshid Quli Khan—as governor of Bengal, Bihar, and Orissa.

Murshid Quli quickly made his mark. Makhsudabad indelibly became Murshidabad, the new power centre in the east, soon a place of palaces and relative prosperity. The settlement grew rapidly to reflect its status as the new capital of Bengal. 'The largest dimensions of the city proper in 1759,' noted *The Imperial Gazetteer of India*, 'are said to have been 5 miles along the Bhagirathi in length and 2½ miles in breadth on each bank of the river, while the circumference of its extensive suburbs has been put as high as 30 miles.'

◆

By 1914, the year O'Malley's *Murshidabad* was published, the former capital of the subah of Bengal, Bihar, and Orissa had given its name to a district shaped like 'an isosceles triangle with its apex pointing to the north-west'. Nominal nawabs ruled the fading town, more jewelled mayors than moguls. Murshidabad wasn't even the district headquarters: that was Berhampore—Bahrampur—less than 10 kilometres downriver, and it remains so today.

But the region's natural features, intrinsic to its history, were largely unchanged. The western aspect of Murshidabad, across the Bhagirathi, stretches towards Birbhum and the Rajmahal hills in an undulating terrain with 'banks of bluffs', a place of 'laterite clay and nodular limestone' as O'Malley describes it. For the Marathas who would soon harass Bengal and its nawabs, in particular Alivardi Khan, to distraction, such land was hardly a deterrent. They swept up from Orissa and for several years plundered land along the west coast of the Bhagirathi seemingly at will, weakening Alivardi's hold and, as we have seen, ultimately wresting Orissa from him.

The varied land was rich. The chief crop further west of Murshidabad was winter rice. To the north, east, and south lay lowland areas of rice and winter wheat, woven together by a network of rivers and channels the most important of which were the Bhagirathi, Jalangi, and Bhairab, all distributaries of the Ganga. Several oxbow or horseshoe lakes, the remnants of an abandoned loop of such rivers and channels were called beel or jheel. Motijheel, and its eponymous palace of which we shall read more, was one such, situated along a loop as the Bhagirathi moved away—Bengal's rivers have long meandered at the will of momentum and siltation. As with the deltaic regions of Bengal the marshes and these waterbodies were lush with submerged and floating water plants. 'The edge of sluggish creeks are lined with sedges and bulrushes, and the banks of rivers have a hedge-like scrub jungle,' O'Malley notes with precision the lay of the land. 'Deserted or uncultivated homestead lands are covered with shrubberies of semi-spontaneous species, interspersed with clumps of planted bamboos and groves of Areca [betel nut], Moringa...and Anona [custard apple].'

There was an abundance of bamboo, banyan, pipal (ficus), babul (acacia), jackfruit, bael (wood apple), tamarind, coconut, date and much kul (jujube), the fruit tree also used to source lac. And, of course, mango. 'Murshidabad has a reputation for its mango orchards,' O'Malley writes. The reputation remains as true today. Vast orchards along the Bhagirathi greet visitors. Varieties like kalapahar, which turns blackish as it ripens, and was reputedly the favourite of both Murshid Quli and Alivardi, are rare. As is the kohitur, of which a handful of trees exist in the garden of a descendant of Mir Jafar, but there are still over a hundred varieties, some grown and grafted since at least the eighteenth century, that find their way to markets. It isn't surprising Clive and his forces decided to set up base at a mango orchard at Plassey. They are ubiquitous on the banks of the Bhagirathi in a stretch to the north and to the south of Murshidabad, where Plassey is.

The thread that strung it all together, from Murshidabad right down to the Bay of Bengal was the Bhagirathi–Hugli. This has always been a tricky river, with varying levels during the wet and dry seasons, ebb and flow of tides, and accumulation of silt that would create char or chor, banks. These were all impediments to seamless passage from Calcutta to Murshidabad. The earliest historical mention of the silting of the Bhagirathi, O'Malley claims, is from a letter of Tavernier dated 6 January 1666. In it, Tavernier mentions that fellow traveller and chronicler Bernier was compelled to travel overland from 'a place near Rajmahal to Cossimbazar' as the river wasn't navigable. 'When the river is low, it is impassable because of a large sand-bank which lies before a town called Suti.'

'Elsewhere,' writes O'Malley, 'Tavernier speaks of the river as a canal...' He notes another account, from 1683, that mentioned the river above Nadia being full of shoals, and that, when he arrived at 'Maula'–possibly Mohula—he went from 'thence to Cossimbazar by palki, a distance of 9 or 10 miles'.

The Bhagirathi channel continued to deteriorate. Charles Stewart's 1813 work, *History of Bengal*, establishes a Plassey-related Bhagirathi factoid. In 1757, right before the Battle of Plassey, Siraj attempted to take advantage of the river's temperamental flow '... believing that the English ships of war might proceed up the eastern branch of the Ganges to the northern point of Cossimbazar island [a large feature formed by an extreme loop of the Bhagirathi] and come down the Bhagirathi to Murshidabad, commanded immense piles to be driven in the river at Suti, by which the passage of that river has been rendered merely navigable by boats, and that only during half the year.'

A post-Plassey record by Major Rennell, in 1781, notes that the 'Cossimbazar river'—the Bhagirathi—was nearly dry from October to May. O'Malley quotes a record, from a 1797 'memoir' on the Ganga by a Captain Colebrook (I take it to mean the officer Robert Hyde Colebrooke, who was also for some time surveyor general of Bengal, and wrote 'On the Course of the Ganges through Bengal'). Colebrooke notes that Bhagirathi was in some years not 'practicable for boats proceeding to Calcutta'. Even the Jalangi, generally more robust had its patchy years too. It was unnavigable in the driest months. These 'Murshidabad' rivers were altogether not 'to be depended on'.

◆

Murshid Quli's reign as subahdar between 1717 to 1727 was highlighted by a major shake-up and reorganization of the revenue administration. Company officials would later adapt it in ferocious spirit, unleashing brutality and even helping to make a bad famine terrible.

By all accounts the nawab was conservative. He was pious to a fault and saw himself as a messenger of Islam. He was a teetotaller, kept away from narcotics, and was devoted exclusively to his wife, a rarity in those times. His plain grave, made so by his order, lies below the eastern steps of the Katra Masjid in Murshidabad in a tiny, dank chamber that is sometimes strewn with straw.

For all his humility and professed simplicity, he dealt harshly with any misdemeanour of citizens. In particular, he was extremely harsh in his punishment of corrupt revenue officials and defaulters, perhaps a holdover from his experience in Dhaka and with prince Azim-us-Shan. Among other histories, I read John McLane's *Land and Local Kingship in Eighteenth-Century Bengal*, in which he refers to the historian Abdul Karim to suggest Murshid Quli was first and foremost firm with officials, minor and senior, from record-keepers to collectors for any slip-ups. Besides being placed under guard, they were denied 'food, drink and "calls of nature"'.

And, from some accounts, Murshid Quli overlooked the brutality of his revenue officers against erring zamindars, although McLane says Karim questioned their single-source credentials of such accounts. For instance, take this description of the actions of one enforcer, Nazir Ahmad, taken from Munshi Salim Allah's *A Narrative of Transactions in Bengal during the Soobahdaries of Azeem us Shan, Jaffer Khan, Shuja Khan, Sirafraz Khan and Alyvirdy Khan*, translated from the Persian:

> He used to suspend zemindars by the heels, and after rubbing their soles of their feet with a hard brick, bastinado them with a switch. In the winter, he would order them to be stripped naked, and then sprinkled with water. He also used to have them flogged, till they consented to pay the money.

Another enforcer, Sayyid Reza Khan, a deputy diwan who married Murshid Quli's granddaughter, was perhaps more insistent, by sometimes placing erring officials and zamindars alike into a pit containing human waste in 'such a state of putrefaction as to be full of worms, and the stench was offensive... He also used to oblige them to wear leather long drawers, filled with live cats. He would force them to drink buffaloe's milk mixed with salt, till brought them to death's door by a diarrhoea...'

Murshidabad lore also attributes a daughter of Murshid Quli, the begum Azim-un-nisa, who was said to have had a peculiar obsession. She ate the liver of young men (another version of the lore suggests male children), hence her commonly-known alias, Kaleja-khaki Begum. Lore has it that it was all to cure an ailment of the heart (a version suggests an attempt to enhance sexual endeavour). This had to be imbibed occasionally (a version suggests: every night). The runaway begum of this runaway tale is said to have been buried alive by her husband in 1730, three years after the death of the appalled— and censorial—Murshid Quli. (Her tomb lies on the way to the tomb complex of Mir Jafar and his clan.)

Company officials, even relatively young officers, did not have to suffer such indignities with the nawab or his allegedly obsessive daughter, but as we shall see, life under Murshid Quli wasn't all smooth sailing, a bit of a dampener for an organization that flaunted a coat of arms with three three-masted ships under full sail protected by a pair of ferocious sea lions—literally, lions with piscine lower bodies.

3

THE NAWAB, HIS BANKER,
THE COMPANY, AND THEIR NEEDS

'...we are resolved to turn our faces to fortune'

Murshid Quli contributed to another development of consequence for Bengal—and, eventually, for Plassey. He patronized a family of bankers, the Seths, a branch of which had moved east as part of a generations-long scattering, from Nagar in Rajasthan to the far west of the subcontinent.

Under Murshid Quli's patronage and that of successive nawabs, the Seths would seamlessly leverage every opportunity and take care to hedge their business as best as possible. They would play all sides to their best advantage and have others fall in line through their influence as financiers—to nearly all parties in India's and Bengal's dynamic equation. They dealt big. 'Described as the "Rothschild of India" by Edmund Burke,' notes a chapter in the work, *Finance and Modernization: A Transnational and Transcontinental Perspective*, edited by Gerald D. Feldman and Peter Hertner, 'the banking house would consider it beneath their "dignity" to lend below Rs 100,000—a colossal sum in those days'. The colonial bureaucrat S. C. Hill quotes contemporary Company records to note: 'Among the leading Natives, the Sets stand out as the great millionaires of their day. Jagat Set was probably worth eight millions sterling, and, as the Rothschild of his time, held a high place in the Council of Murshidabad.'

For several decades the Seths displayed a particular knack to back the winning horse. Even create the winning horse.

Murshid Quli and the banker Manik Chand had formed a friendship in Dhaka, where the latter had established a branch—kothi, literally, house—during the future nawab's tenure there as diwan. When Murshid Quli moved to Makhsudabad, Manik Chand moved with his patron. It would transform his fortunes. Manik Chand was effectively the chancellor of the exchequer, and supervised the collection of revenue. The revenue of Bengal, the richest province of the Mughal empire, passed through his banking house. The innovative banker was reputedly the first to transfer revenue worth several million rupees to Delhi by a hundi—draft—that would be drawn on a correspondent bank there run by the family, obviating the cumbersome process of carting numerous chests of coin under guard. The house quickly emerged as the biggest merchant bankers in eastern India, with the privilege of advising nawabs and with the power to stand up to European merchants who had the weight of their countries behind them. His house would also lend to these merchants, advise them, intercede on their behalf and, occasionally, chastise them.

Manik Chand presided over a banking empire with branches across Bengal in Calcutta, Dhaka, and Hugli, and in other parts of eastern India in Assam and Patna. The house networked with correspondent banks, run by the family, in Kashi (Varanasi) and Delhi; and in the fast-growing Company settlement-towns of Surat, Bombay, and Madras. After Farrukhsiyar became emperor, Murshid Quli interceded on behalf of his banker friend to procure him the title, Seth. It's derived from the Sanskrit shreshthi, merchant. It's today a common surname in northern India. It's also freely applied in western India to mean: chief, or patron.

The Seths used their heft in several visible and invisible ways. Take the matter of minting money. O'Malley, like several other chroniclers, notes the irritation of the Company at its inability to mint coins in this eventual seat of Bengal's nawab. Makhsudabad had, at least since 1679, been a 'mint-town'. This is indicated by a rupee coin from Aurangzeb's reign preserved in the Lahore Museum. J. H. Little, in his detailed biography, *The House of Jagat Seth*, explains that when Murshid Quli (then Kartalab Khan) moved to Makhsudabad from Jahangirnagar–Dhaka and formally transferred Bengal's mint there, it 'deprived Dacca of its last claim to be considered the capital of Bengal and transferred the title to Murshidabad'. (Little wrote of the original site of the mint as being where the Imambara stands today—it was built in 1847 after a mosque complex built by Siraj was destroyed in fires. Little quoted a diwan of an early twentieth century nawab of Murshidabad to suggest that is why the ghat on the Bhagirathi near the Imambara is called Mint Ghat. As I write this, a hundred years after Little published his work, it is still known as Mint Ghat.)

The mint did rather well. The Company contributed to its profits from time to time. For example, in 1706 the 'English at Cossimbazar were induced to pay Rs. 26,000 for the convenience of having bullion, which they imported from Europe, coined into rupees at the Murshidabad mint,' writes O'Malley. Company sources claim that Murshid Quli reneged on a promise he made in 1715—two years before he formally became subahdar of Bengal—to permit the Company to freely coin its own 'siccas', and by 1716 had begun to disrupt the Company's business in Qasimbazar over the dispute.

Samuel Feake, at the time chief of the factory in Qasimbazar, advised his superiors that a balm of Rs 25,000 would help matters. This gift was to be distributed as follows: 15,000 rupees to Murshid Quli, 5,000 to his diwan, Ikram Khan, and the remaining 5,000 to be distributed between various mutsuddis or accountants, and the important keeper of the mint, 'Ragonundun Darogha'—the daroga, Raghunandan.

Feake was following established practice with Murshid Quli: he had more than once put the squeeze on the Company. Once he had raised a demand of 30,000 rupees to permit hindrance- and duty-free trade, in the name of the emperor. The Company offered 20,000 rupees. The nawab declined. Various underling governors and officials had routinely wanted gifts and bribes of smaller amounts, but this was serious. Company 'Consultation' of 18 July 1706 records 'advice from Mannick Chund' that a 'sanad' or permission for 'our free trade in Bengal for a piscash' of that amount. That peshkash, gift, didn't find its way to Murshid Quli. The Company withheld it as, meanwhile, the Mughal emperor Aurangzeb had died in 1707, triggering a war of succession. The officer who carried the money to Qasimbazar from Calcutta was ordered back. Company chiefs in Calcutta didn't want funds squandered. They would wait until the power structure became clear.

Pressure resumed. In 1711, there was a demand for 45,000 rupees to again procure the free-trade farman in the name of the emperor at the time, Bahadur Shah, sometimes referred to as Shah Alam.

There would in addition be 'contingent charges' for several officers, amounting to several thousand rupees. The Company offered 30,000 rupees, and added a threat to withdraw the Qasimbazar factory. We learn from Little's narrative and C. R. Wilson's *The Early Annals of the English in Bengal*, and records of Company minutes and correspondence that on 30 July the Calcutta Council ordered its chief in Qasimbazar, Robert Hedges, to convey to Murshid Quli that the offer would remain at 30,000, all inclusive. Or else they would close down the factory in Qasimbazar and obstruct Mughal shipping from passing Fort William at Calcutta. They would also let the emperor know how his diwan in Bengal was hampering trade. On 6 August, the Council sent another message to Hedges: '...if the Duan [Diwan] will not comply we are resolved to turn our faces to fortune.'

The stalemate was broken a week later by Manik Chand's nephew, Fateh Chand—the first in the family who, in a few short years, would be granted the title of Jagat Seth, literally, Banker to the World. Murshid Quli would request the emperor for a free-trade farman.

(Some chroniclers claim the title, and emerald seal of the Jagat Seth, was granted by Farrukhsiyar. Little disputes this. He refers to family documents, India Office Records, and proof sheets of Wilson's unpublished third volume of *Early Annals* to surmise that, sometime between the end of 1722 and the end of 1723, when Muhammad Shah was emperor, Fateh Chand received from him the title of Jagat Seth. 'The original farman of the emperor which is still in the possession of the family,' writes Little, 'has been thus translated: "At this victorious hour and happy moment, the world-obeyed command of sunny lusture receives the honour of issue that, from the Court of eternal sovereignty, Seth Fateh Chand—with the award of the title of Jagat Seth as a hereditary distinction and the bestowal of magnificent robes of honour, an elephant and a pearl earring, and his son Anand Chand with the title of Seth and the gift of robes of honour and a pearl earring ..."' That 'imperative' arrived from the 'presence of glorious majesty', in the 'fourth year of the exalted reign'.)

The Seths with typical play-all flourish stepped in with a solution to bypass the threat by Murshid Quli to disrupt trade, with a tidy benefit to the banking house through brokerage. '...Futtichundsaw [Saw is a corruption of Sahu] an Eminent Merchant being now with us,' the Council in Calcutta observed, 'and offering to provide our whole Investment now ordered at Cassimbazar for an allowance of 6¼ per cent, he standing to all bad debts at the Aurangs and our goods to be delivered here in Calcutta. It being so late in the Year we judge this to be best and only method that appears to secure these goods for our homeward bound Shipping.'

Hedges went along with this practical solution offered by his bosses. There wasn't another way to bypass Murshid Quli, '...for, if any merchant had supplied the English, he certainly would have been punished by the Duan, who still continues obstinate about the Sunnud'.

Murshid Quli woke up to the tactic, and to potential loss of trade, when Hedges prepared to close the Qasimbazar factory in October 1711. The diwan made a counter offer. A payment of 30,000 rupees for permission from him for duty-free passage of Company goods in Bengal, Bihar, and Orissa—the money to be paid on receipt of this sanad—and a further 22,500 rupees when the emperor's farman came through. This was agreeable to the Council as they realized the 'Duan's interest is very great at Court'. They urged Hedges to agree. A powerful noble on their side was better for free flow of trade across three vast territories of the subcontinent instead of the likelihood of Murshid Quli practising at will the Qasimbazar Shuffle, as it were, across his 'Jurisdiction', and obstructing the purchase and passage of goods. As the Council noted, the nawab '...undoubtedly will impede them very much if we don't agree with him'.

Such impediments, intercession by the Seths and others, irritations and solutions of the moment would continue until Plassey—a very business-like project all around.

Even though the fracas with Murshid Quli over trade was papered over with the help of the Seths, his continued obstruction with the mint didn't sit well with John Company, especially given its desire to expand its business in Bengal. Fort William had become the seat of the Bengal Presidency in 1700. Trade was picking up. The scholar Susil Chaudhuri writes of how saltpetre from the region of Patna, considered to be superior to saltpetre from the Coromandel and Gujarat for making gunpowder, was added to the export inventory from Calcutta. It greatly supplemented the flourishing trade in textiles which would remain the mainstay of the Company's sales in London through the eighteenth century, as we see in documents of the India Office records maintained at the British Library in London. (A remarkably post-colonial comment attends the list in the digital archives of the Library: 'While workers were subjected to the devastating effects of extreme climate, famine and war, the landowners, brokers and the Company grew rich on their skills.')

The Company was poised at the cusp of the Bengal boom, the extent of which would become evident well before Plassey. In his 1953 doctoral thesis on early eighteenth-century Bengal trade for the University of London, Sukumar Bhattacharya noted how the number of trading ships bound specifically for Bengal from Britain grew steadily from 1708–09 to 1739–40—from the reign of Murshid Quli to the beginning of the reign of Alivardi.

However, even as business was picking up, it also became evident to the Company that, for all the surface bonhomie and commercial dealings, the Seths didn't see it in their interest to permit the Company unfettered access to the mint, thereby reducing their hold over it and their income.

Realizing this truth, the Council in Calcutta refused to pay any more facilitation money—bribes—to Murshid Quli, preferring instead to smoothen the way in Delhi and wait for composite imperial permission to trade freely and to use the mint, among other concessions. The Company's embassy led by Surman petitioned the Mughal court in Delhi in 1716 'that the officers of the mint at Murshidabad should at all times, when required, allow three days in the week for the coinage of the English Company's money'. Surman requested use of the mint 'without let or molestation', we learn in Wilson's *Early Annals*.

News of a farman obtained from the emperor Farrukhsiyar by Surman's pathbreaking embassy reached Calcutta in May 1717. Besides granting the Company the right to freely trade in Bengal—the origin of much heartburn later, and part of the mortar of Plassey— the farman, at least to the mind of the Company, opened a door to press for use of the mint in Murshidabad.

'In consideration of a piscash of 3,000 Rupees per annum payable by the Company at Hughly,' goes a translation of the 'Phirmaund for Bengal, Behar and Orixa' from 'Phuruhshir' in the third volume of

Hill's *Bengal in 1756–1757*. 'That all their mercantile affairs together with their gomastahs (factors) have free liberty in all subahships to pass and repass to and fro either by land or water in any port or district through-out the several provinces above said and liberty to buy and sell at their will and pleasure.' The operative phrase mentioned a little later on in the farman was 'custom free'.

The Company had permission to establish a factory and trade in 'whatsoever place they have a mind' and the emperor acknowledged the Company's request for earmarking of land—40 bighas, or a little over 13 acres—for such factories. The 'renting' of Calcutta, including Sutanuti and Gobindapur, was reconfirmed at an annual payment of rupees 1,195 and six annas; and thirty-eight 'towns'—villages, really—'adjoining to the aforesaid towns' would be the Company's for the annual payment of rupees 8,121 and eight annas.

Madras 'siccaes' or siccas would now be considered on par with Surat coinage if they proved to be of similar quality. And Bombay could mint siccas ('On the island of Bombay let there be the glorious stamp on the siccaes coined there, passing them current as all other siccaes are throughout the Empire'.) This was the precedent, along with Surman's petition on the record that the Company hoped to leverage for unobstructed use of the mint at Murshidabad.

◆

There's an interesting anecdote about Surman's embassy in Keay's *India*, which explains some of the behind-the-scenes activities, including the application of multiple pressure points: "'Considering the great pomp and state of the kings of Hindustan, we was very well received,' wrote Surman on arrival in Delhi…and was soon dispensing lavish bribes. Meanwhile, the mission's doctor successfully treated some swellings in the imperial groin. He was handsomely rewarded, but as to the farman, Farrukhsiyar remained infuriatingly indifferent. Only when threatened with the withdrawal of the Company from Surat and its other establishments in Gujarat did he relent. Losing the Company's bullion and trade for the price of a paper was unthinkable. On New Year's Eve 1716, more than a century since Captain William Hawkins had first applied for it, the farman received the imperial signature.'

It could be said that Surman's embassy, which left Calcutta in April 1714—thereafter remaining in Patna for a year before reaching Delhi in the autumn of 1715—was as much a triumph of the embassy's persistence as the application of its medical officer, William Hamilton. A glowing article in the *Indian Medical Gazette* in early 1907 described Hamilton as a medical officer who was 'probably the most famous, and is certainly the one who has been the greatest benefactor of his country' of all the doctors who had served in India in the previous three centuries. Hamilton certainly paid back manifold the three-hundred-rupee-wardrobe allowance to ensure he was presentable at the Mughal court.

Hamilton began treating Farrukhsiyar almost immediately after reaching Delhi. There was simply no opportunity for the embassy to present its requests to an emperor afflicted by ill health. A swelling in his groin was only one of the problems. James Talboys Wheeler's *Early Records of British India* notes a letter dated 6 October 1715 from Surman's embassy to Calcutta:

> We designed to have presented our petition on the first good opportunity, but His Majesty's indisposition continuing, and Mr. Hamilton having undertaken to cure him, it has been thought advisable by our friends, as well as by ourselves, to defer delivering it till such time as it shall please God that His Majesty in some measure returns to his former state of health, which advice, we intend to follow, considering that, whilst he is in so much pain, it can be but a very indifferent opportunity to beg favors of him. The first distemper the doctor took him in hand for, was swellings in his groin, which, thanks be to God, he is in a fair way of curing; but within these few days last past he has been taken with a violent pain, which is likely to come to a fistula; it hinders His Majesty from coming out, so naturally puts a stop to all manner of business, wherefore we must have patience perforce.

Two months later, Surman wrote of the 'welcome news' of Farrukhsiyar's recovery. 'As a clear demonstration to the world he washed himself the 23rd ultimo, and accordingly received the congratulations of the whole Court.' Farrukhsiyar also lavished gifts on Hamilton within a week of this public recovery—among these, a 'culgee' or kalgi set with precious stones to adorn his turban or cap, two diamond rings, an elephant, a horse, and 5,000 rupees, 'besides ordering at the same time all his small instruments to be made in gold, with gold buttons for his coat and waistcoat, and brushes set with jewels'.

While the petition took another year to work its way through channels even with this grateful emperor, at times it appeared as if, besides the matter of intense negotiation that contemporary chroniclers and later-day historians write of, the delays were caused by a Farrukhsiyar who was loathe to let this physician go. More than a year later, with the farman long granted and the embassy preparing to return to Calcutta, on 30 May 1717, Farrukhsiyar gifted robes of honour to Surman and his colleagues (Surman had already received a horse and a 'cunger'—khanjar, dagger, a week earlier) before granting them permission to leave. 'We were ordered to pass, one by one, to our obeisance, then to move from the Dewan,' notes a letter dated 7 June. 'We did so. But when it came to Mr. Hamilton's turn, he was told, the king had granted him a vest as a mark of his favour, but not for his despatch.' It would take artful persuasion by Surman (among other things, the absence of supplies of Western medicine in Delhi and '...the heart-breaking distractions of being parted for ever from his wife and children would be insupportable...') and an undertaking by Hamilton that he would return to Delhi after visiting his family in Britain to finally make Farrukhsiyar relent. That was fortunate, as we learn that Hamilton never married and died a bachelor in December the same year, shortly after the embassy's return to Calcutta.

'When the news of Hamilton's death in Calcutta was reported to the Emperor,' notes an article in the *Medical Gazette*, 'it is said that he sent a special messenger to Calcutta to ascertain whether the report was true, or had been published simply with a view to enable Hamilton to escape fulfilment of his promise to return to Delhi. Farakh Siyar himself, however, was not to enjoy the imperial dignity much longer,' the article drily observes, 'he was deposed and assassinated in 1719.'

Even with the good doctor's ministrations, the farman appears to have cost quite a bit, as the description by Keay hinted at.

Consultations of the Council in Fort St George on 20 August 1756 record a letter written by the Madras Council—purportedly by Robert Orme to Admiral Watson—that the 'embassy deputed by the East India Company to Delhi about 40 years ago, obtained from the great Mogul at more than the expence of £100,000, the rights and priviledges which their Settlements have hitherto enjoyed in Indostan'.

◆

At a congratulatory meeting in the summer of 1717, the Council in Calcutta decided to celebrate the imperial farman, and the decision was duly recorded:

> It being necessary to make some Publick Rejoycing upon the Advice. We have received from Mr. Surman and that all the Country may know Our Phirmauns are actually in Mr. Surman's Possesssion. Agreed That next Wednesday We make a Public Dinner for all the Company Servants and a loud Noise with Our Cannon and conclude the day with Bonfires and other Demonstrations of Joy which we know will be taken notice of in the Wacka and other publick News Papers.

In some ways the celebration may have been premature. We learn from Wilson that on 1 July that year the Company sent twenty chests of bullion for coining under the supervision of Qasimbazar-based chief Feake, but ran into trouble: an order could not be obtained, 'because Jaffercaun's Chief Mutsuddy, Ragonundun, seems to be in a dying Condition and till he recovers or is dead they cannot tell who to apply themselves to'. The only recourse appeared to be the nawab. Little dispassionately takes the story forward, based on Wilson's records. 'In the end they visited the Nawab and showed him a copy of the farman. The Nawab took it, read it and then bluntly refused them use of the mint.'

Murshid Quli had protected his own interests and that of his friendly bankers. When Raghunandan died, responsibility for running the mint passed on to the Seths, who carried on the monopoly, protected by the nawab. They charged a tidy sum for both minting from bullion and for re-coining—known as batta. Its profits, O'Malley notes, were stated in the 'rent-roll' of 1728 for Murshidabad 'to amount to Rs. 8,04,108'.

In Bengal, the nawab of Bengal was the law.

◆

The alliance of the nawab and Seths would remain potent for several decades, even as nawabs and those who ran the banking house changed. The mint remained out of reach to the British, whatever else may have come to them. Little tells us that, some years after the death of Manik Chand, the chief of the Company factory at Qasimbazar declared the Seth's 'adopted son [his nephew and heir, Jagat Seth Fateh Chand] had the sole use of the mint and not another banker or merchant dared to buy or coin a rupee's worth of silver'. (It was not until 1757, after Plassey, that the Company would first strike coins of its own in its new mint in Calcutta, 'but still in the name of the Emperor of Hindustan'.)

In the waning years of Alivardi's stressed rule, the ever-diligent and quick-footed Company representative in Qasimbazar, William Watts, who would conspire against Siraj, tried everything in his considerable arsenal of cash-and-cajole to get permission to mint coin in Calcutta for the Company, as the gambit to do so in Murshidabad had failed for several decades. His letter to the Court in London, routed through the chief in Calcutta, Roger Drake, is a study in Byzantine application and caution, and acknowledges the immense reach of the Seths, then led by Jagat Seth Madhab Rai, that would take John Company the victory at Plassey to finally leash:

> To the Hon'ble Roger Drake, Esq.

> Hon'ble Sir,—As the directions to the Hon'ble the President and Council from the Hon'ble the Court of Directors for the establishment of a mint in Calcutta require the utmost secrecy, I have been obliged to use the greatest caution in the affair, but by all the distant enquiries I could make it would be unpracticable to effect it with the Nabob, as an attempt of that kind would be immediately overset by Juggut Set even at the expense of a much larger sum than what our Hon'ble Masters allow us to pay. He being the sole purchaser of all the Bullion that is imported in

this province by which he is annually a very considerable gainer.

However, that no means might be left unessayed to get so beneficial a privilege for our Hon'ble Masters, I have at last ventured to entrust and consult our vaqueel, who is of the same opinion that it is impossible to effect it here, but said his Master Hackem Beg had a son in great power at Delhie, who might be able to get us a Phirmaund from the King; but that this would be attended at least with the expense of one hundred thousand Rupees, and that on the arrival of the Phirmaund here it would cost another hundred thousand Rupees to the Mutsuddys and Dewans of the Nawab to put that Phirmaund in force, and that this affair must be carried on with the greatest secrecy, that Juggut Set's house might not have the least intimation of it, but I much question whether we could get the mint for any sum with so extensive a privilege as our Hon'ble Masters want.

Cossimbazar,
Dated 8th Feby., 1753.
I am, &c., (Sd.)
WILLIAM WATTS

◆

There is a certain breathlessness that accompanies most descriptions of the Seths, a tradition that has persisted since the eighteenth century. N. K. Sinha, an academic who wrote the introduction to the 1967 edition of J. H. Little's *The House of Jagat Seth*, 'compared their role in money and politics with that of the Fuggers of Augsburg and the Medicis of Florence', writes Subodh Kumar Mukhopadhyay in the introduction to the 2016 edition.

There can be debate as to this Murshidabad-centred banking family being compared to the German house and the Fiorentino they came to replace in European prominence, variously in terms of absolute wealth, political reach, and patronage of a range of things from the church to the arts. However, there can be no doubt that, between 1717, when Murshid Quli became the subahdar of Bengal, Bihar, and Orissa, and 1760 when the nawab Mir Qasim agreed, as a quid pro quo, to a Company mint in Calcutta and effectively robbed the Seths of their monopoly, the Seths were the movers and shakers in Bengal. In 1765, their position would be weakened further as John Company gained the right to collect revenue for Bengal.

It isn't clear what guided Mukhopadhyay, also an academic like Sinha, to make a near-hagiographic claim that Seths were 'liberal in their attitude and never guided by petty interest', unless he means they were guided only by grand strategic interests like their Augsburgian and Florentine spirit-cousins. Mukhopadhayay goes a step further to establish the pious credentials of the Seths. 'They had nothing to do with the plunder of Murshidabad treasury after the battle of Plassey,' he writes, ignoring their established role in the Plassey conspiracy and its aftermath. 'Judging by the prevailing moral standard of the times they certainly stood high above others.'

Little, whose work the two Bengali academics introduce, was well-placed to write his work on the Seths. He was headmaster of Nawab Bahadur Institution in Murshidabad, established in 1825 to educate the children of the nawab and his relatives and courtiers. His tenure permitted him the trust, information, and several records and correspondence of the Seth family, which eventually led to the publication in two parts of his *The House of Jagat Seth*. Perhaps inevitably then, Little writes that the Seths were not 'tainted' with 'greed', 'chicanery', and 'treachery' that accrued to the Plassey plotters.

There is near-unanimity among past and present chroniclers that the Seths' political machinations were driven by the coldest calculation of business and profit—including the events leading up to Plassey. They were eager players in the grand games in which Clive himself excelled, in matters of Bengal, which he conveyed as being a place of 'fighting, tricks, chicanery, intrigues, politics and the Lord knows what'. (The original statement by Clive is actually contained in a post-Plassey correspondence with Orme, in which Clive offers his records: 'I am possessed of volumes of materials for the continuance of your History, in which will appear fighting, tricks, chicanery, intrigues, politics and the Lord knows what. In short there will be a fine field for you to display your genius in...')

In that maelstrom the Seths backed the English with consistency—that grudging acknowledgement alone remains Little's defence of their character. 'It would be fair to conclude,' he writes in the chapter on Jagat Seth Madhab Rai and his cousin 'Maharaja' Swaroop Chand, the two firmly linked to the Plassey conspiracy, 'that their conduct before the battle was not different from their conduct afterwards and hence we can assert that they had been consistently loyal to their engagement with the English and were untainted with the avarice of Omichand and the trickery and treachery of Rai Durlabh Ram and [other conspirators].'

Relations between Company merchants and the nawab of Bengal became 'frequently' strained on account of the nawab attempting to 'extort' money. 'At such times we shall find Jagat Seth acting as mediator between the English and the Nawab and we shall note the fact that whereas the officials of the Government, high and low always ready (as Poohbah would have said) to be insulted with a bribe.' Little is eloquent in their defence, 'the Seths of Murshidabad never demanded money from the English as the price of the services they rendered them,' even though the Company's own records prove otherwise, as we have seen. But yes, generally their return on investment lay in playing the longer game of secured business and profit. In this, as we shall see, they had no compunction in steamrolling the French when they weighed the British to be better placed for power play than their European neighbours and competitors.

To go by Little, it was nearly all preordained for the Seths. He quotes a 'Hindustani' proverb from Herbert Hope Risley's *The Peoples of India*: 'The three-tufted ones (Marwaris), the red-faced ones (Europeans) and the cactus plant cannot live without increasing.' The Seths certainly played their part in a prosperous inevitability.

4

THE PURITAN AND THE PHILANDERER: NOBLE ALIVARDI, IGNOBLE SIRAJ?

'...this excessively blustering and impertinent young man...'

Like grandfather, like grandson? Not Alivardi Khan and Siraj-ud-daulah. Not exactly.

Several chroniclers and historians accept this, following the cue of a couple of references, the memoirs of Jean Law, the French chief at Qasimbazar, and *Siyar-ul-Mutaqherin* by Syed Ghulam Hussain Khan Tabatabayi translated from the Persian into English by Haji Mustapha.

The three-volume *Siyar* richly details characters, politics, and court intrigues. It is sometimes unreliable—Where does fact end and fiction begin? What is reasonable and what is biased?—but it gives us a fine flavour of the times. The author claims proximity to the courts of the nawabs of Bengal (Alivardi and Siraj), and the nawab of Patna (Alivardi's grand-nephew and Siraj's cousin and sometime competitor, Shaukat Jang, of whom we shall read more shortly).

The *Siyar* is very harsh on Siraj, which has led some critics of this work, particularly in the state of West Bengal in India and in Bangladesh, to suggest it has an overlay of obsequiousness to the Company—part of a victor's narrative of justification. Even so, the *Siyar* is in several ways a pillar-work of Plassey. It's not so much for descriptions of the battle, which are scant, alleviated by a few dramatic descriptions. The *Siyar*'s value lies in suggesting the behaviour of the Plassey players, and setting the context of the times.

Perhaps there was for them no other way, but it appears to have been a conscious decision by those who provided follow-on narratives to not provide caveats for information or insights based on hearsay. This resulted in some rather sweeping formulations. Noble Alivardi and ignoble Siraj remained the general tone from the Plassey years up until the late-eighteenth century. From then on, a few historians, particularly in Bengal, began to portray Siraj as a wronged and hapless nawab, although some Siraj-defenders have also been guilty of taking that narrative to the extreme.

Plassey remains central to both sides of the argument. Siraj was the primary cause for Plassey. Or Siraj was a scapegoat for Plassey— or, at the very least, Siraj wasn't the only reason for Plassey. The truth remains in a grey zone between these suppositions, and both comforting and discomfiting certainties.

Alivardi, who was nawab from 1740 to 1756, is mostly portrayed as sensible and puritanical as much as his grandson, heir, and successor Siraj is portrayed as profligate and intemperate. The *Siyar*, for instance, holds Alivardi from his very youth to be 'averse from profligacy and debauch, and from everything that savoured of drunkenness; nor did he seem to have much taste for such amusements and music or dancing, or for the conversation of women'. By all accounts he remained faithful and devoted to his wife, the begum Sharf-un-Nisa, Gift of God.

Away from matters of state he spent time mostly immersed in the Quran, reciting prayer, even reading some history. Naturally these indulgences were possible in the more 'pacific' moments of his reign, the *Siyar* reminds us; a time of relative normality when that other normal, as it were, battling depredations by the Marathas for a decade until 1751—when a humiliating treaty with them bought peace—didn't occupy him to distraction and exhaustion.

Alivardi's day began a couple of hours before dawn, and, after ablutions and prayers, he took coffee with friends. At 7 a.m., it was time for a two hour-long durbar, the royal audience, and interaction with military and civil officers and all manner of petitioners.

Then he would retire for an hour or so with familiars: nobles, a son-in-law, Siraj, if he was in Murshidabad. There was chit-chat, interesting conversation, listening to poetry, a 'pleasing' story. He would personally supervise the menu for his lunch, including selecting meats and spices; food appears to have been Alivardi's other weakness—besides his indulgence of his grandson, Siraj. Imbued with a taste 'very nice and very delicate', Alivardi would ask for specific dishes, which were 'always [prepared] in his presence at the time, to the care of which was appointed either some of the persons then present, or some person freshly come from Persia or any other country renowned for good cookery'. Matters of state would be permitted to intrude whenever 'heads of office, and gentlemen and noblemen of the hall of audience'—who were in attendance as Alivardi took his literary, conversational, and culinary delights—had anything of consequence to say.

When the meal arrived, spread across a large 'napkin' on trays and plates, he would recommend to his favourites-of-the-day the dishes he had supervised, and took no more than a mouthful of every dish for himself. The nawab critiqued each dish for its flavour and finesse; we aren't told the name of the dishes, just that he obsessed over them. On some days he chose to dine in private, in the company of women, 'all being his daughters, grand-daughters, or nieces of relations'.

Then it was time for an hour-long nap, accompanied with storytelling by a professional storyteller. (Here, Haji Mustapha, the translator of the *Siyar*, is severe in a footnote awash in scorn: 'In a country where there are so few books, and where not one man in a thousand can read, and not one in a million has any inclination to read, storytelling becomes a profession very useful to great men. But for what? To learn something? No; only to lull them to sleep.' The Haji was a mysterious Frenchman who converted to Islam, and is also sometimes referred to as Monsieur Raymond. In the preface to the *Siyar* he identifies himself as Nota-Manus: literally, the note hand. He provides the translated *Siyar* with a curious and entertaining overlay of Eastern flair and orientalist approval and disdain.)

Nap over at one in the afternoon, Alivardi would wash, pray, and read a chapter of the Quran. Then he would take a glass of water cooled with saltpetre, or ice that was made possible from November to February with an innovative combination of keeping water in earthen plates to a depth of two feet, sheltered from a breeze and insulated by straw mats. After that, it was time to be reintroduced to the durbar, with men of learning, physicians, and such. Favoured guests were offered the huqqa. A non-smoker, the nawab took coffee. More discussions of the Quran would follow till it was time for the 'learned men' to leave. And then it was again time to return to businesses of state with 'chiefs of offices, the general intelligencer, and the rich banker, Djagat-seat'. They and others 'read and mentioned the news of every part of Hindia' and matters of administration and revenue that couldn't be addressed at morning durbar. Nawazish Muhammad Khan, his son-in-law, married to one of his daughters, Mehr-un-Nisa, better known as Ghaseti Begum, attended from time to time. As did Siraj, her nephew, she would come to despise and do everything within her grasp to unseat as nawab.

The two-hour late afternoon durbar over, it was time for jocular pursuits with the quick arrival of a 'facetious person and other *bon mots* people'. Alivardi's butler was present, as was his 'holsterer' and the chief of the 'candle-and-oil office', 'Mahmud-hedjra' and 'others of that stamp'—the court's favoured eunuchs who, for the pleasure of Alivardi, 'cracked jokes upon each other' and performed 'mutual satires'. The evening concluded with family time, attended by his wife, various princesses and, after Siraj took on a 'consort', occasionally she too. After a relatively sparse dinner of some dried fruits and sweetmeats, it was time for bed.

At this point the *Siyar* heaps praise on Alivardi. The text is lyrical in describing the manner in which the nawab always took care of his own, especially those who had stood by him in his days of 'distress and poverty', rewarding them and their families with jobs, promotions, and presents.

> His administration was so full of lenity, and his attention so intense to the security and quiet of the subject, and of the husbandman especially, that none of them can be said to be so much at their ease on their father's knees, or their mother's lap; nor was there a man in office with him, without excepting his very menial servants, that did not make fortunes by lacs.

Here was a hard but sensitive man who 'understood' the arts and 'never' failed to show regard to artistes. He was 'excellent company', witty and charming, 'hardly equalled by any of his contemporaries'. He was a 'prudent, keen general, and a valorous soldier'. There were 'hardly any qualifications he did not possess' and, as for virtues, 'few are the virtues which shall not be found to have made part of his character,' including prudence and foresight.

◆

And Siraj?

In contrast, there exists little detail in the *Siyar* of Siraj's day except general descriptions of bursts of impetuosity, imperiousness, brutality, abject sentimentality, and sensuous pleasures. It was all aided by quantities of 'wine'—which several telling, sympathetic to or critical of Siraj maintain he gave up at the deathbed of his grandfather, at the dying nawab's express request. It would appear young Siraj spent the year and a half of his troubled reign sober, even though beset in turn by insecurity and rage, some courage and immense confusion, desperate to succeed amidst scant loyalty at court: a callow ruler frightfully jostled by the flow of events. He may have no longer been driven to drink, but power plays provided equally debilitating distractions.

Alivardi appears to have spoilt the boy, the eldest child of his daughter, Amina Begum, and the noble, Zain-ud-din Ahmed Khan, son of Alivardi's elder brother, Mirza Ahmad or Haji Ahmad. (It gets more complicated. In another marriage of cousins, Alivardi's other daughter, Ghaseti Begum, married Zain-ud-din's brother, Nawazish Muhammad Khan, who constructed the fabled Motijheel Palace to please his wife.)

Several accounts relate the story of how, soon after Siraj was born in 1733—the boy was named Mirza Muhammad—Alivardi was appointed naib nazim, deputy governor, of Bihar by the nawab Shuja-ud-din, the son-in-law of Murshid Quli and his successor, who took the masnad in 1727. (It again gets complicated. Murshid Quli had actually named Shuja-ud-din's son, Sarfaraz, as his heir. But upon his death it was felt by leading nobles, Alivardi among them, that Shuja-ud-din was better suited to rule. After a brief power play, the son abdicated in favour of the father! Shuja-ud-din died a natural death in 1739 after a rule largely regarded as benevolent.)

Anyway, Alivardi's appointment as naib nazim, the good fortune of which he emotionally conflated to Siraj's birth, began a lifelong affection for the boy. And obsession, nearly all chroniclers maintain.

In 1740, Alivardi became nawab after what is known as the Battle of Giria, named after the Bengal village near which it was fought. Sarfaraz Khan, the grandson of Murshid Quli, and Shuja-ud-din's son, largely regarded as indolent and a debauch by contemporary and future historians, died in battle against Alivardi's forces. Alivardi's coup is attributed to underwriting by the Seths, to avenge an insult by Sarfaraz. This, some accounts mention, was leveraged by Haji Ahmad, Alivardi's brother, to hatch the plot.

It makes for another of Murshidabad's fascinating stories. John Zephaniah Holwell's *Interesting Historical Events Relative to the Provinces of Bengal, and the Empire of Indostan* contains an arresting hearsay account. He notes that around 1939, the same year Sarfaraz became nawab, Jagat Seth Fateh Chand married off his grandson, 'Seet Mortab Roy'—the future Jagath Seth Madhab Rai of the Plassey conspiracy—'to a young creature of exquisite beauty, aged about eleven years. The fame of her beauty coming to the ears of the Soubah, he burned with curiosity and lust for the possession of her; and sending for Juggaut Seet, demanded a sight of her.' The aged Jagat Seth, whom Holwell describes to be then 'compleat fourscore'—eighty—begged Sarfaraz to desist, 'that the Soubah would not stain the honor and credit of his house, nor load his last days with shame, by persisting in a demand which he knew the principles of his cast [caste], forbid a compliance with'.

It didn't wash. Sarfaraz was both outraged and curious. He surrounded Fateh Chand's house with some cavalry, insisting that 'he might only see her, he would instantly return her without any injury'. Knowing well Sarfaraz's 'impetuosity' and to cauterize the 'disgrace', Fateh Chand consented. '...the young creature was carried with the greatest secrecy in the night to visit him. She was returned the same night, we will suppose (for the honour of that house) uninjured; be this as it may, the violence was of too delicate a nature, to permit any future commerce between her and her husband'. Fateh Chand didn't forget, or forgive, and the 'whole powerful family, consequently became inveterate, tho' concealed enemies to the Soubah'.

Holwell writes that 'Hodjee Hamet'—Haji Ahmad—Alivardi's brother soon heard of the incident. He saw it as an opportunity to seek revenge on Sarfaraz, who he felt had treated him poorly in the wake of the nawab Shuja-ud-din who ruled after Murshid Quli.

The brothers had prospered under Shuja-ud-din whom several historians consider a sort of golden-era nawab. During his eighteen-year rule until 1739, he reorganized the administration after merging the subah of Bengal with Bihar, imparted even-handed justice, and reduced the administrative harshness associated with Murshid Quli. As we have seen, he also raised Alivardi to a high position. And Haji Ahmad came to be Shuja-ud-din's chief counsellor. They were well rewarded by the nawab for their role in his elevation to the masnad. Now Sarfaraz's arrival to the masnad wasn't pleasant for the brothers and other nobles who had participated in, and profited from, the palace putsch against him all those years ago in 1727.

'Hodjee lost no time in procuring a private audience with the dis-affected Seets and Allum Chund [Alamchand was appointed as diwan by Shuja-ud-din and among the angry nobles],' writes Holwell, 'in the course of which he represented in the most lively manner the oppression and extravagant government of Suffraaz Khan, and that nothing but the most deplorable consequences to the provinces could be expected from such an unbridled and tyrannical disposition—and that if he already treated with such insults and contempt, those for whom his father had the highest veneration and friendship—what might not others dread from his future violence?'

And, so, the conference came to the conclusion that '...Aliverdi Khan [whom Holwell subsequently, and repeatedly, refers to as 'Usurper'], as the only one capable of rescuing the provinces from apparent and inevitable ruin.' The die was cast against Sarfaraz, culminating in the battle at Giria.

A similar future would visit Alivardi's grandson, but that is for a little later.

◆

After he became nawab, Alivardi's coddling of young Siraj continued.

'A child may ask...for an elephant, a horse, a child may want to hold the moon in his hand... [kokhōnō hāthi chāye, kokhōnō ghōrā chāye, kokhōnō bā ākāshér chāndkhānā hāthér mōdhhé dhōrité chāye],' Akshay Kumar Maitreya writes in his emotional history of Siraj. 'His grandfather's affection ensured that the seeds of poor upbringing were planted in Siraj's innocent heart. Young Siraj didn't receive the education of controlling his demands—and his nature...' Well, as to his nature, 'From the attitude, behaviour and conversation of servants, friends and relatives young Siraj realized that he was a mini-nawab [khudrō nobāb]!'

The bond appeared to have deepened after Zain-ud-din Ahmed Khan, Siraj's father—and Alivardi's son-in-law, was killed in Patna by Afghan rebels in 1748. A massive counter-attack by Alivardi routed these former soldiers in his pay, who were perhaps spurred on to take Patna by the invasion that year by fellow-Afghan Ahmad Shah, who overran Delhi. Amina Begum, Mirza Muhammad—Siraj—and his younger brother, Mirza Mahdi, were rescued from Patna; they had survived under the protection of a loyalist. This brother, formally Ikram-ud-daulah, had earlier been adopted by Nawazish Muhammad and Ghaseti Begum. The boy died of smallpox at a very young age. Besides the tragedy of the affair, it appears to have upset Ghaseti Begum as she had hoped Ikram would one day be named Alivardi's heir.

In 1752, Alivardi formally declared Siraj as his heir and successor. The boy was between nineteen and twenty.

Siraj, who is usually depicted as a gentle-faced, quite handsome and well-built young man, meanwhile gathered grand titular credentials, helped along by his indulgent grandfather. A royal farman preserved in Murshidabad's Hazarduari Palace records the awarding of the inām or prize of Marapur village in the dominion to Mansur-ul-Mulk Siraj-ud-daulah Shah Quli Khan Bahadur Haibat Jung (Victor of the Land, Light of the Dynasty and, possibly in the more ironical cut, One Who is Fearsome in Battle, or One Who Causes His Enemies to Panic). The grant was formally given him in 1754 by the Mughal emperor Alamgir II, to maintain Qadam-i-Rasul, literally the Footprint of the Messenger—another way of venerating Prophet Muhammad—in this village.

◆

'It is not clear if Alivardi had an understanding of Siraj's character,' Maitreya writes, 'But clever Siraj had keenly studied Alivardi.' He manipulated his grandfather into building him a palace, Hirajheel, the grandly named lake of diamonds—to seemingly match his aunt's palace at the lake of pearls—on the west bank of the Bhagirathi, across from Mir Jafar's palace. (There was some dispute at the turn of the twentieth century about the site, the structure long washed away by the Bhagirathi. Several historians defer to Major Rennel's account for its location.)

There's a story about Siraj trapping Alivardi after inviting him and some courtiers and zamindars to visit his palace apartments for a meal. He practically held the nawab hostage—a colourful story. He relented only after extracting a ransom of half a million rupees from Alivardi and his courtiers. Instead of being angry, Alivardi was delighted by his grandson's chutzpah.

At any rate Siraj's 'pleasure palace', as Maitreya puts it, began to be constructed in Hirajheel. His court would eventually be established here. Maitreya is nearly apoplectic as he describes that future: 'it was in the pleasure palace of Hirajheel that the traitor Mir Jafar took Clive-shāhéb's hand to ascend to the throne...here was the place of the Mussalman's sunset, the place of the English sunrise.'

'As soon as Siraj's intelligence and machinations allied with wealth, it fuelled festivities, with dance and music, wine, and hedonistic companions,' Maitreya continues. He adds: 'With the aid of money, artifice, and temptation many daughters of the land lost everything [at Hirajheel]. This is the great sin for which Bengalis became frightened of Siraj; word of this great sin spread across the land...'

According to the *Siyar*, it all began early for this dreamy-eyed prince whom it portrays as being akin to a street thug—and evidently a bisexual one:

> Patrolling every street and every lane with a cohort composed of Aalyverdy-Qhan's children and grand-children, he fell into an abominable way of life, that respected neither rank, nor age, nor sex, but was calculated to prepare from afar the ruin and desolation of that sublime building of fortune and sovereignty which its founder had been rearing with so much toil and danger. No notice was taken of so flagitious a conduct; and it was on such repeated connivances that the young man commenced a course of enormities that afforded materials, and administered fuel, to the overtaking vengeance of an unerring observer.

The *Siyar* offers no validation for its claims, which has led some Siraj-defenders to question its veracity, labelling it as gossip of a

Company stooge. But there's little else to go by. 'This conduct,' the *Siyar* continues, 'which Aaly-verdy-qhan overlooked in that infatuated young man, turned out to be so natural in him, that at last he became fearless, and was committing daily excesses and violences of all kinds, not only without the least remorse, but also without the least reprimand. He made a sport of sacrificing to his lust almost every person of either sex, to which he took a fancy; or else, he converted them without scruples into so many objects of the malignity of his temper, or the frolics of his inconsiderate youth.'

Even Siraj defenders like Maitreya evidently had little choice but to bow to contemporary chronicles in the absence of other texts that highlight positive character: 'But distracted by the troubles with Marathas, the aged Nawab was unable to stem this tide of pleasure...'

Alivardi would die at eighty-four (some say eighty). He had become nawab at an already advanced age in 1740. Did the tiring nawab give up with Siraj, even though he clearly didn't give up on Siraj?

In particular, Haji Mustapha adds in a conspiratorial footnote that one of Siraj's confidantes and Plassey generals, Mohanlal, 'made a present' of his sister Aleya to his patron. 'Small and delicate,' weighing only '22 seers' or '66 English pounds', the beauty of this apparently ethereal courtesan was legendary. 'For nothing is more common amongst Indians,' writes the Haji in rapture, evidently still too much the Frenchman even with his conversion to a pious Islam, 'when they want to give an idea of a surpassing beauty, than to say, when she ate Paan, you might have seen through her skin the coloured liquor run down her throat...'

She was also evidently one with attitude, and one of the early conveyers of his betrayal at court, 'intriguing' with the nawab Siraj's brother-in-law for which sin the Haji claims she was walled up—'immured'—while alive. This is offered as another example of Siraj's cruelty, but not before a scathingly ironical exchange with Siraj. '"Miss," said the Prince, "I find that you are a whore?" "And so am I," answered disdainfully the poor woman in despair, who had been a dance-woman. "I have ever been so. This indeed might be made a matter of reproach to your mother, but not to me; I am so by trade."'

Some like Jadunath Sarkar chose to discount the characterizations of Siraj by English merchants of Calcutta or that of the author and translator of the *Siyar* as being fanciful, and instead focused on the recollections of Jean Law, chief of the French factory in the suburb of Saidabad in Qasimbazar. As we have seen, Law was a contemporary of Watts, the chief of John Company's factory in Qasimbazar—which was the only substantially fortified one among the trading stations here of the various European East India companies, as Hill tells us. The French factory, and that of the Dutch in the Qasimbazar suburb of Kalikapur, 'were merely large houses lying in enclosures, the walls of which might keep out cattle and wild animals and even thieves, but were useless as fortifications'.

But even here, there's some extreme profiling of Siraj's character. Hill's *Three Frenchmen in Bengal* contains Law's memoirs and records his impressions of the four years from the time Siraj became nawab in 1756, which Law describes as 'painful and exciting'. Law broad-brushes Siraj as a sort of cross between Caligula and a caporegime:

> Siraj-ud-daula, a young man... [was] very common in appearance. Before the death of Aliverdi Khan the character of Siraj-ud-daula was reported to be one of the worst ever known. In fact, he had distinguished himself not only by all sorts of debauchery, but by a revolting cruelty. The Hindu women are accustomed to bathe on the banks of the Ganges [presumably the Bhagirathi, although the main channel of the Ganga–Padma isn't too far to the east]. Siraj-ud-daula, who was informed by his spies which of them were beautiful, sent his satellites in disguise in little boats to carry them off. He was often seen, in the season when the river overflows, causing the ferry boats to be upset or sunk in order to have the cruel pleasure of watching the terrified confusion of a hundred people at a time, men, women, and children, of whom many, not being able to swim, were sure to perish. When it became necessary to get rid of some great lord or minister, Siraj-ud-daula alone appeared in the business, Aliverdi Khan retiring to one of his houses or gardens outside the town, so that he might not hear the cries of the persons whom he was causing to be killed.

(Hill writes that he came by a copy of Law's memoirs in the British

Museum, along with those of Law's colleagues, Renault de St Germain, appointed governor of Chandannagar in 1756, and Jacques Ignace Courtin, the factory chief in Dhaka. Hill freely maintains that he had to add both style and grammar to these memoirs he translated, but he attempted to preserve both their 'form' and 'spirit'. In any case, even with that caveat, and some inherent biases in the tellings, the memoirs, especially that of Law, make for fascinating glimpses into the dynamics that crafted Plassey. Especially, as it comes from a French perspective, a country and company that Siraj at one time or another demanded assistance from—even pleaded with for help—to counter the British. One should also take into account the fact that the French lost their mercantile and political grip on Bengal and India on account of Plassey.)

There's another account from the time Siraj conquered Calcutta, and in a coordinated move his forces also proceeded to overpower the Company enclave in Dhaka. By his own account and that of others, Law, upon the urging of Courtin, his colleague in Dhaka, secured through his goodwill at court the release of English prisoners there. French gallantry appears to have been at its apex here, countering the nawab's roving eye as much as his rage. 'Siraj-ud-daula,' recounted Law, 'being informed that there were two or three very charming English ladies at Dacca, was strongly tempted to adorn his harem with them.'

◆

The accounts I have quoted make Siraj appear to be his grandfather's hatchet man and enforcer—an entitled young rogue about town in Murshidabad. It isn't as though he was unique when it came to cruelty or deceit. Alivardi wasn't exactly free of these blemishes, having deposed his master for the masnad of Bengal. He tricked the Maratha raiders led by Bhaskar Pandit to a meeting in 1744 to discuss détente, and then slaughtered the entire Maratha party. These two incidents are counted as the most prominent of his hard-nosed exploits. Tapping Siraj as his successor would have meant keeping things in the family, and, in the calculating manner of such things, it was strictly business.

Did Alivardi overlook Siraj's alleged abduction and other excesses despite being a pious Muslim? It's hard to say anything with certainty as everyone who has a view appears to be quoting the same source—largely, Law's account. Besides, for all of Alivardi's conservative bent, it didn't prevent him from appointing Hindus to prominent positions in his administration, much like Siraj would. There appears to be scant logic by any yardstick for Alivardi to permit his grandson to routinely drown subjects for entertainment. Such gratuitous acts would likely have been a recipe for administrative disaster for a nawab already beset by war, rebellion, and age.

At any rate, the dirty linen, real or imagined, of Alivardi's self-proclaimed Afshar dynasty, obsessed contemporary and several later chroniclers and historians keen to gather every reason for the destruction of that two-nawab house, the end of Bengal's administrative and political autonomy, and the spectacular success of Clive & Co. Going by modern-day notions it is perhaps attractive to think of Siraj as bipolar or an alcoholic in difficult remission. Indeed, Hill refers to the eighteenth-century Company official Luke Scrafton's *Reflections on the Government of Indostan*, where he mentions that Siraj indulged in 'all sorts of debauchery' till his promise to Alivardi at the latter's deathbed. 'He likely kept his oath,' notes Hill, 'but probably his mind was affected by his previous excesses.'

Siraj could even be regarded as a bullying boy-man who became terminally afraid of the English only after being attacked by Clive's forces in Calcutta in February 1757—some time before Plassey was even a plan for Clive and, certainly, Siraj.

◆

Going by Law and Hill, Siraj and the English—the Company—appear to have had a difficult relationship from his days as a teenage prince. For instance, Hill tells us that European nations and merchants alike, including chiefs of all factories in Murshidabad, worked with their vakils (local agents and petitioners) at the court in Murshidabad. It was accepted practice as it was the most practical. A vakil carried local language skills, knew the durbar's etiquette and nuances of court, knew which noble or officer to approach and how to influence the person to further the case of a client. But the English, insists Hill, kept away from Siraj. Indeed, their vakils did too '...whilst applying to other nobles for patronage and assistance, studiously refraining from making any application to Siraj-ud-daula when English business had to be transacted at Court'.

Hill refers to Law's memoir for the bully-boy-Siraj rationale, as well as to provide the reason as to why the English would shy away from petitioning Siraj for favours at the Murshidabad court. Indeed, the English took on the prince in any way they could:

> On certain occasions they refused him admission into their factory at Cossimbazar and their country houses, because, in fact, this excessively blustering and impertinent young man used to break the furniture, or, if it pleased his fancy, take it away. But Siraj-ud-daula was not the man to forget what he regarded as an insult.

Law notes that Siraj made plain his anger at such past slights when he became nawab, and went after the English in a sequence that set up the showdown at Plassey. 'The day after the capture of the English fort at Cossimbazar [in early June 1756], he was heard to say in full Durbar, "Behold the English, formerly so proud that they did not wish to receive me in their houses!" In short, people knew, long before the death of Aliverdi Khan, that Siraj-ud-daula was hostile to the English.'

But, curiously, he didn't have the same attitude towards the French or the Danes, who appear to have treated him with courtesy even when pressed against the wall. Law maintains Siraj was 'very well disposed towards us'. It was all about attitude, adjustment and building a relationship. 'It being our interest to humour him, we had received him with a hundred times more politeness than he deserved.' Law says that Siraj's associates Durlabh Ram—eventually a Plassey conspirator—and Mohanlal advised him to petition Siraj for important matters. The French also gave him presents from time to time and this 'confirmed his friendship for us'.

Indeed, Law recalls that 1755 had been a 'very good one' for Siraj, on account of the Danes on whose behalf he claims to have interceded. That year the Danish trading company set up an establishment in Srirampur by the Bhagirathi–Hugli, between the British settlement of Calcutta to the south and the French settlement in Chandannagar to its north. 'In fact, it was by his [Siraj's] influence that I was enabled to conclude this affair.' And Alivardi Khan permitted his grandson and heir to 'retain all the profit from it'.

'So I can say that I had no bad place in the heart of Siraj-ud-daula. It is true he was a profligate, but a profligate who was to be feared, who could be useful to us, and who might some day be a good man.'

◆

The *Siyar*, for its part, much like Company-glory tellings, introduces disparaging remarks about Siraj beginning it all: belittling and battling the British when he ought to have had better sense. It suggests that even Alivardi acknowledged his beloved grandson's faults especially with regard to his attitude towards the Company:

> ...he knew with how sparing a hand providence had bestowed on Seradj-ed-döulah his share of knowledge and prudence; and he was fully sensible of the manner he would govern the people of God, and upon what bad terms he was already with the Military Officers, besides how prone he seemed to fall out with the English of Calcutta...and to assure in full company that as soon as himself should be dead, and Seradj-ed-döulah should succeed him, the hat-men would possess themselves of all the shores of Hindia.

Here Ghulam Hussain Tabatabayi insists that he recounts the truth. 'As I was myself in Seradj-ed-döulah's service, and fully apprised of his turn of mind, as well as often in his company, and that of his grandfather's, I remember to have that assertion from that Prince's [Alivardi's] own mouth.' He adds, in a further pitch for veracity: 'Nor is my testimony a slight one; it will be supported by several persons, then present, to whom I shall refer, and in fact the prediction came to be verified just as [Alivardi's] mind had foreseen.'

The *Siyar* raises the instance of a key general of Alivardi's, Mustafa Khan, being of a similar mind as Siraj's, and who had 'boundless influence' on the ageing nawab, suggested he 'take Calcutta, and to put all the English to the sword'. (Mustafa Khan would rebel against Alivardi in the mid-1740s, after he was denied the governorship of Bihar as a prize for his help to slaughter the Maratha embassy. Siraj would have been eleven at the time.)

Alivardi didn't answer then or even at a later time when the general insisted upon that course of action to show the English their place, claims the *Siyar*. It happened in the presence of two of Alivardi's sons-in-law whom the general brought along to underscore his argument. There is a lengthy rebuttal in Alivardi's sage voice in the wake of the general's departure from the room, counsel for treating the English and the Company with tact and patience:

> My dear children, Mustapha-qhan is a soldier of fortune, and a man in monthly pay, who lives by his sabre; of course he wishes that I always have occasion to employ him...but in the name of common sense, what is the matter with your ownselves, that you should join issue with him, and make common cause of his opinion? What wrong have the English done me, that I should wish them ill? Look at yonder plain covered with grass; should you set fire to it, there would be no stopping its progress; and who is the man then who shall put out a fire that shall break forth at sea, and from thence come out upon land? Beware of lending an ear to such proposals again; for they will produce nothing but evil.

The same passage in Charles Stewart's *The History of Bengal* is worded a little differently.

> My child, Mustapha Khan is a soldier, and wishes us to be constantly in need of his service; but how come you to join in his request? What have the English done against me that I should use them ill? It is now difficult to extinguish fire on land; but should the sea be in flames, who can put it out? Never listen to such advice as his, for the result would probably be fatal.

Stewart, fluent in Persian and Arabic, concludes:

> In consequence of these sentiments, the Europeans were little molested during his government, and were permitted to carry on their commerce according to the tenor of the farmāns they had received from the Emperor on making the usual present.

This appears to be somewhat of an overstatement. As we have seen, the Company had a long history of run-ins with Bengal's nawabs on a wide range of matters.

◆

The pious sentiments quoted a little earlier do not tell the whole truth. Alivardi wasn't entirely pacific towards the Company. Indeed, the British from time to time got under his skin, and he under theirs.

In this O'Malley is more even-handed. He cites Reverend James Long's *Selections from Unpublished Records of Government (1748-1767)* to demonstrate that there was an occasion of 'a serious quarrel' between that nawab and the Company. By Long's reckoning, in 1748, 'an English man-of-war seized some vessels laden with the goods of various Hooghly merchants, Muhammadan and Armenian, and also containing things of value belonging to the Nawab'. Alivardi Khan sent a stern order—'parwana'—to the governor of Fort William in which irritation and 'menace' was made clear, and even as it reached Calcutta, Company operations in Dhaka were being squeezed:

Translate [*sic*] of the Nabob's perwannah to Governor Barwell received the 9th January 1749:

The Syads, Moghuls, Armenians, &c., merchants of Houghly have complained that lakhs of Goods and Treasure with their ships you have seized and plundered, and I am informed from Foreign parts that ships bound to Houghly you seized on under pretence of their belonging to the French. The ship belonging to Antony with lakhs on Board from Mochei, and several curiosities sent me by the Sheriff of that place on that ship you have also seized and plundered. These merchants are the kingdom's benefactors, their Imports and Exports are an advantage to all men, and their complaints are so grievous that I cannot forbear any longer giving ear to them.

As you were not permitted to commit piracies therefore I now write you that on receipt of this you deliver up all the Merchants' Goods, and effects to them as also what appertains unto me, otherwise you may be assured a due chastizement in such manner as you least expect.

According to Long and O'Malley, the Calcutta Council reached out to Alivardi with a gift of a 'fine Arab horse' (and, at the same time, 'contemplated measures of retaliation' against Armenian merchants of Calcutta—of which more shortly).

A despatch of 27 January 1749 from Fort William to the Court in London notes:

> The gentlemen at Dacca, in a letter dated the 8th instant, advised that positive orders arrived there from Muxadabad to put a stop to their business in general. In reply to the above letter, we acquainted the gentlemen at Cassimbazar that we should not be against their keeping the Durbar easy if it be done on reasonable terms, and sent them the horse, which they informed us would be agreeable to the Nabob, to lay hold of a proper opportunity to present it to him.

Alivardi wasn't mollified. He soon began to stop the boats of British merchants, and cut off the supply of provisions to the British factory in Dhaka. Alivardi's troops surrounded the factory at Qasimbazar, reminiscent of the time of the nawab Shaista Khan, and not unlike what Siraj would do in a few short years. The Company capitulated. 'The English got off after paying to the Nawab, through the Seths, twelve lakhs of rupees,' writes Long—though some accounts mention the amount as being a tenth of that.

The latter seems more likely. The Company's Consultations of 31 August note:

> The English trade being stopped and the factory at Cossimbazar surrounded with troops by the Nawab owing to the dispute with the Armenians the English try through the Seets to propitiate him, but his two favorites demand a large sum of money Rs. 30,000 for themselves and 4 lakhs for the Nawab, at last after much negotiation the Armenians expressing themselves satisfied the Nawab becomes reconciled, but the English got off after paying to the Nawab through the Seets...

Ever the eager intermediaries.

(The Company would try the equine approach again some years later, in 1754, when the Calcutta Council had enough of what they perceived as 'the Durbar...making use of any frivolous pretence for a stoppage of our business'. On 20 December 1754, the Council agreed to 'send the Nawab a present of a Persia Horse and some fine wax work, also to the Fousdar of Hoogly and his Duan Nundoo Coomarry [the diwan Nandakumar, who would on account of his association with the future governor-general Warren Hastings, gain fame and infamy as Maharaja Nandakumar or Nuncomar].' There weren't any horses at hand, the minutes of the meeting noted, the 'Hon'ble Company's Horses being both dead'. But two horses were on the market for '2,500A. [Arcot] Rupees', which, it was agreed, would be purchased straightaway with cash.)

The Company's Consultations in Calcutta in March the same year—1749—indicate Alivardi's financial outreach, as well as the continuous expenditure on war and rebellions that drained Bengal's treasury and prompted frequent requests for funds. 'Eyles Chief of Cossimbazar writes respecting the impossibility of their getting a Bill on Patna, the Shroffs having absconded on account of the extortions of the Nabob who is now at Culfia (Cutwa)...but cannot prevail on his forces to go on without paying them more money,' the meeting noted. 'That upon his hearing the Mirattoes had taken Tanner's Fort [the Tanna Fort in what was Dhana Makua, not far from the Botanic Gardens in Howrah, across the Hugli from Calcutta] he had Nowarries Mahomud Cawn [Nawazish Muhammad Khan, Alivardi's nephew] to send for their Vucuels [vakils] and enquire into the reason why the English suffered them to come so near them, adding it would be a very acceptable piece of service to drive them from thence...'

The Consultations on 2 May indicated how the push for money would continue across the food chain, with Alivardi projected as being too distracted to be of any succour:

> Yesterday we received a letter from Edward Eyles, Esq., Chief of Council at Cossimbazar dated the 29th April, advising that our merchants, gomastahs at Malda have complained that some of the Nabob's people had been there and treated them very ill for refusing to comply with their demands for large sums of money, and threatening to plunder their effects in case they stood out. That on receipt of their letter they informed Newarris Muhomed Cawne and Chamerage thereof and requested them to write to the Nabob about it, to which they answered that they should

be very willing to comply with their request but apprehended the Nabob's affairs were in such a state at that time that their writing to him would avail but little.

These Company records extracted by Long offer priceless insights into the times and circumstances in the run-up to Plassey. O'Malley has another story that reflects the turmoil that existed in Bengal during this period, the nawab pushing, the Company trying to push back—and the other way around, in a continuous game of gaining advantage: 'On another occasion, Ali Vardi Khan demanded the estate of a Musalman who had died at Calcutta intestate and without relatives.' Thereafter, in 1751, after his claim had been 'paltered with' for several years, Alivardi threatened to attack the factory at Qasimbazar. Company-wallahs in Fort William backed off. 'The Council forthwith paid over the value of the estate, and were compelled to add a further sum on account of interest.'

The Company resisted whenever it could. Company Consultations from 30 May 1751 considered a letter from Alivardi earlier that month, in which the nawab demanded the Company hand over Ramkishan Seth, a merchant he considered a smuggler as the man hadn't paid government dues. Here's the letter as translated by Company writers:

To the Hon'ble A. Dawson, President of Council.

I have heard that Ramkissen Seat who lives in Calcutta has carried goods to that place without paying the Muxidavad Syre Chowkey duties; I am greatly surprised and imagine he stands in no fear of any body for which reason I write you and send a Chubdar to bring him and desire you will be speedy in delivering him over, as he may be soon here; be expeditious and act exactly as I have wrote.

ALLYVERDI CAWN.
Muxidavad,
20 May 1751

Long mentions that the Governor of Calcutta declined, insisting on a point of commercial relationship. The Seth's father and grandfather were the Company's merchants—specifically, 'dadney' merchants who were contracted in advance to deliver goods at a certain time and at certain prices. Besides, the merchant himself was a 'great debtor' of the Company. Surrendering him could mean considerable loss to the Company. Alivardi accepted the argument.

The nawab attempted to keep a leash on the French too, and put the squeeze on them from time to time. Just days before his letter to Dawson, he sent troops against the French factory in Qasimbazar. Company representatives naturally kept track of it as they did all movement of, for and against the French and other competitors, and would write to the Court in London on 20 August 1751:

> Under date the 11th May, the gentlemen at Cossimbazaar wrote us that the Nawab had surrounded the French factory with his forces for some time and stopped their business at all their settlements on account of a dispute with the Durbar, which, as they were informed, was accommodated for 50,000 Sicca Rupees.

To be fair, at times the nawab interceded to settle a dispute that erupted into a messy situation of prestige and loss of face that led directly to loss of business. In the spring of 1755, for instance, a year shy of Alivardi's death, a situation arose from a dispute between a merchant, John Wood, and an official of the raja of Bardhaman, or Burdwan. Long writes that the official, a gomasta of the raja, Ramjiban Kabiraji, owed 6,367 rupees to Wood, 'the payment of which could not be secured'. Wood obtained a 'warrant of sequestration' from the Mayor's Court in Calcutta and with that authority sealed the raja's 'house and effects' in Calcutta.

The raja, Tilak Chand ray, was enraged. How dare an Englishman seal his property on account of a dispute with Kabiraji, his underling whom the Company variously referred to as Rambujan Cubbarazy and Ramjeebun Cubbrage? Tilak Chand ray had in 1753 received the title of Maharajadhiraj, King of Kings (in English, diluted to His Royal Highness), from the Mughal emperor, but was really a zamindar who, like most such landlords, received honours and were transformed into royalty. Ray, like other landlords of the subah, had to kowtow to Murshidabad, but he wielded enough local power to stop the Company's trade in Bardhaman, shut down the Company's aurungs, and seized the Company's goods along with its agents. There was nothing Company executives could do except fulminate at a meeting on 1 April 1755 that Tilak Ray's decision was by 'no means warrantable and extremely insolent'. The only way out, they decided, was to approach Alivardi. They expressly did.

By 5 May, they received relief in the form of a letter from Alivardi to the raja, asking him to reverse his orders. The nawab also threw in a minor but, in the context of the heartburn that would soon follow with Siraj, remarkable lecture on the necessity of trade with Europeans. 'This manner of acting is contrary to your interest and very wrong, as it is by no means allowable that a zemindar should take such a step without an order first had from me,' Alivardi wrote in a letter. The Company obtained a copy of the letter:

> The English are foreigners and have settled in our Country on a dependence of our protection in their Trade; and if they are treated in this manner, the consequence will be their withdrawing themselves and their Trade, on which account I positively direct that on the immediate receipt of this Perwanah you remove the Chowkeys you have put on their factories, and let their business have the usual currency without any further trouble.

◆

Alivardi's various frictions with the Company, and his occasional attempts to smoothen matters to carry on trade—and, as we have just seen, even chastising Bardhaman's zamindar—would seem to have been, more often than not, the give-and-take manner in which the British and Indian rulers in the region dealt with one another. It's just that, with Siraj, there were a number of other reasons that led to an altogether different train of events. As we shall see, from Siraj doing a Shaista, with his attack on Calcutta; imperatives of an European war that primarily drove the British and French against each other in Bengal as elsewhere in and around the subcontinent; and a realization through wars in southern India, which we will discuss a little later, that Indian armies could be outmanoeuvred and outmatched by their European counterparts.

◆

And to think that less than five years before Plassey, Siraj was received with great civility by the Company during a formal visit to Hugli, during which he made 'great professions of friendship to the English'. In a despatch to the Company's Court in London on 18 September 1752 (key despatches were, of course, sent by sea, including news of the victory at Plassey, in triplicate and by different ships, notes Long), officials at Fort William noted in great detail how the president in council at Calcutta waited upon the teenage heir apparent:

> The Nobab Sarajee Doula whom Allivirde Cawn appointed to be his successor being arrived at Hughley where he was invited by the French and the Dutch Governors with a present equivalent to his dignity, and the President having received letters from the Phausdars [faujdar] and Coja Wuzeed [Khwaja Wajid, the Armenian merchant], the purport whereof is entered upon our consultation of the 31st August, from whence we judged it highly necessary to pay the Nabob the compliment required, and therefore agreed that the President should prepare himself accompanied by Messrs. Cruttenden, Beecher and the Commandant, and that a present should be made the Nobab that might prove satisfactory.
>
> This morning the President returned from the visit where he was received with the utmost politeness and distinction far superior than was paid the Dutch or French, and if these people's words are ever to be confided in, we flatter ourselves that the expense we have been at on this occasion has procured you great favor and will be the means of your Honor's business being conducted without any interruption from the Government for some time to come, and we beg leave to offer our sentiments that a greater intimacy well timed with the heads of the Government (not before practised) when opportunity offers either here or at the head subordinates may be greatly conducive to your Honor's interest at a small expence, for it is chiefly those about the Nabob who are in power that urge circumstances to our disadvantage and stir up his resentment and when any large sum is paid they receive the greatest share.

This last was about smoothening the Company's way with some well-placed presents quite apart from the periodic baksheesh that was occasioned by every permission, or solution to a problem, whether innocent or opportune. Siraj, whom the Company already refers to as nawab—or, here, nobāb in the Bengali manner, possibly a reflection of a Bengali writer or a British one with a keen ear for Bengali—was offered generous tokens. These and related expenses are meticulously recorded in Company ledgers.

As Long notes:

> In the accounts of presents to Suraja Doula and his officers on their visit to Hugly are entered 35 gold mohurs, = Rs. 677; ready money Rs. 5,500; wax candles Rs. 1,100; a clock Rs. 880; looking glasses 2 pairs Rs. 550; 2 marble slabs Rs. 220; pistols 1 pair Rs. 110; a diamond ring Rs. 1,436; to Alliverde's wife and women 26 gold mohurs,= Rs. 429; fukiers Rs. 184; the Dutch Military servants Rs. 756; Phausdar of Hugly Rs. 770; the sum total in ready money amounted to Rs. 15,560.

In return the president of the council in Calcutta received a robe of honour and an elephant.

Alivardi was so pleased with the reception accorded to Siraj and his entourage that within weeks he had sent a parwana 'in favor of the Company's trade'. It is particularly interesting—and ironical—to note the positive tone in the address, which arrived on 8 October 1752 for Roger Drake, Company chief in Calcutta. It arrived even as the letter from the Council to Court in London that mentioned the procurement at 'small expence' of 'great favor' and the advantage of this 'greater intimacy' was on the months-long voyage home for memos and men alike.

> Of all merchants the greatest and the picture of friendship, Mr. Drake, Governor of the English Company, whom God preserve.
>
> By the favor of the Almighty the bright eyes and soul of Nabob Munsoor An Mullick, Bahaudur [Mansur-ul-Mulk, or Victor of the Country, one of Siraj's titles], arrived at Muxadavad on the 24th Secandar Son paunch; your friendship, praises, presents, and going to meet him, he has told me a great deal about so much that I cannot express it. I am extremely pleased and delighted with you and a thousand thousand times remain

sensible of it, and in return by the grace of God the Company's business I will be very favorable to.

Siraj too wrote to Drake, adding his pleasure to a parwana: '...you are a great man, and that greatness becomes you, the head of all merchants, and the standard of merchants.'

Siraj was then a friend as much as any nawab, established or on the make, could be a friend, strategically fêted and suitably befriended. The teenager hadn't yet been magically transformed into the demon the British—and their eventual allies, who contributed to creating a history of victors—loved to hate, the man whose forces would pressure Drake and most of his colleagues to abandon Calcutta less than four years later.

Maybe Siraj-ud-daula was unpredictable, perhaps a mystery. Even when he became relatively better known to the Company, the political nuances and personalities of Bengal evidently remained as arcana to the board of directors in London. Piers Brendon wryly observes, '...one Company director did ask if Sir Roger Dowler was really a baronet.'

5

COMPANY VERSUS COMPAGNIE VERSUS KOMPAGNI

'...not to make war in these parts with any
European nation is very wrong...'

In Bengal, John Company and the Crown were also wary of other foreign businesses and communities besides the French. The relationships were complicated.

As we have seen, the Mugs (or Magh, and Mog in Bengali) from the region of Chittagong and Arakan in Burma, were 'a subject of continual anxiety' to Calcutta. They were feared throughout deltaic Bengal, and even Jahangirnagar–Dhaka. Pirates and marauders not unlike the British Sea Kings and Dutch Corsairs, they rampaged across much of the first half of the seventeenth century, and they 'leagued with enterprising Portuguese [whom the British in South Asia barely tolerated at the time] from Chittagong'. They pillaged villages and towns, and plundered 'all boats and vessels that fall in their way'. (Even with enhanced prestige after the victory at Plassey, records show that in 1760 the Government in Calcutta ordered defences against the Magh by placing a boom across the river just south of Calcutta.)

However, the Portuguese, besides their harassment in concert with the Magh or by themselves, weren't much of a power in the subcontinent by the mid-eighteenth century. They were restricted to their outposts on the west coast of India in Goa, Daman and Diu, having 'yielded the palm to Dutch and English enterprise', as Long puts it. 'The Portuguese had ceased to be conquerors; many of them became pirates, others traders, others topasses or gunners, and others were famous as cooks, some were good fiddlers.' At the time of the Company's surge in the east they only had one settlement, in Bandel, not far north of Hugli, a former Portuguese base.

Even at the peak of their influence in Bengal for much of the sixteenth century and early part of seventeenth century the Portuguese largely remained pirates and slave traders. They would sail up the 'Mutla' (Matla River) past Port Canning, and the 'Vidiadurry' (Bidyadhari), and pillage or trade. Indeed, they travelled up the Bidyadhari and established a base by the Salt Lake near what was yet to be the Company settlement in Calcutta. Whatever trade they found here and near Hugli was insufficient, so '...they engaged extensively in a slave trade in the Sunderbunds [the Sunderbans],' Long notes, 'their scouts were then to be seen along the banks of some of the beautiful Sunderbund rivers, hauling away men and boys from their homes and exporting them to the Slave Mart at Goa, or retaining them in Bengal to swell that non-descript class of persons called Portuguese; they leagued themselves with the Mugs in these forays of man hunting, and hence one cause of the depopulation of the Sunderbunds' alongside cyclones and inundation.

Company records from 1748 show a river near Diamond Harbour called Rogue's River—'probably because it was resorted to by Portuguese pirates and Mugs'. Major Rennell, the British geographer, simply marked a tract of the Sundarban east and south of 'Calna' (Khulna in Bangladesh) as 'land depopulated by the Mugs'.

And, although Phiringhi or Féringhi is the Bengali catch-all term for Portuguese, derived from the generic Persian for European foreigner, some among the British had other ideas. Holwell, the survivor-dramatist of the Black Hole, for example, was derisory and presumptuous in his references to the Portuguese in India. In 'Consultations' on 16 June 1755 to clarify matters for the Mayor's Court in disputes between those of other ethnicities and religions against 'Feringees', he defined the 'Feringy' as 'black mustee Portuguese Christians, residing in the settlement as a people distinct from the natural and proper subjects of Portugal, sprung originally from Hindus or Mussulmans, who by the law of nations cannot by their conversion to Christianity, be exempted from their allegiance to the Mogul, their natural Lord.'

There was even speculation among the British, relates Long, that in the event of a future war with France, Portuguese women who had been permitted to enter Fort William for security during the siege of Calcutta by Siraj, would hesitate to 'take up arms against an enemy of their own religion'—they being Roman Catholic, like a majority of the French. A bizarre ban on Roman Catholic priests in Calcutta was 'remonstrated against' by the Court of Directors. (But the 'Portuguese' couldn't entirely be dismissed. In the pre-Plassey and Plassey era there were relatively few Bengali writers, or clerks, to manage the accounts, so several Portuguese were employed. For a while, writes Long, Portuguese was widely understood in Calcutta and was even lingua franca 'among servants'.)

For their part, the Armenians were largely tolerated by the British in Bengal, though they squabbled from time to time, even quarrelling over 'restitution money' granted them after the retaking of Calcutta by Clive & Co.

These traders, perhaps because they were relatively less snobbish than Europeans—Long speculates it was on account of them being 'Asiatics'—mixed more freely with 'natives' than did the British. Consequently, they penetrated deeper into the hinterland.

In 1748, a quarrel flared up between the Armenians and the British. The British navy had seized two Armenian ships in the Persian Gulf that were on their way to Bengal. The Armenians in Bengal appealed to Alivardi who, as we have seen, went into a rage and stopped the Company's trade and charged them with piracy. Long believes the nawab 'aimed at making a profit out of both parties', leveraged the incident to squeeze cash. It's instructive to see how the incident played out, as it gives us insights into how the various players in Bengal conducted themselves in regard to one another. After the initial provocation, the British government in Calcutta threatened to prevent Armenian ships from passing through Calcutta. When the Armenians appealed to the Calcutta Council and its president, they were asked to sign a document to convey to Alivardi that they were 'satisfied' with the resolution of matters. The Armenians refused. The Calcutta government threatened to eject the community from Calcutta. This was an empty threat, Long suggests, because the Company would have lost money if the Armenians stopped using the port: 'five per cent, on the great importations made by them of raw silk, and of the goods on the Coast of Coromandel.'

It was getting messy. And the Company was anyway losing money with the nawab disrupting its trade. Eventually, as we have seen, the

Council in Calcutta settled with Alivardi even though the Company had no control over the original incident in the Persian Gulf—they were not the Company's ships but the Crown's ships over which they had no authority. The Council even tried to blame the French for the interdiction, a ploy that didn't work. By August that year they settled with Alivardi.

It didn't make for a happy denouement. The British continued to keep the Armenians at arm's length. The Company even prevailed upon their political appointees to toe the line after the upset at Plassey. Long notes that in 1760, before he turned on John Company, their approved nawab 'Kasim Ali Khan' [Mir Qasim] ordered that 'it is contrary to all custom to give a zemindary to an Armenian'. Why? asks Long, 'unless for the same reason that in 1765 the jealousies of trade caused the Government to forbid the Armenians residing at Aurungs'.

Less complicated was the British relationship with the Danes in the Plassey years. Their west bank settlement up the Hugli was nearest to Calcutta, in the 'salubrious shades' of Srirampur. Or Fredericknagore to the Danes, after their king. (The earlier settlement of Dannemarksnagore near Chandannagar had collapsed with the second edition of the Danes' East India Company.) Wars in Europe in the early nineteenth century would see the occupation of Srirampur by the British—they simply crossed the river from the bastion of Barrackpore on the opposite shore. In 1844, the third edition of the Danish business enterprise in Asia—Asiatisk Kompagni—would exit Bengal after selling assets and rights to the English Company. But from the 1750s onward, until the Danish exit, Srirampur was a place of trade, and, in the British mind, a place of leisure with inexpensive food and beverage in welcoming tavernas. In Company records, reference to the Danes 'occurs chiefly in connection with some row when a British subject strayed into their territory and committed some trifling outrages, which to them at once rose to the importance of a national affront,' writes Long.

Like many—including Siraj—the Danes suffered collateral damage when the English were at war with the French—especially as the Danes wished to trade with the French. It was 'a frequent source of misunderstanding,' we learn, 'the doctrine of neutral bottoms was not then acted on.' It was a twisted time and relationships were cynically opportunistic. After the Plassey fires cooled, the Danes actually applied in 1760 to the British in Calcutta for 'cannon and ammunition', as they 'expected an attack of the Mahrattas on Serampore'.

◆

The Dutch East India Company, or Vereenigde Oostindische Compagnie, had its settlement in Chinsurah (Chuchurā in Bengali), just north of Chandannagar. Their relationship with the British was conflicted—and this is a Company point of view—largely because of what items to trade and their share in the trade. 'The Records teem with long correspondence and complaints regarding their due share in the Saltpetre Trade, and the interference of English Gomasaths [a typographical error: gomasthas] with their purchasing goods,' observes Long. Notwithstanding their bickering, they were far more cordial with the English than with the French. Indeed, Company records show that in 1748 the Dutch had actually approached the British in Calcutta for the protection of Chinsurah against the French; because the French had been attacking Dutch shipping in Batavia— former Jakarta.

Sometimes things got downright petty between the French and the Dutch. Consultations in Calcutta on 3 January 1749 noted how the French had forcibly taken possession of the Dutch Garden at Chinsurah:

> Huyghens, Director of the Dutch Settlement at Chinsura, informs the Deputy Governor of Calcutta, the Honourable Barwell, that the French at Chandernagore have by force of arms taken possession of their Company's garden [in Fort Augustus] whereby they have broke the neutrality of the Ganges.

We shall discuss it at length a little later but this neutrality, if not complete amity, between the various European powers in India, which was shattered by events in the run-up to Plassey, insulated the settlements and trade of all European entities against wars in Europe. And, quite incredibly, this neutrality in Bengal persisted even when the British and French were fighting each other in southern

India in the 1740s in what turned out to be a trailer for Plassey.

The Calcutta Council agreed to tell Alivardi 'of the neutrality being broke by the French' because they were concerned the French might someday move against them ('...and as the Dutch are our allies from their acting in such manner with them we have reason to apprehend they would do the same by us when in their power.')

Even so, common interest would occasionally bring the sniping companies to a shared platform, as even a relatively minor incident could become a troubling precedent that affected all. For instance, on 14 July 1755, when the Company considered a joint appeal with the French and Dutch to Alivardi:

> On the 12th instant, we received a letter from Mr. Nicholas Clerembault, Chief, &c. Council at Dacca, dated the 7th, informing us Meer Abou Taleb, Naib to the Nabob Kissendass, on a pretence of a demand of some considerable present from the Dutch Factory there, had seized a writer belonging to the Dutch and confined him in the Kellah [fort] till the Dutch Chief made a promise of complying with their demand. As it is a most violent and unprecedented proceeding to an European, they have reason to apprehend it may greatly endanger their future residence there if a proper complaint be not made to the Great Nabob Mohobut Jung at Muxadavad. That Mr. Ysinck, the Dutch Chief, having informed the French Chief and Mr. Clerembault that he should inform the Council at Chinsurah and desire the application to us and to the Council at Chandernagore in order to obtain our and their consent to a joint complaint to the Great Nabob at Muxadabad.

For his part, Alivardi generally encouraged, and even attempted to enforce, such neutrality. It all began to fall apart when the English and French prepared for hostilities as a result of the build-up of tension that finally led to the Seven Years War in Europe in 1756, and put Siraj on edge. In the months before Plassey and later, some British militarists—including Clive—and chroniclers, and even the Council in Madras which sent Clive to Bengal, suggested that the mutual neutrality of Europeans in the subcontinent in general, and Bengal in particular, was impractical.

The Dutch would largely remain off the British register of threat perception during the Plassey years, but came back strongly in the aftermath. In November 1759, the Dutch and British actually fought pitched land-and-river battles near Chinsurah; the land battle was called the Battle of Bidera. Siraj's disaffected general, Mir Jafar, who replaced Siraj as a quid pro quo for conspiring with John Company to hand Siraj a defeat at Plassey, had opened a back-channel with the Dutch Company to counter Clive & Co.'s demands for funds and concessions—the Company's trade-off for backing Mir Jafar against Siraj! In Bengal's radiating ripple of conspiracy enhanced by the European penchant for mercantile militarism, nearly 2,000 troops under the Dutch flag, of which 1,500 were Dutch and Malay troops, arrived from Batavia and fought a little over 1,300 troops and cavalry under the British flag. Both sides employed warships. The Company decisively won over Compagnie, the key land battle being led by Colonel Francis Forde. 'They [the Dutch] made a bold stroke for ascendancy in Bengal in 1759, and might have got it but for the promptness of Colonel Forde,' Long tells us. A couple of escaping Dutch ships—the remainder were grounded, or surrendered—were intercepted at the mouth of the Hugli by arriving British ships.

As a result of this, Mir Jafar would lose his nawabship, courtesy of Clive & Co. the following year to his son-in-law, Mir Qasim, who would in turn lose it back to Mir Jafar in 1763. All these were examples of business-led regime changes that became case studies over two hundred years before the unlovely examples led by American and European corporations and consortiums in the twentieth century!

◆

As far as the Germans were concerned, they were simply not welcome in Bengal. The Company did everything to discourage the Germans from the time they made attempts to trade in 1751. They met 'determined hostility from the English,' notes Long. And it appears that the British had all the encouragement they needed from Alivardi, the subahdar of Bengal, Bihar, and Orissa.

A revealing letter from Alivardi dated 19 August 1751 actively demands the Company's intercession to prevent the passage of German ships on account of their marauding of vessels that answered to the nawab—an example of their outright aggression to belatedly muscle in on the Asian mercantile game of their European neighbours. To go by this letter's translation and record with the Company, for all of Alivardi's professed push for non-aggression between European powers along the Ganga–Bhagirathi–Hugli, it was all a matter of expediency—if something worked for the state, it worked. It isn't idle speculation, therefore, to wonder what the busy minds of the Company, and that of other European companies, might have been thinking. Self-serving policy worked both ways. If they needed the subahdar, the subahdar also needed them—until the domino effect of European politics and Siraj's ire upset the edgy but relatively cosy geopolitical and geo-economic applecart of Bengal. Here's Alivardi's letter in translation:

TO THE FIRST OF MERCHANTS MY FRIEND MR DAWSON

My Friend,—have heard from Hooghly some time past news that Mr. Acton and Mr. Mills, both English under the protection of the Germans, are coming with three ships of war that hoist German colors from the Franks country to Hooghly, and design to lay in the road, to stop the river and seize the Musselmen ships; on this account I have already sent Perwannahs to you and the other European nations which by this time must be arrived with you, since which I have received your arrived act by which I find my intelligence is true; but what you will, that the company have ordered you not to make war in these parts with any European nation is very wrong, for in time past in Sujah Cawn's [Murshid Quli's son-in-law, the nawab Shuja-ud-din Muhammad Khan's] time, the English and Dutch chiefs both entered into methods for destroying the German chief and engaged him to join with you, on which account the German chief absconded; now you will write me so different a story, it is not right or reasonable. If the Germans come here, it will be very bad for all the European, but for you the worst of all, and you will afterwards repent it, and I shall be obliged to stop all your trade and business, and shall get an order from the king for so doing. It will be proper for you now to consider of your trade from Patna and Bengal how if these troubles happen, you are to carry it on; therefore, take care that these German ships do not come into the road [Balasore Roads, a gathering point for ships off the coast of Orissa before entering the mouth of the Hugli] or stop the way; do you act in such a way, and such a manner as to punish them before they arrived in the road.

Long notes that Adam Dawson, Drake's predecessor at Fort William, ordered the Company's pilots on the Hugli to 'on no account to take charge of or show the way to any Allaman', and hoped that the French and Dutch would also uphold this blacklisting of the Germans. 'God forbid that they should come, but should this be the case, I am in hopes they will be either sunk, broke or destroyed.'

The boycott would be cemented in a few short years with London's imprimatur. In 1757, the Court of Directors sent an order to the effect that there would be no 'commercial dealings of any kind' with German ships.

6

THE BATTLE OF MYLAPORE: LESSONS FOR PLASSEY

*'The Moors, unaccustomed to such
hardy and precipitate onsets, gave way...'*

Robert Orme doesn't pretend to be anything but a chronicler of British glory and ascendancy. His *A History of the Military Transactions of the British Nation in Indostan* is dedicated to the monarch at the time, George III, and he declares the work as an 'attempt to commemorate the successes of the British arms in Indostan'.

He is also brutal about those who governed India before the British, a judgement levelled with the comforting certitude of the civilized occidental who always stoops to conquer. Orme, while prejudiced about the character of Indian rulers, sharply assesses the issue of information about their rule:

> Hence the public in Indostan, deprived of authentic evidence, are left to judge of the actions of their rulers either from probable conjectures, or from the general idea of their characters. The constitution and defects of the government have rendered poisons and assassinations, in the practice of the great, the common method of removing those who stand in opposition to the ambition of others; insomuch that a history of one century in Indostan, would furnish more examples of this nature than can be found in the history of one half of the kingdoms of Europe since the time of Charlemagne.

Orme's comments also give away the symbiotic link between the Company and the Crown, commerce and military, and demolish to a great extent the argument that pro-colony chroniclers offer to justify every action by placing the onus of bloodthirsty deviousness at the door of the rulers of Bengal—indeed, of India. Consider Orme's introduction to his works:

From the year 1745 to the conclusion of the late peace, the English have been continually engaged in war, in one or other of these divisions [Bombay, Madras, Calcutta]: and the preservation of their commerce in the East-Indies absolutely depended on the conduct and success of the wars of Coromandel and Bengal... We have therefore thought that a general history of their military transactions in Indostan, during this period, would not be unacceptable to the public; more especially as there is no part of the world in which the British arms have, of late years, acquired more honour.

Orme's accounts enable our understanding of the dynamics of the subcontinent, egos and machinations of its rulers and usurpers, the chutzpah and military craft that European merchant-soldiers applied to bring them great riches along with greater political domination. Even accounting for Orme's bias, he gives credit where it is due, especially when it bolsters his argument. Take, for example, his description of the Battle of San Thomé in October 1746, named after the early sixteenth century basilica constructed by the Portuguese, which the faithful believe contains the remains of the apostle Saint Thomas. It is also known as the Battle of Adyar, after the river where the French troops faced the ineffective artillery of the Nawab of Arcot; and the Battle of Mylapore after the area where the last phase of the battle was fought.

The battle is an acknowledgement of French prowess against forces of 'the Moors'. This is significant as Muslim rulers in Delhi, eastern India, and southern India were at the time symbols of a politically dominant religion, with the Maratha clans the only politico-religious bulwark against them. Orme portrayed the battle as one of European prowess against a numerically superior Indian force. This is an interesting observation by him as it actually followed from the French capture of the British garrison-settlement at Fort St George, the seat of the Madras Presidency and as crucial a post to safeguard the commercial and strategic interests of John Company along the Coromandel coast, Bay of Bengal, Ceylon, and trade routes to Southeast Asia and China as Pondicherry was to the French.

Chroniclers of the time often used different yardsticks for different combatants. Battles among old European foes in the Orient were matters of mutual valour, a battle of equals with unequal results, the French winning some with a combination of intrigue and military, the British winning others with equal application including, ultimately, the grand prize of India. But a major victory against locals was something else altogether—a matter of great import. The Battle of Mylapore was in some ways a portent of Plassey.

The First Carnatic War between 1746 to 1748 along the Coromandel coast and its hinterland that in the present day includes areas of the provinces of Andhra Pradesh, Tamil Nadu, and Karnataka was when Robert Clive began his journey as an ordinary John Company employee transformed by opportunities of battle into a military man of extraordinary reputation.

Conflict had broken out among the French and British in the Carnatic. It was spurred by the War of the Austrian Succession that began in 1740 in the wake of a disintegrating Hapsburg empire, a pan-European war in which they were on opposing sides. The French had allied with Bavaria and its claimant to the Hapsburg crown, Charles Albert, the British with Austrians and their queen, Maria Theresa, on the opposite side—the British were wary of French domination in Europe and France's competing commercial and military interests elsewhere in the world. The French and British fought each other only in 1744, after the formal declaration of war by France against Britain. Then it got intense on land and sea, and in their overseas holdings, and in turn upset the mutually beneficial détente that the British East India Company and its French counterpart, Compagnie Française des Indes, had thus far maintained. British naval forces began to blockade France, and raid French merchant shipping on their routes to trading outposts, such as in India and the Caribbean. The British, with the help of militias in their American colonies, took Forteresse de Louisbourg, a significant fortress and commercial port on the northeastern edge of Nova Scotia in present-day Canada. In 1746, French troops had laid siege to the British settlement in Madras; in September the British surrendered. (A later French foray into Cuddalore—which was centred on Fort St David—the British settlement south of the major French base at Pondicherry, failed.)

Complicated as all this was, it was made more so by the governor of Pondicherry and, by extension, chief of French interests in India,

Joseph François Dupleix. Several British- and pro-British historians and chroniclers credit Dupleix, who may have taken to science if his father's influence hadn't procured for him in 1720 a position with the French company in Pondicherry, with setting the subcontinental template for Clive & Co. Although, going by Orme's description, the British spooked Dupleix into war against them in this particular instance, of which more to follow shortly. Dupleix and Clive would clash more than once in a series of battles that would seal in gold Captain, Major, and then Lieutenant Colonel Clive's reputation by the time he arrived in Bengal in late 1756: a star of the Second Carnatic War (1749–54) and the man who contributed to outsmarting and outgunning Dupleix.

Before Dupleix's appointment as governor in Pondicherry in 1742, he was for eleven years chief at Chandannagar and knew both subcontinental dynamics and British ambitions well. Around the time of his arrival as governor in Pondicherry, France was already deeply committed in the War of the Austrian Succession, and he aggressively pursued a policy of extending the French sphere of political and military influence as a corollary to securing for the Compagnie its commercial influence. One of the ways in which he did so was by occasionally offering his services to one nawab or ruler over another. Dupleix would manage to extend French territory along the Coromandel coast, specifically the area known as the Carnatic and Northern Circars, and French influence along much of present-day southern India excluding the kingdom of Travancore (the southern half of present-day Kerala and southwestern Tamil Nadu). A crucial part of the equation was the nawab of Arcot, Muhammad Anwaruddin Khan, who was an appointee of the nizam of Hyderabad, who ruled much of the Deccan quite like Murshid Quli and Alivardi ruled Bengal: autonomously, with an occasional, nominal doff and tribute to the fading Mughals.

From several accounts, the elderly yet vigorous Anwaruddin, who became nawab in 1744 at the age of seventy, wasn't above intrigue, including assassination, the allegations of which never entirely left him despite his protestations to the contrary and his patron, the nizam, standing by him. And much like the elderly yet keen Alivardi in Bengal—who at this time was four years into his nawabship and battling the Marathas—Anwaruddin wasn't keen on the European powers feuding on his territory as a result of their entanglements in Europe, or mercantile competition, or the ego of a grasping administrator-merchant like Dupleix. The nawab of Arcot generally preferred to be even-handed towards both Company and Compagnie. But events in Europe would begin to tip his hand, as it would that of Europeans in the region of the Indian Ocean and Bay of Bengal. Among the more balanced accounts of this widening ripple comes from Orme. It appears that, whatever overreach Dupleix is accused of during his run for Indic fortune and fame, in this instance he was spooked by the British.

As a consequence of the War of the Austrian Succession, 'a squadron of English men of war appeared in the Indian seas,' Orme writes, '...two 60 gun ships, one of 50, and a frigate of 20 guns.' Led by a Royal Navy commodore, Curtis Barnett (Orme refers to him as Barnet), who had earlier made his reputation interdicting French shipping on its way to the Caribbean, they passed by India and headed out instead to two strategic locations, the Strait of Malacca between the Malay peninsula and the present-day island of Sumatra in Indonesia, and the narrow Sunda Strait between Sumatra and the island of Java—not far northeast of the island-volcano that would in some decades develop a fearsome reputation, Anak Krakatau.

They attacked French shipping: three ships on their way from China to Europe; one returning to Pondicherry from Manila from which they realized 180,000 pounds sterling from the cargo; and a third ship at Aceh, on the northwestern tip of Sumatra, near the northern entry to the Strait of Malacca—and converted the merchant ship into a warship with forty cannon. Raids done and point made, the ships rendezvoused at Batavia. The re-formed squadron then 'appeared on the coast of Coromandel in the month of July 1745,' writes Orme, 'at which time the garrison of Pondicherry consisted of no more than 430 Europeans, its fortifications were not completed, and no French [naval] squadron had hitherto appeared in India'.

This, and reports of reinforcements from Britain, 'alarmed' Dupleix. 'He prevailed on the Nabob An'war-odean to insist with the government of Madrass,' Orme recounts, 'that the English ships of war should not commit any hostilities by land against the French possessions in the territories of Arcot; but the Nabob at the same time assured the English, that he would oblige the French to observe the same law of neutrality, if their force should hereafter become superior to that of the English.'

This posed a problem to the chief of Fort St George, Nicholas Morse. He made a distinction between Britain's fleet that owed allegiance to king and country, and his own employer and overlord, John Company. The distinction would become blurred by quid pro quo and expediency as the Eurasian conflict gathered momentum in southern India and, in just over a decade, travelled up the coast to Bengal. The Company chief in Madras conveyed to Anwaruddin that he could only do so much: he could acquiesce to the nawab's wish on behalf of Fort St George, 'but that Mr. Barnet, the commander of the English squadron, was the immediate officer of the King of Great Britain, by whose orders and commission he acted, independent of the East India company's agents at Madrass.'

That didn't wash with the nawab, who equated the Company with its country of origin. As Orme puts it: 'The Nabob replied, that all officers of the English nation who came to the coast of Coromandel were equally obliged to respect his government in the Carnatic; and that if Mr. Barnet, with his squadron, should venture to act contrary to the orders he had now given, the town of Madrass should atone for their disobedience.' The threat worked. Officials at Fort St George managed to convince Barnett to 'confine his operations to the sea'.

Evidently miffed at such a reality, the restless commodore despatched one of his ships away from the nawab's eyes and concerns to the seas off Balasore in Orissa, along the 'Gulph of Bengal'. It was a strategic point near the Gangetic delta where 'she took two or three French ships returning from different parts of India to the French settlements in Bengal'. The remainder of the British fleet went away to Mergui in Burma, a port town east of the eponymous archipelago, where it gained safe harbour in the face of approaching storms. But the ships returned to the Coromandel coast in early 1746 where they were reinforced by three ships arrived from Britain. Before a French squadron of ships appeared later that year, in an escalating response, Barnett would die of an illness in April 1746 at Fort St David in Cuddalore—other accounts mention it as May, aboard a ship anchored off that fort.

A fleet of nine French ships reached the Coromandel coast on 25 June, commanded by a person Dupleix disliked but could do little to reign in at this point: the governor of the French territory of Mauritius (Île de France) and Reunion (Île de Bourbon), Bertrand-François Mahé de la Bourdonnais. The 'Mahé' in his name, so goes a story, accrued from his role in capturing for France the eponymous enclave on the Malabar coast surrounded by the present-day state of Kerala.

After a brief battle, which led to deaths and damage to ships on both sides, the British squadron's commander retreated the following day to the vast Trincomalee harbour on the east coast of present-day Sri Lanka, a region which remains dry in the southwest monsoon months, for repairs and resupply. According to Orme, an aggressive intent to fight, a tactical feint, by la Bourdonnais fooled them. The Frenchman '...practised to deter the English from doing what he most dreaded; for most of his ships had expended the greatest part of their ammunition, and several of them had not victuals on board for twenty-four hours.'

Later that night when the French ships reached Pondicherry, it led Dupleix to become concerned about another matter, that a rival in full 'command of his armament' had a likelihood of gaining both wealth and reputation, which 'created jealousy in the mind of Mr. Dupleix'. The two dissented on various matters, notes Orme, but la Bourdonnais (for whom Orme has only praise—for his seamanship, tactics, gallantry, and honour—quite unlike the snide tones he reserves for Dupleix), maintained the peace in the interests of France.

La Bourdonnais judged that his fleet too needed refitting, and re-arming with more cannon, to be effective against the British squadron or any other British force. He sailed from Pondicherry on 24 July. By 6 August he had come by the British squadron, which had meanwhile been refitted and supplied. Orme writes that the British avoided an engagement as they noticed the 'addition of cannon' to the French ships. He refers to la Bourdonnais's account to note that the two squadrons sailed within sight of each other for three days, before the British ships, on account of 'sailing better' than the French, 'disappeared'.

And here la Bourdonnais may have precipitated an encounter,

going by Orme's submission. He returned to Pondicherry, remaining alert to the danger of elusive British ships also returning to the Coromandel coast as a deterrence to French attacks. 'But encouraged by their shyness at the last meeting,' Orme writes, la Bourdonnais 'now determined to lay siege to Madrass.'

The British discovered these plans and appealed to Nawab Anwaruddin for intercession. But they slipped up, writes Orme, by not making a counter-offer:

> ...neglecting to accompany their application for his assistance with a present of money. This ill-judged parsimony left the Nabob so lukewarm in their interests that although he did not give Mr Dupleix a positive permission, he refrained from making any preparations, or even from using menaces to prevent the French from attacking Madrass.

◆

And so fell another domino in the series of events that would contribute to the future history of Plassey, especially in terms of acquiring knowledge about the use of men and materiel and in how far to push envelopes in the subcontinent.

La Bourdonnais lay ill in Pondicherry as French ships arrived off Madras on 18 August and cannonaded that settlement. They failed to damage anything. There was awkwardness to their manoeuvres, feels Orme, because la Bourdonnais was absent.

But it was enough to bring the town to a level of 'consternation'. The Company settlement had been around for nearly a hundred years. Orme writes of it as being about 5 miles (8 kilometres) along the coast and a mile inland. The premium real estate was, of course, Fort St George and its vicinity—'White Town' in parlance, a template replicated in Calcutta—where the British and other Europeans 'under their protection' lived. It was a complex of about fifty houses, the Company factory, the factory residence, other Company buildings, and Anglican and Roman Catholic churches. This was enclosed by a 'slender' wall and 'slight' bastions and batteries. To the north of this lay 'Black Town'—another template that would be followed in numerous trading-post-and-colonial settlements—which in the case of Madras was 'worse fortified' than White Town, and contained 'many very good habitations' of Armenian merchants and 'the richest of the Indian merchants'. This, too, was Company land. Further to the north lived 'Indian natives of all ranks'. Company land also included a couple of villages, populated entirely by Indians.

This nervous settlement was eagerly awaiting help from the British ships which had been last reported to have been sighted around 23 August in the area of Pulicat, north of Madras, where there was a Dutch settlement, but had then disappeared. We learn it was on account of at least one large man of war, with sixty cannon, that was 'so leaky' the impact of firing her cannon might have sunk her. Instead the ship and the squadron headed up to Bengal. 'The consternation of the town was therefore little less than despair,' relates Orme. The 250,000 inhabitants of this thriving, teeming Company territory now awaited their fate, with the British at this time, in this place, outgunned on sea and land. There were just 200 British soldiers in the garrison, with only 'two or three' of the officers having experienced 'any other service than that of the parade'. A hundred more British residents were civilians. The remainder were Indians, apart from an estimated three to four thousand Indian Christians, Orme writes with an unkind cut presumably reserved for some Goans of the day and other Indian converts in Portuguese territories in the subcontinent 'who call themselves Portuguese, and pretend to be descended from that nation'.

Against this motley bunch the French poured several thousand soldiers and sailors, European, African—'Caffre', the slur which in South Africa would be transformed into Kaffir—and Indian. Some troops were landed by ship on 3 September at a place a little over 20 kilometres south of Madras, and after a day were within 'cannon shot' of the settlement. They were now joined by other troops under French command, in all '1,100 Europeans, 400 Caffres, and 400 Indian natives disciplined in the European manner'. The rest of the force, 1,800 European mariners, remained on board. They prepared for a siege of Madras.

La Bourdonnais, who was by now recovered, directed the attack. It began on 7 September with a bombardment of White Town, by a battery of mortars to the west of the settlement, situated about 450 metres from the fort's walls. By the next day, the French had cleaned up British artillery to the fort's south, and by the following morning two British residents came to 'treat' with la Bourdonnais. It didn't work, and the bombardment continued through the day and the night of 9 September, except for a couple of hours of intermission during which another unsuccessful peace conference took place.

Fort St George finally capitulated to la Bourdonnais's terms on the morning of 10 September: 'It was agreed that the English should surrender themselves as prisoners of war: that the town should be immediately delivered up; but that it should be afterwards ransomed. Mr. De la Bourdonnais gave his promise that he would settle the ransom on easy and moderate terms.' French forces thereafter left the British and others under their protection alone, and took over the Company's warehouses and stores of ammunition. Orme writes that no one in the French camp lost their lives in the battle, and the British lost 'four or five' in White Town. He also notes with post-Plassey hindsight the situation and object lessons that the Company and Crown learned during the episode in Madras: 'From this period it is useful to contemplate the progress made by the English in Indostan, both in the science and spirit of war.'

◆

But first, there was some confusion and crossed-messages, and arguments among the French, essentially la Bourdonnais, and the French Council in Pondicherry under the influence of Dupleix. On the very day the British governor in Madras sued for peace, the nawab's messenger reached Pondicherry with a stern query for Dupleix: How could the French presume to attack Madras without his permission? They would require to lift the siege or face the nawab's army.

'Mr. Dupleix sent directions to his agent at Arcot to pacify the Nabob, by promising that the town, if taken, should be given up to him,' Orme tells us, 'and by representing that the English would certainly be willing to pay him a large sum of money for the restitution of so valuable a possession.' It pacified the nawab for a time, but when word of it reached the British, they were upset that Dupleix had taken upon himself the right to dispose of British territory in India as he pleased—a source of considerable bad blood in subsequent years.

To add to the complication, as we have seen, la Bourdonnais had struck his own bargain with the British in Madras: of being ransomed and be done with it. In this he disagreed with the suggestion of the French Council in Pondicherry and Dupleix that, in the interests of France, and 'not private advantages' as la Bourdonnais sought, Madras must be razed to the ground. (Clive would employ similar logic eleven years later when he pressed for an attack on Chandannagar on his way to Plassey.)

While disputes among the French continued, the British, according to Orme, managed to find a touch of good fortune in the longer-term, larger scheme of things. Although Madras would for the time being remain in French hands, the Treaty of Aix-la-Chapelle negotiated primarily by Britain and France on 18 October 1748, swapped conquered territories in the Americas and Asia.

Indeed, Orme's extreme suggestion is that, had the bickering among the French not continued, the Company and Crown enterprise in India might have been in jeopardy; and Compagnie, instead of Company, may have had the run of much of the subcontinent.

For one thing, three large and well-armed French men-of-war with over 1,300 mariners and troops arrived in Pondicherry on 27 September 1746, providing la Bourdonnais enough firepower, feels Orme, to have 'conquered the rest of the English settlements in Indostan'. La Bourdonnais wanted to, but was 'contradicted' by 'Mr. Dupleix, and the council of Pondicherry'.

Meanwhile, there was still the matter of ransoming Madras, which la Bourdonnais was keen on, and Dupleix not—for reasons mentioned earlier. There was also the matter of weather. The winter monsoon—northeast monsoon—would soon be setting in. And there was a period of calm during this switchover from the summer monsoon—southwest monsoon—and then the onset of this 'retreating' monsoon with stormy weather, typical of the southeastern part of India and eastern Sri Lanka. So, la Bourdonnais was caught in a bind: he wished to remain in Madras until his proposal of ransom-and-release had been met, and yet, he didn't want his ships to be trapped by foul weather.

The storm arrived around the midnight of 2 October, and devastated la Bourdonnais's ships. Of the six ships off Madras, none were seen in the morning. One was entirely driven away. Four other ships, including one with seventy cannon, lost their masts. A sixth sank with a handful of crew managing to escape. Twenty other ships flying the flags of other nations were forced ashore, or sank. This affected la Bourdannais's plans, but he still retained firepower, as the ships newly arrived from Europe and moored off Pondicherry escaped—there was relative calm in Pondicherry as the storm raged in Madras. He had also agreed to a treaty of ransom with the British a day earlier, agreeing that the French would leave Fort St George by 4 October, and the remaining 'artillery and warlike stores' would be divided among the French and the British.

But Dupleix wouldn't have it, and wanted Madras to remain in French hands. After the storm, la Bourdonnais essentially told the British they were better off signing a treaty with him than being left without a treaty, and at the mercy of Dupleix. The governor-marauder evidently offered more honourable terms than the governor-merchant, because the Council at Fort St George signed a treaty with la Bourdonnais on 10 October 1746. Orme writes that la Bourdonnais had already taken on board all Company merchandise his forces found, and all the 'naval' stores—which had already been decided upon before the storm. That amounted to 130,000 pounds sterling. The French also took gold and silver worth 31,000 pounds sterling. The French share of the division of artillery and military stores, a split decided upon before the storm, was computed at 24,000 pounds sterling. Other merchandise was 'relinquished' to the owners. The agreement also called for the French to leave Madras by the end of January 1747, 'after which the English were to remain in possession of it, without being attacked by them again during the war [of the Austrian Succession]'.

La Bourdonnais also squeezed a very business-like reparation from the Company with this agreement—although naturally it was much less, as we shall see, than the squeeze the Company put on Murshidabad's post-Siraj nawabs. The governor and Council of Madras would pay the equivalent of 440,000 pounds sterling ['1,100,000 pagodas': the gold pagoda or coin issued by the company in Madras was usually at a premium to the contemporary French and Dutch issues, or that of the Arcot pagoda]. Six equal instalments would need to account for 240,000 pounds sterling paid at Pondicherry before October 1749; the remainder, 200,000 pounds, to be paid on bills were drawn on the Company in London, 'payable a few months after they should be presented'. The English provided hostages as guarantees for the treaty.

And then la Bourdonnais made his curious exit from Indian shores and equations. On 12 October 1746, he left Madras after handing over charge to a Pondicherry Council member, cleared for this purpose by Dupleix, reached Pondicherry three days later, and by 20 October, had sailed on with seven ships. The plan was to sail to Aceh, but la Bourdonnais's own ship was deemed unseaworthy for the voyage. The squadron split up, one group carrying on to Aceh, the other, with la Bourdonnais on board, making for Mauritius. (When he subsequently arrived in France in 1748—after being captured en route by the British and paroled—he was arrested on charges of corruption. He spent over two years in the Bastille before acquittal in 1751. Among his other legacies: Louis-Charles Mahé de la Bourdonnais, a grandson of our Bertrand-François, was an acknowledged European chess wizard. But that is another story.)

◆

Two days after la Bourdonnais's departure from Indian shores, Nawab Anwaruddin's forces formed up outside Fort St Geroge, and attacked it.

To have Orme tell it, 'very soon' after the French had taken Madras, the nawab 'began to suspect, or had discovered' that Dupleix's pledge 'to put him in possession of the town, was a fraud employed to divert him from giving the English any assistance during the siege'. In any case it had become clear that the French would hold on to Fort St George and the surrounding area as long as possible. Here Orme offers the underpinning of his logic for the European termination of a subcontinental myth:

> He [Anwaruddin] determined to revenge this affront by laying siege to Madras; which he made no doubt of taking from the French, with as much ease as they had taken it from the English: for measuring the military abilities of the Europeans, by the great respect and humility with which they had hitherto carried themselves in all their transactions with the Mogul government;

he imagined that this submission in their behaviour proceeded from a consciousness of the superior military prowess of the Moors.

(This is generally correct, though to be fair, the Company's transactions hadn't always been carried with humility. There was the instance of the Company being chased away by Bengal's Mughal governor Shaista Khan, several run-ins with the nawab Murshid Quli, and relatively minor run-ins with Alivardi that were matters of record at the time of the Battle of San Thomé. Besides, the subcontinent was already witnessing the laying bare of Bengal and its western flank by rampaging Marathas, spoiling, devastating raids which repeatedly outmanoeuvred, extended, and exhausted the 'Moor' Alivardi.)

A livid Anwaruddin sent an army of 10,000 to Madras led by his eldest son, Mahfuz Khan—Maphuze in Orme's telling. Dupleix had sent word to the French governor at Fort St George to 'refrain' from hostilities. That, and two emissaries sent to negotiate with him may have led Mahfuz to misinterpret it as a sign of weakness on the part of the French.

The nawab's forces replicated the French approach of positioning artillery near the walls of White Town, and planned to 'escalade'— scale the walls of—Black Town. They also planned to drain a part of the river (a branch of the Cooum) that ran to the settlement's west and decanted into the Bay of Bengal several hundred metres to the south of Fort St George. Here the nawab's forces took their cue from what the British did: cut a channel through the sands to drain the river whenever required. They also took control of a spring north of the settlement, a source of 'good water' for the settlement. Orme condescendingly remarks: 'These measures shewed a degree of intelligence very uncommon in the military operations of the Moors.' At any rate, Mahfuz Khan thought he was placed perfectly for a siege. It would be just a matter of time before the French caved in.

The French attacked first, with a volley of cannon. The drop in the level of water in the river and spring water being 'interrupted' gave them clues as to what was about to happen. The nawab's forces retreated wherever fire was directed at them. The day proved to be a stalemate. That was on 21 October. Orme provides a racy account of what followed:

The next day, being the 22nd of October, a body of 400 men, with two field pieces, marched out of the town, and attacked that quarter of...the Nabob's army, which was encamped to the northwest, between the town and the spring. Their cavalry mounted on the first alarm, and uniting their squadrons, advanced with the appearance of resolution. Having never experienced the effect of field pieces, they had no conception that it was possible to fire, with execution, the same piece of cannon five or six times in a minute; for in the aukward [sic] management of their own clumsy artillery, they think they do well if they fire once in a quarter of an hour. The French detachment concealed their two field pieces behind their line, until the enemy's cavalry approached near enough to feel the full effect of them; when the line opening to the right and left, the field pieces began to fire: two or three of the enemy's horses were killed by the first discharge, which threw the whole body into confusion: however they kept their ground some time, as if waiting for an intermission of the fire; but, finding that it continued with vivacity they took to flight with great precipitation. The French plundered their tents and baggage without interruption, and took two pieces of cannon, so little fit for service, that they flung them into a well. They did not lose a man in the attack, and killed about seventy of the Moors.

Mahfuz had evidently had enough, and retreated to the west of the settlement, but after hearing that French reinforcements were on the way, moved a few kilometres to the south, in the area of San Thomé, near the Adyar.

Orme continues:

On the 24th of October the French detachment arrived, by break of day, at the bank of the river opposite to St. Thome, and found the Nabob's troops, horse and foot, drawn up on the other side, to oppose their passage... The river was fordable, and they passed it without loss, notwithstanding they were exposed to the fire of the enemy's artillery, which, as usual, was very ill served. As soon as they gained the opposite bank, they gave a general fire of their small arms, and then attacked with their bayonets.

The Moors, unaccustomed to such hardy and precipitate onsets, gave way, and retreated into the town, where they again made a shew of resistance from behind some pallisades which they had planted in different parts...

The French gave chase with concentrated fire. They boxed in the nawab's troops in the narrow lanes of the town and they retreated in a general melee, under fire. Several were killed. It was soon a rout, as the nawab's panicked army poured into the plains to the west.

Their general, Maphuze Khan, mounted on an elephant, on which the great standard of the Carnatic was displayed, was one of the first who made his escape. They were scarcely fled out of the town before the detachment from Madrass arrived, and assisted in the pillage of the enemy's baggage, among which were some valuable effects: many horses and oxen, and some camels were likewise taken. It is said, that the French troops murdered some of the Moors whom they found concealed in the houses they were plundering. This defeat struck such a terror into the Nabob's army, that they immediately retreated some miles from Madrass, and soon after returned to Arcot.

Orme then delivers the coup de grâce:

It was now more than a century since any of the European nations had gained a decisive advantage in war against the officers of the Great Mogul.

Orme is triumphant on behalf of the French even as he recounts the possibility in strategy and tactics, and the thoughts of command and control that the expedition triggered in the British.

The experience of former unsuccessful enterprizes, and the scantiness of military abilities which prevailed in all the colonies, from a long disuse of arms, had persuaded them that the Moors were a brave and formidable enemy; when the French at once broke through the charm of this timorous opinion, by defeating a whole army with a single battalion.

◆

After this triumph, Dupleix sent emissaries who 'declared null' the treaty the council at Fort St George had signed with la Bourdonnais. Nearly everything, except 'movables, cloaths, and the jewels of women', now belonged to the French.

Payback would arrive manifold in the Second Carnatic War even with the taking of Pondicherry by the British in 1761. Before that finale, there would be the decimation of the French in Bengal by the British, as a corollary of Plassey. The so-called neutrality of the Ganges, an informal arrangement that sought to provide safe passage for European ships in Bengal even if a state of war between, say, Britain and France, existed elsewhere, would be in tatters. And Siraj would lose the only Europeans he thought he could count on: the French.

BOOK II

THE
BUILD-UP

7

THE ENEMY TERRITORY OF MURSHIDABAD

'...the means of overturning his power,
whether by art, by force, or by treason'

Sometimes, ruins get recycled.

Nawazish Muhammad Khan, Alivardi's son-in-law, built Motijheel Palace using stones, mostly black marble or basalt, and other material from the region of Gaur, the administrative heart of Bengal from the seventh century CE until the sixteenth century. Specifically, the eponymous medieval capital, Gaur, which had its glory days till the mid-sixteenth century before it was abandoned. Even its name, the *Siyar* claims, was considered 'inauspicious' by the second Mughal emperor, Humayun, who changed it to Jinnatabad.

Motijheel was an oxbow loop of the Bhagirathi that remained once the course of the river moved away. It provided the backdrop for the eponymous palace, and gave the area its name, the lake of pearls. Along with a rich haul of rice, mango, mulberry with which to nurture silkworms for the region's famous silk, mustard flower, sugarcane, and tobacco, the area was known for cultured pearls—golden-hued seed pearls mainly, but on occasion, pearls of value, as British colonial sources for the British Indian district of Murshidabad tell us.

The *Siyar* adds that the complex also contained a stone hall or sangi dālān, mahalsarai—harem—offices, a mosque.

And it was all for the pleasure of Nawazish's 'beautiful wife', as the *Imperial Gazetteer of India* describes her, the pertinacious Ghaseti Begum. Formally known as Mehr-un-Nisa (literally: sun of women, a person of great beauty), she was the eldest daughter of Alivardi, and sister to Siraj's mother, the begum Amina.

A rare description of Motijheel comes to us from a penetrating and mildly disapproving letter by Jemima Kindersley, a keen traveller to India, written in September 1766, a time when Francis Sykes was the Company's resident at Murshidabad's court. Mrs Kindersley, whose letter was quoted by bureaucrat-orientalist Henry Beveridge in an essay, *Old Places in Murshidabad*, appears in one place to have confused Nawazish Muhammad, the creator of Motijheel, with the nawabs Alivardi and Siraj, but there is complete clarity as to her note of irony and mild triumph:

> Just above Cossimbazar is Motte Gill (Mottee—pearl, Gill—lake) or the lake of pearl, one of the prettiest of the Mahomedan Palaces, and now the habitation of the English resident at the Durbar: the spot has its name from a lake of clear water which surrounds it on every side except one small entrance. It was made by a former Nabob of Murshidabad. In case of war, this was a place of security for his wives and children to retire to. The buildings are in the style of the country. Along the middle of the ground, at certain distances, are different sets of apartments. Most of the rooms are small and dark, but what I most disapprove of is the useless expense they have been at for walls, for from every set of apartments are extended two long heavy walls, which reach on each side to the water's edge; this is the taste in most of their palaces. The walls do not answer the purpose of our garden walls in England (for they plant no fruit-trees against them), nor any other purpose that I can conceive, but to divide the gardens into smaller parts and by that means lessen the beauty and increase the heat. The most pleasing amongst their buildings are those in the open style, apartments which are not surrounded with a wall, but the roofs supported with double and triple rows of light pillars, which have a very elegant effect. We may easily suppose that the Nabob, who expended such great sums of money to build, to plant, and to dig that immense lake, little foresaw that it should ever become a place of residence for an English Chief, to be embellished and altered according to his taste. Much less could he foresee that his successors on the musnud should be obliged to court these Chiefs, that they should hold the Subahship only as a gift from the English, and he by them maintained in all the pageantry without any of the power of royalty.

A description of the atmosphere around Motijheel comes to us from John Shore, a subsequent resident at Murshidabad's court—and a likely resident at Nawazish's palace to love and folly. (O'Malley in his *Murshidabad* writes that in 1768 the palace was temporarily abandoned in favour of a residence in Maidapur on account of its 'unhealthy situation', but it was later re-occupied for a few years.) From Shore's observations, O'Malley believes it's likely that he lived there between 1771 and 1773, as in a letter written at the time, he mentions being a resident in a garden house of the nawab about 6 kilometres from Murshidabad. 'Here I enjoy cooing doves, whistling blackbirds and a purling stream,' Shore wrote. 'I am quite solitary and, except once a week, see no one of Christian complexion.'

O'Malley in his punctilious manner believes this is to be 'poetic license', as the 'purling stream can only have been the Bhagirathi, which in the hot weather'—the letter was written in April—'is a mere thread of water'.

By the end of the next decade, Motijheel Palace appears to have already been in ruins, as mentioned in the *Riyazu-s-Salatin*. Nothing remains of the palace today.

Motijheel is an apt setting for revisiting Plassey for several other reasons. Siraj marched to Plassey from here. His nemesis, Mir Jafar, built here a pleasure palace—no sign of it remains either. A co-nemesis, Clive, stayed at Motijheel Palace, the *Gazetteer* tells us, when he arrived in 1765 to 'negotiate the transfer of the Dewani to the Company', and again the following year to mark the first time the British formally conducted the ceremony where the annual settlement of land revenue—punya—was made.

Motijheel Palace had, meanwhile, been the residence for a few years, from 1758 onwards, of Warren Hastings, who was appointed British resident in Murshidabad. (He would, in 1772, become governor of Bengal and, in a run that lasted till 1785, eventually governor-general of British India administered from Fort William.) From 1757 to 1786, Motijheel remained the residence and office for British officials.

But, above all, Motijheel remains in Plassey memory as the residence of Ghaseti Begum, a revenge-minded aunt to Siraj, and his co-nemesis along with Mir Jafar and Clive.

◆

It appears from the *Siyar* that Ghaseti Begum began to be greatly alarmed about her future as soon as her father, Alivardi, 'fell into a dropsical habit of body' in 1756.

The nawab evidently tried to fight off his debilitating state by abstaining from water for a time, but upon realizing that such 'distemper' was incurable in a man of eighty, simply gave up his special diet and any medication. Widowed, the protection of her father visibly ebbing, Ghaseti Begum began to insure herself from Siraj's influence from her redoubt at Motijheel Palace.

Going by such accounts, the begum Ghaseti's dislike, and subsequent hatred, even fear, of Siraj has roots in her disappointment at her young son's premature death. As we have seen, Ikram, younger brother of Siraj, was adopted by Nawazish and Ghaseti. The boy's death emotionally broke Nawazish. He was diwan of Dhaka but for several years left the administration in the hands of his deputy, Hussain Quli Khan. Ikram's passing appeared to have kindled in Ghaseti an abiding bitterness: her son wouldn't be nawab. Siraj, made heir by Alivardi in 1752, would. The *Siyar* notes that she bore Siraj 'an invincible hatred'.

That bitterness received a focus, the *Siyar* maintains, after the killing of the family confidante and—by this account—Ghaseti's long-time lover, Hussain Quli. Or former lover. And her husband's lover. It's complicated.

The scandal rocked the court and incensed the family, the *Siyar* says. Siraj's grandmother, Sharf-un-Nisa, 'consort to Aaly-verdy-qhan, went so far, as to ask leave to put to death the two obnoxious brothers, meaning Hussein-culy-qhan, and Haider-aaly-qhan. The old Viceroy, by one of those neglects that cannot be ascribed to anything but an unavoidable fate, contented himself with answering that such an affair could not be done without Nevazish-mahmed-qhan's consent.'

After having 'extorted her husband's tacit consent' Sharf-un-Nisa approached Nawazish, her son-in-law, by his consort, who was her daughter. Ghaseti Begum acquiesced, the *Siyar* claims, as at that time 'there had happened a little misunderstanding between her and Hossein-culy-qhan for an inconsiderable subject, which it would be improper to mention'. She was 'so dissatisfied' with the man that she joined her mother in persuading Nawazish.

Haji Mustapha, the *Siyar*'s translator and no slouch in matters of court gossip, adds that what 'the author calls an inconsiderable subject, is by no means an inconsiderable one for ladies'. The Haji describes that delicate matter:

> Hossein-culy-qhan, who was, what they call in English, a handsome, stout, black man, had quitted this Princess, for her younger sister, Amna-begum, of amorous memory, mother to Seraj-ed-döulah. But there was another subject of discontent between her and the handsome stout man, although it looks somewhat ludicrous. The stout man had the talent of fencing with either hand; and whilst actually in intrigue with Gahassity-biby, the wife, he had a great deal of business to transact with the husband, who was an impotent man, addicted to feminine joys. This husband was Nevazish-mahmed-qhan, eldest nephew as well as son-in-law, to Aaly-verdy-qhan; and he had more than once serious quarrels with his consort about the ambidexter nobleman. There are at Murshedabad to this day several persons who remember of sharp dialogues that happened on that very strange subject between the husband and the wife; but although they are exceedingly curious, and not quite uncommon in this country, they prove, however, to be of such a nature as English paper would not admit.

Siraj detested this 'ambidexter nobleman', and even accused him of trying to kill him. That isn't far-fetched—after all, it chimes with the conspiracy theory that his aunt actually wanted her adopted son, Siraj's biological brother Ikram, to be nawab. When Ikram died, it became a anyone-but-Siraj scramble in that begum's mind. By that logic Hussain Quli, a lover and de-facto co-governor of Dhaka, could well have been part of a conspiracy to get Siraj off the fast track to nawab that he clearly was on. Siraj evidently thought so, and, writes Sarkar, when he heard Hussain Quli was at court, actually entered Alivardi's durbar with 'armed retainers carrying lighted matches for their muskets' to kill Hussain Quli right there.

Alivardi pacified his 'darling grandson' and—here Sarkar draws on the telling of one Yusuf Ali—suggested a less public place might be more suitable for his death. Siraj had him assassinated in the streets of Murshidabad around April 1754.

The *Siyar* describes this in its usual florid fashion. It claims Nawazish, '[who was] at all times a weak man, and now was discontented with both earth and heaven', consented to the action against his 'intimate friend' that the *Siyar* believed would damn him in both realms. Preparations had to be made for the assassination to be carried out successfully. The key one was for Alivardi to have an alibi. 'Aaly-verdy-qhan, to save appearances, as he fancied, and to conceal his share in the perpetration of the crime, went to Radjmahl, on pretence of a hunting party... Seradj-ed-döulah then on his grandfather's departure, made a visit to his uncle, Nevazish-mahmed-qhan, and having received his consent, he was returning home in the evening; and this was in the beginning of the year 1168 [A. H., corresponding to 1754-55].' As it happened, Hussain Quli's house lay on the way, and 'that poor wretch, who expected his death these many days' had remained at home, out of sight. Siraj stopped at the house and ordered both brothers to be brought to him. The crowd gathered outside the gate of his residence alarmed Hussain Quli and he fled to the house of a Haji Mehdi, who was Nawazish's usher. Hussain Quli asked Haji Mehdi to go immediately to Nawazish and warn him of the danger his 'friend' was in.

'The usher did so,' we read in the *Siyar*, 'but received no succour for Hussain Quli. Meanwhile, Siraj's associates broke into his house as well as the adjoining ones, found the man, and brought him to Siraj.' The prince immediately ordered Hussain Quli, by then in tears and begging for clemency, killed—'hacked to pieces', we learn, as was Siraj's wont as a 'cruel, relentless, remorseless monster'. Hussain Quli's brother, Haider Ali Khan, who was blind, was also brought before Siraj who immediately ordered his death. But not before the man, unrepentant and unbowed unlike his brother, got in some tongue-lashing:

...he gave his murderer foul language, and loaded him with taunting reproaches, in which he severely reflected on his person, his mother, and his family. Thou worthless fellow said he, if it is thus that thou murderest brave men? He was not suffered to say more, but was instantly cut down.

The disconsolate Nawazish's health, already affected by the loss of his son, deteriorated. Physicians detected 'symptoms of an hydropsy'—edema. Alivardi had him, his wife, and his entourage, including a 'favourite actrisse', brought to his palace. Nawazish's condition worsened. Ghaseti Begum, 'although actually in her father's house, trembled lest Seradj-ed-döulah should confine her in that very palace, now resolved to provide for her safety; and putting herself in a covered chair together with her dying husband, she carried him to her own lodgings' in fabled Motijheel. He died shortly, in 1755. Nawazish was buried by the grave of his son, Ikram-ud-daulah.

◆

Now Ghaseti Begum went about her business of buying insurance. 'She had this longwhile cantoned herself at Moty-djil, where on seeing how matters went, she had distributed elephants and lacs of rupees to the troops of her deceased husband, in hopes of engaging them to stand by her, against Seradj-ed-döulah.' The *Siyar* claims she received their 'solemn promises' and 'oaths'.

The *Siyar* also maintains that other nobles too rushed to Alivardi realizing he was 'drawing to his end', eager to have the dying nawab put in a word of recommendation to his grandson. Alivardi smiled and—'so well did he know the man's character'—suggested they wait three days after the nawab's death to see if Siraj was in that time 'upon good terms with his grand-mother', Alivardi's wife Sharf-un-Nisa. If he did, then they would have a 'chance'.

Alivardi died at five in the morning on 10 April 1756 (according to the *Siyar*, 'ninth of the month of Redjeb'—or Rajab—in the Islamic year A. H. 1169).

A premonitory letter that Hill gathered from records in Pondicherry is an indication of the political situation in Murshidabad at the time of Alivardi's passing and Siraj's accession. 'His nephew, who is also his grandson, has succeeded to the subahdari of Bengal without the slightest opposition, contrary to our expectations,' said the letter of 26 April from the French Council at Chandannagar to their colleagues in the council of Masulipatnam, or Machilipatnam. 'Instead of the revolution with which we thought the country was menaced at the death of the old Nawab, everything appears to be quiet and to submit to his successor.'

That would change shortly.

◆

The *Siyar* mentions that among the first things Siraj did—'the first operation of his government'—after assuming the subahship following the period of mourning, was to get after his aunt, Ghaseti Begum. Her attempt to insure her future against Siraj by lavishly paying off key nobles and generals led nowhere.

Siraj sent troops to Motijheel with 'injunctions' to remove 'Bibi Gahassity' from the palace, following which the officer commanding this foray was to 'seize every thing belonging to her, jewels, money, as well as furniture' and transport it all to the 'public treasury'. The *Siyar* is scathing about Ghaseti Begum's foolishness in expecting bribery to protect her even as it implicitly highlights Siraj's marauding character: 'It was then that the silly woman found the consequence of having so liberally distributed her money.' All those who took her money to fight Siraj on her behalf now had 'no stomach' and withdrew to 'places of shelter' purchased with those funds. With them went their followers. Some, like Mir Nazar Ali, engaged some 'Commanders of character' with handsome presents to intercede with Siraj on their behalf, and 'procured' their escape from Siraj's wrath for associating with the begum. Nazar Ali, one such, is thought to have escaped with anything between 1.2 to 1.5 million rupees worth of jewels and an uncharted amount in cash. Impoverished by gambling in Varanasi, he would return to Murshidabad in 1780, to be looked after by an acquaintance—a former dancing girl, as the *Siyar* notes. At any rate the mini exodus left in the Begum's employ only a few mercenary-loyalists.

◆

Hill speculates in *Three Frenchmen of Bengal* that Ghaseti's hatred of Siraj may have escalated—ultimately planting in her a robust seed of what would flower into the Plassey conspiracy—with Nawazish's death shortly before the death of Alivardi Khan, 'that it was supposed he was poisoned to ensure Siraj-uddaula's accession'.

The translation of a letter written in French to a Monsieur Demontorcin, dated 1 August 1756 at Chandannagar, notes a curious validation of the theory of Nawazish's hastened death, besides offering a lengthy description of the French view of Siraj's assault on Calcutta. This letter also claims Siraj's grandmother urged him to settle his differences with his aunt Ghaseti—still influential and still wealthy despite Siraj's purported raid on her treasury—as his masnad was far from secure. There were threats from the west driven by the Mughal emperor, Marathas were still a danger, and so were some influential officers of the realm, like the diwan in Dhaka after Hussain Quli, Raj Ballabh—who was loyal to Ghaseti.

The letter notes:

> All these reasons induced him to come to terms with the Begum of Moti Jhil all the more so as the Begum of his grandfather, Aliverdi Khan, strongly urged him to do so, representing the danger he ran of being driven from his throne... Consequently she spoke to her daughter, widow of Nawajis Muhammad Khan, who had been Nawab of Dacca and had died eight months before from taking a little soup which Aliverdi Khan gave him to ensure the kingdom to this young prince. His aunt, this same Begum of Moti Jhil, of whom we have spoken above, and widow of this Nawajis Muhammad Khan, willingly agreed to the accommodation which was unexpectedly presented to her, and the affair terminated amicably by her paying over a sum of money.

There was nothing amicable about anything between Siraj and his aunt, the *Siyar* claims. Indeed, she had asked for it—'just retribution', that text suggests in rare camaraderie with Siraj, as well as a sexist twist. It was all a mis-step on her part: she should have reached out to the young nawab 'instead of hating her nephew, ought to have considered him as her own son'. Besides, she had practically egged Siraj on. Her dalliance with Hussain Quli was tantamount to 'having consented' to his 'unjust death'. The widow's sexual drive, that made her 'guilty of an infinity of infamous actions, with which she had dishonoured her character and family', was an indignity that justified her being 'disrobed of her rank and honour', and much of her wealth confiscated. She should have had the good sense to sue for peace as had her younger sister, Rabia Begum (also known as Munira Begum, Alivardi's third daughter), whose daughter was a widow of Siraj's younger brother, Mirza Mahdi, the *Siyar* notes. As a result of this, she felt humiliated, practically incarcerated, and seethed in her confinement, her hatred for Siraj chiselled ever sharper. There would be more conspiracy even before Plassey.

◆

Changes soon followed at Siraj's court, with a great shuffling of high officers. Mir Jafar, the mir bakshi, paymaster general of the nawab's forces, lost his office to Mir Madan, who was brought in from Dhaka. Mohanlal, chief of Siraj's household, was made diwan and prime minister.

Such appointments by the young nawab upset the status quo beyond the resentment already present on account of Siraj's 'levity, his profligacy, as well as his harsh language, and the hardness of his heart'.

The *Siyar* mentions that 'Commanders of character' all deserving respect and regard, were all 'thoroughly estranged from him by his harsh language, and his shocking behaviour'. Other prominent citizens of Murshidabad were similarly ill-used, 'especially' the Jagat Seth Madhab Rai. He was slapped by Siraj at court when he expressed his inability to raise thirty million rupees from the Company and the merchants of other countries—this episode is mentioned in Company documents, as we shall see. Another version states that Siraj asked for a loan of that amount from Madhab Rai. Either way, the assumption is that funds were required to top up a stressed treasury, and to petition the Mughal emperor for a farman to be formally declared subahdar of Bengal, Bihar, and Orissa. The Mughals, as we have seen, were as fond of gifts as anyone else.

All these were tired of living under such an administration, and wished no better than to be rid of such a government, by Seradj-ed-döulah's death; so that whenever they chanced to perceive any appearance of discontent anywhere, or any hatred against the present Government, they would send secret messages to the party, with exhortations to contrive some mode of deliverance;

under promise of their being heartily and effectually supported. Mir-djaafer-qhan, as the most considerable and the most injured of the malcontents, was the foremost amongst them. Djagat-seat had underhand promised to support him vigorously; and they formed together a confederacy.

Such intrigue gathered momentum as Siraj continued to 'mismanage'. For a change the *Siyar* is blunt in its description of the growing resentment among the dislocated and distraught at court—the 'military and financial elites', as described by the scholar Joel Bordeaux in his account of the zamindar of Nadia, Raja Krishnachandra Rai.

◆

Krishnachandra of Nadia is painted by hagiographic poetry as being almost Akbar-like in his mien. A just ruler, patron of the arts, a great supporter of Vaishnavism in its battle against Hindu orthodoxy, an epicurean, patron at court of a famous wit, Gopal Bhnar, a Falstaffian character whose exploits, real and apocryphal are even today a staple read in numerous Bengali homes. The raja may have had a dark side, as it were, one which places some Bengali nationalist historians, staunch Hindus, in particular, in a quandary, when they attempt to balance this pride of Bengal, a Hindu aristocrat in an overwhelmingly Muslim era, with his concurrent avatar as an alleged Plassey conspirator.

Bordeaux's work has the prominent Bengali scholar and emancipator, Ishwar Chandra Vidyasagar, emerging as an influential denier of Krishnachandra's role as conspirator, in his 1848 work *Bānglār Itihāsh* (History of Bengal), referred to in the introduction. Bordeaux notes that the Plassey portion of the work was 'rendered back into English by G. T. Marshall two years later as *A Guide to Bengal*'. 'Sourcing the denial to Vidyasagar in this way presumably made it more authoritative,' observes Bordeaux, 'despite being practically a word for word translation of [John Clark] Marshman's original'. In it, Vidyasagar didn't just clear Krishnachandra of conspiracy, following Marshman, he cleared all of Bengal's zamindars:

> As the Hindoos have an idea, that it was their Zemindars who invited the English to take the country and deliver them from Seraj-ood-dowla, it is necessary here to state in the most positive

terms that not one of the Zemindars of Burdwan, or Nuddea, or Rajshahye, or any other district had any share in this revolution. How could they? They were mere Collectors of revenue.

In the published record available to us there is never any reflection of the resentment of the citizenry, whose comments on Siraj are entirely absent in contemporary and later accounts. Plassey remained, as the *Siyar* reminds us again, a matter for the elites:

> ...and everyone of them sowed in his breast the thoughts of getting rid of so improper a Ruler; in so much that none remained attached to him, but a few young men, as profligate and as giddy as himself, all of whom had been suddenly raised to power and influence by his means. For as to the principal men in the city and army, every one of them, shocked to see such a man on the throne, were only intent on finding out the means of overturning his power, whether by art, by force, or by treason. And soon fortune favoured their wishes.

◆

Among the first efforts at destabilizing Siraj that the elites of Murshidabad got off the ground was to incite Siraj's cousin, Shaukat Jang, the naib nazim of Purnea in Bihar. This prince had succeeded his father, Saiyid Ahmad Khan, Alivardi's nephew, as deputy governor on 27 March 1756, just about a fortnight before Alivardi died on 10 April 1756.

Ghulam Hussain Khan Tabatabayi claims that when he was in Shaukat Jang's court, where he was engaged as minister, a letter arrived from Mir Jafar exhorting the callow deputy governor of Purnea to 'stand up, and to wrest the whole of Aaly-verdy-qhan's estate from Seradj-ed-döulah's hands.' He notes that the letter 'mentioned several Commanders and Grandees, who, as well as Mir-djaafer-qhan himself, looked upon Sayd-ahmed-qhan's son as their only resource against the growing and daily cruelties of Seradj-ed-döulah's; and he pledged himself that he would be strongly and unanimously supported, as the enterprise was easy, and it only wanted some one to sit on the throne; in which case all the others would undertake to place him thereon, under certain conditions and stipulations, which he mentioned at length.'

Tabatabayi doesn't elaborate as to what these conditions were, but a safeguarding of the conspirators' interests would seem, logically, to be part of the quid pro quo. It is for what-if speculators to muse that, had Shaukat Jang succeeded against Siraj, Bengal may have remained merely a commercial advantage for Company and Crown with an obtuse, crass and pliant nawab at hand, instead of the political and commercial victory it quickly became on account of a relatively more belligerent and assertive nawab.

Shaukat Jang, emboldened by the overtures of the confederacy of conspirators in Murshidabad, would play out the first of several major moves against his embattled cousin. He leveraged his father's connections at the Mughal court in Delhi and managed to reach Ghazi-ud-din Imad-ul-Mulk, vazir to Emperor Alamgir II. The vazir agreed to consider his plea to be formally appointed subahdar of Bengal, Bihar, and Orissa.

The vazir was quite the mover-and-shaker. We learn from multiple sources that his machinations led to the deposing of the previous emperor, Ahmad Shah—he was blinded before being imprisoned—and the enthroning of Alamgir II in 1754. (In 1759, the vazir would have Alamgir II assassinated and replaced by Shah Jahan III. He would conspire with the nawab Mir Jafar to attempt the capture and killing of the Mughal prince Ali Gauhar; the prince managed to escape, and took the throne as Shah Alam II. And so on, in a myriad of Mughal conspiracies.)

Not that Shaukat Jang would have exactly been a step up from Siraj, nor would he have made a better nawab to follow Alivardi, the *Siyar* maintains. The cousins were alike, 'equally proud, equally incapable, and equally cruel'. Their brief battle, spurred in some measure by Ghaseti Begum, was really a roulette of misfits, and 'smoke was already seen to rise' from Alivardi's 'generation and house'.

Tabatabayi maintains he was stuck between two dangerous and unbalanced people, Shaukat Jang and Siraj. He was in Purnea, but after Saiyid Ahmad Khan died and his son Shaukat Jang succeeded him as deputy governor, 'not thinking proper to remain in that young Prince's service', he—'the Poor Man' in his self-description—decided to go to Azimabad where his family was settled. But he changed his mind upon learning en route that his two younger brothers and a maternal uncle had been banished from there by Siraj's order, and he became 'fearful of that Prince's resentment'. So he returned to Purnea, and, with great reluctance declared himself to the service of Shaukat Jang—as he was equally afraid that the churlish prince, a cousin to Siraj, might otherwise do him harm. Tabatabayi claims Shaukat Jang 'made it a point to manage all his affairs mostly by my counsels, or at my desire. So that like the Vezir [equivalent to the Queen] in the game of Chess, I was close to a wooden King, that could neither think, nor act, by himself.' As Shaukat Jang couldn't read or write well, he claimed to have been both his 'school-master and his Minister'. His tutor.

Tabatabayi was a peerless raconteur of such matters, bordering on voyeurism. In one incident reminiscent of Siraj, Shaukat Jang berates his commander-in-chief in public.

> One day, sitting in full Court and at noon-day, at which time the hall of audience is always crowded, he turned towards the Commander-in-Chief, Carguzar-qhan, and said: 'Doubtless, Car-guzar-qhan, after the conquest of Bengal, shall compliment me with the pay of his new raised men.' The officer, surprised at this speech, but without losing his presence of mind, answered directly: 'Yes, my Lord, and Master; for I hope they shall get so much booty, that they will not grudge such a portion of their pittance.' 'You are mistaken,' replied Shaocat-djung; 'I am not such a sot as Aaly-verdy-qhan, who always used to give to his men every thing that was found in an enemy's camp. For my part, I will not part to them with so much as a handful of straw, above their pay.'

(The Purnea nawab's household appear to have escaped with lesser indignities than the 'most obscene and most infamous language' reserved for his commander and officers, according to Haji Mustapha, reserving for them no other abuse than what was 'used by women'. Such as childless woman or man. Husbandless. 'Sir-mondi; Qhandi; hairless, or head-shaved; she-laughter; and to be shaved, or without a head of hair, is a great opprobrium amongst all kinds of women; and to laugh is accounted a piece of levity amongst women of distinction, who are allowed only to smile.')

Things had got so bad at Shaukat Jang's durbar, we are told, that several commanders and the chief had openly begun to hold meetings against him, not always in a treasonous manner but more to express their anger and exasperation at being treated with contempt, humiliated. When word of it travelled back to Shaukat Jang, he was rattled, and realized his grand ambitions could be at risk. So, he offered to behave better.

◆

Siraj played a counter-move. He had got wind of the conspiracy to place Shaukat Jang on the masnad of Murshidabad, and his cousin's outreach in Delhi to undercut him with a farman. In May 1756, Siraj set out with an army towards Purnea.

His cousin wasn't ready. He backed down. Siraj received a 'dutiful' message from Shaukat Jang around 22 May 1756, writes Sarkar, echoing the *Siyar*. It was enough for Siraj to withdraw his forces and deal with the 'defiance of the English merchants in Calcutta'. He would attack Calcutta that June. The battle with Shaukat Jang, who was far from done with his ambition—and his sponsors in Murshidabad with theirs—would wait until October.

◆

Among the best-informed people in Bengal, the Frenchman Jean Law notes in his memoirs, 'were the bankers and merchants, who by their commercial correspondence had been in a position to learn many things.' The house of Jagat Seth was well placed to help the British—or anyone else—but they were in particular 'likely' to help the British, Law maintains, as both were 'joined' in the range of complaints and needs against Siraj.

Like several European chroniclers of the time, as well as a few after, like Little, who wrote a definitive book on the Seths, Law describes the banking house with a degree of awe. Till Alivardi's death the Seths enjoyed the 'greatest respect'. The house ran 'almost all' the nawab's 'financial business'. They also moved and shook things up, puppeteer-like, to safeguard the family's business. The Seths, maintains Law, 'had long been the chief cause of all the revolutions in Bengal'.

Law would note elsewhere in his memoirs of the anti-Siraj mechanics of Plassey and the bankers' role in it: 'They are, I can say, the movers of the revolution. Without them the English would never have carried out what they have.' Siraj's overtures to the Jagat Seth after the British recapture of Calcutta in January 1757 had only a limited effect, in Law's opinion, as the British had, meanwhile, made their overtures too. The bankers were in a sweet spot. 'The Nawab began to perceive that the bankers were necessary to him. The English would have no one except them as mediators, and so they had become, as it were, responsible for the behaviour of both the Nawab and the English.'

The Seths, according to the sharp-eared Law, liberally spread their wealth to ensure information from those 'nearest to the Nawab'.

> From what came to the knowledge of the Seths it was easy to guess what he intended, and this made them tremble, for it was nothing less than their destruction, which could be averted only by his own. The cause of the English had become that of the Seths; their interests were identical. Can one be surprised to see them acting in concert?

Law reminds us that the banking house had engineered the putsch that 'overthrew' Sarfaraz Khan and brought Alivardi to power. Alivardi consequently gave them great acknowledgement and entrusted the financial management of his subahs to them. But Siraj wasn't versed in the wizened ways of his grandfather, and thought himself beyond the 'assistance of mere bankers', observes Law. He didn't appear to fear them either. His behaviour towards the 'Bankers to the World' remained bereft of the 'slightest politeness'. To have Law tell it, it seemed the young nawab salivated after their vast fortune and it seemed certain that one day he would 'seize it'. Law and others among the European chroniclers don't offer anything beyond opinion, not even corroborated opinion for this claim: the confiscation of Ghaseti Begum's fortune and palace appears to have been the guiding principle for the assertion. Even so, the insult meted out to Jagat Seth Madhab Rai at court, and Siraj's relative recklessness towards the British, appear to have been enough of an unacceptable risk. Whatever the reason, the bottom line became clear for the house of Jagat Seth, Law observes: 'These bankers, then, were the persons to serve the English.'

'They could by themselves have formed a party, and, even without the assistance of any Europeans, have put another Nawab upon the throne and re-established the English, but this would have required much time,' Law offers an elegant, if somewhat dramatic, analysis. 'Business moves very slowly amongst Indians, and this would not have suited the English. The bankers also were Hindus, and of a race which does not like to risk danger.'

More than conforming to racial stereotypes, the bankers were most likely just being bankers: trying to ensure good money wasn't being poured after bad. 'To stimulate them to action it was necessary for the English to commence operations and achieve some initial successes, and as yet there seemed no likelihood of their doing so.'

The British would simply have to bide their time and, meanwhile, accept harsh terms from Siraj. And Siraj wasn't about to budge unless push came to a massive shove.

Siraj's attitude wasn't derived only from an upper hand, but also from 'the most extravagant contempt' for all Europeans, observes Law. '(A) pair of slippers, he said, is all that is needed to govern them.'

That would all change with the arrival in Bengal of Lieutenant Colonel Robert Clive and Rear Admiral Charles Watson.

8

THE CONFLICT IN CALCUTTA

'...the British (in Calcutta) had exceeded their rights'

In the *Ain-i-Akbari,* a record of administration during the reign of the Mughal emperor Akbar, what would become the enclave of Calcutta is mentioned as a 'rent-paying village named "Kalikatta" under Sarkar Satgaon'. The year was 1596, as Maulavi Abdus Salam, the translator of *Riyazu-s-Salatin,* a history of Bengal from the first Turkic conquests in the thirteenth century through the early 1770s, observes in a footnote. He writes that in 1686, 'in consequence of a rupture with the Musulman authorities at Hughli port, the English merchants, led by their Chief, Job Charnock, were obliged to quit their factory there and to retreat to Sutanati [now a northern quarter of Calcutta].' Charnock and his colleagues would for a while retreat southward from Sutanati too. The retreat was the continuation of the fallout of a major disagreement with the governor Shaista Khan, which led to his taking over the Company's Qasimbazar factory and Charnock's narrow escape to Hugli—which we read about earlier.

The new settlement soon extended itself 'southwards'. It first absorbed the village of Kalikata—'between the present Customs-House and the Mint': 'now' and 'present' being the early 1900s when the translation of *Riyaz* was published. The settlement then absorbed the village of Gobindapur, 'which existed to the south of the present site of Fort William'.

In 1689, a year after Shaista's departure from Bengal, it would become the Company's headquarters in Bengal, the ritual completed with the Company flag unfurled there in 1690—usually considered the year of Calcutta's birth. In 1696, construction for the original Fort William would begin, more than fifty years after the establishment of Fort St George in Madras, an indication of the primacy of the Company's Madras presidency over that of the Calcutta Presidency, which would last until Plassey. (Calcutta would remain the centre of

Britain's subcontinental empire until 1911, when the decision was taken to shift the capital to Delhi.) A refurbished fort replaced the original Fort William in 1742—Siraj would attack this one. Charnock is usually portrayed as the founder of Calcutta. Posterity would dispute this, holding that Charnock, who went somewhat 'native', evidently besotted with his common-law Indian wife, wasn't the one. In 2003, a bench of the Calcutta High Court dispelled that assertion on the basis of litigation in the 'public interest' by a group of descendants of one of the 'original' families which petitioned the court as Sabarna Roychowdhury Paribar Parishad. The Court's sesquicentennial souvenir of 2013 notes:

> In May 2003, the High Court accepting the report of an Expert Committee of Historians headed by Prof. Nemai Sadhan Bose, held that Calcutta does not have a 'birth day' nor one simple 'founder'. It was a process in the 17th century in which Charnock, who settled in Sutanuti, Eyre and Goldsborough, on Englishside, and Lakshmikanta Majumdar who developed the tract; the Sett and Bysack families who lived in Gobindapur, and Sabarna Choudhuri who sold the villages to the English were all involved in the process of establishing Calcutta.

Charnock's location, even if pestilential, and several bends down the river from the original trading station at Hugli, would prove to be a strategic master stroke. From being north of Chandannagar, a potential French choke point, the British were now to the south of it. With Fort William and the settlement, Calcutta was the southernmost of the settlements of any European nation on the river. The merchant and military shipping of every nation moving upriver from the mouth of the Hugli at the Bay of Bengal to Chandannagar, Chinsurah, Bandel, Srirampur, even shipping under the direct protection of the nawab of Bengal after relocation of the capital of Bengal subah from Jahangirnagar to Murshidabad, would have to pass the British at Calcutta. And downriver too, of course. To the east lay the great Salt Lake, a natural barrier. Even factoring in the initial surge of Siraj, and threats from the French and, briefly, the Dutch, Calcutta, a place of swamps, mosquitoes, and disease, would over the years prove to be far from Charnock's Folly for Company and Crown.

Calcutta was a continuous work-in-progress, and its environs for Company-wallahs a series of discoveries. The tributaries and distributaries of rivers, channels, the sinews of commerce, and the Bhagirathi–Hugli, its winding backbone, were part of this evolution of new places, and quirky names for new places quite in keeping with the tradition of quirky names in Bengal. At a meeting in Calcutta in December 1754, Company brass expressed surprise at several such—'where are they?'—along, and off, the Hugli when the time for an annual survey came around: Fisherman's Creek, Hangman's Point, Mingo Bibby's Creek, Dean's Town, Dover, Rogue's River...

Within a few decades after Charnock's move, Calcutta had become a thriving town of grand buildings in its aspirational White Town, with the northern and eastern peripheries of Black Town forming a sort of support and strategic buffer similar to Fort St George in Madras. Even with all the irritations of the location, commerce prospered. Perhaps more so the lifestyle of Company employees.

Indeed, matters had slipped to such a dissolute level that the Company mandated a behaviour code for its officers. We learn from Long's compilation that 'Covenanted servants were ordered in 1754 "to attend office from 9 to 12 in the morning, and in the afternoon when occasion be". They were also recommended a more frugal manner of living, indispensable for early hours at office. An early ride at day-break, breakfast at 8, office from 9 to 12, dinner at 2, sleep, tea, ride, visiting and supper filled up the day at that period.'

The good life had permeated even to lowly 'writers'—clerks— the Company's most junior employees in India who were expected to be 'regularly bred to writing, accounts, French and other accomplishments'. They were often disciplined over their luxuries. 'Palankins, horses or chaises were at first prohibited to writers going to office, under pain of dismissal from office, but they were afterwards allowed in the hot and rainy seasons,' Long notes. He also notes that they received 'frequent wiggings' from the Court in London regarding their 'loose hand'. As the Court pointed out, 'the books, papers and accounts with regard to method, as well as writing, are faulty to a degree we are quite ashamed of', that 'their copying is done in such a hurry, that in general it is unfit to be seen, and many parts are scarcely legible', and that 'Consultations for these several years past wrote in such a vile manner as not to be legible in many places.'

A letter from the Court dated 25 March 1757 advised writers at the Calcutta Presidency to record matters, 'the general books and consultations, general letters, and all other books and papers of consequence, in plain, full round hands like what is practised here, and at Fort St. George, and Bombay, and not in the same loose hand which is too generally used at your Presidency.' At any rate London had to put up with what they received from cadet Company-wallahs in Calcutta, because, as Long notes, there was 'a prejudice against entrusting the copying of confidential documents to black writers'. As it happened 'black' writers were dismissed from office by an order in 1759.

Young Company clerks were also evidently somewhat lacking in responsibility. A biography of a familiar of Clive, Raja Nabakrishna, mentions some Company recruits being ruined on account of 'pillaws and harems'. As far as treating rare Company documents went, on occasion these were used as toilet paper. In February 1756, the Court wrote an outraged letter to Calcutta:

> An original letter from the Chief and others at Patna, and a leaf torn out of the original Diary of Mr. Surman's Embassy to the Great Mogul were picked up in a public necessary house which the Writers make use of, and are now in our hands, where, we are informed, many fragments of papers of great importance have likewise been seen. We cannot avoid taking this notice that you may prevent such idle mischief in future...

The following year, 1757, in which one of its former writers and current overachievers, Clive, would come into lasting fame and infamy at an age just shy of thirty-two, the Court in London wrote about the 'luxurious, expensive and idle manner of life which too much prevailed'. Word went out to disallow all 'expenses about cook-rooms, gardens, lately observed on the face of the bills'.

◆

Robert Clive arrived as a callow writer of eighteen on the shores of India on 31 May 1744, aboard the *Winchester*. When the ship moored off Fort St George on that day, after a near-disastrous and bizarre voyage that also saw the ship being run aground in Brazil and remaining there for nine months before it could again set sail that February, Clive was already discomfited. He had once fallen overboard during the voyage and as the British Library's lead curator for Company records, Margaret Makepeace noted in a chatty backgrounder of Clive, lost his 'buckled shoes, hat and wig'. He had also 'nearly drowned'.

The teenage Clive was diligent and recovered smartly. From an account dated 1 June 1744, Makepeace noted 'sundries' purchased from the captain of the *Winchester*: 'two pairs of black stockings, one hat, one wig, one pair of silver buckles, and one piece of duroy'—a coarse woollen cloth and etymological parent of corduroy—'and trimming'.

Clive's private papers note another set of purchases on 11 June at Fort St George: glasses for wine and water, decanters, 'half a hogshead of Cape wine', ten yards of 'camblet', a looking glass, half a dozen pewter spoons, one 'firkin' or small cask of butter, and a dozen 'cocoa' knives and forks made of coconut wood. Clive also listed several 'sundries' that were necessary for him to function as a proper young writer, Makepeace notes:

> Many fabrics are detailed: long cloth, cambric, handkerchiefs, black dimity for breeches, silk for lining clothes, gingham for bedding, curtains, cotton and lace for bedding. He purchased 'wastecoats to write in the Office', eight China plates, and some furniture: six chairs, a cot, a couch, and a table.

And staff—writers hired an array of domestic staff, which Clive too records: a dubash or translator, a 'cook boy', washerman, women to bring in water, a barber for shaving and powdering. The indulgent writer could easily get carried away with the expatriate life even with the modest salaries that writers drew from the Company— another cause for rampant business-on-the-side episodes in the early Company years across India, and the eagerness for rewards, and loot as a corollary of war.

Writers weren't the only ones with a yen for the good life. In the thriving party-town of Calcutta, soldiery weren't above a little leisure either, enough for the Company to take note. As a prophylactic warning, those who contracted syphilis had to pay higher fees in hospital. But doctors 'got only half the head money allowed for common diseases', which was evidently meant as another bizarre prophylactic—a reluctance to treat those who had contracted the disease. Syphilis was just one of the consequences of the hard carousing the English got up to in Calcutta. Bar room brawls weren't unknown. The Company's Consultations for 12 December 1748 notes a letter from Robert Wilson, Esq., to the Hon'ble William Barwell, Esq., President and Governor of Fort William, and the Council. The letter, with a dateline of the Apollo, a taverna in the Lal Bazar area of the city, which Long describes as 'fashionable place then' at Calcutta, is a study in outrage.

> Hon'ble Sir and Sirs,—Last night a great number of seamen belonging to the Company's ships assembled together in a tumultuous manner ashore headed by the Boatswain of the Lapwing, threatening to destroy Her Majesty's subjects under my command, to cut the ship adrift, and set her on fire, upon which I sent for a guard to protect the people then ashore, which was refused. Two of my Officers who were repairing on board were met by them, but beaten and so ill treated that their lives are despaired of. I therefore demand immediate satisfaction for the great insult offered Her Majesty's ships and subjects.

Drinking, in the 'shape of arrack' and hooch, was very common, Long notes. 'It was considered as a cooling drink in the great heat, when they had no punkahs and all the doors were thrown open.' It had an effect on preparedness, Long continues. 'It was found very injurious to seamen in 1754. A captain applied to come from Kedgri [Khejuri, by the mouth of the Hugli, across the vast stretch of the river from Sagar Island] to Calcutta in August, "as many of his people was down in fluxes, and as at Calpi [Kulpi, south of Diamond Harbour] sailors had the opportunity of intoxicating and killing themselves with pariah arrack, generally fatal to the health".'

Company-controlled arrack was evidently better. A despatch

from Calcutta to the Court of Directors in 1752 actually requests equipment for distilling arrack:

> Mr. John Knox, who purchased your Honours' arrack farm, having petitioned us to request your Honours will send him two stills of 400 gallons each with three worms of a size proportionable thereto, and being willing to pay 25 per cent, on the prime cost thereof, we enclosed send your Honours his petition, as we think his request reasonable.

Whatever the provenance of the arrack, troops and sailors imbibed it to some distraction. After the taking of Chandannagar on the way to Plassey, Clive had to move his camp and troops 'about a mile to the northward of Chandernagur,' he would write in a letter dated 16 April 1757 (signing off as 'R. Clive from Camp, Chandernagore'), to put a stop to the 'disorders among the military by the too easy procurance of arrack in the town'.

Gambling was another activity the puritanical Company frowned upon in its doctrine of human resource management. Company representatives in Calcutta were reprimanded on that account, and the message went home.

A despatch to the Court in London on 25 February 1750 by the grandees of Fort William is a study in contrition.

> ...a spirit of gaming prevails against your servants here, and assure you that had we ever observed the least appearance of this vice we should have suppressed it in it [sic] infancy, your orders on this head shall be punctually observed if we shall hereafter find any of your servants guilty thereof, as we concur in opinion with your Honours that no trust or confidence can be placed in persons guilty of a vice so pernicious.

◆

Nothing, though, led to trouble quite as much as Company employees, even private European and Indian traders, making money by misusing the dastak, or trading permit, earned by Surman's embassy that allowed the Company duty-free trade in Bengal.

It upset Alivardi, and upset Siraj to fury, as it denied the treasury legitimate revenue. It was also frowned upon by the Company as such activities, while they enriched Company employees who effected a wink-and-win principle with dastaks, affected the revenue and profit of the Company.

Long refers to an instance from 1753, when a ship in the Portuguese fleet 'had been fallen in with by the Commodore sailing without hoisting any colors'. When she was seized, he writes, it was 'found to be an English ship from Calcutta sailing without a pass'.

Company directors in London would, in as proximate a time to Plassey as 31 January 1755, write to the chiefs in Calcutta about the issue:

> In short, we have too much reason to believe our servants at the several subordinates in one shape or other unfaithfully interest themselves at our expense in the investments and we are the more induced to believe so from the observation we have made upon the deelolls [dalals, brokers] of Jugdea's complaint against Messrs. Bayley and Playdell which was under your examination upon the departure of the Falmouth, together with some hints which have been given us of unfair practices at Dacca, which we are not yet sufficiently enough apprized of to mention, to all which add the very extraordinary instance of Mr. Wogan's raising from nothing such a fortune at Dacca as it is generally reported he has brought home, although so young and low in the service. Upon the whole, there appears a real necessity that their future conduct should be well looked after and a scrutiny made into their past management.

Mr Wogan appears to have been wayward even by the profiteering standards of the day: he misused Company privileges to profit from the Dutch. The Court was incensed:

> With regard to Mr. Wogan, we are not surprised at the large fortune he has acquired in so short a time, having been informed that he supplied the Dutch with their Dacca goods on which he got at least 15 percent. This practice of furnishing our rivals, the Dutch, with goods, we have great reason to believe, has been for some time past and is at present carried on by our servants, greatly to our prejudice, by furnishing the Dutch with

those very goods which we ordered and were provided with our Dadney...and particularly the best in quality.

As ever, money talked loudest. On 29 December 1756, the Court wrote with some amazement of the 'very great remissness in our pilots during the last war'. These pilots, who had the crucial task of navigating ships up the treacherous, shoal-ridden Hugli would make money in any way they could, charging 'exorbitant price' for any 'foreign or country ships' they came by in Balasore Roads, along the coast of Orissa not far from the mouth of the river. Point Palmiras was the name of the location near which the pilots waited. 'By these means our ships, which at that season were daily expected to arrive, were totally neglected, insomuch that our commanders have been obliged to put a confidence in, and trust the care of their ships to, an enemy's pilot.' That was unacceptable.

◆

Most historians refer to published records and correspondence, almost entirely derived from the British East India Company, and the French factor at Qasimbazar, Jean Law, to list a series of annoyances that finally led to Siraj's 'rupture' with the English—as Sarkar puts it.

One such purported annoyance was the young nawab feeling insulted when the Company chief of the Bengal Presidency, Roger Drake, didn't follow protocol and presented a gift to Siraj on his accession. Another, as we have seen, appears to have been the refusal of the English in Qasimbazar to permit Siraj the crown prince to enter their premises and homes for fear of the damage that he (the 'drunken disorderly youth,' as Sarkar descibes him) could cause. A third was the continual misuse by Company employees—by the Company's own admission—of its duty-free permit.

The fortifications (and repairs to fortifications) being worked upon by the Company to its settlement in Qasimbazar, and Fort William in Calcutta were also a cause. They were begun at the instance of the Council in Calcutta in early 1756 who were galvanized into action by the threat of war in Europe between Britain and France. The Council urged the repairing and bolstering of defences at Fort William by the Hugli—to the west of the present-day General Post Office. To the north was the Maratha Ditch, a feature designed to stem any attack by Maratha marauders in the preceding decades, but now 'half-choked' with disuse.

Besides readying the ditch there was also the matter of constructing earthworks, writes Sarkar, 'specially a redoubt and drawbridge, called Perring's Redoubt across the Ditch at Baghbazar'—at the time an extremity of Black Town and today among the city's most congested areas, with the Hugli to its west, and just north of the enclave of Kumartuli, a famous hub of idol manufacture for Bengal's numerous festivals of the gods. Such activity by the Company was 'a clear violation' of the terms under which the Mughal government 'had allowed them to live in Bengal'.

The tipping point, though, seems to be the safe harbour given to Krishna Ballabh, son of Raj Ballabh, a deputy to the governor of Dhaka. This development had a complex back story like so much else connected to Plassey. Nawazish, who, as we have seen, doted on his wife Ghaseti Begum, was a 'sickly imbecile,' maintains Sarkar, and left the running of Dhaka to the begum and her 'favourite', Hussain Quli Khan. Others have been less coy, as we know, outing Hussain Quli as one of several of the begum's lovers. And there's the matter of his death at the insistence of Siraj.

That is how Raj Ballabh succeeded Hussain Quli. Raj Ballabh had earlier been superintendent of the Bengal fleet 'establishment' for which the Bengal government granted 1.4 million rupees a year. In his new capacity Raj Ballabh also looked after Ghaseti Begum's interests.

Siraj remained quiet as long as Nawazish Muhammad was alive. After his hated aunt's husband died in 1755, Siraj brought the charge of embezzlement and financial mismanagement against Raj Ballabh. On the face of it the charge seemed 'plausible,' writes Sarkar, because there was precedence even in the early years of the reign of Murshid Quli, who became nawab in 1717—the administrators of the jagirs, or estates that financed Bengal's army and navy 'were known to have peculated their collections'.

Alivardi was on his deathbed. And Raj Ballabh happened to be in Murshidabad at the time. Raj Ballabh was arrested in March 1756. Sarkar claims it was all the old nawab could do to postpone his beheading—at least until the Dhaka accounts had been scrutinized—

but he sent men to attach Raj Ballabh's property and take his family into custody. They managed to evade the arresting party. Krishna Ballabh, his son, escaped to Calcutta with 'the women and the treasures of the family', relates Sarkar, 'on the pretext of a pilgrimage to Jagannath'—the coastal temple town of Puri in Orissa. Sarkar writes that he arrived in Calcutta on 13 March and by 'bribing M. Drake, the governor secured an asylum'.

John Malcolm in his laudatory *The Life of Robert, Lord Clive*, actually pins responsibility for Krishna Ballabh's asylum on William Watts, chief of the Company's Qasimbazar factory in the Plassey years and keen competitor to the French company's representative, Jean Law.

> The person the Nabob alluded to was Kishendass, the son of the late Dewan of the Nabob of Dacca, who visited Calcutta on his way to Juggernath [which we know from chroniclers to be a journey of more than a month at the time]; and as he was strongly recommended to Mr. Drake, the President of Calcutta, by Mr. Watts, the Chief of Cossimbazar, on account of services rendered by his family to the Company, he was treated with kindness and attention.

Robert Orme, in his second volume of *History of the Military Transactions of the British Nation in Indostan*, a root text for Plassey, backs up the escape:

> A Gentoo, named Rajabullub, had succeeded Hossein Cooley Khan in the post of Duan or Prime Minister to Newagis... doubtful of the event of the impending contest he determined to place his family and treasures out of the reach of danger; and not deeming them in safety at Dacca, where they had remained for some time, he ordered his son Kissendass to remove them from that city, under pretence of going [for] a pilgrimage to the Pagoda of Juggernath, on the coast of Orixa.

The young man, also a 'Gentoo'—an archaic Anglo derivation of the Portuguese gentio, or gentile, to mean Hindu—left Dhaka on a relay of boats, found his way to the Ganga–Padma, slipped into the Jalangi River and then made his way to Calcutta.

It was a massive insult to the authority and ego of Siraj, and he held the Company responsible. As he perceived it, an 'under trial' subject of the realm—his realm—was given refuge, in defiance of his authority, in a place within his realm. Through a review of contemporary records, Sarkar notes that Siraj sent an emissary to Drake demanding Krishna Ballabh be handed over to him. But it all appears to have descended to a farce. The emissary was Narayan Das, who Sarkar says was the brother of Siraj's intelligence chief. The man was also tasked with investigating unauthorized fortifications in Calcutta. Das entered in disguise and 'when he was brought before the Calcutta Council, he could produce no diplomatic credentials. So he was turned out of the settlement as a spy'. The date was 16 April, six days after Alivardi's death. It was the first major instance of British defiance Siraj faced as nawab. (Sarkar maintains Siraj learned of this on 20 May, while still on the campaign against his cousin, Shaukat Jang.)

Siraj, evidently, went nuclear with rage. The English in Calcutta refusing to hand over Krishna Ballabh was as much a trigger as their refusing to diminish fortifications and other defensive measures, including the Maratha Ditch (the work for which had begun in 1742, notes Orme; it was a time when Alivardi was beset by the Marathas and evidently saw reason in such a defensive measure for Calcutta). 'The rumour ran that M. Drake replied to the messengers that, since the Nawab wished to fill up the Ditch, he agreed to it provided it was done with the heads of Moors. I do not believe he said so,' Law writes, 'but possibly some thoughtless young Englishman let slip those words, which, being heard by the messengers, were reported to the Nawab.'

'Accordingly, no sooner had the Nawab heard the contents of the answer from the English, than he jumped up in anger, and, pulling out his sword, swore he would go and exterminate all the Feringhees,' Law recalls.

Law maintains he was 'assured' that Shaukat Jang, the nawab of Purnea and among Siraj's arch enemies, had spilled the matter to Siraj in the form of some letters the English had sent him. As incredible as this is—unless it was a sophisticated ploy to gain Siraj's trust, trigger an expedition by Siraj to Calcutta and, thereby, leave

Murshidabad's masnad vulnerable to takeover—Law holds that such information reaching Siraj is 'how the match took fire'.

◆

Siraj's concerns were legitimate, writes Hill, his views notable for their exception among Company or Raj historians for actually faulting the attitude of Drake, the Calcutta Council, and even their representative in Qasimbazar, the generally nimble-footed Watts.

Indeed, to bolster this point Sarkar and other historians who maintain John Company's defence of these actions as expedient, often quote Hill, a more balanced classical commentator, if you will, of Plassey dynamics among Plassey-era and Raj-era British. Although Hill dismisses Siraj's irritation and anger at the British as 'pretexts for war' he criticizes the behaviour of the nawab's opponents in Calcutta with equal emphasis: 'As regards fortifications it is quite clear that the British (in Calcutta) had exceeded their rights.'

'As regards the abuse of trade privileges,' Hill adds, 'it must be confessed that the British had used the dastaks or passes for goods free of custom in a way never contemplated by the farmans.' Sarkar and others of his persuasion also quote Hill for another Company transgression, that of providing refuge to Krishna Ballabh.

> Concerning the protection given to the servants of the native government...the English had no right to shelter the servants of Government from the authorities in (their) own country. It will be seen, therefore, that Siraj-ud-daulah had a show of reason in all the pretexts he alleged for his attack on the British.

In his *Three Frenchmen in Bengal,* Hill notes that Watts was recklessly belligerent, both before and after Siraj became nawab—'not only foolish enough to neglect him, but carried his folly to extremes.' (Watts recovered much later, in the pre-Plassey months of 1757, to outmanoeuvre the French as well as to skilfully create firm opposition to Siraj.) Watts made no pretence of his opposition to Siraj's accession. On the contrary, the English factory chief 'is strongly suspected of having entered into correspondence with Ghaseti Begum'.

Hill is among the strongest votaries of Watts being a key Plassey conspirator from the time he is believed to have supported Nawazish's candidature for nawab. Later, he is believed to have pitched in, much like Ghaseti Begum and Mir Jafar, to encourage Purnea's nawab Shaukat Jang to move against his cousin Siraj. Hill notes that Watts went further still: '...he advised Mr Drake, Governor of Calcutta, to give shelter to Kissendas [Krishna Ballabh], son of Raj Balav, who had fled with the treasures in his charge' when Raj Ballabh was ordered by Siraj to 'account for' Nawazish's property and his own.

(Hill suggests that Siraj was a wealth-snatcher, he coveted others' wealth so much that several nobles had 'fled to the English, or were suspected of secretly having sent their treasures' to Calcutta. Hill and some other British or 'Company' chroniclers accuse Siraj of coveting the wealth of all trading outposts and particularly that at Calcutta. As we shall see, this is a grey area of assertion as with so much to do with narratives around Plassey.)

Watts's manoeuvres on behalf of the Company led him to recommend to the chiefs in Calcutta that fortifications be beefed up in Qasimbazar, in great part to ensure security in case of hostilities with the French in Europe spilled over to India. Watts would stand fast—and recommend to Drake he ought to do so too—when Siraj demanded all recently completed and ongoing Company fortifications be demolished. This, even as the French complied with Siraj's orders with regard to their Qasimbazar post as well as the settlement in Chandannagar, as Law's memoir claims.

> I immediately drew up an Arzi, or Petition, and had one brought from the Council in Chandernagore of the same tenour as my own. These two papers were sent to Siraj-ud-daula, who appeared satisfied with them. He even wrote me in reply that he did not forbid our repairing old works, but merely our making new ones. Besides, the spies who had been sent to Chandernagore, being well received and satisfied with the presents made them, submitted a report favourable to us, so that our business was hushed up.

As we read a little earlier, Siraj was on his way to Purnea to deal with Shaukat Jang—the expedition left Murshidabad on 10 May 1756—when he heard of his messenger-spy being ejected by Drake from Calcutta. This was on 20 May, according to Sarkar, around the time that he received a conciliatory message from Shaukat Jang.

Siraj withdrew from his campaign against Shaukat Jang and turned towards Murshidabad, to prepare to take on the Company. He sent word to lay siege to the Company factory in Qasimbazar—from his perspective he had lost too much face; the Company had defied the legitimate authority of the nawab of Bengal. Siraj also ordered his army to prepare itself for the march to Calcutta.

'At the same time he gave orders for the march of his army, and appointed several Jemadars to command the advance guard,' Law continues the narrative from the time Siraj was enraged upon learning of Drake's purported comment about filling up the Maratha Ditch with the heads of Muslims.

> As in his first burst of rage he had used the general word Feringhees, which is applied to all Europeans, some friends whom I had in the army, and who did not know how our business had ended, sent to warn me to be on my guard, as our Factory would be besieged. The alarm was great with us, and with the English at Cossimbazar. I spent more than twenty-four hours in much anxiety, carrying wood, provisions, etc., into the Factory, but I soon knew what to expect. I saw horsemen arrive and surround the English fort, and at the same time I received an official letter from the Nawab, telling me not to be anxious, and that he was as well pleased with us as he was ill pleased with the English.

Siraj's forces arrived at the Company's Qasimbazar factory on 24 May. Sarkar goes with the narrative that, while some factors managed to escape, other Britons were shortly 'made prisoners in violation of a solemn promise'; and the factory was 'occupied and looted'.

A day later, Watts and his colleagues would manage to slip a letter through to the Council at Fort William from their base in Qasimbazar. They had managed to obtain intelligence that Siraj had moved quickly after receiving a letter from Drake and one from the French director. The letter mentions how Siraj was 'extreamly angry' and 'immediately sent orders to Roy Doolob [Rai Durlabh] to stop our business at Cossimbuzar and to Mohunlol [Mohanlal] to write to the Nabob at Dacca to stop our business there, and has likewise ordered Cossim Alli Cawn [Mir Qasim] with a body of forces to march to Tannahs Fort [near Calcutta] and has advanced them two months pay.' Even as they wrote it, Watts and his colleagues added new information: 400 cavalrymen had arrived at the factory. They asked for a 'supply of ammunition' as the garrison at the factory was 'very weak'.

A week later, they would write to the Council that more forces had arrived 'and put a stop to all provisions coming in'. The vakil of the British Company at court conveyed a message:

> ...that unless your Honour &c. will fill up the ditch and pull down the new works which he hears is begun upon, he [Siraj] is determined to attack us, therefore if your Honour &c. are determined not to comply with his demand, we request you will send us a supply of men, as our garrison is very weak, however we think it adviseable for your Honour &c. to write a letter to the Nabob immediately.

Another letter followed the same day, confirming the orders had been sent to Dhaka to stop the Company's business, and their concern that some nobles at court may have exaggerated the degree of the fortifications in Calcutta, including work on the ditch. They were unable to say more. 'We hear the Nabob is near Rajamaul [Rajmahal] and it is very uncertain when he will return and what his schemes are.'

◆

As to 'schemes', Siraj appears to have had a very clear idea. He wanted to clip the wings of the Company. He wrote a series of letters from Rajmahal and on his way back to Murshidabad, to the influential Armenian merchant Khwaja Mohammed Wajid.

The Khwaja (a gentleman of distinction, often referred to by Europeans as Coja or Khoja) was a leading light of the small Armenian community in Bengal, and, according to the historian Sushil Chaudhury, among 'one of the three merchant princes—the others being the Jagat Seths and Umachand—who collectively dominated the commercial life and hence, to a great extent, the economy of Bengal' from the 1730s through the 1750s. Khwaja Wajid had a monopoly of trade in salt and saltpetre, commodities that interested Indians and European companies alike. He operated from Hugli town. Through his connections at the court of Alivardi, observes Chaudhury, he also gained 'virtual control' of the economy of Bihar.

The merchant did extensive business with the French and the Dutch, writes Chaudhury, 'and through' Umachand '...with the English'. 'Extremely devious as he was, he had a passion for extending his commercial hegemony at any cost and was ready to swing his allegiance at the slightest prospect of commercial advantage.' Chaudhury notes that after Plassey, the merchant who turned against Siraj—he didn't think it a good business proposition to offend the Company—cosied up to Mir Jafar, who continued his monopoly. He offered to share the monopoly in saltpetre with the Company in exchange for its pressuring the Dutch to buy exclusively from him. In 1758, the Company would take away his saltpetre monopoly.

Now Siraj wrote several letters to this man, treating him as an intermediary with a message to Europeans in general, and the British in particular. These letters, as recorded by Hill, are revealing not only in terms of intent but also for their fluency of thought and language—the original being written in Persian—which few of Siraj's critics give him credit for:

Letter from the Nawab to Coja Wajid, dated Rajmehal 28 May,1756.

It has been my design to level the English fortifications raised within my jurisdiction on account of their great strength. As I have nothing at present to divert me from the execution of that resolution I am determined to make use of this opportunity; for which reason I am returning from Rajahmaul and shall use the utmost expedition in my march that I may arrive before Calcutta as soon as possible. If the English are contented to remain in my country they must submit to have their fort razed, their ditch filled up, and trade upon the same terms they did in the time of the Nabob Jaffeir Cawn [Murshid Quli]; otherwise I will expel them entirely out of the provinces of which I am Subah; which I swear to do before God and our prophets. Should any person plead ever so strongly in their behalf it will avail them nothing, as I am fully determined to reduce that nation to the above mentioned conditions and I require that you will not on any account speak in their favour. Enclosed you will receive perwannahs for the French, Dutch, and Danes, in which I have assured them of my favour. I request you will deliver them, and see they are well used in their trade and other respects. Endeavour to engage those nations to prevent the English resettling themselves after I have drove them out.

(The following paragraph was wrote at the bottom in the Nabob's own hand.)

I swear by the Great God and the Prophets that unless the English consent to fill up their ditch, raze their fortifications and trade upon the same terms they did in the time of Nabob Jaffeir Cawn I will not hear anything in their behalf and will expel them totally out of my country.

Upon reaching Murshidabad he wrote again to Khwaja Wajid, who evidently interceded on behalf of the Company. Siraj asked him to return the gift of a horse the Company had sent along, and stuck to his stand of ridding Bengal of the Company. And, most importantly for posterity, spelled out specific grouses against the Company and urged the merchant to ask the French to attack the British. He wrote the letter the day before he sent a force of artillery to the Company's factory in Qasimbazar.

Letter from the Nawab to Coja Wajid dated Muxadavad 1 June, 1756.

I have received your letter acknowledging the receipt of my indent for broad cloth, horses &c., that my chawbuck swar [chabuk sawar: literally whip-rider, but more rough rider] had seen and approved of two horses in Calcutta and that the English had sent me one of them as a present by the chawbuck swar... The horse which the English have delivered... I direct you to return them again, as they have neither regarded my orders nor live with me upon a good understanding, for which reason I will not accept of their present and therefore insist on its being sent back. I have three substantial motives for extirpating the English out of my country, one that they have built strong fortifications and dug a large ditch in the King's dominions contrary to the established laws of the country; The second is that they have abused the privilege of their dustucks by granting them to such as were no ways entitled to them, from which practices the King has suffered greatly in the revenue of his Customs; The third motive is that they give protection to such of the King's subjects as have by their behaviour in the employs they were entrusted with made themselves liable to be called to an account and instead of giving them [up] on demand they allow such persons to shelter themselves within their bounds from the hands of justice. For these reasons it is become requisite to drive them out.

Siraj reiterated the point he had made in the earlier letter about the necessity of the Company sticking to the terms during the reign of Murshid Quli, or else. He even threw in a potent threat, a message for the French to break the neutrality and attack the Company in concert with Siraj:

I recommend it to you to endeavour by good usage to engage the French to attack the English on the river while I besiege them on shore; and the easier to induce them thereto, you may promise from me, that I will deliver the town of Calcutta into their hands as soon as I have made myself master of it.

He then added with his own hand a note at the bottom of the letter to underscore his resolution to drive the Company out if they ignored his orders:

Please to acquaint the English minutely of my resolutions. If they are willing to comply with those terms they may remain, otherwise they will be expelled [from] the country.

When the Company did not back down, Siraj took over its facilities in Qasimbazar—a repeat of what Shaista Khan had done nearly seventy years earlier. After Siraj marched for Calcutta on 5 June, within a fortnight of receiving news of Drake's response at Rajmahal, he wrote again to the Armenian merchant, exhorting other Europeans to join his expedition against Calcutta and the Company:

I have seized Mr. Watts, the English Chief at Cossimbuzar (who has acted very unlike a Chief), and have delivered him over to the charge of Hussein Ally Beg Cawn.

A letter dated 3 June to the Dutch Committee at Hugli from the Dutch deputy resident at Kalikapur, George Lodewijk Vernet, and others of the Dutch Council there, notes that Company officials had initially sent word to Durlabh Ram that they would stand their ground. But that lasted only until the evening of 2 June when Watts gave in:

> ...when their Chief had the infamy to allow himself to be prevailed upon by the lamentation and tears of his wife so far as to write a cowardly letter to Durlabh Ram, in which he entirely submitted to the will of the Prince, and one hour after date at the invitation of the said Durlabh Ram, he went with his steward like one distracted, in his nightdress, having only two foot soldiers before him, to meet him.

In this letter extracted from the Vernet Papers at the Hague by Hill, the Dutch note that Siraj met Watts and then sent him into custody to remain there until he 'should have signed three machalcas'— machalka, a bond, with penalties on forfeiture—'one to surrender the family and rich possessions of Raja Balav, one to raze their works at Calcutta and one to pay thenceforth the inland trade tolls.' (Three days later, on 6 June, Vernet and the Kalikapur Council would write to the Council in Hugli to 'speedily' send '60 military and 2 quarter-gunners and 40 arquebusiers, 10 cannons with a sufficiency of balls and grape-shot for the aforesaid pieces, linstocks [poles for firing the cannon], rammers with sponge-heads, a few hand-grenades and 1,000 lbs. of powder' to prevent any likelihood of the 'fury of that raging tyrant' falling upon them.)

A Company employee's letter to the Council in Fort William on 4 June is devoid of any mention of the reasons the Dutch gave for Watts's capitulation. Instead, the British at Qasimbazar presented it as a consequence of Siraj's forces being overwhelming. The same letter observes that Watts was made to march in the vanguard of Siraj's forces led by Rai Durlabh, and that they expected Siraj to march the following day, leading a force that altogether numbered 50,000 men.

A separate letter of 4 June, written by Francis Sykes, who

would after Plassey be the British resident at Murshidabad's court, mentions a slightly different series of events, although he confirms the number of 50,000 troops marching upon Calcutta. Sykes writes that one of Siraj's officials arrived at the Qasimbazar factory on 2 June and informed Watts that the nawab wanted to 'talk to the Chief'. 'They obliged Mr. Watts to sign a machulka, which to the best of my remembrance signifies as follows, 1st No protection is to be given in Calcutta to any of the Nabob's subjects, 2^{d} The draw-bridge at Perrings and the new fortifications are to be demolished, and 3^{d} no dusticks to be given to any of the black merchants.' Watts wasn't permitted to return to Qasimbazar, and Siraj's officials insisted that others in Qasimbazar's Council had also to sign the undertaking. When they reached Murshidabad, an order arrived from Siraj for the factory to deliver up all weapons and ammunition. The factory gave up a cannon and powder too.

William Tooke, a Company employee who would later in 1756 provide Orme with a detailed account of what transpired before and during Siraj's attack on Calcutta, perhaps has the most colourful, though not sensational, account: 'Upon Mr. Watts's going before the Nabob, with his hands across and a handkerchief wrapt round his wrists, signifying himself his slave and prisoner (this he was perswaded [*sic*] to do by...Radabullub, and others, who assured him it might be a means of pacifying the Nabob, his appearing before him in an abject submissive manner), he abused him very much and ordered him to be taken out of his sight, but...[upon] telling the Nabob he was a good sort of a man, and intended on hearing of his arrival from Rajamull to have come and embraced his footsteps (Hat bandky Sahebka kuddum puckkerna)'—a phonetically admirable version of the Hindustani hāt bāndhké Sāhéb-kā kadam pakarnā—Watts was taken away to sign the machalka.

To continue with Siraj's letter to Khwaja Wajid, in which he again wrote of his intention to expel the Company:

> I now dispatch Nazir Mahmud Daliel to you and direct you to seize all ships, sloops and vessels belonging to my subjects and deliver them to Mahmud Beg; desire the French, Dutch and Danes to be expeditious in getting their vessels of force in readiness to accompany my land army and attack the English

by the river while I besiege them on shore. I have sent them perwannahs likewise to that purport; and (God willing) I shall soon appear before Calcutta.

(The following paragraph was wrote in the Nabob's own hand at the bottom of the letter.)

I swear by the Majesty of God I will not permit the English to remain settled in my country.

9

TURNING POINT

'"Calcutta is yours...I give you that place and its dependencies..."'

Siraj marched for Calcutta on 5 June 1756.

He reached the outskirts of Calcutta with the battle train an impressive eleven days later—'using unexpected promptitude', Sarkar notes somewhat churlishly. It's perhaps also a hint that, at the time, Siraj's speed of movement in the past weeks had caught nearly everyone off guard. Certainly the French. A letter between an official in Chandannagar and another in Dhaka dated 19 June shared a joke about how Siraj may 'still be shut up in his Harem' because there wasn't news of him for several days after he left Murshidabad for Calcutta. But on 15 June news arrived of the nawab having 'slept the night in a garden opposite Chinsurah'.

◆

According to Law, Siraj did his best to enlist French support to boost morale and strengthen his army as he feared Calcutta might not be a pushover—as we have seen, this is supported by his letters to Khwaja Wajid. 'He wrote to me in the strongest terms to engage the Director of Chandernagore to give him what assistance he could in men and ammunition.' According to the Frenchman, Siraj went further, mixing entreaty with threat. He cannily reminded Law that the French were 'always' at war with the English in Europe and, more recently, in India on the Coromandel coast. "Calcutta is yours," he said to our agent in full Durbar; "I give you that place and its dependencies as the price of the services you will render me".'

Refusal to help would be interpreted as a sign of 'little interest', Siraj warned. He offered to do 'as much good' as Salabat Jang, the fourth nizam of Hyderabad, who had favoured the French in the Deccan. In exchange for French military aid against Maratha raids—as well as more assistance, including against chiefs the English had backed—the nizam had, in addition to concessions on fees on the French even conferred the title of Saif-ud-daulah Umdat-ul-Mulk (Sword of the Dynasty and Support or Protector of the Realm) on the French commander, and future governor of Pondicherry, the Marquis de Bussy-Castelnau. Refusal could also mean grave trouble for the French ('"...you will soon see me fall on you and cause you to experience the same treatment that I am now preparing for others in your favour..."').

Law managed to finesse his way out of a possible predicament by gently reminding Siraj that the matter in southern India was 'settled amicably', and the English in Bengal had given the French 'no cause of offence'. And so help wouldn't be coming.

Siraj remained hopeful of French help. Law mentions that, just before the nawab left for Calcutta and its conquest, he sent word through an emissary that he 'still counted on our assistance, and he sent me a letter for the Governor of Pondicherry, in which he begged him to give us the necessary orders'. Given that it would take several months for such a request to reach Pondicherry and a reply to arrive, and even more time, theoretically, for a French force to arrive from Pondicherry, Law was plainly relieved. He had bought time.

(Like several of his colleagues, Law's behaviour towards the British at this time was exemplary—even though it didn't subtract from British belligerence in less than a year, as John Company and His Majesty's troops and sailors demolished Chandannagar to secure the British rear on the way to Plassey. Several British historians and chroniclers, including Holwell—whose fervid account of the Black Hole incident would provide the post-Plassey moral outrage for the retaking of Calcutta by a joint force of the Company and Crown, freely praised Law for the succour he provided the British. Law provided shelter to Mrs Watts and others of her family, indeed anyone from the English factory in Qasimbazar who managed to make their way to the French factory. When Siraj sent Holwell and a few other survivors of the so-called Black Hole on to Murshidabad as prisoners, Law helped the ragged band. 'After Mr. Law had given us a supply of clothes, linen, provisions, liquors, and cash,' Holwell would write in a letter on 28 February 1757, 'we left his Factory with grateful hearts and compliments.')

Over the next several days, spurred by red-flag messages from Qasimbazar, the Council at Calcutta requested help from the Council at Madras and the Dutch Council in Hugli. Drake and Holwell were signatories in nearly all such correspondence.

'We are likewise extreamly deficient in musquets, shot, bayonets, small field-pieces, mortars, and most kind of military stores, a proportionable quantity of which we shall likewise expect from your Honour &c.', the Council wrote to Madras on 8 June. They added an equally desperate postscript:

> P.S.—As it will be impossible to make gun-powder should our town be closely invested, and as it is probable the quantity we have by us and shall be able to make before his arrival, will all be expended by the time your reinforcement comes, we think it would be proper for your Honour &c. to send us likewise as much of that article as you can.

The Dutch turned down the request for help. A letter dated 8 June arrived from Hugli to Calcutta, in which the Dutch Council pleaded their inability to help. These were fraught times and they needed whatever resources they had at hand. They could not find the mutual agreement the British invoked to seek help. And, the Dutch wrote, in any case 'our Superiors charge us to remain neutral in all cases that do not concern us, we cannot see that the reasons upon which your Honours rely necessitate that we, who are established here as simple merchants, should on that account be obliged or feel it our duty, to expose ourselves to dangerous troubles from which we are not sure we shall remain exempt...'

They received an angry response, dated 13 June, which invoked Crown and Country: '...and we regret to see your Honour and the Council so cool and indifferent. Your Honour should consider the alliance and friendship between His Britannic Majesty and the States-General of the United Provinces,' goes part of the letter extracted from Dutch records. 'We cannot believe...that you are withheld from offering a helping hand to a colony of Great Britain, attacked and brought into great straits as it now is without the least grounds upon a specious pretext...'

While there wasn't any question of the French helping the British, they, like their colleague Law, decided not to help Siraj either—the 'neutrality of the Ganges' would be maintained with Siraj too. 'Whatever the advantages he [Siraj] offers us on this occasion, as it is not in our power to conform to his wishes without having been in the first instance authorised to do so by our Superiors,' the Council in Chandannagar wrote on 9 June to their colleague in Patna, 'we have agreed that the Director should write and thank him for his favourable disposition towards us, and at the same time excuse ourselves for our absolute inability not only to accept his obliging offers but also to supply him with the assistance he demands. Not knowing what effect our refusal will have on the Nawab's mind and fearing he may take it in bad part, we think we cannot take too much precaution against the resentment he may possibly feel towards us and which must be expected from a man so violent and passionate. It is for this reason, Sir, we advise you to be on your guard against whatever may happen, and to take every precaution which may seem advisable for the security of your Factory and your own persons.'

French neutrality in Bengal would in the longer term help the British, but as correspondence blazed across the Hugli, Siraj arrived near Calcutta. The British were on their own.

◆

The British were quite clear, writes Sarkar and others, that they would defend White Town, the European enclave, primarily around later-day Dalhousie Square and to its east and south. The collateral damage for their defences was Black Town, to the north, where Indians lived, mostly in bamboo and straw huts. These they set fire to, Hill writes, 'to clear the town as much as possible' to create space for defensive manoeuvres. They also set fire to parts of the town on the night of 16 June, to prevent Siraj's men from approaching.

'Next day, the British destroyed all the native houses to the eastward and the southward, and the Nawab's plunderers set fire to the Great Bazar'—Sarkar explains this was the old Burra Bazar area, north of present-day Fairlie Place. British women were by then already in Fort William. The following day, the 18th, they were joined by Portuguese and Armenian women and children. It wasn't an act of charity. Portuguese and Armenian militiamen refused to fight unless their families were first taken to the fort.

Every hand mattered, even though Holwell would later note: '...100 were Armenians [and] were useless, as were the black boys and slaves, most of whom could not handle a musket.' At this time, he and other Company officials in Calcutta would surely recall that the Court in London had written in February 1756, reminding them of the need to form a proper militia—an initial suggestion was made as far back as 1752—'as at this time in particular a regular militia may be of the greatest importance for the defence of the settlement, you are without delay to cause a plan to be formed for the purpose, and you are to carry the same into execution as far as shall appear useful and practicable.' It would, of course, be all too late.

Hill refers to records of correspondence and various memoranda at the India Office in London to arrive at an accounting of the military in Bengal as on 29 February 1756, less than four months before an angry Siraj arrived. At Calcutta there were 260 listed as 'Officers and Soldiers, Europeans', and 225 of such listed as 'Blacks'. Company servants were counted as 'about 45'. Altogether, 530 of these, besides whatever militia could be rounded up, faced off against several tens of thousands of Bengal troops.

The contingent of 40 at Qasimbazar (24 Europeans, 16 'Blacks') had already been overpowered. The 46 at Dhaka (31 Europeans, 15 'Blacks') were themselves besieged and too far and too few to be of any use in Calcutta. The post at Luckipore—Lakhipur—with 31 (20 Europeans, 11 'Blacks') was too distant to help. In all Bengal the Company could count on less than 650 to wield weapons.

As to Fort William, it had a long history of being inadequately equipped for battle. In January 1751, a dispatch to the Court in London explained why it was impossible to come to the aid of colleagues in Cuddalore: 'It was entirely out of our power to send them at Fort St. David any fire-arms, as we have not more in our military stores than 200 firelocks fit for service, exclusive of the arms of this detachment.' And yet they sent 201 soldiers, Reverend Long notes, 'as this part of Bengal is quite settled at present and there being no appearance of any immediate troubles'. The soldiers needed some inducement. They 'refused to embark without receiving a bounty of

20 rupees a man', the same bonus paid to those earlier sent on to Bombay. Desertion was an ever-present risk.

In January 1753, Consultations at Calcutta noted that stocks of gunpowder were so low they had to be conserved, avoiding the traditional salute even to British ships. ('Having but a small quantity of gun-powder in provision and esteeming the salutes of our own country ships expensive and unnecessary. *Resolved* that in future the Fort return no salutes to any of our own country ships.') Attempts to manufacture gunpowder locally, near Bag Bazar, met with 'little success', Long writes.

There was also the matter of morale. As late as February 1755, the Council at Fort William wrote to the Court about how 'Subaltern Officers of our establishment' were dispirited by the 'present method of sending out annually Gentlemen from Europe with Military Commissions superior to theirs'.

Besides, the fort itself was in need of renovation, as a February 1755 missive to London noted:

Colonel Simson, Engineer of the Fort, reports—

The whole Fort when finished will be a narrow slip on the side of the River, and in order to build it, the whole south side of the Factory which contains the apartments for most of the young Gentlemen in the Company's service, the Magazine for arms and Military stores, the shop for medicine, smith's shop, &c., must be pulled down immediately, as also the Church and Hospital; as all these buildings are in constant use, they cannot be well spared, and it would be difficult to supply their place immediately.

There was some need for urgency, Long explains, as information at this time had been received, as Company officials in Calcutta noted, 'that great fleets and many forces are suspected to be preparing in France for this part of the globe'. A Colonel Scott submitted a scheme at a cost of Rs 75,000 for 'enclosing Calcutta with a ditch, redoubts, drawbridges; the ditch was to be 36 feet wide and 12 feet deep,' observes Long. 'The Council rejected it as too expensive.' In any case it was accepted that, as Fort William had so many private residences of Europeans so close to it, any 'strong fortification' would require demolition of several of these houses. 'A Captain Jones wrote in 1755 a long memorial on the state of the Fort,' writes Long. '... the walls could not bear guns, and the guns sent out from Europe lay without carriages in the Fort, while goods were sold by public outcry at the Fort Gate.'

That August, the Council wrote to London that it was 'highly necessary to send three or four expert Gentlemen educated in the branch of Engineering and carrying on in the most regular manner Plans of Fortification'. They were to be backup, as engineers simply didn't live very long in the climate:

> ...experience teaches us to verify this general observation that men's lives advanced to or nigh the age of Forty are very precarious in such a change of climate from their native Country, therefore successors should be appointed to prevent the inconveniences we now labor under. It has hitherto been very unfortunate to this Settlement that every Gentleman who has had capacity has been appointed by our employers to fortify this place, has not lived even to make a beginning on the plans proposed.

From 12 June 1756, Fort William went to work with whatever was at hand. While a large group of militia were stationed within the fort, groups of capable officers and troops, and volunteers, were stationed to the north, east, and south of the fort along with batteries—the few cannon the fort possessed.

◆

The first shot, as it were, in this battle for Calcutta wasn't fired by Siraj's forces, but by the Company. And not in Calcutta, but across the river Hugli at Tanna Fort, manned by the nawab's forces. And, even before Siraj arrived in Calcutta.

Company shipping had been interdicting and searching non-British and non-European boats since the beginning of June. On 13 June, the Company sent four vessels to attack this strategically located fort downstream of Calcutta. The troops they carried took Tanna Fort without a fight, and destroyed whatever little weaponry they found there. But the following day they retreated upon the arrival of between 3,000 and 4,000 of Siraj's forces, many of whom had crossed the river north of, and at, Chandannagar and carried on south along the western bank of the Hugli. The British contingent withdrew to Calcutta, which lay on the eastern bank and joined the cluster of ships near Fort William.

The battle of Calcutta really began on 16 June with an exchange of cannonade between Siraj's forces and the ketch, *Fortune,* and the sloop, *Chance.* The British forces repulsed every attack that day, and even led a midnight raid to the south of White Town after destroying cannon and inflicting casualties, as they had through the day. But to the north it was a different story, as Siraj's troops advanced past several landmarks, including Umachand's Garden, that merchant-prince's palatial retreat. That night and through the day on the 17th, Siraj's forces advanced through Black Town but kept away from British batteries, as recounted in the journals of Captain Alexander Grant in Stuart Reid's book, *The Battle of Plassey.* (About two-thirds of the book comprises appendices of several Company documents, narratives and journal entries of Company officers, and musters of troops, mostly sourced from compilations like that of Hill, which also records Captain Grant's account. The Captain was an ancestor of Reid.)

Tooke, whom we earlier referred to for a version of Watts's predicament in Murshidabad, and a volunteer in the defence of Calcutta, later submitted this in his account to Orme:

> June 17th we caused all the buzars and cajan houses [thatched with palm leaf, Hill helpfully explains] to the eastward to be burnt, as likewise to the southward, almost as far as Govinpoors [Govindapur] where many of our people being detected plundering were instantly punished with dicapitation.

A decision was enforced to give no quarter to Siraj's forces: no prisoners, they were to be killed; the fort was already too burdened to hold prisoners. It was also the day that Umachand gave himself up to the protection of the British, and was kept under guard in Fort William.

But the night of 17th, as Grant's journal recollects, was a poor one for the British.

This night all our peons deserted us, and in short every black fellow, who could make his escape, abandoned us. Upwards of 1,000 bearers left us in one night, on being ordered to carry the powder from the Magazeen [which lay to the north of Fort William] into the Fort.

18 June was a day of chaos for the British, compounded, it appears by some accounts, by Drake, the governor-merchant, and Holwell, the physician-volunteer. Even as British forces to the north, around the saltpetre godown and south, in the residential area that lay beyond the Great Tank—later the centrepiece for Dalhousie Square—engaged in fierce fighting, street to street and sometimes house to house, Siraj's forces, taking far greater casualties than the British, began to slowly push them back. In the east the onslaught by Siraj's forces was intense, and Holwell and Drake's gauged resistance was becoming impossible. Orders went out to spike the cannon and retreat towards the fort, which some officers later maintained was premature; but it may have simply delayed the inevitable.

The British also held a council of war that day to take stock of the situation. Tooke provided a remarkable account of it to Orme:

> About 8 o'clock in the evening a council of war was held, whereat were present Mr. Drake and his Council that remained, all the military officers, and some of the principal inhabitants of the town; when it was debated what were the safest steps to be taken in the present exigency of affairs; when the first enquiry made was from the Captain of the Artillery, Lawrence Witherington, for the quantity of ammunition there was in the garrison, who reported that at the rate it had been expended there was sufficient for about two days more at furthest, but if husbanded a little, might be made to serve for three. Thereupon a retreat was considered of, and proposed by Mr. Holwell to be made the next day or next night, and that it might be done in a safe and calm manner, and the interval employed in sending the Company's papers, treasure, &c., on board the different shipping they had taken up, and that the same might in due time also be made publick to every one; but this was rejected at about 1 or 2 o'clock in the morning (owing in some measure to a cannon

shott passing through the Consultation room) with the utmost clamour, confusion, tumult and perplexity, according to custom without coming to any determination or resolution, but good naturedly leaving every member to imagine his proposals would be followed and put in execution.

◆

On 19 June, the British caved in. Siraj's forces had begun a cannonade that landed in areas close to the fort, destroying among other buildings a church that stood to the northeast. It had become dangerous at the bastions of the fort, and along the curtain (wall). Defeat was a matter of time, and there was concern that as the British had given no quarter, they couldn't expect any. Between 9 a.m. and 10 a.m. there began an exodus.

Drake didn't prove himself much of a 'chief-man'—as he was called at Murshidabad's court, the *Siyar*'s translator tells us; it was at the time the 'etiquette expression'. Drake left. So did several officers, including Captain George Minchin, the captain-commandant, and Captain Alexander Grant, a senior engineer, several of the militia, 'with most of the principal inhabitants', Tooke noted.

Those who remained were furious, he added. 'Upon the Governour's going off, several musketts were fired at him, but none were lucky enough to take place.'

In any event it led to further chaos, with a sort of desperate order returning among those who remained. It would soon be Holwell's hour of glory—or self-glorification, depending on the point of view. Again, Tooke offers a description of what transpired:

> Those who were in the way, upon hearing the foregoing gentlemen had quitted the factory, as also of those who quitted it the night before, and seeing every ship dropping down, imagined the retreat to be general; which prompted many to go also that otherwise never intended it; for who could judge a Governour and most of his Council with his two first officers and engineer, as also most of the militia officers, would be the first to desert the garrison.
>
> Upon Mr. Drake's ship getting under sail, every ship

followed his example, and in less than an hour's time not a boat was to be seen near the factory, nor a vessell in condition to move, but the Company's [the *Prince George*, which led the attack on Tanna Fort less than a week earlier] which run ashore shortly after, when those who were in the factory's retreat was entirely cut off. Upon which a council of war was called by those who remained, at the head of whom was Mr. Pearkes who yielded up his right to Mr. Holwell, declaring he did not think himself qualifyed for command in such distracted affairs. Mr. Holwell therefore was unanimously appointed to act in his stead, and Captain Lewis, master attendant (Captain Graham having carried away one of the Company's sloops before the attack), and the defence of the place was carried on briskly, under the new commanderie...

10

THE BLACK HOLE: HORROR OR HOAX?

'The dreadful suffering that followed, the madness...'

By noon on 20 June, British officers and troops were outmanoeuvred. They were in any case outnumbered. Twenty-five were killed, seventy wounded, the artillery crews decimated. Holwell realized he wouldn't be able to hold out for long, and managed to get Umachand to write a letter to Manikchand, 'one of the Nawab's favourites', to intercede.

An emissary appeared around two in the afternoon—at least one other account mentions it as 4 p.m.—and made gestures to stop firing. Holwell assumed this was on account of Umachand's letter, and thought he could use the ensuing quiet to refresh what remained of his troops, perhaps even hold out until nightfall and effect a retreat. Holwell writes that he accordingly raised a flag of truce, but even as they rested, word arrived of Siraj's soldiers gathering near the ramparts. A gate leading from Fort William to the Hugli had 'burst open' with troops guided by a Dutch sergeant called Hedleburgh, who had deserted the British the previous day along with other Dutch mercenaries. Even as Holwell took stock, troops using bamboo ladders poured over the walls of the fort ('with precipitation scarce credible to Europeans', in Holwell's words) and set about killing anyone wearing red coats, the uniform worn by troops of the Company and Crown.

Holwell, whose other notable act—notable for trivia mavens that is—appears to have been the purchase of Perrin's Garden for 2,500 rupees in 1752, which Long suggests was the precursor to the future Calcutta landmark of Eden Gardens, was looking forward to leaving Calcutta. In September 1755, he had given a year's notice for his return to Britain, a procedure that had by then become the norm. Long notes that 'Mr. Holwell intended to leave in September 1756, little anticipating he would be a prisoner at Murshedabad then.' Or among the dramatis personae of the Black Hole, for that matter.

Holwell and other British 'gentlemen' at the fort expected to die fighting, expecting 'no mercy from the Nawab', but were instead given the opportunity to surrender by one of Siraj's officers. 'Mr. Holwell was taken to a part of the ramparts from which he could see the Nawab, to whom he made his salaam,' writes Hill. 'This was courteously returned.'

◆

And with that Fort William—and Calcutta—capitulated.

Siraj entered the fort on a litter from the side of the river to the west. Holwell had three interviews with Siraj that afternoon, Hill relates, citing Holwell's own account.

> To the first Mr. Holwell had been brought with his hands bound. The Nawab released him from his bonds, and promised him on the word of a soldier that no harm should befall him. On the other hand, he expressed great anger at the presumption of the British in resisting him, and much displeasure against Mr. Drake.

This was evidently against Drake's resistance in general and also at ordering the Government or 'Factory House' to be burnt. 'He admired the European houses, and said the British were fools to force him to destroy so fine a town.'

Siraj left after a while, and took up residence in a house that had belonged to a Mr Wedderburn.

Hill writes that some of the nawab's troops set about a sort of controlled mayhem: they 'plundered the Europeans of their valuables but did not ill-treat them'. Indeed, he writes that the Portuguese and Armenians 'were allowed to go free and disappeared, and several of the Europeans simply walked out of the Fort, making their escape' to the Hugli or 'the ships at Surman's'. [This is Surman's Garden, to the south of the old Fort William, as an account from June 1756 by a Mr Grey Junior, a Company employee notes, and not Surman's Nullah, a canal later known as Tolly's Nullah. Surman's Garden, Henry Elmsley Busteed's *Echoes from Old Calcutta* informs us, later became the 'more modern Hastings']. This assertion is used by Indian nationalist historians to debunk the Black Hole narrative, of which more shortly.

The *Siyar* maintains that 'the vilest part' of Siraj's army went on a looting spree, but that the nawab himself didn't benefit from 'so much wealth in merchandise and money' taken from the homes and warehouses of English, Indian, and Armenian merchants.

The *Siyar* also mentions one act of chivalry that would go some way in the days before Plassey. Some English ladies ('bibi') were captured by Mirza Amir Beg, an officer with allegiance to Mir Jafar. He is described as being a gentleman, and kept the ladies 'decently and untouched; but in secret'. Later that night he is said to have told Mir Jafar about them, and the general gave leave for a large and swift boat, a bhovaliah that, depending on its size, would be rowed by between twenty and sixty rowers, to spirit them away. Mirza Amir is said to have undertaken some subterfuge to hoodwink sentries, pretending to have the boat accidently caught by the downstream current.

Eventually they drifted and rowed a dozen 'kos', about 40 kilometres, downriver where Drake's ship had anchored. Mirza Amir refused the modest gifts that the grateful British, several of them husbands of these bibis, offered the gallant officer ('...I have done nothing but what was required by a sense of honour; and what might entitle me to your remembrance,' as the *Siyar* tells it). This naturally went down well with the British, who added this to their good books, as it were, by extension eyeing Mir Jafar as being sympathetic to their cause.

◆

The fate of Holwell and other prisoners changed within a few hours, around sunset. 'Some European soldiers had made themselves drunk and assaulted the natives,' writes Hill. There was speculation it could have been the Dutch who had earlier deserted—the jury is out on that, as even soldiers faithful to the Company had earlier gone on a bit of a binge in preparation for what appeared to them like a fight to the finish. Indeed, the account by Grey Junior notes that, 'At the time the fort was taken there was not above the number of 20 men upon the walls. The greatest part of the souldiers were drunk, and those that were sober were quite fatigued with continual hard duty, and want of a regular distribution of provisions.'

The 'natives' complained to Siraj, 'who asked where the Europeans were accustomed to confine soldiers who had misbehaved in any way. He was told in the Black Hole...'

'...and, as some of his officers suggested it would be dangerous to leave so many prisoners at large during the night, ordered that they should all be confined in it.'

This was taken literally. The nawab's officers were said to have in any case been enraged by losses suffered during the siege; Hill compiles Holwell's and other estimates to offer a range of between 7,000 to 15,000 troops, even though it seems excessive. The officers piled 146 persons without any care of status or gender into a cell measuring '18 feet square' on 'one of the hottest nights of year', and they remained there until relief arrived on the morning of 21 June. Hill separately cites the 'exact dimensions' offered by C. S. Wilson in the *Indian Church Review* as being 18 feet by 14 feet 10 inches, an even tighter fit than what Holwell assumed. Hill writes with uncharacteristic emotion:

> The dreadful suffering that followed, the madness which drove the prisoners to trample each other down and to fight for the water which only added to their torture, the insults they poured upon their jailors in order to induce them to fire on them and so end their misery, and the brutal delight of the native soldiers at a sight which they looked upon as a tamasha, are all told in Mr. Holwell's narrative, than which nothing more pathetic is to be found in the annals of the British in India. From 7 o'clock in the evening to 6 o'clock in the morning this agony lasted, for even the native officers who pitied them dared not disturb the Nawab before he awoke from his slumbers.

Hill, like many others, quotes Orme here to mention that when Siraj finally woke and paid attention to the matter, 'only twenty-three of one hundred and forty-six who went in came out alive, the ghastlyest forms that were ever seen alive, from this infernal scene of horror'.

The bodies of the dead, Britons and Anglo-Indians alike, were removed and buried without ceremony in a nearby ditch.

Holwell would later construct a memorial to the dead, Hill writes, 'on or near the spot where their bodies were buried, just outside of the east gate of the Fort'. The brick monument, built sometime in 1758–59, was demolished in 1821 by Francis Rawdon-Hastings, governor-general of the presidency of Fort William at the time. The monument had deteriorated and was also struck by lightning. In 1902, the viceroy of India, George Nathaniel Curzon, who effected modern India's first formal politico-religious schism when he partitioned Bengal in 1905, had a white-marble replica of the Holwell monument erected a short distance from the Black Hole in the southwest corner of Dalhousie Square—present-day Benoy-Badal-Dinesh Bag, or B. B. D. Bag, named after three colonial-era Indian revolutionaries. On account of public protests it was relocated in 1940 to the grounds of St John's Church on Council House Street, south of Dalhousie Square. A modest tourist attraction, it remains there today, at the site of one of the earliest public structures constructed by the Company, after Calcutta became the capital of British India in 1772.

(The Black Hole is now absent, access to the area restricted as it's an area of government offices, but there are photographs of where it used to be. There's one, for instance, of a small rectangle adjacent to the north wall of the General Post Office. The image of the rectangle with wrought-iron fencing is credited to Stereo-Travel Co., a Long Island, New York-based imaging business, and dated 1908.)

Curzon's Holwell monument, if you will, acknowledges it is a 'reproduction of the design of the original monument' and that it was raised by the 'surviving fellow-sufferer J. Z. Holwell, Governor of Fort William/On the spot where the bodies of the dead/Had been thrown into the ditch of the ravelin'—a smaller fortification, usually in the shape of an spearhead, placed ahead of the main 'curtain' or wall, and a ditch.

Holwell—and, by extension, Hill—painted Siraj as a money-grubbing upstart who placed a greater value on loot over lives; the very accusations that would quickly accrue to the Company and, in a few short years, to the Crown. Holwell, the survivor, was summoned by the nawab who asked him about the lack of riches in the fort, 'for his men had found in the Treasury of the richest of the European Settlements only the miserable amount of 50,000 rupees, or about £6,250.' Holwell pleaded ignorance. Siraj would have none of it. He ordered that Holwell and three others be handed over to his commander and confidante, Mir Madan—the general who would in posterity emerge as a tragic hero of Plassey in the patriotic-Indian telling. Holwell writes that thereafter they were treated abominably, force-marched in the hot sun before being held in an open balcony for a couple of days—'here their bodies burst out into terrible boils' writes Hill—before being shipped upriver to Murshidabad.

Siraj returned to his capital on 11 July. Holwell and his colleagues had by then been imprisoned for ten days. The nawab met them again on 16 July. Again, Holwell himself offers an uncharacteristically gallant appraisal of Siraj at that audience, a change from the picture of the callous despot at the time of the Black Hole incident less than a fortnight earlier:

> The wretched spectacle we made must, I think, have made an impression on a breast the most brutal, and if he is capable of pity or contrition his heart felt it then. I think it appeared, in spight of him, in his countenance. He gave me no reply, but ordered a sootapurdar and chubdar immediately to see our irons cut off, and to conduct us wherever we chose to go, and to take care we received no trouble nor insult; and having repeated this order distinctly, directed his retinue to go on.

Hill speculates that Siraj's grandmother, Sharf-un-Nisa Begum, and his mother, Amina Begum, prevailed upon the nawab to be gentler to the captured British. (They took a longer, more practical view as the two ladies evidently kept up commerce in Calcutta. For instance, he quotes a Company source to illustrate 'how very angry Amina Begam was with Omichand for getting the better of them in the sale of some opium and saltpetre at Calcutta.') There were others at court who counselled the nawab to simply send Holwell back to Calcutta and have Siraj's governor there, Manikchand, pressure him to give up the treasure they thought was secreted somewhere in the Fort. At the very worst, Holwell and his colleagues would be worth an impressive ransom.

'It may be,' Holwell recounts Siraj as saying. 'If he has anything left, let him keep it. His sufferings have been great. He shall have his liberty.'

It was done. The prisoners were allowed to make their way to the

Dutch factory. In some days they would make their way to Calcutta, the city now renamed Alinagar by Siraj in honour of his grandfather.

Calcutta was by then a no-go area for Europeans. Siraj had on 21 June ordered they all leave the settlement, on 'penalty of losing their nose and ears', relates Hill. That day he renamed Calcutta as Alinagar. He also gave orders to build a mosque within the fort, for which a part of the east curtain was pulled down 'to make room for it'.

The nawab relented in a few days, and permitted European residents to return, but the order was again reversed for a time on 1 July: punishment for 'a drunken soldier' having killed 'a Muhammadan', Hill writes.

In the second week of August, Holwell and his party reached Falta, the tiny village downriver where the other escaped Britons were camped.

◆

Just how many died in the Black Hole? How many were there to begin with? A macabre arithmetic has since remained with the incident. Some historians and chroniclers take Holwell at his word, some discount the numbers, and some dismiss the very idea, suggesting instead it was a fevered and resentful imagining by Holwell that played to Company galleries and provided the moral outrage necessary to plan revenge for the humiliation the British had suffered at Calcutta.

Hill follows Holwell's count of twenty-three, although he acknowledges other estimates, such as Drake's, which counts twenty-five survivors.

There is also the matter of degree. Although such a preoccupation can appear ghoulish, it has become a touchstone to credit or discredit alibis and moral judgement.

A total of 146 went in, twenty-three came out alive, claimed Holwell. Hill's account isn't as certain.

It is difficult to estimate the actual loss of the British. In the Black Hole 123 perished, of whom we can trace the names of only 56; between 50 and 100 must have perished in the fighting or died of their sufferings during the siege or at Fulta, and, if, general rumour can be trusted, many whites and half-castes were drowned in the effort to escape.

For this last, Hill discounts the estimate of Pierre Renault, the French governor, or director, of Chandannagar, who put the numbers at 200 Europeans (Renault estimated that 3,000 'refugees', a mix of Armenians, Portuguese and 'half-castes' made their way to the French settlement after the fall of Calcutta). Deaths are difficult to document in a melee of this sort, but attention has been focused on the Black Hole numbers for reasons mentioned a little earlier.

More doubt is sown by the 'Black Hole' monument. A visit to Curzon's Holwell monument will show that it lists twenty-seven names of those 'Who perished in the Black Hole prison' and clarifies that these are 'in Excess of the list Recorded by Governor Holwell Upon the original monument'. The reference to Holwell's title is one that came to him later as governor of Fort William—effectively, governor of Bengal after Clive's first departure from the province in 1760. It was clearly the Company's reward for 'Councilman' Holwell, a former surgeon who with considerable courage stood up to Siraj. The inscription adds: 'The additional names, and The Christian names of the remainder Have been recovered from oblivion By reference to contemporary documents.' These names include even those who died later. As Hill suggests, the viceroy took some liberties with names: 'Lord Curzon adds to this list the name of Eleanor Weston, and a few of the names of those I have given as being killed during the fighting,' he explains in his book *Bengal in 1756-1757* in the section where he details the siege of Calcutta by Siraj, the Black Hole incident and several other aspects of events of the summer of 1756, including the time of difficult and even desperate refuge of the escaped British at Falta.

It was clearly a time of some confusion and emotion, and deaths on account of the siege of Fort William at times appear to have been conflated with deaths from confinement at the Black Hole.

Hill overrode his evident disdain for Siraj, disgust at horrors linked to the Black Hole incident, and his own office as a senior employee of the British Indian empire to collate information and, frequently, analyse it with distance. In that vein Hill begins by discounting the statement of the French chief at Qasimbazar, Jean

Law, about Siraj being 'strongly tempted to adorn his harem' with some 'very charming' English ladies in the settlement at Dhaka as 'probably a libel'. 'It was not the custom of the Muhammadans to ill-treat ladies, and Siraj-uddaula had had in his grandfather a good example of chivalry to the women-folk of his enemies and as a matter of fact the whole of the party [from the Company factory and residences at Dhaka] escaped safely to Fulta, where they arrived on the 26th August in a sloop lent them by M. Courtin'—Jacques Ignace Courtin, the French chief at Dhaka.

Siraj took from the British factory at Dhaka 'merchandise and silver worth 1,400,000 rupees,' Hill quotes French sources as saying, 'which will give the reader some idea of the value of the British up-country trade'. John Company's losses in Bengal, on account of Siraj's punitive expedition were later estimated at 'at least 95 lakhs of rupees'—9.5 million rupees—Hill writes, and also that Clive 'wrote home that the losses of private persons exceeded £2,000,000,' about sixteen million rupees.

The stock of the British in Bengal was entirely diminished at this point. The only settlement that escaped Siraj's attention was a small British operation in Balramgachhi (or Balramgarhi) on the Buribalam River, near Balasore in present-day Odisha. While the British factors in Balasore left for the refuge of Falta on the Hugli, the sub-factory continued uninterrupted in 'Balramgurry'—and, as the *Imperial Gazetteer of India* of 1908 informs us, was even briefly proclaimed the seat of the Presidency!

Back to the matter of the Black Hole.

Hill refers to the instance of several ladies whose deaths, as clearly suggested in different accounts, were caused by suffering during the siege. As far as Hill could ascertain, only one lady, a Mrs Carey, was in the Black Hole. She survived, while her husband, Robert Carey, did not. A Mrs Knox is mentioned in the *Calcutta Gazette* of 19 October 1815 as having died after being the last survivor at the 'horrid scene of the Black Hole in 1756'. She was fourteen, 'and the wife of a Doctor Knox'. Hill writes of this claim made several decades after the siege and cited even later, in 1897, in a chronicle of the city, Busteed's *Echoes from Old Calcutta*: 'Probably the reference to the Black Hole is an amplification, for in the careless talk of Calcutta the

Black Hole and Fort William seem to have been often confounded.'

There appears to be similar cases of confusion or exaggeration with stories that allude to the barbarity of Siraj and his generals and troops, even though there can be little doubt that several women 'of the lower classes', as Hill describes them, died of hardships caused by the siege. Some may have drowned in the Hugli during a panic-stricken escape. Some others may have been carried off by troops as war trophies. But there were certain exaggerations. Hill writes:

> A French account says that 100 white women and as many white children were carried up country. It is hardly necessary to point out that there were not so many white women or white children in Calcutta, and the lists of the refugees at Fulta show that almost all the white ladies and children were on board the ships that escaped.

These assertions, and the absence of any mention of the Black Hole incident in any contemporary Indian account, like the *Siyar*, are seized upon by critics of the Black Hole as proof of either exaggeration by Holwell's fevered mind or outright fiction portrayed by Holwell and others after deliberate thought. It gave the Company and Crown a compelling reason for outrage and provided the moral basis and opportunity to not only retake Calcutta but enter into every manner of arrangement to secure the East India Company and Britain the dominions of Bengal, Bihar, and Orissa by overthrowing Siraj, extracting vast reparation and concessions, and establishing a series of puppet nawabs for the good of Company and Crown.

For his part Haji Mustapha, the *Siyar*'s translator, in an extensive footnote expresses deep disappointment that the author didn't mention 'a word of those English shut up in the Black-hole, to the number of 131 [another numerical discrepancy], where they were mostly smothered.' This is taken by several later historians and commentators of the subcontinent—though not, notably, pro-Raj commentators like Nirad Chaudhuri—as evidence of the entire Black Hole of Calcutta incident in a cramped space in the old Fort William being a figment of the British imagination, cooked up by Holwell, propagated by British chroniclers, and digested by generations of Britons. Especially, as it strains credulity that the decidedly anti-

Siraj author of the *Siyar*, who spared no occasion in his sprawling work to damn that nawab, would pass up such a plum opportunity to damn the man some more.

Indeed, Haji Mustapha's own words are taken as revealing by those who consider the Black Hole incident to be fiction, or at least exaggerated in both content and form. Here is what the *Siyar*'s translator tells us about the incident:

> The truth is, that the Hindostanees wanting only to secure them for the night, as they were to be presented the next morning to the Prince, shut them up in what they heard was the prison of the Fort, without having any idea of the capacity of the room; and indeed the English themselves had none of it. This much is certain, that this event, which cuts so capital a figure in Mr. Watts's performance, is not known in Bengal; and even in Calcutta, it is ignored by every man out of the four hundred thousand that inhabit that city; at least it is difficult to meet a single native that knows any thing of it; so careless, and so incurious are those people. Were we therefore to accuse the Indians of cruelty, for such a thoughtless action, we would of course accuse the English, who intending to embark four hundred Gentoo Sipahees, destined for Madras, put them in boats, without one single necessary, and at last left them to be overset by the boat, where they all perished, after a three days' fast.

Ergo, maintain critics of the Black Hole theory (with what is in the present day colloquially known as 'whataboutery'), even if we were to entirely believe British narrators, that the Black Hole incident did happen, and deaths took place, it was at worst an accident. And, in an echo of the assertion that the *Siyar* not mentioning the matter suggests it did not take place, for these critics the ignorance of Calcutta's contemporary 'native' population about the tragedy suggests it was not an incident predicated on truth.

Jadunath Sarkar is among the foremost of these critics, even though his own account is sometimes overlaid by gratuitous criticism of the British. Like Hill and several other Western chroniclers, he holds the Calcutta Council responsible for initiating the siege of the settlement by their obduracy, but also a high degree of brutality 'by ordering their soldiers not to take any prisoners,' essentially because, as we have seen, it was claimed that they didn't have space for prisoners. Neither did the 'Murshidabad troops', but they didn't resort to such an 'inhuman course', Sarkar muses. And, even when attacked by Europeans (which eventually led to the incarceration of all Europeans in the Black Hole) they didn't take recourse to their 'legitimate right under International Law which makes prisoners of war liable to be shot if they assault their guards'. It isn't clear what international law Sarkar refers to, as the first of the Geneva Conventions governing the laws of war was signed only in 1864; he perhaps meant common practice. 'With oriental humanity they merely put restraints on the rowdy Englishmen,' is how Sarkar defends the actions of Siraj's troops using the logic of the fog of war, 'but in the unsettled conditions of a fort taken by storm, with fires raging outside, they had no time to separate the sheep from the goats, and the prison was left in charge of the common soldiers throughout the night.'

Sarkar, like Hill and Little, has trouble reconciling the actual numbers of the dead, but declares it more bluntly than Hill—that the figure of '123 dead out of 146 confined' as 'given out and accepted in Europe' as 'manifestly an exaggeration'. Little went further: he called it a 'gigantic hoax', which is now among the most quoted remarks on the episode, present in numerous commentaries and studies.

Sarkar maintains that there 'could not have been' that number of British 'left in Siraj's hands' three hours after the surrender at 4 p.m.: the numbers don't add up considering the deaths during the siege, evacuation before surrender, and the fact that numerous people were simply allowed to leave by the nawab once the surrender came into effect, as we have seen. Grey Junior's account notes the following:

> Some rushed out at the gate towards the river to take possession of a boat that lay half in and half out of the water, and in an instant it was so laden that it was impossible to get it off. In the meantime the Moors surrounded and shewed them signs of quarter, upon which they delivered themselves up. Some of them went to the Nabob himself and were by him pardoned, and others whilst the enemy were busy about the plunder got

into a boat and went down the river to the ships at that time lying off Surmon's Gardens.

Sarkar's second factor for accepting or rejecting what had been put about is a strange, if compelling, empirical approach. He refers to an experiment conducted by Bholanath Chandra (also referred to in some instances as Bholanauth Chunder), a chronicler and contemporary of the iconic Bengali writer, Michael Madhusudan Dutta, and the writer, Bhudev Mukhopadhyay, at Calcutta's Hindu College. Chandra, a landlord, and sometime employee of a British-owned mercantile firm, and also a member of the Asiatic Society of Bengal is known for his two-volume *Travels of a Hindoo to Various Parts of Bengal and Upper India*, published in 1869.

Sarkar explains that Chandra 'fenced round an area 18 feet by 15, with bamboo stakes, and counted the number of his Bengali tenants who could be crammed into it'. The number was found to be 'much less than 146, and a Bengali villager's body occupies much less space than a British gentleman's'. Moreover, Sarkar insists, there exists no mention of a list or 'headcount' of those who remained after 4 p.m. on 20 June, and so many had simply walked away. He notes that even Holwell was offered a chance to escape (Hill writes that a Company carpenter offered Holwell a secret passage out, but he gallantly chose to remain with his colleagues and defend the fort.) 'It is a very reasonable supposition,' Sarkar concludes echoing Hill's thought, 'that all the former British residents of Calcutta whose manner of death could not be clearly ascertained in that week of confused fighting, administrative breakdown, and loss of home and records, were afterwards set down as "perished in the Black Hole".'

◆

The weakest link in the Black Hole story remains Holwell, whose accounts are the cornerstone of all doubt.

In *The Black Hole of Calcutta*, published in 1935, Saiyid Amin Ahmad offers five different accounts—in this book, cross-checked and supplemented with the records from which these are sourced. These were given by Holwell, he notes, 'at five different times' and with these he seeks to prove Holwell's inconsistency and, therefore, his dishonesty about the whole matter.

Holwell's first account is reported by Francis Sykes in his letter dated 8 July 1756 to the Council then camped in Falta. Sykes was then in Qasimbazar, and that very morning had met Holwell and three of his colleagues who had 'passed by on their way to Muxadavad prisoners and in irons'. He notes that Holwell also wrote to Law for 'a little bread and butter and other necessaries as they had had only rice and water since they left Calcutta which is upwards of 15 days. They were in an open boat exposed to all weathers.' Sykes provided the following 'purport' of Holwell's conversation with him:

> As soon as the Nabob arrived in the Fort he found with covenanted servants, soldiers and officers to the number of 160 who were put into a place called the Black Hole and jammed so close that out of 160 put in alive the next morning 110 were brought out dead for want of air. Jenks, Reveloy, Law, Eyres, Bailie, Cooke, Captain Buchanan, Scott and all our other military officers and Covenanted servants dead. The writers and officers behaved bravely. A prodigious number of Moors are killed. All the night our poor gentlemen were in the Black Hole, the Nabob's people kept firing at them through the window.

The second instance, Ahmad notes, was dated 17 July 1756 with a dateline of 'Muxdavad'. Hill writes that these were identical letters Holwell had written to the Councils in Bombay and Fort St George in Madras.

> The resistance we made and the loss they suffered so irritated the Nabob that he ordered myself and all the prisoners promiscuously to the number of about 165 or 170 to be crammed altogether into a small prison in the fort called the Black Hole... from whence only about 16 of us came out alive in the morning the rest being suffocated to death—amongst those myself, Mr. Richard Court, Mr. John Cooke, Mr. Lushington, Ensign Walcot, Mr. Burdett (a young gentleman volunteer), Captain Mills, Captain Dickson, and about 7 or 8 soldiers blacks and whites; amongst the dead Messrs. Eyre and William Baillie, the Reverend Mr. Bellamy, Messrs. Jenks, Rively, Law, T. Coales etc. our 3 Military Captains and 9 Subalterns, many of our volunteers

and inhabitants, of whom particular lists shall be forwarded the Honourable Company as recollection enables me.

This, as Ahmad notes, implies Siraj gave the order for the incarceration of prisoners in the Black Hole. 'Myself, Messrs. Court, Walcot and Burdet were sent to the camp the 21st in the morning, there put in irons and marched three miles to town the 22nd, in the sun and our irons, with no covering to our heads, and hardly any to our bodies. At the Dock Head we were detained the 22nd, 23rd and 24th, and the evening of that day put on board an open boat for this city destitute of a rupee or any necessary of life. On the 7th instant we arrived there (our subsistence on the way up on rice and water)'—this is consistent with what he told Sykes—'and were deposited under a guard in an open stinking cowhouse, a spectacle to the whole city (and hardly escaped a second smothering), untill the 11th'—three days after he met Sykes—'when we were removed to the jemidar's house under whose custody we were. On the 15th we were again remanded to the cowhouse, flattered with hopes of knowing our ultimate fate, there we remained that night and yesterday [had our fetters struck off and] were once again blessed with liberty and freedom to go where we pleased. The humanity and friendship we received here from the gentlemen of the French and Dutch factorys will ever require our most grateful remembrance.'

While the latter part, which is additionally placed here to provide a sense of continuity and context, is consistent with Sykes's recall, the part about the Black Hole is not, as Ahmad maintains. He goes as far as to claim Holwell knew he had erred (here Holwell actually owned up to having committed 'errors and omissions' while being in a 'wretched state'), and with his increasingly enabled recollection, he wrote a lengthy letter from Hugli to the Council at Fort St George on 3 August 1756. In it Holwell also clarified several comments he had earlier made about the Black Hole, including numbers, and Siraj's culpability:

> I over reckoned the number of prisoners put into the Black Hole and the number of the dead; the former being only 146 and the latter 123, many recovering after air was let in by opening the door in the morning; and many more I doubt not might

have recovered had any means or care been taken of them. I charged the Nabob with designedly having ordered the unheard-of piece of cruelty of cramming us all into that small prison; but I have now reason to think I did him injustice. His orders I learn was only general, 'That we should be imprisoned that night, our number being too great to be at large.' And being left to the mercy and direction of his jemidars and burkandosses [barkandāz, or matchlock-men], their resentment for the number of their brethren slain took this method of revenge; and indeed they ceased not insulting us the whole night, though witnesses of horrors which bar all description.

Holwell's clarifications weren't enough, Ahmad maintains. What about the matter of being fired upon ('the Nabob's people kept firing at them through the window', in his version to Sykes) that was now 'toned down' to the troops merely being insulting. Indeed, he points to Holwell's pages-long letter of 17 July in which he details numerous incidents with time and date—hardly the condition of a man in a wretched state. Ahmad also points out the confusion over 'Mrs Carey' that we read about a little earlier.

Admittedly Ahmad, like many critics, is harsh on Holwell—but he is attempting to prove Holwell was harsh on Siraj—and the unsaid aspect of so many accounts finding their own wings with future readers, especially everyday readers who did not benefit from comprehensive sources, naturally going with whatever proved to be easily available or was more salacious—especially an account published in 1764, the clincher so far as Ahmad was concerned that much of the British view of the Black Hole was embroidered and exaggerated.

The document that outraged Ahmad was titled, 'A genuine narrative of the deplorable deaths of the English gentlemen and others who were suffocated in the Black Hole in Fort William, at Calcutta, in the kingdom of Bengal, in the night succeeding 20 June, 1756, in a letter to a friend by J. Z. Holwell, Esq.' This story-length letter had a preface by Holwell in which he claims it was written by him to his friend, William Davis, on 28 February 1757, while Holwell was on a sloop called *Syren*. The third volume of Hill's *Bengal in 1756-1757* contains the entire letter.

It's a dramatic tale that provides far more 'detail' than any of

Holwell's other accounts of the hours before his incarceration in the Black Hole, and more so each agonizing hour in the Black Hole, Holwell's own selfless acts, and that of others towards him in particular and to the incarcerated company in general—but mostly the horror of the experience. In this account Holwell stays with the count of 146 prisoners imprisoned, and 123 dead by the following morning. He writes:

> Figure to yourself, my friend, if possible, the situation of a hundred and forty-six wretches, exhausted by continual fatigue and action, thus crammed together in a cube of about eighteen feet, in a close sultry night in Bengal, shut up to the eastward and southward (the only quarters from whence air could reach us) by dead walls, and by a wall and door to the north, open only to the westward by two windows, strongly barred with iron, from which we could receive scarce any the least circulation of fresh air.

There was only one person, Holwell writes, an aged guard, who showed compassion. Holwell offered him baksheesh for mercy.

> I called him to me, and, in the most persuasive terms I was capable, urged him to commiserate the sufferings he was a witness to, and pressed him to endeavour to get us separated, half in one place and half in another; and that he should in the morning receive a thousand rupees for this act of tenderness. He promised he would attempt it, and withdrew; but in a few minutes returned and told me it was impossible. I then thought I had been deficient in my offer, and promised him two thousand. He withdrew a second time, but returned soon, and (with I believe much real pity and concern) told me it was not practicable; that it could not be done but by the Suba's order, and that no one dared awake him.

After 9 p.m., he writes, the situation had become even more unbearable, with thirst taking over. The old guard took pity again, and asked for some water to be brought in skins. The only way it could be delivered was through the bars. It triggered a madness.

> Oh! my dear Sir, how shall I give you a conception of what I felt at the cries and ravings of those in the remoter parts

of the prison, who could not entertain a probable hope of obtaining a drop, yet could not divert themselves of expectation, however unavailing! And others calling on me by the tender considerations of friendship and affection, and who knew they were really dear to me. Think, if possible, what my heart must have suffered at seeing and hearing their distress, without having it in my power to relieve them; for the confusion now became general and horrid. Several quitted the other window (the only chance they had for life) to force their way to the water, and the throng and press upon the window was beyond bearing; many forcing their passage from the further part of the room, pressed down those in their way who had less strength, and trampled them to death.

Holwell meanwhile kept time. He writes that by a half past eleven, desperation descended to the next level of hell. He confesses to drinking his own urine to quench thirst, but preferred instead the taste of sweat ('...whereas no Bristol water could be more soft or pleasant than what arose from perspiration.')

They all now found that water, instead of relieving, rather heightened their uneasiness; and, 'Air, air,' was the general cry. Every insult that could be devised against the guard, all the opprobrious names and abuse that the Suba, Monick Chand, &c. could be loaded with, were repeated to provoke the guard to fire upon us, every man that could, rushing tumultuously towards the windows with eager hopes of meeting the first shot. Then a general prayer to heaven, to hasten the approach of the flames to the right and left of us, and put a period to our misery. But these failing, they whose strength and spirits were quite exhausted laid themselves down and expired quietly upon their fellows...

Holwell writes that he survived on the kindness of others, who made place for him for a little more air.

When the day broke and the gentlemen found that no entreaties could prevail to get the door opened, it occurred to one of them, (I think to Mr. Secretary Cooke) to make a search for me, in hopes I might have influence enough to gain a release from this scene of misery. Accordingly Messrs. Lushington and Walcot undertook the search, and by my shirt discovered me under the dead upon the platform [there was a slim platform that ran the length of the cell]. They took me from thence, and, imagining I had some signs of life, brought me towards the window I had first possession of.

But as life was equally dear to every man, (and the stench arising from the dead bodies was grown intolerable) no one could give up his station in or near the window: so they were obliged to carry me back again. But soon after Captain Mills (now Captain of the Company's yacht) who was in possession of a seat in the window, had the humanity to offer to resign it. I was again brought by the same gentlemen and placed in the window.

By six in the morning, with Siraj awake and made aware of the situation, the nightmare ended for those who survived it.

◆

In this account Ahmad, like some others, homes in on Holwell's accusation that the merchant Umachand was behind it all, in particular his continued incarceration. It was an act of revenge for Holwell not releasing Umachand from his arrest at the fort. (And here Holwell repeats again an accusation that Siraj was somehow directly responsible for the whole thing—another reversal of his stand.)

> My being treated with this severity, I have sufficient reason to affirm, proceeded from the following causes. The Suba's resentment for my defending the Fort, after the Governor, &c. had abandoned it; his prepossesion touching the treasure; and thirdly, the instigations of Omychund in resentment for my not releasing him out of the prison as soon as I had the command of the Fort, a circumstance, which in the heat and hurry of action, never once occurred to me or I had certainly done it, because I thought his imprisonment unjust. But that the hard treatment I met with may truly be attributed in a great measure to his suggestion and insinuations, I am well assured from the

whole of his subsequent conduct; and this further confirmed to me in the three gentlemen selected to be my companions, against each of whom he had conceived particular resentment; and you know Omychund can never forgive.

'But perhaps Holwell had forgotten all this, when he attended the Select Committee meeting held on the 10th April 1757,' Ahmad notes, as he praised Umachand along with two key players of Plassey, one as a conspirator and commanding officer, the other as a commander, who were present. They noted with relish a significant contribution provided by Umachand in the British capture of Chandannagar in March 1757, on the way to Plassey.

Present:—

Colonel Robert Clive,
Major Kilpatrick,
J. Z. Holwell Esqr.

We the servants of the East India Company should always be grateful to that noble-minded and wealthy merchant of Calcutta, Omichand. It was through his agency that we succeeded to secure the assistance and co-operation of Diwan Nuncoomar, Phoujdar of Hoogly. A body of Subahdar's troops was stationed within the bounds of Chandernagore previously to our attack of that place. These troops belonged to the garrison of Hoogly and were under the command of Diwan Nuncoomar. If these troops were not withdrawn, it would have been highly improbable to gain victory.

Holwell is inconsistent, is the overall message of his critics. The bulk of them portray Holwell as an expedient liar who with his pamphleteering helped the cause of Company and Crown while at the same time glorifying his own role.

But that's a version. Unlike Holwell's versions, but still a version. While it may reclaim some honour for Siraj, Plassey was always about a lot more than amplified justification for revenge for the Black Hole incident. Even Holwell's revenge.

11

MAYBE A MATTER OF MONEY

*'...the greatest moral certainty that the Nabob never
intended to drive the English out...'*

Siraj turned belligerent towards the companies of other Europeans
after seizing Calcutta which he renamed Alinagar in the memory of
his grandfather. Law maintains that as soon the nawab had his victory
there he began to pressure the French in Chandannagar and the Dutch
in Chinsurah. The message was simple: the settlements would have
to fork out 'contributions'—it was Siraj's way of defraying expenses
for his Calcutta foray, among other things—or risk having their flags
taken away and the forts at these places demolished.

From Calcutta he even wrote a threatening parwana dated 22
June 1756 to the Dutch chief, Adriaan Bisdom. It reached the Dutch
a day later.

> Chief of the merchants and harbinger of friendship Adriaan
> Bisdom, Director for the Holland Company, live happy and
> contented!
>
> I have too frequently written to you from Moorshedabad
> that you were to join your power to the King's army for the
> destruction of the wicked English by water, though your not
> doing so is of no account whatever, and you were asked only
> to put you to the test, for by God's blessing and help I am
> so strongly provided that I find myself able to exterminate
> ten such nations as these English, and if you wish to ensure
> the continuation of the Company's trade in this country, you
> will have to act in accordance with what I caused to be made
> known to you through my friend Faggeruttojaar [fakhr-ul-tujjar,
> chief or pride of merchants], Choja Mhameth Wajed [Khwaja
> Mohammed Wajed—the Armenian Khwaja Wajid]; but in
> the contrary case, it will be all over with your trade in this

Soubaship, which is a true warning concerning which you must know your own mind.

Siraj left Calcutta for Murshidabad on 11 July, leaving Manikchand in charge of Calcutta, and a force estimated at between 8,000 to 9,000 foot-soldiers, and 5,000 cavalry. Manikchand, formerly diwan to the Raja of Bardhaman, was according to the *Siyar*, 'presumptuous, arrogant, destitute of capacity, and wholly without courage'. The *Siyar* maintains that his cowardice was already proven when he abandoned Alivardi when that nawab was set upon by Maratha marauders near Bardhaman. In any case, Siraj's choice of Manikchand to oversee Calcutta appears to have been a point of disappointment for other commanders, including Mir Jafar and two other senior commanders.

Siraj had compelled the French to pay him 350,000 rupees and the Dutch, 450,000 rupees as levy, a matter that didn't particularly endear him to these European merchants along the Hugli. But the fact that he left the settlements untouched interests those such as Hill. He is also surprised that Siraj for all his belligerence over fortifications constructed by the English in Calcutta, didn't bother to raze them—or fill the Maratha Ditch, for instance. Perhaps it was because he had made his point. Perhaps he didn't expect to cede control soon, and thought these tactically advantageous.

Perhaps—and Hill uses this instance to further buttress the point—all Siraj really needed was diplomatic handling. 'This proves that if the English had shown the humility and readiness to contribute which he desired, he would have left them in peace at the first, or, after the capture of Calcutta, have permitted them to resettle there without further disturbance.' Basically, it was all about a show of authority which turned into an opportunity for 'satisfying his greed'. His already vast wealth was of no consequence in this regard, maintain both Law and Hill. Much like his grandfather, Siraj squeezed whomsoever he could, and the European trading companies in particular, believing they had 'inexhaustible' wealth.

This point escapes the *Siyar* and other critics of Siraj. According to the *Siyar*, Siraj was so incompetent and monomaniacal that he embarked on the expedition to Calcutta 'of his own contriving, and without consulting anyone'. In their view, it was an expedition that could have entirely been avoided had more circumspect and mature minds prevailed.

After all, the matter with Drake could have been easily sorted out, 'this dispute with the English might have been terminated by a few words in a conference, by the least of his Ministers and Commanders, without it becoming necessary to recur to force and to war', and the 'guilty race' of Alivardi 'should be deprived of an Empire'.

Perhaps Tabatabayi was unable to reflect the views of the communique by Watts and his colleague Collet to the Court of Directors in London, in which they castigated their colleagues in Calcutta, while offering a defence of their own conduct in Qasimbazar. (Drake and the Calcutta Council had, meanwhile, severely reprimanded them, perhaps to minimize their own deficiencies.) The letter is dated 16 July 1756, and was written at Chandannagar—the location yet another instance of the French, although studiously neutral, offering refuge to the British. (So did the Dutch: indeed, Hill notes that the Dutch chief's house had so many European refugees from Calcutta his wife took to sleeping on a bajra, or bojrā, a kind of houseboat, on the Hugli.)

Watts and Collet wrote of how Siraj could have perhaps been mollified with money:

> We are persuaded this dismal catastrophey of Your Honours' estate in Bengal being plundered, your Settlements lost, your servants destroyed and ruined with some hundred thousands of Calcutta inhabitants might have been prevented had the Governour and Council thought proper to have compromised matters for a sum of money. And as a proof, the Nabob touched nothing at Cossimbuzar but the warlike stores or at any of the other factorys or aurungs till he had taken Calcutta.

They mentioned that Rai Durlabh, who commanded the 'van' of Siraj's forces, frequently asked to see Watts when he was a prisoner in the Bengal camp. 'Smiling', he told Watts the Company would need to pay up 'a crore of rupees'. When told the Company's 'whole estate' didn't match that figure, the demand dropped from ten million rupees to two million rupees. Watts again begged off. 'The duan then desired to know what they could afford to pay,' to which Watts replied saying he would need to first consult with the Council in Calcutta—so could he please be permitted to write? Rai Durlabh denied this request, but instead suggested that, should the Council reach out first with any 'proposals of accommodation', Watts could write to Calcutta as often as he pleased.

As it turned out, the letter from Watts and Collet mentioned they had no opportunity to write or make any kind of contact until they had arrived near the settlement of Hugli, 'where we got permission to write to the Dutch Director for some provisions, to whom we sent a letter to be forwarded to Calcutta wherein we wrote that if the Governour and Council would send a proper person to the camp or empower us to act, we flattered ourselves that even then the dispute with the Nabob might be finished for a sum of money.' They claimed that the chief of the Dutch settlement assured them the letter was delivered to Drake along with a letter of his own, the import of which was that after the 'disgrace the Company had suffered at Cossimbuzar by the taking of their factory and imprisoning their servants, they were resolved not to come to any agreement' with the Company. The Dutch wouldn't take the risk of antagonizing Siraj by being seen to aid the Company. The English were on their own.

Watts and Collet also backed up their claim of 'the greatest moral certainty that the Nabob never intended to drive the English out of his province but would have been satisfied with a sum of money' by invoking the unsalutary experience of Khwaja Wajid:

> Coja Wazeed, a considerable merchant and one who has great influence with the Nabob, his duan also told us that he was sent by his master four times to Calcutta to persuade the gentlemen to pay a sum of money and pacify the Nabob, but without effect, and the last time was threatened to be used ill if he came again on the same errand...

Watts and Collet insisted that if indeed more proof was required one could easily see Siraj's treatment of the French and Dutch as corroboration. They were both ordered to pay up two million rupees each after Siraj's taking of Calcutta. But the French and the Dutch protested, saying they simply couldn't afford the sum but were instead willing to pay a generous amount on the lines of a nazar, a gift, usually made when a nawab took the masnad, for instance. Siraj was greatly angered with the response, but was finally calmed with a much lesser amount than he originally demanded:

> ...he appeared so incensed that he ordered ten thousand men into the Dutch Town with directions to demolish and plunder the houses and people on the first signal. He then demanded their guns, ammunition and colours but was at last pacifyed with a present of four hundred and fifty thousand sicca rupees. The French were threatened and treated much in the same manner, and were obliged to pay three hundred thousand siccas; this account we can affirm to be true as we had it from the gentlemen themselves.

◆

Whatever the *Siyar's* bias against Siraj, it's difficult to ignore its repeated assertion that the young nawab, whether on account of his immaturity, impetuosity, or cussedness, decided to disdain, attack and, if need be, demolish Murshidabad's entrenched elite—indeed, Bengal's entrenched elite. His victory at Calcutta and subsequent victory over his cousin, Shaukat Jang, of which more shortly, appears to have cemented this attitude.

Such elites, maintains the *Siyar,* continued to be shocked by what they perceived as his impoliteness, aided by the 'insolence' of the 'upstarts that had taken possession of his mind'. There was also the young nawab's propensity 'not to ask any one's opinion,' (although he did appear to consult those he trusted). For their part, the elite held back their distress as well as their counsel, in most affairs adopting a posture of diplomatic aloofness, and were 'in general ill-intentioned', wishing 'miscarriage' of policy and orders, 'as well as their Ruler's downfall'.

'He was so ignorant of the world, and incapable to take a reasonable party,' the *Siyar* tells us, 'being totally destitute of sense and penetration, and yet having a head so obscured by the smoke of ignorance, and so giddy and intoxicated with the fumes of youth and power and dominion, that he knew no distinction betwixt good and bad, nor betwixt vice and virtue.'

With this, and Siraj's penchant for confiscating the wealth of those he disliked or thought dangerous—the incident with Ghaseti Begum again assumes importance—all the young nawab really earned by the barrelful was bad blood. Such ill-will fed and fattened conspiracies.

'Was it possible for such a man to keep his throne?' the Frenchman Law asks rhetorically.

In his memoirs, he writes that when Siraj was formally granted a farman by the Mughal emperor to be lord of the three subahs of Bengal, Bihar, and Orissa, Europeans were 'forced' to assume that it must have been on account of some 'great virtue' that balanced his 'vices'. But the 'young giddy-pate', as Siraj is described by Hill, was quickly seen by his critics as having 'no talent for government except that of making himself feared,' and so 'every one longed for a change,' to be rid of what they saw as this most 'cowardly' of men.

Law goes as far as to suggest that the change ought to have been effected straightaway, before Siraj could settle down. It would have brought 'happiness and tranquillity' for Bengal and would have in general been good all around. The Dutch could have been roped in for such a project, and it may have saved them misfortunes 'which have since happened to us'. He, of course, meant the British, who with their belligerence against Siraj had such an impact that they became de facto overlords, the wealthy-beyond-belief puppetmasters of Bengal, and all other European powers lost significance in Bengal and, in quick order, eastern India.

Law mused:

Three or four hundred Europeans and a few sepoys would have done the business. If we could have joined this force to the enemies of Siraj-ud-daula we should have placed on the throne another Nawab—not, indeed, one wholly to our taste, but, not to worry about trifles, one to the liking of the house of Jagat Seth, and the chief Moors and Rajas. I am sure such a Nawab would have kept his throne. The English would have been re-established peaceably, they would certainly have received some compensation, and would have had to be satisfied whether they liked it or not. The neutrality of the Ganges assured, at least to the same extent as in the time of Aliverdi Khan, the English would have been prevented from invading Bengal, and from sending thither the reinforcements which had contributed so much to their success on the Madras Coast. All this depended on us, but how could we foresee the succession of events which has been as contrary to us as it has been favourable to the English?

Neither did Siraj. That much is certain—at least, not to the extent the British blowback demolished his rule and utterly destroyed him. It remains a monumental what-if.

◆

It became clear that, with the French and the Dutch—the other significant European player in eastern India at this time—out of the equation for any logistics or military support against Siraj, the Company was left to its own devices. Any pushback to recover ground in Calcutta and Bengal would depend on what colleagues in Madras, Bombay, the board of directors in London, and the British government were to decide. The Mughal emperor in Delhi, Alamgir II, who ruled in the Plassey years (from June 1754 to 1759) was little more than a cipher for his vazir, Imad-ul-Mulk, with whom both Siraj and his cousin Shaukat Jang were currying favour. In any case, Delhi was worth little more than the emperor's seal by now, the empire's power, as we have seen, visibly eroded across the subcontinent: it mattered little as to who controlled which part of India away from Delhi, so far had the regions travelled from the Mughal matrix.

As it happened, a series of fortunate events would begin to coalesce for the Company in India. Rear Admiral Charles Watson had arrived in Bombay in November 1755 at the head of a fleet designed to safeguard Britain's subcontinental interests. Concerns over increasing conflicts such as the wars in the Carnatic, and the political atmosphere in Europe that made a continental war imminent—with the danger of it spilling over in South Asia—were the key imperatives. Within months of his arrival the admiral joined his colleagues from the navy, the Company's army, and the Maratha government of the Peshwa Balaji Bajirao to take on the forces of the rebel Maratha admiral Tulaji Angre, whom some Western records refer to as Angria, like his vaunted predecessor Kanhoji Angre, over January and February 1756.

Clive had returned to India for the second time after three

years at home. He was already a bonafide hero in England. The clerk who escaped the siege of Fort St George that presaged the Battle of Mylapore, and later displayed heroics against the French at the siege of Fort St David at Cuddalore in early 1748 to earn a commission in the Company's army as an ensign (he had impressed the commander of British forces in Madras, Stringer Lawrence), had emphatically become what might be described as a merchant-militarist. In September 1751, Clive only twenty-six and now a lieutenant, displayed great resoluteness (after a few months of rest and recuperation in Bengal to recover from nervous exhaustion) to first take the fort of Arcot and then defend it against a siege led by the far larger forces of Chanda Sahib, a sometime ruler of Tanjore and now a contender to rule the Carnatic, and his French allies—with the governor of Pondicherry, Dupleix, pulling the strings. The young lieutenant effected what would become his tactical hallmark, a surprise attack at night or early morning, and panicked his enemies into fleeing. They regrouped, and then Clive led his smaller number of men into defending the fort for several weeks.

When Clive returned to India in July 1755 it was as Lieutenant Colonel Clive, and the designated governor of Fort St David. His reputation was further enhanced by his participation with Admiral Watson in the battle against Tulaji and his forces at the fort of Gheria (Vijaydurg, a four-hour drive north of Goa). Clive led the troops while the admiral oversaw the cannonading of the fort, an approach they would later employ in their recapture of Calcutta in January 1757 and the demolition of Chandannagar in March that year. As we shall see, the admiral and the colonel would, within weeks of news of the loss of Calcutta, be formally tasked by the Council at Fort St George in Madras to travel up the coast to relieve the destitute at Falta and recover Calcutta.

Meanwhile, however, life at Falta was harsh. Lived largely onboard various ships and vessels that had escaped Calcutta, it was abject. Long writes about it as being along Falta's 'pestiferous' shores.

Not that Calcutta was any less pestiferous. In August 1757, just weeks after Plassey, Clive would write to the Court that the 'unhealthiness' of Calcutta at that time of the year had compelled him to station most of his force away from the city as 'the lives of men are very precious at this critical juncture'. Long writes of Calcutta in autumn as being a 'second Batavia, the Golgotha of India'. (There's even a letter between French officials that describes Siraj's conquest of Calcutta as: 'The factory at Golgotha held out for three days only.') It was a place of raging fevers and le mort de chien—cholera—made worse by awful sanitation, the neighbouring 'Chowringee jungle' and the reeking mudbanks of the Hugli. Orders would go out for better sanitation, and to cut trees with the exception of fruit trees.

But there was infrastructure, after a fashion, in Calcutta. Falta had none and illness and death were rampant. Provisions were supplied at some risk to those who had benefited from the Company, like Nabakrishna—as Long writes, 'the Nawab prohibited under penalty of death any one supplying the English'. Such loyalty to the Company would, as we shall see, hold Nabakrishna in excellent stead.

The exiled government of Calcutta was onboard too. Detailed records were maintained of both death, life and whatever passed for lifestyle. When it all ended, and Calcutta recovered, the Council would, like employees of any company, consider the expenses of that exile. The proceedings of 14 February 1757 record a few such, broken down into the denominations of rupee, paisa and anna:

Captain Peter Dickson delivers in the following accounts, viz.:—

1 Bill for allowances for the inhabitants on board from 1st October to 31st December at Rs. 50 per mensem each, amounting to Rs. 1,708-5-3.

1 ditto for diet expenses of the inhabitants on board for part of the month of September, amount Rs. 142-0-0.

Mr. Colin Campbell likewise delivers in the following accounts, viz.

Expenses of the sloop Dragon from 26th July to 16th December 1756, amount Rs. 742-0-8.

1 Bill for wages as Commander of sloop Dragon from 6th June to 6th December at Rs. 75 per month, amount Rs. 450-0-0.

1 ditto for diet expenses of the inhabitants on board from 26th July to 26th September, amount Rs. 364-0-0.

Dr. George Gray sends in a note for wine, &c., for the use of the sick, amount Rs. 336-0-0.

While all this was going on, the Council met regularly and kept up a constant correspondence with colleagues in exile in Chandannagar, or those under the watchful eye of the court in Murshidabad, like young Warren Hastings, or in faraway Madras, where several messages were sent offering explanations for the disaster, and desperate requests to reverse that disaster.

Within two months of the defeat at Calcutta and the Black Hole incident, on 22 August 1756, Consultations held aboard the *Phoenix*, a schooner, by the Bengal Council recorded the following observations. It included a letter of outreach to Siraj, as surprising as that may appear, while at the same time noting that outreach must be conducted with several other officials—including eventual Plassey conspirators and commanders—and observations that ammunition, weapons, and men would soon be on their way from Madras. It was all very businesslike, just as Siraj's destruction would be:

At a Committee, present—

The Hon'ble Roger Drake, Esq.
William Watts, Esq.
Major James Kilpatrick.
John Zephaniah Holwell, Esq.

Met by appointment of the Board for the better despatch of affairs of the country and for the receiving of intelligence and advice.

The Honorable George Pigot, Esq., and Council at Fort Saint George in their general letter of the 7th instant received the information that they had sent down by the Sea Horse sloop, Captain Oliphant, 120 barrels of ammunition, and that Admiral Watson has consented to the sending down His Majesty's ship the Bridgewater, which would be despatched in a few days with further supplies of men and ammunition.

Major Kilpatrick on the 15th instant wrote a complimentary letter to the Nabob Surajed Dowla complaining a little of the hard usage of the English Honorable Company, assuring him of his good intentions notwithstanding what had happened, and begging in the mean time, till things were cleared up, that he would treat him at least as a friend, and give orders that our people may be supplied with provisions in a full and friendly manner. This letter to the Nabob he enclosed to Mr. Bisdom, the Dutch Governor, to have it translated into, Persian, but Mr. Bisdom in his answer excuses himself, and advises him to send it up to Mr. Warren Hastings at Cassimbazar, assuring him at the same time in the genteelest and strongest manner that he might command him in every thing unless where his honorable master's interest interfered.

The Consultations also noted an offer of help Major Killpatrick received from the merchant Umachand—'assuring him of his good intentions and of the desire he had to serve him'—which letter he sent down by Khwaja Petrus Arathoon, another prominent Armenian merchant who helped the exiles (he was usually referred to as 'Coja Petross' and sometimes as 'Armenian Petrus'); and Abraham Jacobs, a Jewish merchant, an agent of the Company and another provider to the exiles.

> These people promise great things from Omichand as greatly in the interest of the Honorable Company, and advise the Major to write complimentary letters to Raja Manick Chand, Juggerseat, Coja Wazed and Raja Dewlap [Rai Durlabh], which letters Omichand would get rendered into Persian and delivered with the originals.

The executives and officers of the Company proved unusually resilient and were impressive in their ability to clinically think matters through when the Bengal enterprise was in great jeopardy. The meetings and consultations at this time of exile, largely on the *Phoenix*, provide an insight into how the British analysed and prepared their response to the immense political churn that was taking place.

For instance, take this meeting aboard the *Phoenix* a little over a week later, on 31 August 1756, that decided to deepen the intelligence network to keep track of developments concerning Siraj's forces in and around Calcutta—which were already expecting a pushback led by the British navy—matters in Murshidabad, and with other European companies:

Mr. Robert Gregory to Major Kilpatrick from Chinsura of the 19th instant received the 24th advices that oft the 17th at Calcutta they [Siraj's forces] had received a reinforcement of 300 horse; that they were daily sending up goods and money from thence to Chinsura being under great apprehensions from the expected men-of-war, and that Manick Chand had expressly wrote to the Dutch Governor but the night before to supply the English with no manner of provisions or ammunition, severely threatening him if he did.

Advices received of the 26th from the same gentleman at Chinsura of the 23rd mention that boats were getting ready to fall down upon our fleet and set it on fire: that Manick Chand was going down to Bugee-Bugee [Budge-Budge, between Calcutta and Falta], from whence he intended to surprise us: that he always kept three fishing boats in sight of the fleet to observe our motions, and that it was there reported that he had sent down Mr. Mackcett's banian as a spy.

And yet, Long observes, Manikchand was at this time in friendly correspondence with the English. And, like the merchant Umachand, he 'negotiated at this time between the Nawab and the English... understanding how to run with the hare and keep with the hound'. The meeting continued its observations:

A letter received this day from Mr. Gregory of the 28th mentions that the Nabob had sent to the Dutch to take off his hands all the effects he had plundered from the English, which they say they have wrote to be excused in, but that they fear he will compel them to it.

Agreed that Mr. William Forth, be appointed also to procure intelligence among the Dutch and French, and to transmit the same by every opportunity, and that Mr. Warren Hastings at Cassimbazar be directed to remain there in order to observe their motions at Muxadavad, and learn as far as he is able what they are doing there, documents of which he will transmit to the Major [Killpatrick] by every opportunity or by express.

Within the week, on 5 September, the Consultations noted a

breakthrough in communications, and a softening of the stand by Manikchand, which mirrors Long's assertion, and suggests high-powered back-channel negotiations—and confirms it. There is also the record of a matter of immense significance. As the British stewed in Falta, Shaukat Jang, Siraj's cousin and the nawab of Purnea, appeared to be on the warpath again, carried along by his own ambition and strategic direction from Murshidabad's conspirators. The meeting recorded the crucial reason for Jagat Seth Madhab Rai's displeasure against Siraj: a demand to raise thirty million rupees. The military elite, including Mir Jafar, stood by the banker after Siraj, in perhaps his greatest act of folly, publicly slapped the Jagat Seth. The meeting also noted how precarious the Company's reach was at this time, and how delicate a public relations outreach in Murshidabad might need to be. The parentheses in these minutes are Long's:

> Omichand writes (through Coja Petros and Abraham Jacobs) he did not think it right to forward the letters for Juggerseat, Rajah Dewlap and Coja Wazed which he therefore returned. The bearers (Omichand's messengers) further observed that some small presents of cutlery and chintz from the Major (Killpatrick) would be both very useful and acceptable to people it was necessary to employ...

A letter arrived the same day for the major, who had clearly taken on the role of coordinator for the Falta exiles, from Manikchand, Siraj's governor in Calcutta. The letter was written on 2 September from Alinagar, the renamed Calcutta, and contained 'many complaints' and 'the strongest assurance of his assistance'. This remarkable crack in Siraj's political bastion in the afterglow of his greatest triumph—driven perhaps by a sense of doom on the part of Manikchand of both the inevitable fightback by the Company or the success of conspirators in Murshidabad—carried an offer of help for the exiles. 'He sent at the same time a boat with a dustick,' notes the Consultations, 'with orders for the opening a bazar and for the supplying us with provisions of all kinds'. As we have seen, Siraj had specifically forbidden any interaction with the British ousted from Calcutta, or for anyone to sell them food or any other provision.

A day earlier, word had also arrived from Bisdom, the Dutch

chief at Qasimbazar, conveyed through a Company intermediary. The information was of 31 August and suggested more cracks in the bastion: Shaukat Jang was on the warpath against his cousin, and, by Bisdom's word, Siraj's insistence on funds and his public humiliation of the Jagat Seth had now ensured the banker had become a formidable enemy:

> ...[Bisdom] is informed that the Nabob of Pyrnea was appointed by the King, Nabob of Bengal; that he was joined by another considerable Raja, and that he had begun hostilities and taken about 200 boats; that upon news of this Surajed Dowla had ordered Jaffer Alii Cawn and other principal officers to march with a force to oppose him, which they did, but returned on the 29th on account of a dispute between the Nabob and Juggerseat, in which the former reproached the latter for not getting a phirmaund and then ordered him to raise from the merchants three crore of rupees, but Juggerseat pleading the hardships of his already oppressed people received a blow on the face and was confined. Jaffer Alli Cawn [Mir Jafar] returning upon this went with other principal officers and insisted on Juggerseat being set at liberty but were refused, on which they declared that they would not draw their swords in his service till he should be appointed Nabob by the King.

This amounted to open defiance of Siraj's authority. And, if Bisdom's communication is taken at face value, the 'principal officers' also insultingly reminded Siraj that the Mughal emperor had not formally recognized him as subahdar. His cousin Shaukat Jang had that privilege.

That battle line was clearly drawn, and preparations were being made for a campaign against Shaukat Jang. A thousand of Siraj's forces had already been asked to move north to Murshidabad. Warren Hastings, then a junior Company official in Qasimbazar, had separately confirmed that preparations were on:

> Mr. Warren Hastings writes from Cassimbazar that great preparations were there making for a war with Shocut Jung, the Nabob of Pyrnea, who has had the Nabobship of Bengal, Bahar, and Orissa, conferred upon him by the King of Dily,

whose eldest son is appointed Subah of the province; that Sajatel Mulhut has sent 6,000 horse to his assistance and the most of the Rajas near Pyrnea were in the same interest, having deserted Sorajed Dowla.

◆

As Siraj focused on pouring his rage on the Company, Shaukat Jang, the nawab of Purnea, who had bought reprieve and time in May 1756 with a letter of submission, had focused on procuring a farman from the emperor in Delhi to legitimize his claim. Some future Plassey conspirators also worked to incite Shaukat Jang to again invade Murshidabad.

Meanwhile Shaukat Jang had procured the farman through vazir Imad-ul-Mulk's blessings—and by extension, that of the Mughal emperor Alamgir II. 'He soon obtained from thence leave to take possession of the three provinces governed by Seradj-ed-döulah, under condition of sending to the Presence the latter's confiscation, and of forwarding regularly an annual tribute of one coror [crore, or ten million] of rupees,' the *Siyar* notes. Just how much this incensed Siraj is indicated in the Company's Consultations, as we just read: upon his return to Murshidabad he practically held the Jagat Seth responsible for it.

Transaction sealed, the royal order received, Shaukat Jang planned to march against his cousin even though his own army of regulars and mercenaries was in some turmoil. Like Siraj, he had succeeded in upsetting key commanders including a few who had deserted Siraj. Some of the provocations were petty such as the nawab insisting upon being addressed as Alampanah, protector of the world, instead of the usual 'Nawab namdar, selamat'—renowned nawab, greetings. The *Siyar*'s translator, Haji Mutapha, claims that Shaukat Jang sent the vazir a letter requesting that he be addressed as Alampanah in all future correspondence ('...I hope that you shall condescend to make use of it, in writing to me.'). He made sure to have the request underscored with a nazar of eleven ashrafis, gold coins. He stressed the seriousness of the matter by telling two of his 'protectors' at court, that 'whoever should use any other title than that, would receive no answer, and would have his letter torn to shreds.'

But Shaukat Jang was nevertheless an alternative to Siraj, and that alone appeared to be attractive to Bengal's deep state, as it were.

In a play that sought to hedge bets, the Company decided to reach out to Shaukat Jang, the first formal move towards a planned coup against Siraj. This took place several months before the Plassey conspiracy was signed, sealed, and quickly delivered. The decision was taken on 15 September 1756 during consultations on board the sloop *Grampus* at Falta:

> The Board agreed to send a letter in Persian to the Pyrnea Nabob with presents, hoping he might defeat Surajed Dowla. Warren Hastings writes, 'the English at the Court of Moorshedabad were never mentioned there but; with pity or contempt.'

The Calcutta Council also began to fancy its chances of retaking Calcutta with a steady stream of information from various sources about the situation in the city. As we have already seen, about a thousand of Siraj's troops were pulled out of Calcutta for a possible campaign against Shaukat Jang. On 20 September, consultations at Falta took note of a report of four days earlier from a Padre Bento at Chinsurah. The padre related what he had observed during his stay at Calcutta for most of August. There were '1,000 or 1,500 sepoys and that they had mounted most of the Honorable Company's cannon on the battery facing the river for which they had made new carriages, very bad and unfit for service; that there were few guns mounted on the bastions and none on the curtain' facing the town.

The padre later learned that the numbers were more like one thousand in Calcutta's garrison. He reported that at Tanna Fort there were '200 men, 11 guns, four 2-pounders, one 24-pounder, and six more unfit for service; with only four Portuguese gunners'. Elsewhere too, the numbers masked a certain hollowness: '...that at Bujee-Bujee [Budge-Budge] there were 800 men, about 20 good guns and 50 or 60 Portuguese little better than coolies: that at Hughly there are 500 men, of which 40 are in the fort, the rest being quartered on the gunge, a place a little above Bandel; they have there also ten unserviceable guns and some old Portuguese gunners. He further adds that the sponges for the guns [cannon] were that day sent up to Muxadavad and that the four forts seemed all ready to run away upon the first alarm.'

There was some anger too, at Siraj rubbing salt in a gaping Company wound:

> This day received a letter from Mr. Hastings of the 13th instant wherein he says that they were making an outcry of the furniture of our factory [at Qasimbazar], which was bought up by the Armenians and others; that the Nabob, to engage the Dutch and French to purchase also, had put peons upon their factories and threatened their Vaquills with the chaubuc.

Chabuk. Whip.

On 7 October, the Council was pleased with news of a further chink in Siraj's armour, during a meeting on the *Grampus*: 'Omichand writes from Chinsura that Coja Wazed and other merchants would be glad to see the English return, were it not for fear of the Nabob.' Long notes that, in anticipation of a British fightback, Khwaja Wajid Wazed moved with 'all his women and effects from Calcutta to Tanna Fort, as did several "Moor merchants"'. Evidently, they thought it a safer place than Calcutta even though that small fort was technically in Siraj's control. Umachand moved his family to Chinsurah feeling safer in the redoubt of the Dutch. Even Manikchand, Siraj's appointed governor of Calcutta, was 'afraid to remain at Calcutta'—'they all expected the English soon back'.

Energized, the Council decided to write a letter in Persian to the 'Raja' of Balasore, Mansur Ali, who presided over a crucial gateway to the Hugli on the Bay of Bengal, 'to engage him in the English interest'.

◆

This time Siraj didn't march pre-emptively against Shaukat Jang, but sent an emissary. His demand: hand over the charge of Purnea to his emissary, Rai Rasbihari. By several accounts Shaukat Jang sent back a reply, instead asking Siraj to give up the masnad in his favour. Siraj could then move to Dhaka as his governor—or just retire from public life.

In response, Siraj sent his generals and an army. Mohanlal, a loyalist through to Plassey, along with another unshakeable Siraj-loyalist, the deputy governor at Patna, Ram Narain, and several other loyalist landlords of the region.

The battle took place on 16 October 1756 (the same day Watson and Clive set sail from Madras with reinforcements) at a place a little to the north of Manihari by the Ganga, in present-day Katihar district of Bihar. It began well for Shaukat Jang's forces but went quickly awry. Shaukat Jang, whom some chroniclers credit with more courage than capability, decided to rally his forces for a breakthrough. Shaukat Jang was leading them atop an elephant when he died of a musket-shot to his head. His war was lost.

Siraj's foes, especially the Europeans were sobered by this turn of events. Siraj's fortunes were now clearly ascending. The nawab of Purnea had died rashly against his cousin's more disciplined troops. Siraj's foes lost their momentum and their moment, while Siraj defeated a significant enemy.

The young nawab whom everybody had written off even before his accession as incompetent had, within six months of taking the masnad, first cowed Shaukat Jang, then ejected the British from Calcutta, dominated all other Europeans, and then defeated Shaukat Jang, the claimant of the masnad backed by the emperor's seal. The incident made it clear to his principal foes and European merchants in Bengal, declared Law, 'that the change so much desired could be effected only by the English'.

But they were in Falta, destitute, waiting for deliverance from Madras.

◆

For the British the situation was getting desperate.

On 30 October, the Council at Falta received news from the merchant Abraham Jacob, who had by then taken refuge in Chandannagar, that Manikchand was preparing to march south to Budge-Budge. He had been spooked 'upon news coming to Calcutta of the arrival of an English galley with soldiers, who were immediately landed, and of the flags being hoisted without anybody's being molested...' Manikchand, who had earlier responded to overtures, 'then gave orders for an extraordinary look out and held a Council in which it was determined to send the greatest part of their force to Bujee Bujee with all their horse, who were at least a thousand, where the Raja himself was to go with an intention to surprise us.'

Manikchand and his colleagues were clearly taking no chances. During consultations at Falta on 23 November, the meeting learned of a letter sent to Holwell, courtesy of the Company's intelligence network, as to how the Bengal forces had placed 'four chests of powder' under each bastion. There were also plans to sink two vessels on the Hugli off Tanna. The channel there was narrow. Another communication, a contradictory one as Long notes, advised that at Calcutta they were 'in the greatest tranquillity, everybody imagining that a treaty with the English was on the carpet, and that all differences would soon be made up'.

It was also agreed during the meeting that Major Killpatrick would again write to 'Jujjeseat' [Jagat Seth Madhab Rai]. This outreach was more like a plea: '...to assure him that our dependence was upon him, and upon him alone for the hopes we have of resettling in an amicable manner'.

Fortunately for the British in Calcutta, ever since news of the reverses reached Madras, gears had begun to churn emphatically in that presidency which still held policy sway over Calcutta—and would until the 1770s when the situation was reversed with the great ascendancy of the Company in Bengal.

Help was finally on the way.

◆

Letter from Colonel Clive to his father dated 5 October 1756, Fort St George:

Honoured Sir,—The expedition to Bengal which I am upon the point of undertaking will not allow me to write a long letter.

I hope to write you fully and to your satisfaction by the next conveyance.

I have desired my attorneys to pay you the interest arising from all my moneys in England and the Bishop of Clenforts [Clonfert, in Ireland], annuity which is all in my power at present, having lost over £3,000 on the Doddington and I fear a greater sum at Bengal. This expedition if attended with success may enable me to do great things.

It is by far the grandest of my undertakings. I go with great forces and great authority.

I have desired Mrs. Clive, who has nothing else to do, to write you all particulars and I am with duty to my mother and affection to my brothers and sisters.

Honoured Sir,—Your most dutiful and obedient son, Robert Clive.

The Nawab of Murshidabad's boats on the Ganga. Courtesy: The San Diego Museum of Art.

Coloured engraving of Fort William in Calcutta by Jan Van Ryne, published by Robert Sayer in London in 1754. Courtesy: Rijks Museum.

The coat of arms of the British East India Company. Courtesy: INTERFOTO/Alamy Stock Photo.

The coat of Arms of the French East India Company circa 1600s. Courtesy: Wikimedia Commons.

The capture of the French settlement of Chandernagore (Chandannagar) in Bengal by British forces, March 1757, during the Seven Years War (1756–63). Artist Dominic Serres. Oil on canvas. Courtesy: Wikimedia Commons.

The British settlement of Fort St George at Madras, 1754. Artist Jan Van Ryne. Hand-coloured etching. Courtesy: Wikimedia Commons.

The trading post of the Dutch East India Company in Hugli, Bengal c. 1665. To the left is the Bhagirathi-Hugli. To the right is an encampment with an Indian dignitary in a tent, horses, cows, elephants and camels. Artist Hendrik van Schuylenburgh. Oil on canvas. Courtesy: Rijks Museum.

Equestrian portrait of Aurangzeb (r. 1658–1707), 17th century. Illustrated album leaf. Courtesy: The MET

Emperor Farrukhsiyar (r. 1713–19) bestows a jewel on a nobleman, c. 1713–14. Artist Chitarman II (Kalyan Das-Active at the court of Emperor Muhammad Shah in Delhi, c. 1700–45). Courtesy: The MET.

Murshid Quli Jafar Khan (r. 1717–27), also known as Jaffar Khan Bahadur Nasiri, the first independent nawab of Bengal in the Mughal era. Courtesy Wikimedia Commons.

A painting of Peshwa Balaji Bajirao, Prince of Wales Museum, Mumbai. Courtesy: Redtigerxyz/ Creative Commons.

Nawab Alivardi Khan (r. 1740–56) with his grandson Siraj-ud-daulah sitting opposite his nephew Sayyid Ahmad Khan (Saulat Jang) and two nobles, one possibly Shaukat Jang, Sayyid Ahmad's son. Murshidabad, c. 1756. Courtesy: Wikimedia Commons.

Portrait of Siraj-ud-daulah (r. 1756–57). Courtesy: Wikimedia Commons.

Siraj-ud-daulah with a concubine. Date unknown. Courtesy: Wikimedia Commons.

Lord Robert Clive, Baron of Plassey. Sir Eyre Coote, an officer of His Majesty's 39th
Artist Thomas Gainsborough c. 1764. Regiment of Foot. Courtesy: Wikimedia Commons.
Oil on canvas. Courtesy: National Army
Museum, London.

Joseph François Dupleix, governor general
of the French establishment in India in the
eighteenth century. Courtesy: Wikimedia
Commons.

A French East India Company cannon.
Courtesy: Wikimedia Commons.

RIVER HUGHLEY

to the Eastward

Avenue leading

Plan for the intelligence of the military operations at Calcutta when attacked and taken by Siraj. *Source:* Robert Orme, *A History Of The Military Transactions Of The British Nation In Indostan From The Year MDCCXLV*, Vol. 2, London: Wingrave, 1778.

Plan of the Old fort with the existing buildings in 1903. *Source*: C. R. Wilson (ed.), *Old Fort William in Bengal*, Vol. 1, Published for the Government of India, London: John Murray, 1906.

The Black Hole incident that took place on 20-21 June 1756, during which several dozen Britons and Eurasians were kept in a small cell in Fort William, leading to numerous deaths. Courtesy: Wikimedia Commons.

Robert Clive on the roof of Siraj's hunting lodge at Plassey, examining the enemy lines, 23 June 1757. Artist: Richard Caton Woodville II. Courtesy: The Print Collector/ Getty Images.

Siraj's artillery at Plassey on its movable platform, drawn up against Clive's troops, 23 June 1757. Lithograph by Richard Caton Woodville II, c. 1923. Courtesy: Wikimedia Commons.

A painting depicting the meeting of Mir Jafar and Robert Clive after the Battle of Plassey by Francis Hayman. Oil on canvas, c. 1760. Courtesy: Wikimedia Commons.

On 16 August 1765, Mughal Emperor Shah Alam II signed the Treaty of Allahabad with Robert Clive which awarded the diwani of Bengal to John Company. Courtesy: Wikimedia Commons.

Mir Qasim with a mistress, entertained by musicians and dancers. Watercolour on paper. Courtesy: Wikimedia Commons.

Watercolour of the Nawab Mubarak-ud-daula, or Nazam-ud-daulah (1770–93), with his son Baber Ali Khan in the Nawab's durbar with British Resident, Sir John Hadley. Inscribed on the back in ink and pencil is: 'Nabob's Durbar and reception of the English Resident at Morshedabad'. Courtesy: Wikimedia Commons.

A panoramic painting of the Motijheel Palace, lake, mosques, and tombs c. 1790–1800. Anonymous artist. Inscribed on the back in ink and pencil: Bird's Eye View of Motijeel. Courtesy: Wikimedia Commons.

A tableau of Siraj's army on the march to Plassey, at Motijheel tourist complex, Murshidabad. Courtesy: the author.

Namak Haram Deori, or Traitor's Gate, entrance to the house of Mir Jafar in Murshidabad. Courtesy: the author.

A Maratha temple to Eklingji—Shiva— across the Bhagirathi from Hazarduari Palace, Murshidabad. Courtesy: the author.

A mural commemorating the battle at Plassey railway station. Courtesy: the author.

The House of Jagat Seth, Murshidabad. Courtesy: the author.

Bust of Siraj-ud-daulah on a pedestal, by the Plassey memorial compound. Courtesy: the author.

The statue of Siraj-ud-daulah at Motijheel tourist complex. Courtesy: the author.

The grave of Siraj-ud-daulah at Khosh Bagh, near Murshidabad, where he was buried on 3 July 1757. Courtesy: the author.

The obelisks of three of Siraj's generals—Nauwe Singh Hazari, Bakshi Mir Madan, and Bahadur Ali Khan at Murshidabad, constructed by the Nadia District Citizens' Council over 1972–73. Courtesy: the author.

Plassey battlefield in the present day. Courtesy: the author.

12

WHEN CLIVE (FIRST) FOUGHT SIRAJ

'...former inactivity did not proceed from fear'

On 13 October 1756, a week after Clive wrote to his father, he received formal orders from the Council at Fort St George for his expedition to Bengal. It was signed by the governor of Madras, George Pigot, Clive's military mentor, Stringer Lawrence, his friend and later, Company chronicler, Robert Orme, Henry Powney, William Perceval and Robert Palk.

Rear Admiral Charles Watson of the British Navy, freshly arrived from Bombay, was tasked to lead a squadron of ships, 'judging the re-establishment of the Company's Settlements at Bengal to be of the highest importance to their welfare'. The admiral would also shepherd the Company's ships—*Walpole* and *Marlborough* and the ketch *Boneta*—assigned to the expedition. They would altogether carry 528 European officers and men, '940 sepoys and 160 lascars with twelve field-pieces, one haubitzer [howitzer], and a necessary quantity of ammunition'. Clive would be commander-in-chief of the land forces, as the Council had 'full confidence' in his abilities.

They would in all likelihood meet most of the former Calcutta Council when they reached the Hugli, the two commanders were advised. Five of them, Drake, Colonel Lawrence, Watts, Manningham, and Becher had been made members of a Select Committee 'for the management of all matters relative to the protection or preservation of the Company's estate, rights and privileges'. This committee had in turn been appointed by the 'Secret Committee of the Honourable East India Company'.

Now this Secret Committee had the future charted. It was a stunning example of the Madras-based subcontinental arm of a joint stock company headquartered in a suite of rooms in London's Leadenhall Street directing an expedition of its own forces and that of the British government against the nawab of one of the subcontinent's largest and most prosperous provinces who owed nominal allegiance to one of the greatest empires in the world, crumbling though it was. The course of action was spelled out in a separate letter to the Select Committee that awaited Watson and Clive at Falta, in which the commanders would be able to 'observe our intentions in fitting out this armament, and this letter will serve to guide you in acting up to the spirit of these intentions'.

Essentially, a treaty would need to be signed with Siraj to the best advantage of the Company, and, if required, the threat of arms would freely be used to ensure Siraj signed that treaty:

> Conformably to these intentions we have desired the gentlemen of the Select Committee appointed as before mentioned to form and deliver you a plan of such treaty, as they would recommend to be made for the best advantage of the Company with the Nabob of Bengal, and likewise a plan of such military operations, as they shall judge to be most likely to compel the Nabob to consent to the terms of the said treaty. They will probably desire your presence at their Councils. We need not recommend to you to assist them with your best advice, and we most earnestly require you to endeavour to preserve a good harmony throughout.

In other words, the admiral and the lieutenant colonel had been instructed to politely listen to whatever the Select Committee in Bengal had to say, but, if they felt such suggestions were impractical and slow, they could simply override the committee:

> If any part of the plans you shall receive from the gentlemen before mentioned shall appear to you not to lead by the most speedy and effecatious [sic] way to obtaining the hoped for advantages to the Company you will explain particularly your sentiments to those gentlemen, pointing out to them such alteration as you think will better answer the purposed end, in which alteration we flatter ourselves they then will concur. If not, you are empowered, and we do hereby empower you, to pursue such measures as you shall judge most conducive to the Company's benefit...

Clive therefore was authorized to pursue matters according to his own judgement, although he would remain accountable to the Madras Council.

Speed was crucial. The Madras Council expected an update of the situation with France, perhaps a declaration of war. (News would arrive of war with France a few months after the expedition's departure in mid-October. Watson would receive word of the war that had begun in May 1756, on 19 January 1757, when Calcutta was already retaken.) As and when news of the war reached Calcutta, the Madras Council was clear that Clive and most troops would be needed back in Madras for the defence of the Coromandel coast. He would then leave behind the minimum force required for the 'immediate' defence of Calcutta, 'notwithstanding any thing that may be urged to the contrary by the gentlemen of Bengal, for in such circumstances we cannot but regard the certain possession of the Establishments under our authority on this Coast, and in this country, to be an object of too great importance to the Company...'

'Enclosed is a copy of a Council of War, held here by the officers of His Majesty's squadron the 30th September and 2nd October'—the order continued with another order of business: share of plunder— 'concerning the disposal of what may be taken from the Moors, with copies of three letters which passed between Mr. Watson and us on the same subject'. The order spelt out the precise shares of the sea and land forces, and the chain of command in case 'reprizals' were to be ordered.

Clive would need to ensure receipts for all expenses, from allowances to troops, to provisioning for them. There was a sum allowed—'On the ships *Marlborough* and *Walpole* we have laden Arcot rupees 400,000 (two lacks on each ship) consigned to you for the service of the expedition.' He could, of course, ask the Calcutta Council for more funds should he have the 'occasion'. Besides, Clive was always at liberty to ask for more funds from Madras.

He would carry a letter from the president at Madras as well as a letter from Salabat Jang, the nizam of Hyderabad, to be delivered to Siraj at a time he would 'judge most proper'.

And, just for good measure, in case Siraj proved intractable and cussed about benefits due the Company, Clive would also have in his possession an attested copy of the original farman by Farrukhsiyar:

> We deliver you likewise a copy attested by the Caugee [Qazi, chief judge] of Delly of the Mogul's phirmaund to the Company for the possession of their several Settlements, and a book containing a translation not only of the phirmaund, but also of the orders sent from Delly at the same time to the officers of the several subahs, enjoining them to put the Company in possession and permit them to enjoy the priviledges granted by the said phirmaund. By this book you will be particularly informed what the Company have a right to pretend to in the province of Bengal, which will be a great assistance in your negociations with the Nabob. When you return to the Coast you are to leave both the Persian copy and the book of translations in the hands of the Select Committee at Bengal.

◆

It wasn't smooth sailing.

First, a colonel of His Majesty's 39th Regiment of Foot, John Aldercron, refused to answer to Clive. He considered Clive inferior, and irregular. As we have seen, Clive had received a 'King's commission' as a lieutenant colonel of infantry only in 1755 before his return to India. Aldercron was reluctant to hand over control of a part of his troops to Clive, and therefore, cede control of the King's troops to the Company. He was also upset at Clive, a Company man, being given command of all land forces for the Bengal expedition. Indeed, he refused to allow government troops to embark for Calcutta, and insisted on guns and ammunition already loaded to be unloaded. (A detachment of the 39th Foot had already left for Calcutta under the command of Major Killpatrick, but it was intended more as reinforcement than as a liberating force. Calcutta hadn't fallen when they left Madras. This accounted for the presence of Major Killpatrick and his troops of the 39th Foot in the campaign up the Hugli and into Plassey.)

Admiral Watson was content with his joint command of all ships, government and Company, and for them to carry mixed troops. And, as Reid notes, he overcame Aldercron's defiance by smartly insisting the colonel 'release three companies of his regiment to serve on board as marines!' The admiral also readily provided navy ships for this joint venture of the Company and Crown.

On 13 October, a joint fleet of five royal naval ships and five of the Company, began to embark its passengers, battle-cargo, and supplies. A journal of the expedition preserved by a member of Clive's family notes that the 'King's ships' consisted of the *Kent* (carrying 65 king's troops, 77 Company troops, and 59 'sepoys and lascars'), *Cumberland* (97, 150, 67), *Tyger* (56, 146, 70), *Salisbury* (58, 147, 57), and *Bridgwater*, which carried 96 Company troops. The Company ships carried sepoys and lascars: the *Walpole* (413), *Marlborough* (360), *Protector* (132), the snow—also snaw, a two-masted ship with a small 'trysail' or 'snow' behind the mainmast—*Lapwing* (90), and the ketch, *Boneta* (60). Altogether, the fleet carried 276 King's troops, 616 Company troops, and 1,308 sepoys and lascars.

The fleet set off from Madras on 16 October.

And almost immediately sailed into bad weather. Admiral Watson had earlier pressed for a delay of the expedition citing monsoon seas and storms. The fleet was blown off course.

'In this season the only way to get Bengal, is to steer across the bay to the shore of Tannasery and Arracan [Tenasserim and Arakan in Myanmar], along which the currents slacken, and sometimes even tend to the northward,' Orme writes, '...and milder weather than in the middle of the bay enables the vessel to gain the latitude of the sands at the eastern mouths of the Ganges; from whence tides help across to the road of Ballasore, and from hence assure the entrance into the river Hughley.'

By 10 November, Admiral Watson had to give orders to ration food and water. 'Two days later, the fire-ship, unable to stem the violence of the monsoon, bore away to Ceylon; and the *Marlborough*, one of the company's, failing very heavily, was left on the 16th by the rest of the fleet...' The *Marlborough*, with its crucial load of cannon, sailed to Bombay for repairs. The remainder of the fleet arrived in the 'soundings' off Point Palmiras, near a reef close to Balasore Roads by the mouth of the Hugli, on 1 December. 'But the *Cumberland* and *Salisbury* not having kept the wind so well as the others, struck on the dangerous sand which extends several miles from that point out to sea.' Both ships managed to re-float, but strong winds forced the *Cumberland* 'away to Vizagapatam'.

The *Kent* and *Tyger* managed to reach Balasore Roads but they were compelled to wait for 'spring tides' until 9 December when, under the guidance of British pilots who had been on the lookout for the ships, they travelled up the Hugli. The two ships reached Falta on 15 December. The remainder arrived on the 20th, except *Cumberland* and *Marlborough*, whose absence greatly impaired the force of the armament for the *Cumberland* was not only the largest ship in the squadron, but had on board 250 European troops; and the greatest part of the field artillery had been imprudently shipped on board the *Marlborough*.

◆

In the end, the re-taking of Calcutta by Clive & Co. right after New Year's Day 1757 was anti-climactic. Manikchand, whom the *Siyar* described as 'wholly without courage', abandoned Calcutta with all his troops. But he didn't turn tail in the beginning. He briefly got the better of British troops before he literally got the fright of his life.

Soon after arriving at Falta, the letters that Clive had carried from Madras, 'accompanied by one from himself and another from Mr. Watson, full of threats,' relates Orme, 'were sent open to Monickchund, the governor of Calcutta, in order to be forwarded to the Nabob. Monickchund replied that he dared not send letters written in such menacing terms; and on receiving this answer, it was determined to commence hostilities.'

Orme notes that the absence of the troops on board the *Cumberland* was in 'some measure' filled by troops under Major Killpatrick's detachment, and by seventy volunteers, who landed at Falta.

On 27 December, Watson and Clive began the push up the Hugli from Falta. On the 28th they arrived at Mayapur, about 16 kilometres south of Budge-Budge. The plan was to attack Budge-Budge, with ships attacking it from the river, and Clive leading troops overland. The following day at dawn after a sixteen-hour march the troops arrived at the outskirts of the town. They thought they were well-placed in the fields of outlying villages. The fatigued troops settled in to rest in a large hollow—without taking the precaution of posting sentinels.

After about an hour, they came under fire from matchlocks. A section of Manikchand's troops, who had travelled south from Calcutta to bolster Budge-Budge were on the attack. It was all Clive's troops could do to hold on. Several died and many more were injured. Thereafter, cajoling by Clive for a determined push led to a bayonet charge which saw his troops pushing through the villages. Fire from field-pieces added to the retreat of Manikchand's troops, who 'fled as fast as they could to join a large body of horse', as Orme describes it.

This contingent of cavalry, he continues, 'was now discovered advancing from the south towards the hollow; but, on perceiving the fugitives coming from the village, this cavalry halted at a distance of half a mile. On this the English troops, with the field-pieces, formed regularly on the plain, and advanced towards the enemy, who were commanded by Monickchund. They stood several shot from the field-pieces, until one chanced to pass very near the turban of Monickchund, who immediately gave the signal of retreat by turning his elephant, and the whole body marched away to the northeast; and returned to Calcutta.'

The fort fell to the British that night.

It's quite a story even in Plassey's string of interesting stories. Captain Eyre Coote had hoped to lead the battle for the fort—he had even asked Clive for permission, but was denied. At 7 p.m., Clive issued orders to storm the gateway at daybreak under the covering fire of two nine-pounders that had meanwhile been unloaded from the *Kent* at sunset. The attack would be led by 'the King's troops, the Grenadier company, 200 seapoys and 100 seamen'. As it happened, both Clive's plans and Coote's eagerness were upstaged by an ordinary sailor from *Kent*, called Strahan. Coote's incredulity and mild outrage are reflected in his journals:

> ...I then had the command and as my opinion was all day for storming the place, I was in hopes then to have the honour of doing it, but the Colonel sent me word he'd have nothing done till the morning; upon which I went to him to represent how things stood, and that the sailors were all landed, and that our men would suffer from lying out all night; he sent me then

on board the Admiral to know if he would have the sailors sent on board till morning; while I was on board a sailor that was drunk stole away to the fort gate, and fired his pistol and cried out the place was his ['...giving three cheers...' notes Clive's records], upon which the King's [troops], who were next the gate, entered the fort without any opposition; thus the place was taken without the least honour to anyone...

The Bengal troops had melted away at dusk.

Captain Coote did reclaim a little 'honour'. He took command of the fort that night.

As ragged as the Company troops were, Manikchand's experience of the encounter evidently changed the 'contemptible opinion' he harboured of British soldiery, especially after the victory of Calcutta six months earlier. '...and on his return from Buz-buzia to that place he remained there only a few hours,' Orme resumes, 'and leaving 500 men to defend the fort, went away with the rest of his command to Hughley, where having likewise communicated his own terrors, he proceeded to carry them to the Nabob at Muxadavad.'

On 30 December, the fleet travelled upriver from Budge-Budge and anchored at a spot near Tanna Fort on New Year's Day, 1757. Tanna hardly presented a problem. Manikchand's panic had clearly been infectious: the fort was abandoned without a shot being fired, even though the Bengal troops had placed several cannon there.

On the morning of 2 January, Clive landed at Aligarh on the eastern bank of the Hugli, and began a march north to Calcutta with most of the Europeans troops, volunteers and sepoys. By 9 a.m., the *Kent* and *Tyger* had anchored off Fort William, but there was a slight problem: '...for want of wind could not immediately present their broadsides,' Orme relates. That disadvantage made the ships vulnerable to 'brisk' cannonades from Siraj's troops positioned by the river. Nine men died on *Kent,* and seven on board *Tyger.*

The crisis for the British ships was relatively brief as they were able to finally bring their cannon to bear, and opened fire. The intensity of fire from the British ships began to overpower that of the Bengal forces. A little before eleven the remainder of Manikchand's troops deserted Fort William—and, in short order, Calcutta.

Captain Coote led a detachment of troops from the ships into the fort, as Clive and his troops hadn't yet arrived. 'English colours' were hoisted. 'The next day,' writes Orme, 'Admiral Watson put Mr. Drake, and the former members of the council, in possession of the government.'

In a week, Clive & Co. would raid and sack the town of Hugli, removing the last significant outpost of Siraj's forces from the vicinity of Calcutta.

◆

Remarkably, the Calcutta Council was soon back to taking decisions with an eye to the future.

At a meeting on 26 January, only days before a clash with Siraj, it was decided to form a militia under the guidance and charge of Major Killpatrick. Economic activity too was deemed necessary. As the Council noted: 'This being a proper time to encourage the residence of weavers within our bounds, Ordered the Zemindar to advertise that we will protect their possessions and show them favor and encouragement.' A few days earlier, 'Black merchants and other natives' were also allowed back in Company territory, but with provisos. Those who declined to help the Bengal camp during the Company's 'troubles' would be restored their houses and property as is—'found in the place'. But those who neglected to 'secure the outskirts of the town, when they were required to do it, or to lend any assistance in the defence of the place' would forfeit any 'restitution'.

Company servants had to be taken care of, naturally, after several months of exile. A meeting in mid-February would permit a special allowance to non-military personnel:

> The Factory House, Company's house, and all the apartments for the senior and junior servants being entirely destroyed by the Moors, the Board are of opinion that an allowance should be made for the covenanted servants in lieu of habitation and in consideration of the late calamity by which the articles of provisions and other necessaries are grown dearer than formerly, whereby the inhabitants are rendered incapable of subsisting themselves. Agreed the following allowances be made:—

The President ... Rs. 300 per month,
Each Member of Council ... 100
Senior and junior Merchants ... 70
Factors and writers ... 40
to commence from the 1st January 1757

In late-February the Council would even write to the Company's Court of Directors in London about the necessity to send civilians in its service in Bengal to Basra in Iraq to properly learn Persian: 'The great utility of having Europeans skilled in the Persian language we have been more than ever sensible of during the late transactions with the country government.' For such 'transactions', which we shall shortly address in detail, local talent simply wasn't good enough, it was felt, teachers 'not being masters' of this language.

Orientalism and an evolving template for the Indian Civil Service were already on their way. But first there was the matter of the nawab of Bengal, and not only with his language.

◆

News of the attack on Hugli on 10 and 11 January had spurred an 'exasperated' Siraj to move quickly, Orme writes in an unparalleled account of this stage of the conflict. Siraj marched again for Calcutta, bringing with him loyalists as well as disaffected generals and officials like Mir Jafar and Rai Durlabh—by some accounts, to keep them close.

Nearly all historians and chroniclers liberally refer to Orme for descriptions of the battle over Calcutta, as they do for so much of the Carnatic Wars and some aspects of the battle at Plassey. This work is no exception. Although some critics disparage him as a Company historian, Orme's aggregation of information and records, eyewitness accounts of key Company-and-Crown players, and narrative ability remain admirable by any era's yardstick. (Unless otherwise indicated the quoted material in this chapter is from Orme's account.)

Now the Seths and Umachand were both caught in a bind. The situation was delicate. Even as they chafed under Siraj's domination, they couldn't be seen to be against him—certainly to appear as 'friends to the English', as Orme puts it. So, they played the double game. The Seths asked their trusted agent Ranjit Rai to 'attend' Siraj and at the same time, 'ordered him to correspond with Colonel Clive'.

For his part Umachand, both a merchant and wealthy landlord in Calcutta, wanted to recoup his losses on account of the siege of Calcutta the previous June. In order to do so he maintained links with the British, as we have seen, and also found it profitable to travel to visit Murshidabad, where he cosied up to Mohanlal, Siraj's confidante. He managed to regain some of the property confiscated after the siege. Beholden to both Siraj and the Company, he had every interest in 'promoting the pacification'.

Meanwhile, the British, now reinforced and rejuvenated, with Clive and Watson both at hand, prepared for Siraj. A fortified camp was established, with several outposts, a kilometre-and-a-half north of Calcutta, and less than a kilometre inland from the Hugli. The large lake and adjoining marshes to the east of the 'Morattoe' Ditch (eastern suburbs of the present day), ensured that Siraj's army would have to pass this camp. Artillery was boosted by the arrival of the *Marlborough*—the ship that sprang a leak after leaving Madras—which brought several dozen cannon and more troops.

As the British prepared to meet him, one part of Siraj's army began to cross the river north of the destroyed settlement of Hugli on 30 January, while the rest continued south, on the eastern bank. There was some concern among the British that the French would join Siraj as the force on the west bank passed Chandannagar, but the French still maintained the decorum of neutrality of the Ganges, even with news of the war in Europe having reached Bengal. They also declined military assistance to Siraj (a dynamic we shall shortly discuss in the chapter 'The French Connection'). They did this, Orme observes, even though it was certainly in their interest to have done the opposite 'without delay'.

But Clive fretted, as was typical with him in uncertain situations: '...he despaired of victory,' Orme continues. Even with British reinforcements Siraj still had the numbers.

Clive wrote to Siraj the same day proposing peace—an initiative of Ranjit Rai. 'The Nabob answered with expressions of cordiality; but continued his march.'

A flurry of messages continued between the two parties carried, among others, by Khwaja Petrus. There was a brief lull on

2 February as Siraj took stock, and appeared as if he would receive representatives. That went nowhere. On the following morning his van was seen in 'full march' towards Calcutta, framed by the flames of villages it had passed. Then his forces split as they approached the ambush Clive had prepared for them—the fortified camp. One branch took a road on a rise, the other carried on to the corridor British forces had planned. 'Colonel Clive, perhaps not imprudently, unwilling to divide his force, and equally so to break off the negotiation with the Nabob, suffered the troops in sight to pass unmolested,' relates Orme, 'who spread themselves without the Morattoe ditch, and a body of their Louchees, or plunderers, who are armed with clubs, passed into the company's territory about noon, and attacked the houses of the natives in the northern part of the town.' It was similar to the approach of the previous June—the only possible overland approach for attacking Calcutta, with water bodies and marshes to the east and British naval firepower dominating the Hugli. Company forces met them at Perring's redoubt, and in the skirmish that followed, several of the Bengal soldiers were killed and about fifty taken prisoner. This stopped Siraj's attack.

But his army continued to fill the plains north of the city, and to the east and southeast of the British advance camp. It's here that part of Siraj's forces then entrenched itself in a garden. This 'insult' provoked Clive into an attack with a large number of his troops. But the Bengal troops had nine cannon which began their fire. Cavalry lined up on either side of the garden. Clive saw it was 'hazardous' and 'restrained the action to a cannonade'. It continued for an hour. Both sides drew some blood, but Clive withdrew to make his camp before dark.

On the morning of 4 February, the main body of Siraj's troops followed the corridors that the van had taken a day earlier. Siraj himself was still several kilometres to the rear. He sent a letter inviting British representatives for a parley—a gesture the British expected would be made two days earlier—at Nababganj, a village to the north, deep inside the territory his troops controlled. '...Mr. Walsh and Mr. Scrafton were immediately sent,' writes Orme.

When they arrived, however, they discovered Siraj had already moved elsewhere. They followed a stream of his army to finally reach his 'quarters' in the evening to discover that the nawab was much closer than anyone expected: Siraj had set up camp at a garden belonging to Umachand which the 3 February log of Captain Alexander Mcleod, captain of the *Marlborough*, records as 'Hamel Johns Gardens'—within the Company's territory, south of the Maratha Ditch. Siraj had surprised Clive twice in two days.

Orme gives a dramatic account of the moment Walsh and Scrafton were brought to Siraj's camp:

> Here they were introduced by Rungeet Roy to the prime minister Roydoolub, who suspecting that they intended to assassinate the Nabob, desired to examine whether they had pistols concealed, and then insisted that they should quit their swords; but finding that they would not submit to this humiliation, he conducted them to the Durbar, where the Nabob was sitting in full state, accompanied by all his principal officers: many others of inferior degree, such as were of the largest stature, and bore the greatest marks of ferocity in their countenances, had likewise been selected to attend on this occasion; who, to appear still more terrible, were dressed in thick stuffed garments, with enormous turbans, and during the audience sat scowling at the deputies [Walsh and Scrafton], as if they only waited the signal to murder them.

The two envoys pointed out to Siraj that he had entered the Company's territory even as he was 'amusing Colonel Clive with offers of peace'. Orme picks up the story:

> ...after which they delivered a paper containing their proposals, which the Nabob read, and having whispered to some of his officers, desired the deputies to confer with the Duan, and dismissed the assembly. As the deputies were going out, Omichund, who had been present at the audience, advised them to take care of themselves; adding, with a very significant look, that the Nabob's cannon was not yet come up. The deputies suspecting that the Nabob intended to detain them prisoners, ordered their attendants to extinguish their lights; and instead of going to the tent of the Duan, hastened along the high road within the Morattoe ditch to Perring's redoubt, and from thence to the camp.

This decided the matter for Clive. He would attack early next morning, the 5th of February.

◆

So began a strange encounter that would rattle Siraj as no other until the denouement at Plassey.

Six hundred sailors armed with firelocks were landed from the ships at midnight. They joined 650 European troops, a hundred artillery men, and 800 sepoys. They carried half a dozen six-pounder field pieces. They marched three abreast. The sepoys were divided to the front and rear of the column, where the field pieces, artillery men, lascars—Indian ship's crews—and European sailors were. The lascars carried ammunition for the field pieces on their heads, and were guarded by their European colleagues so they wouldn't desert in the dark; other sailors pulled the guns along. Clive positioned himself in the middle of the column.

A section of Siraj's forces, along with Mir Jafar, were within the Maratha Ditch, and a large force was stationed near Umachand's garden to protect Siraj. The remainder were camped in a disorganized manner between the ditch and the lake.

Orme resumes:

A little before the dawn of day, the English line came upon their advanced guards, stationed in the ditches of that part of the high road which leads from the bridge at the head of the lake, to the Morattoe ditch. These guards, after firing their matchlocks, and discharging some rockets, ran away: but one of the rockets striking the cartouch-box of one of the Sepoys, set fire to the charges, which blowing up, communicated the mischief to several others, and the dread of catching this fire threw the whole division into confusion: fortunately none of the enemy were at hand to take advantage of it, and Captain Coote, who marched at the head of the grenadiers, immediately in the rear of the Sepoys, rallied them, and restored the line of march.

It was soon daybreak. And then microclimate intervened: thick fog, common in many places of Bengal at that time of the year, rolled in. The column reached Umachand's garden without incident. Then they heard cavalry at full gallop to their right. The column stopped.

> ...this cavalry was a body of Persians excellently mounted, and
> stationed as an outguard to the Nabob, under that part of the
> Morattoe ditch, which encloses Omichund's garden: they were
> suffered to come within thirty yards before the line gave fire,
> which fell heavy, and killing many of them, the rest instantly
> dispersed in great confusion. The line then proceeded slowly,
> platoons constantly firing on either hand; whilst the field-pieces
> in the rear fired single balls forward, but obliquely outward, on
> each side of the line; but all without any immediate object; for
> the fog prevented any man from seeing beyond the ground on
> which he trod.

That's when chaos struck Clive's troops. About a mile to the south of
the garden was a narrow causeway, raised several feet above adjacent
land, and with ditches on either side. This led east into the area held
by Siraj's forces, and was blocked by them. Clive intended to clear
this obstruction and then return to attack Siraj's camp within the
garden. The column turned east. Only, as the field pieces at the back
of the column were still firing 'obliquely', the fire now tore into this
eastbound line. Several sepoys were killed. While troops at the head
of the line took shelter in the ditches on either side of the causeway,
the troops that followed, unaware of what was happening, kept on
marching. Clive finally managed to regain order when he heard of the
confusion, and brought the troop together 'into one irregular heap'.

Clive waited for the return of some officers sent ahead to examine
the barricade set by Siraj's troops. The assembly then came under
attack:

> ...the troops were unexpectedly assailed by a discharge from
> two pieces of heavy cannon, loaded with langrain, and mounted
> within 200 yards, upon a small bastion of the Morattoe ditch,
> to the right of the barricade, which killed and disabled 22
> Europeans; another discharge soon followed, with less, but
> however with some effect. This annoyance instantly overset
> the resolution of storming the pass; and the line immediately
> began to extend itself again, as well to present the fewest bodies
> to the cannonade, as to gain, without delay a broad high road,

which, about half a mile to the south of the causeway, crosses the Morattoe ditch into the company's territory, and then joins the avenue leading to the fort of Calcutta.

But it was tough going in the fog, with confusion and exhaustion setting in. The field pieces, so sharply placed at the beginning of the march, now seemed like liabilities. The open ground between the causeway and the road Clive's troops wished to gain for their retreat was dotted with small rice fields. Each field, then as now, has what in Bengali is known as āl—an enclosing bank. The field pieces had to be dragged across these fields and over these numerous banks. It was still foggy. The two heavy cannon of Siraj's forces were still firing at them.

When the fog cleared after 9 a.m., the persistence in hauling the field pieces over the rice fields paid off, as they could be quickly positioned to repulse the cavalry, now seen to their left. Then two more cannon joined the attack against Clive's forces. Their trial was far from over:

> At ten, after much fatigue and action, the troops, having abandoned two of the field pieces, which had broken down, arrived, and formed in the high-road leading to the avenue, where a body of horse and foot were posted in front to defend the passage across the Morattoe ditch. Several very large bodies of cavalry likewise assembled in the rear, acting with more courage than those in front, and pressed hard upon one of the field-pieces, which was gallantly rescued by Ensign Yorke, with a platoon of Adlercron's regiment. The fire of few other platoons dispersed the enemy in front; and the troops being now within the company's territory, might have proceeded along the road on the inside of the ditch, quite up to Omichund's garden, where the Nabob still remained, surrounded by a large body of cavalry; but Colonel Clive thinking that they had already endured too much fatigue, continued marching straight along the avenue to the fort, where they arrived about noon.

Clive's troops had received quite a mauling. Twenty-seven including several sailors and eighteen sepoys were killed. And seventy, including a dozen sailors and thirty-five sepoys, were wounded. Two captains of the company's troops were also killed, as was Clive's secretary, a Mr Belcher. A civilian employee of the Company had a leg shot off by a cannon ball.

◆

The officers and men among Clive's forces were demoralized. They thought their commander had exposed them to 'risques' to 'very little purpose', and the expedition was in any case 'rash, and ill-concerted'. Orme agreed, and briefly castigated Clive, his colleague from Madras, for a range of missteps, from taking the wrong route to exposing the expedition to needless danger when there were defences which could have reduced casualties.

But he conceded Clive's position that it was necessary to convince Siraj their 'former inactivity did not proceed from fear'.

As it happened, Siraj and his army were troubled even after having dispersed the British attack. Casualties were high. Orme claims the Bengal army had lost '22 officers of distinction, 600 common men, four elephants, 500 horses, some camels, and a great number of bullocks. The Nabob himself having never before been so near the tumult of a battle, regarded the attack of his camp as an effort of uncommon intrepidity, accused all his own officers of cowardice, and would have immediately retreated out of the company's territory, had they not promised to be better prepared in future.'

The firing of the Bengal army's cannon and muskets from the night of the 5th until daylight the next morning deterred Clive from attacking again.

It was again time for negotiations. The first move came from Siraj, conveyed through Ranjit Rai, the agent of the Seths. A letter chastised Clive for the attack and yet proposed peace. To which Clive responded with equally glib facility, claiming the raid wasn't intended as anything but a proof of character and capability of British troops. Wasn't it proof enough that his troops had 'cautiously' hurt none, except those that directly attacked him? Certainly, Clive added, he was open to negotiations.

This exchange of messages, carried back and forth by Ranjit Rai and Umachand continued for several days. Siraj postured by moving some of his troops to the northeast part of Calcutta, within reach of

British troops. Clive kept his peace.

The psychological battle that was the stalemate paid off in a major gain for Clive & Co. On 9 February, what came to be known as the Treaty of Alinagar was concluded. Siraj agreed to restore whatever effects in the Company's factories had been taken by his troops—such effects as officially recorded by his government. The Company would be able to restore and build fortifications in Calcutta. He permitted the Company to mint gold and silver coins there. And he fully acknowledged the farman of Farrukhsiyar for duty-free trade for the Company in Bengal, as well as the grant of thirty-eight villages. 'The oaths of the Nabob, Meer Jaffier and Roydoolub, were the only pledges or security for the execution of the treaty,' writes Orme.

It was a humiliating, and somewhat perplexing, climbdown for Siraj who, accompanied by two members of the imminent Plassey conspiracy, withdrew several kilometres to the north of Calcutta on 11 February. He had, for all practical purposes accepted that it was better to work with the British. More treaty-making took place the following day, as Siraj and the British sealed a deal—again, cosmetic, as future history would quickly show—to come to the aid of the other in situations of conflict.

Orme writes that Clive also threw in a query to Siraj, conveyed by Umachand, to 'sound if the Nabob would permit the English to attack the French settlement of Chandernagore; for there was time before the setting in of the southern monsoon'. Clive expected to return to Madras as quickly as possible. That aspect, and Clive's reasoning and determination to utterly dominate the French, will be addressed in detail in the following chapter, but here's a presentation by Orme of the next major stage in the run-up to Plassey—a British eye-view as compared to the French perspective we shall soon see.

Here Orme portrays Siraj as being both jittery and duplicitous:

> The Nabob detested the idea of a British attack on Chandannagar, but dreading an immediate renewal of hostilities, temporized; and pretending that Mr. Bussy from the Decan, and a squadron from Pondicherry, were coming to Bengal, he requested that the English would prevent them from entering his dominions; and, as a farther disguise, he requested 20 English gunners to serve in his own artillery; he likewise recommended, that

Mr. Watts might be appointed the company's representative at his court choosing him from a persuasion that he was a meek man, without guile [if this reasoning were true, then Watts was exceptionally talented in deception, and Siraj exceptionally naïve]. The next day he continued his march to Muxadavad, and Colonel Clive having received no positive injunction to the contrary from the Nabob, determined to prosecute the enterprize against Chandernagore.

Once he had taken the call, Clive moved quickly. On the 18th, Company and Crown troops crossed the Hugli at a point several kilometres north of Calcutta to the western bank of the river. They set up camp there, positioned for the northward thrust to Chandannagar. The French had meanwhile tracked the movement and, greatly alarmed, despatched a series of letters to Siraj who was on his way back to Murshidabad. The French plea was direct, as Orme notes: '...as he valued his own safety, to protect their settlement'. The messengers from Chandannagar found Siraj about 60 kilometres south of Murshidabad. The prompt made Siraj halt there, and he 'immediately wrote a letter' to the British, 'peremptorily commanding' them 'to desist from their intention'.

Watts meanwhile set off for Murshidabad, accompanied by a crew of artillery that Siraj had apparently requested to 'disguise' his intentions—the implication here is that Siraj still looked to the French for succour but was going along with the British for the sake of appearances. Umachand travelled with Watts. The merchant's behaviour since the fall of Calcutta and, most recently, the taking of Calcutta and during subsequent negotiations with Siraj, writes Orme, had for the Company 'effaced the impression of former imputations, insomuch that Mr. Watts was permitted to consult and employ him without reserve on all occasions'.

(Watts would also evidently travel in appropriate style when the occasion demanded, as appearances had always to be maintained. On 28 February 1757, a Council meeting in Calcutta would clear the expense of Rs 400 for a fancy palanquin set with silver tassles for the use of the Qasimbazar factory.)

Umachand would soon work his way to greater favour with the British—if not Clive. When the British party stopped near the settlement of Hugli on 18 February, by Orme's account, Umachand came by a sign of Siraj's double game (or a hedging of bets, which the Company had itself practised more than once in recent months). Orme tells us that Umachand came to know of a messenger who had arrived a day earlier carrying a present of 100,000 rupees to the government of Chandannagar. He also discovered that the governor of Hugli, who would in two decades gain fame and infamy at the impeachment trial of Warren Hastings as 'Maharaja' Nandakumar (or Nuncomar, as the British referred to him), had received orders from Siraj to 'assist the French, in case the English should attack them'. Siraj's troops were also on the way to reinforce the Bengal garrison at Hugli.

The British decided to immediately neutralize the threat in Hugli, and despatched Umachand for the purpose. Umachand visited Nandakumar, Orme tells us, and by 'pompous representations of the English force, by assurances of their protection and favour, and the promise of 12,000 rupees to be paid as soon as Chandernagore should be taken, won him over to their interests'. It was a relatively small sum for a person who was very well compensated as faujdar of Hugli and for Orme clearly represented the 'extreme venality which prevails even amongst the highest ranks in Indostan'.

Umachand then enacted a bit of theatre for his master—the Company, not Siraj—that was as redolent of misdirection and dissembling as Orme accuses Siraj of. When Siraj learned about the British plan to attack Chandannagar, he summoned Umachand to his camp—he still hadn't reached Murshidabad. Siraj asked the merchant whether the British would break both the neutrality of the Ganges, and the treaty they had just signed. 'Omichund told him that the English were famous throughout the world for their good-faith,' Orme continues, 'insomuch that a man in England, who on any occasion told a lie, was utterly disgraced, and never after admitted to the society of his former friends and acquaintance.' Umachand continued his dramatic turn and capped it with local colour. He called in a 'Bramin' who happened to be near the tent. He touched the Brahmin's feet in a gesture of piety and, using that prop of traditional trust—'among the Gentoos', as Orme notes—'swore that the English would never break the treaty'. Siraj appeared to be mollified by this display and declaration, and said 'he would revoke the orders he had given to Meer Jaffier, to march with half the army to Chandernagore; and instructed Omichund to assure Colonel Clive, that the troops which had marched two days before, were not intended to assist the French'.

The next day he received a letter from Clive—also a 'disguise', to borrow from Orme—that deferred to Siraj. The colonel would not attack Chandannagar without his concurrence. Siraj resumed his march home.

Watts and Umachand kept up the pressure, although by now it had evolved to working channels at court, to swing a decision in favour of attacking the French, Orme notes. As Clive had undertaken to not attack Chandannagar without Siraj's permission, that permission was now assiduously sought through the mechanism of court intrigue. This brought about great tension at court, as the French, led by their representative Law, wouldn't give in easily. They realized fully the implication of losing Chandannagar to a British attack. Here Manikchand is paraded as a lobbyist for French interests, ostensibly to insure his loot after Siraj's attack on Calcutta in June 1756; and so are Khwaja Wajid, who conducted much business with the French, and the Seths, to whom the French owed 1.5 million rupees. Orme writes that such a relationship ensured their support for the French cause—the protection of Chandannagar and they continued 'counteracting the practices and petitions of Mr. Watts and Omichund' and the 'remonstrances of Colonel Clive'. (As we shall see, the French had the opposite perspective.)

At any rate, both sides accuse Siraj of encouraging 'intrigues'. The British, in particular, were exasperated by Siraj's desperate balancing act: a message suggesting they had leave to attack the French would be countered by another that forbade hostilities. This continued until the end of February, when news arrived that an 'army of Pitans had taken Delhi, and intended to conquer the eastern provinces of the empire'. (The Pathans in this case were the Rohillas, settled near Delhi. When the Afghan warlord, Ahmad Shah Abdali, invaded Delhi in January 1757 and took control of the Mughal seat—the emperor was practically imprisoned—the Rohilla-Pathan chieftain, Najib-ud-Daula, allied with him. The alliance would deepen that April as the Afghans and Pathans played emperor-maker in Delhi). This panicked Siraj into requesting Clive for help 'and offered to allow a hundred thousand rupees a month for the expences of the English troops'.

Meanwhile, the British were reinforced by the arrival of the *Cumberland* from Madras to Balasore Roads on the coast, and three ships from Bombay carrying companies of infantry and artillery. Clive now felt more confident about an expedition to Chandannagar. There was now no question in his mind that formalizing a treaty of neutrality of the Ganges with the French would serve any purpose. 'Colonel Clive therefore immediately dismissed the French deputies, who were then with him, waiting to sign the treaty, which was even written out fair, and which they supposed had been intirely concluded: he at the same time wrote to the Nabob, that he would join him as soon as the news concerning the approach of the Pitans should be verified, and that he should in the mean time proceed as far as Chandernagore,' notes Orme. 'Accordingly the troops quitted their encampment opposite to Calcutta on the 7th of March, while the artillery proceeded in boats, advancing slowly, that the Bombay detachment might have time to come up the river, before they entered the French limits.'

As Clive & Co. plotted their moves, Siraj remained mute over his concerns about Chandannagar, as his concerns about a possible Pathan-led attack on his subah were greater. Nandakumar at Hugli, now bought over to the British cause, assured him that all was well: they had no hostile intentions. And, while Watson dithered over attacking Chandannagar—greatly upsetting Clive as we shall see—he wrote to Siraj complaining that the French had invoked the nawab's name for neutrality of the Ganges.

'The Nabob, perplexed with the angry style of Mr. Watson's letter, made use of these words in his answer,' Orme writes, 'If an enemy comes to you and implores your mercy with a clear heart, his life should be spared; but if you mistrust his sincerity, act according to the time and occasion.'

This letter, which was interpreted by Watson as providing leeway for a British attack on Chandannagar (and demonstrated yet again a sophisticated level of communication from Murshidabad that Siraj's critics deny him and his court) was contradicted by another that quickly followed. The French lobby had evidently interceded. '...but Mr. Watson,' Orme observes, 'considering this contradiction as an indignity, ordered the ships to move.'

Chandannagar, in the way of Clive & Co., was doomed. Orme offers a clinical note: 'The detachment from Bombay having joined Colonel Clive commenced hostilities.'

It was 14 March 1757.

13

THE FRENCH CONNECTION

'...to show you the necessity we were reduced to of
attempting his overthrow'

In *Decline and Fall of the British Empire*, Piers Brendon writes of how both Britain and France 'exploited and exacerbated' the disorder in the subcontinent. As we have seen, they formed alliances with local rulers in southern India, and fought pitched battles on their behalf. 'And they fought increasingly for political as much as for commercial ends, though these ends were inextricably intertwined since,' writes Brendon, 'according to the mercantilist orthodoxy of the time, wealth was crystallised power.'

The formula, he maintains, was simple enough: 'This cash from commerce paid native troops (sepoys) to take territory which yielded tax revenues and opportunities for further gain.'

Irfan Habib views the matter with more magnification. He offers the following table in his *Indian Economy Under Early British Rule, 1757–1857*:

Average annual export of bullion to India (Bombay, Madras and Bengal) and value of commodities imported therefrom by the English East India Company (Annual averages by decades in Rupees, converted from £ Sterling at £1 = Rs 8)

Decades	Export of bullion (Rs)	Value of India commodities imported
1708-17	24,33,690	27,31,202
1718-27	29,52,395	37,88,650
1728-37	26,91,474	43,15,881
1738-47	31,35,578	49,85,374
1748-57	43,61,830	42,24,097

Sources: For bullion exported to India: Bal Krishna, *Commercial Relations between India and England*, p. 317; for value of commodities imported from India: K. N. Chaudhuri, *The Trading World of Asia*, pp. 508–10.

To Habib, this table says it all: the steady increase in the export of bullion—silver and gold, coined and uncoined, by the Company to India, to offset its increasing imports from India between 1708 and 1757. In the last decade, as shown in the chart, the bullion outgo for the Company actually exceeded the value of its imports.

The growth in the English Company's trade did not, however, Habib observes, 'translate into corresponding profits'. In the years 1751–55, he notes that the French earned far greater profit with a 'much smaller' volume of sales. There were reasons beyond plain business. The Company 'had to advance low-interest loans of large amounts to the British government to preserve its monopoly of Asian trade and thwart all aspiring rivals within Britain, while it was also obliged to increase its expenditure on military establishments in the East to keep its European rivals at bay'. The dividend paid to shareholders reduced in the 1750s.

'In such circumstances, the temptation to make use of its military and naval power to secure financial gain was irresistible,' Habib maintains. 'If tribute could be levied by force on Indian rulers and their territories, this could save the Company its expenditure on the large quantities of treasure that had annually to be sent from England to India, and, in effect, secure to it imports from India with the costs paid out of India's own resources. So followed the Carnatic Wars (1746–61) and the Battle of Plassey (1757), and thereafter, the onset of colonial rule.'

◆

Even accounting for the economics of war, a curious détente existed in Bengal between the British and French companies until the arrival of Clive and Admiral Watson from Madras. It was in the interest of the British in Calcutta to keep things low-key and avoid overt conflict, a studied position also maintained by the French.

Whatever happened in Europe between their governments, the two companies would maintain neutrality if not cordiality in Bengal. This had seen the French and the British merchants through a largely adversarial relationship of their countrymen elsewhere, including southern India. The détente persisted through the churn of the First Carnatic War (1746–48) and the Second Carnatic War (1749–54), times when the two countries were not at war in Europe but continued a proxy war with the help of their company-and-country forces—and which earned Clive fame, and his title of Mahabat Jang, Horror in War, from the nawab of Arcot.

There were, of course, slights even in times of peace. For instance, in 1750, evidently riding on the angst of the First Carnatic War and the Treaty of Aix-la-Chapelle that did little to dispel hostility, 'blacks in Calcutta were prohibited dealing with the French,' Long observes. But it was only after the declaration of the Seven Years War in Europe in May 1756, news of which reached India in late 1756, conflated with the British loss of Calcutta, the need to retake it, and to secure trade with a favourable political environment, that matters spilled over in Bengal too. It's what Long colourfully described as the 'feelings of international bitterness, so strong in Europe last century were transferred to India; hence French and English regarded each other as national enemies; they fought for the expulsion of each other'. Hill also employed the phrase claimed by Arabs and Europeans alike: 'Two swords cannot be in one sheath.'

For their part, the French beset by the on-again, off-again entreaties and threats from Siraj, appeared keen to not place 'any unnecessary obstacles', as Hill mentions by way of explanation, in the way of seeing the nawab 'well beaten', and yet safeguard their interests. The strategy was, of course, very chancy and evolved with every throw of the dice in Bengal; and it was specifically aimed at attempting to protect their position primarily in relation to the British. There is even a suggestion, through Hill's interpretation of French affairs, that the French were paranoid about the possibility that, if the British demanded reparations from Siraj after their recapture of Calcutta, the nawab might simply permit the British to capture French settlements to clear that debt. Renault, the chief of the French settlement at Chandannagar, urged Law to ensure that in the event of a treaty between Siraj and the British, a clause be inserted guaranteeing 'neutrality of the Ganges' and prevent such an occurrence.

As we shall see, it echoed the coup d'état fantasies of Law in another context. That of Siraj being replaced by a more sensible, agreeable nawab who might prefer negotiation and détente over cussed belligerence—and also insist on peace between warring

European powers in his domain and thereby protect the commercial interests of all.

There would be no such clause in the Treaty of Alinagar signed on 9 February 1757, by which Siraj formally acknowledged the regaining of Calcutta by the British. 'Neutrality of the Ganges' would remain mere words, to be considered according to the will, or the lack of it, of the British, French, and Siraj. But the French persisted, and proposed just such an agreement with the British beyond the scope of the Treaty of Alinagar. They would persist up until the time Clive decided to attack Chandannagar and, as we have seen, asked the French negotiators to leave Calcutta.

◆

Hill notes that the 'English had no intention of creeping quietly back into the country'. He cites Clive's letter dated 11 October 1756 to the Company's Secret Committee in which he wrote, 'I hope we shall be able to dispossess the French of Chandernagore.' The letter was written five days before the expedition set sail for Calcutta.

There's another reinforcing letter, from the Select Committee in Madras to Admiral Watson, dated 13 November 1756, which was received in Calcutta on 13 January 1757, eleven days after the recapture of Calcutta by the British. In it the Committee wrote of how they had only the previous day received 'by way of Bombay', the declaration of war by their government against France. It passed on some belligerent advice:

> If you judge the taking of Chandernagore practicable without much loss it would certainly be a step of great utility to the Company's affairs and take off in great measure the bad effects of the loss of Calcutta by putting the French in a position equally disadvantageous.

In a letter written a day later, the Madras Committee formally conveyed to the Calcutta Committee its brief to the admiral. It was a prime example of what Reid pithily terms 'mercantile soldiering'.

Altogether it was shaping up to be another arena of glory for Clive, who, as Brendon writes, was a man who won the 'devotion' of his troops and even that of sepoys 'although he spoke no Indian tongue'. He led by 'relentless dynamism and hypnotic charisma', and employed every trick in the book—'as much bribery as force'—to defeat the opponents of Company and Crown and reach the plane his personal motto described: Primus in Indis. First in India.

Hugli and Bandel, both prosperous towns and settlements, the first described by Clive in one of his letters as the 'second city in the kingdom', and Bandel, a Portuguese trading post, would be devastated by Clive and Watson after their return to Calcutta—actions that drew Siraj to his unsuccessful campaign to retain Calcutta. Chandannagar was spared during this sortie but it seemed more a calculated slight, as if the French wouldn't dare to be drawn to battle here one way or the other, and suffer to be mopped up at the will of the Company's commanders. 'So it is evident that he came with this intention to Bengal,' insists Hill.

The French in Bengal would have to go. At the very least their military and political influence would need to be diminished to such an extent as to allow the interests of the Company and Crown an unhindered run. Neutrality would be moot when faced with this attitude.

To be fair, the tide of opinion was turning for the French Company too—back home, that is. When Thomas Arthur, also Comte de Lally, was sent as governor general of France to India in the wake of hostilities between France and Britain in 1756, we learn from Long's compilation of the French Company's unambiguous instructions to the count: 'All English fortifications to be destroyed, all other English places to be demolished, all English soldiers, sailors, writers to be sent to the Island of Bourbon.' We learn that Louis XV, the king of France, was agreeable to this, and the decision that any British territory captured would be depopulated of Britons.

Count Lally would reach India after Plassey was a fâit accompli, and ran a disastrous campaign in India, including a defeat for the French at the Battle of Wandiwash (Vandavasi, southwest of Madras) in 1760, and the French surrender of Pondicherry to the British the following year. He would also be beheaded upon his return to France. But while that strand of history is a minor digression, the aggression behind orders is not.

◆

Even with Clive's obvious belligerence and the charter of aggression he carried from Madras, the Calcutta Council discussed with complete seriousness the French proposal for neutrality in Bengal. We learn that the Council favoured it—'The treaty was drawn up, agreed on unanimously, and before signature, was sent at once to Admiral Watson,' notes Long.

The admiral objected, indeed, refused to ratify the treaty on the grounds that such an agreement would need to be ratified at the French subcontinental 'capital' at Pondicherry, which entailed a minimum delay of two months. Besides, there was every chance the council there would decline to ratify it. And, that such an agreement, even if ratified, might not be honoured by commanders of French ships who answered to their government, not the French company. As Long puts it, '...a number of Members of Government considered the French...notorious for breach of faith and violation of treaties.' Admiral Watson also questioned the sureness of Siraj's guarantee on such a pact of neutrality ('...and the Nawab's guarantee would be little worth,' Long notes, 'as he was of a fickle and uncertain disposition').

◆

The attack on Chandannagar that eventually took place can be largely attributed to Clive. Through masterful manoeuvring and wordplay, even hinting that he would return to Madras, his home. Clive would place his views on the danger the French presented in a letter to the Select Committee at Calcutta on 4 March 1757. It became part of the Committee's Proceedings the same day. In the letter, Clive displays great irritation and impatience, besides sealing once and for all the debate that the Company and Crown interests were conflated:

As Mr. Watson has declined accepting of the expedients proposed to him by us in refusing either to attack Chandernagore immediately or enter into such a neutrality with the French as we have recommended to him and which we think greatly for the benefit of the East India Company both in these provinces and on the Coast of Coromandel, I think he has taken the consequences of miscarriages upon himself, as in so doing, if I am not misinformed, he runs counter to His Majesty's instructions, which require that he should give attention to all representations made to him by the Company's Agents in India for the good of their service.

As the admiral was hesitant, Clive added, as commander of land forces he might as well return to Madras with as many troops as possible. In any case it was getting late in the season for sailing back to Madras. But, should Admiral Watson refuse neutrality, an 'immediate attack' of Chandannagar would become 'absolutely necessary'. Clive then appealed to the perception of the world at large about the hesitation—even weakness—of the Company and the British to arrive at a decision. They would lose credibility: they had invited the French for discussions on neutrality, a project blessed by Siraj, and yet wouldn't sign the treaty.

> Do but reflect, gentlemen, what will be the opinion of the world of these our late proceedings. Did we not, in consequence of a letter received from the Governor and Council of Chandernagore making offers of a neutrality within the Ganges, in a manner accede to it by desiring they would send deputies, and that we would gladly come into such a neutrality with them; and have we not since their arrival drawn out Articles that were satisfactory to both parties, and agreed that each Article should be reciprocally signed, sealed, and sworn so? What will the Nabob think? After the promises made him on our side, and after his consenting to guarantee this neutrality, he and all the world will certainly think that we are men of a trifling, insignificant disposition, or that we are men without principles.

So, Clive insisted, either sign the document of neutrality immediately and be done with it, or prepare to immediately attack Chandannagar should the offer of neutrality be declined by the Calcutta Council. The French wouldn't wait to ally with Siraj, or he with them—and, indeed, if Siraj had any intention to honour neutrality or 'articles of peace' in the first place.

> You may be assured the instant the French find their offers of a neutrality refused, they will immediately assist the Nabob in all his designs against us if he has the least intentions of not complying with the late articles of peace. It may then be too

late to wish Mr. Watson had been pleased to pay more attention to our representations.

While Admiral Watson had done well by Company and country, Clive insisted that any 'future operations' against Siraj would largely depend on Clive's troops. And, to take on both the French and Siraj together would be a 'very precarious' undertaking, even if all troops despatched to Bengal were counted, as the numbers would still not be robust. (But, of course, they would be enough to attack Chandannagar: 'The detachment from Bombay having joined Colonel Clive commenced hostilities on the 14th of March,' is how Orme records it.) The British had to move quickly, Clive insisted, and attack. Or else Clive wouldn't be responsible for any 'misfortune':

> I must therefore request you will join with me in desiring Mr. Watson a third time to ratify the neutrality in the manner agreed upon, and if he refuses, to desire he will attack Chandernagore by water immediately, as I am ready to do by land with the forces under my command. If he refuses this likewise, he becomes responsible for every misfortune that may happen to the Company's affairs.

(So, what will it be, gentlemen? —Clive's tone again pressed for a decision and reminded the Council of the disadvantage of any enterprise of war without his troops. Attack, or not? Please make up your mind so I can either take the battle to Chandannagar and Siraj, or return to Madras with most of the troops. Good luck to you, and, by the way, could you please arrange transport for my trip back to Madras?)

> This done, I propose leaving all the forces I can possibly spare for the defence of the Company's settlements, rights, and privileges in Bengal, and return with the rest immediately to the Coast, agreeable to the positive orders received from the President and Committee of Madras, and I must request you will order proper conveyances for the purpose.

I am, &c.,

Calcutta, 4th March, 1757. (Signed) ROBERT CLIVE.

♦

As it turned out, Long notes, 'The Council altered their opinions under these circumstances and resolved to attack Chandernagore.'

The attack on Chandannagar began on 14 March 1757, and by the end of the action the French settlement was devastated. All French shipping was sunk, either in an abortive bid to deny the British fleet led by Admiral Watson easy access, or by British naval bombardment. (Watson would write to the British Admiralty some days later from his flagship *Kent* which, with the *Salisbury* and *Tyger*, led the British attack on Chandannagar's fort as Clive led the land forces: 'Besides the ships and vessels sunk below to stop the channel up, they sunk and run ashore five large ships above the Fort, and we have taken four sloops and a snow.')

However, it wouldn't be a walkover like the retaking of Calcutta was, or the skirmishes the Company and Crown forces engaged in during the move north from Falta—even the relatively chaotic defence of Calcutta against Siraj's forces. The French stood their ground for several days until a betrayal in the ranks permitted Clive's forces to gain access to the fort that had, meanwhile, faced a steady barrage from British naval ships even as French artillerymen attempted to give back as good as they got. Watson's dry recounting of it to the Admiralty acknowledged as much: 'The enemy had killed in the Fort 40 men and 70 wounded. We also have suffered in some degree, the *Kent* had 19 men killed and 49 wounded, the *Tyger* 13 killed and 50 wounded. Among the number killed was my First Lieutenant Mr. Samuel Perreau, and the Master of the *Tyger*. Among the wounded was [Admiral] Mr. Pocock slightly hurt...' Other colleagues had limbs shattered or 'shot off' by cannon fire.

Having won Chandannagar, the Company decided to altogether obliterate the French threat in Bengal. On 31 March, Admirals Watson and George Pocock, and Clive and Major Killpatrick, would write to the Select Committee at Fort William from Chandannagar:

> Gentlemen,—Having taken into consideration the disposal of the Fort of Chandernagore we imagine it will be for the interest of the Company and of the nation that it be demolished. For should the Nabob from the capriciousness of his disposition

once again turn his arms against [us] or should the French be able to send a force into this Province two garrisons will be more than we can well maintain, especially after the departure of the squadron and return of the Madras troops. We should be glad to know your sentiments on this subject, and are, &c. &c.,

Charles Watson, G. Pocock,
R. Clive, J. Killpatrick.

The decision taken to destroy the fort at Chandannagar and the Company firmly entrenched on French territory along the Hugli, on 16 April 1757 Clive would write to the Court in London justifying the attack:

When Chandernagore is considered as the granary of the Islands, and Pondichery as mistress of a great trade to Europe and round India, as a large and opulent colony already, and which seemed to promise to increase, the loss of it must be acknowledged a very severe blow to the French Company and nation. The destruction of this flourishing colony will, I am persuaded, be attended with many signal advantages to the trade of the East India Company.

Politics and war. As ever, just business.

And yet, once the ugly business of conspiracy and war for business and strategic advantage was done, the bitter rivals in Europe, and bitter business rivals in India, could get back to what passed for civilized behaviour. Proceedings of a Council meeting on 9 May 1757 in Calcutta notes that 'handsome' table expenses were allowed the French governor and Council after their capture after the battle of Chandannagar:

The French Director and Council being kept here as close prisoners, and requesting their Table expenses may be supplied by the Company, it is thought reasonable to subsist them in a manner suitable to their rank. Ordered Mr. Boddam therefore to take the care of that affair upon him, and to provide them with a handsome table during their remaining in Calcutta as prisoners.

◆

In the build-up to Plassey, the French were in Bengal's twilight zone. They desperately attempted to balance Siraj and the British. The British continued to be wary that the French would stand with Siraj. And Siraj remained perplexed as to why the French weren't. Much of this is explained by the background of the build-up to the attack on Chandannagar and, subsequently, preparations for Plassey, when Clive's and Siraj's actions are matched with the French point of view.

As it turned out, Clive had played his cards right; and that is acknowledged quite clinically by the Frenchman Law. He saw through the weakness of a proposed treaty of neutrality along the Ganges given the existing political circumstances, and, therefore, even with his often-stated aversion to Siraj's personality, Law suggested allying with the nawab. 'The neutrality was by no means obligatory, as no treaty existed,' on account of the Calcutta Council ultimately rejecting it, he recalled in his memoirs. Law wrote to Renault, his colleague in Chandannagar, urging a pact with Siraj—'the Moors'.

'In fact, what confidence could we have in a forced neutrality, which had been observed so long only out of fear of the Nawab'—like Alivardi and unlike the current nawab, Siraj—'who for the general good of the country was unwilling to allow any act of hostility to be committed by the Europeans? Much more so when the English were at war with the nawab himself. If they managed to get the better of him, what would become of this fear, the sole foundation of the neutrality?'

As we have seen, Law was unable to bring the British to agree to the French need for neutrality of the Ganges, and that the treaty Siraj signed with the British on 9 February 1757 after he was stung at Calcutta on 5 February, unsettled by Clive's surprise early morning raid, mentioned nothing about neutrality.

Through all of this, Renault and the French Council were too cautious to throw their lot in with Siraj. Instead they suffered British disdain and Siraj's suspicion in turn.

When after the retaking of Calcutta, Clive & Co. bypassed Chandannagar to sack Hugli just upriver from the French settlement, Siraj was suspicious it was on account of a French agreement with the British. But Siraj was mollified when he was able to reach the French administrators through Renault after the attack on Hugli. It proved to him that his suspicion of a Franco-British compact against him was groundless.

Indeed, Siraj repeatedly reached out to the French, from the time he retreated from Calcutta, up until a few days before Plassey.

Watts managed to access the letters Siraj purportedly wrote to the French, and provide updates and translations to Clive, who became increasingly convinced that the French had to be neutralized and so too Siraj.

◆

Espionage played a key role in setting the scene and the pace for Plassey—and, in helping Clive to make up his mind and press for action from Admiral Watson and the Calcutta Council. The Company encouraged intelligence gathering. A Consultation in Calcutta on 1 February 1753 actually records such encouragement. Alongside cutting trees on roads, clearing and repairing the 'tank' at what would become Dalhousie Square, orange trees for the park, a whimsical expense of 9 paise for 'Govind Chand's Cat'—I was unable to trace the purpose—and purchase of confiscated belongings of prostitutes at public auction or 'outcry', the Council also listed 10 rupees 12 annas and 6 paise towards 'the Mores employed for secret services'.

Indeed, one of the great concerns at Fort William after the recapture of Calcutta in early 1757 was that the cipher used to communicate with Watts and Scrafton had been compromised. We learn from Orme and a record in Hill's *Bengal* that the cipher, in which letters were transposed with numbers, went like this: a: 19 b: 15 c: 27 d: 30 e: 20 f: 39 g: 28 h: 18 i: 38 k: 33 1: 16 m: 29 n: 32 o: 23 p: 25 q: 37 r: 34 s: 31 t: 24 u: 35 w: 22 x: 17 y: 26 z: 36 &: 21

Double letters were represented by using the number 4. And the Roman 'I' could imply a stop 'where necessary to avoid mistaking the sense'.

Some capital letters signified key players and places. A was used for Watts, D for Mir Jafar, B for Umachand, C for Siraj, G for the French, E for Murshidabad and F for Qasimbazar.

◆

Clive himself would write to the Court in London in August 1757:

Some of Suraja Dowla's letters to the French having fallen into my hands, I enclose a translate of them just to show you the necessity we were reduced to of attempting his overthrow.

Reverend Long reproduced several of the letters Siraj wrote the French that would come into the Company's possession. Here's one Siraj is believed to have written to Charles Joseph de Bussy, the commander of Pondicherry, in the second half of February, just days after signing the Treaty of Alinagar with the British. A time when the next tactical step as being argued by Clive & Co. was an expedition up the Hugli to Chandannagar:

> Suraja Dowla to the exalted in station, greatest among great Officers, the support of friendship, Monsr. Busie, Bahadre.
>
> These disturbers of my country, the Admiral and Colonel Clive, Sabut Jung, whom bad fortune attends, without any reason whatever, are warring against...Monsr. Rennault, the Governor of Chandernagore. This you will learn from his letters. I, who in all things seek the good of mankind, assist him in every respect, and have sent him the best of my troops that he may join with them and fight the English, and if it becomes necessary I will join him myself. I hope in God these English, who are unfortunate, will be punished for the disturbances they have raised. Be confident. Look on my forces as your own. I have written you before for two thousand soldiers and musqueteers under the command of one or two trusty Chiefs. I persuade myself you have already sent them as I desired. Should you not, I desire you will do me the pleasure to send them immediately. Further particulars you will learn from Monsr. Rennault. Oblige me with frequent news of your health.

Siraj would write again to de Bussy—a letter believed to have been written in mid-March, a time when the French commander was thought to be on his way up the coast in an attempt to secure Chandannagar. It would be too late, of course. On 14 March, the initial skirmishes between Clive's forces and the French had already begun, with the capitulation of Chandannagar, on 23 March, just over a week away. The letter acknowledged 'news' of de Bussy's arrival 'near the Orissa country, with a powerful army of soldiers, Telingas,

& c., to the assistance of the Commander of Chandernagore' and looked forward to a meeting that would 'confirm the great friendship between us'. Siraj wrote that he had 'ordered the Naibs of the Soubah, the Phouzdar, and Zemidars of Midnapore to wait on you and assist you on your march'.

A third letter to de Bussy is supposed to have been written at the end of March, by which time British forces had defeated the French and occupied Chandannagar. Siraj would follow up this letter with another one ordering his officials to 'obtain good intelligence' about de Bussy's movements and arrival, and to not 'impede' de Bussy and his army.

> I am advised that you are arrived at Echapore [Ichhapur in Orissa]. This news gives me pleasure. The sooner you come here the greater satisfaction I shall have in meeting you. What can I write of the perfidy of the English? They have, without ground, picked a quarrel with Monsr. Rennault and taken by force his Factory. They want now to quarrel with Monsr. Law, your chief at Chandernagore, but I will take care to oppose and overthrow their proceedings. When you come to Ballasore I will then send Monsr. Law to your assistance, unless you forbid his setting out. Rest assured of my good will towards you and your company...

Interestingly, Hill has a different take on all this. He is emphatic that Siraj 'foolishly' walked into the British script by marching upon Calcutta to 'fight them on their own ground', and trying to take them head on at Plassey after the British sacking of Hugli, instead of adopting the wiser tactic of blocking their supply route, or by decree forbidding his subjects to resupply the British. Siraj could have 'starved them out of Calcutta in a few months', Hill writes with some astonishment. It's open to question whether the combination of Colonel Clive and Admiral Watson would have capitulated to such a blockade, but this remains among the what-ifs of Plassey.

◆

Law remained convinced that the English were driven to attack the French in Bengal on account of the Seven Years War in Europe.

As we have seen, news of the war reached Bengal in January 1757 right after the retaking of Calcutta by the British. There was also the concern that Renault was pushing for an agreement with Siraj. Although elsewhere in his memoirs Law appears to acknowledge that Clive and Watson were actually more concerned about his moves at Murshidabad's court, in one instance he sidesteps this supposition by shifting the blame onto the British.

> It would appear from the English memoirs that we corrupted the whole Durbar at Murshidabad to our side by presents and lies... As a matter of fact, except Siraj-ud-daula himself, one may say the English had the whole Durbar always in their favour.

'The dethronement of the Nawab had become an absolute necessity (for the British),' Law reiterates. 'To drive us out of Bengal was only a preliminary piece of work. A squadron of ours with considerable forces might arrive. Siraj-ud-daula might join his forces to it. What, then, would become of the English? They needed (as) Nawab a man attached to their interests. Besides, this revolution was not so difficult to carry out as one might imagine. With Chandernagore destroyed, nothing could be more easy...'

But Law acknowledges that the French may not have proved a major impediment to British interests and even their various plans to dethrone Siraj. Merely a 'junction' of the British with anti-Siraj forces, 'the crowd of enemies whom he had, and amongst whom were to be counted the most respectable persons in the three provinces' of Bengal, Bihar, and Orissa would have sufficed.

In any case, the French attempt at influencing Siraj appears to have failed, according to Law, on account of the Seths. In addition, the French were unable to get those like Rai Durlabh, said to have 'feared' to 'fight the English' after the February fiasco in Calcutta, to say any 'even a single word' in favour of the French at court. According to Law, the failure was primarily on account of Jagat Seth Madhab Rai and his cousin Swaroop Chand who had everybody sewn up and primed for manipulation. Even Siraj, against whom they used a 'refined policy' to 'conceal their game'. Law says the banking family frequently bad-mouthed the British in front of Siraj 'so as to excite him against them'. It was to both mislead the nawab and gain his confidence.

According to this telling, it worked. 'The Nawab fell readily into the snare, and said everything that came into his mind, thus enabling his enemies to guard against all the evil which otherwise he might have managed to do them.' It bolstered the British position—and the British were in any case casting their own net snaring Mir Jafar and other nobles—but the strings all led, in one way or another, back to the bankers, 'attached to them by their presents or the influence of the Seths'. This included ministers of Alivardi's court who ran afoul of Siraj's arrogance and temper and even most of the secretaries, who were crucial in communicating the nawab's wishes.

Understandably, this Plassey lore attributes great importance to Siraj's scribes, with some chroniclers attributing to the court secretaries, opportunities to deliberately obfuscate or misdirect a word, leaving room for interpretation. As we have seen, such lore imputes a method readily adopted by the British, for instance, to lay siege to Chandannagar. In any case, while correctly ascribing Machiavellian success to the British, the Company's Qasimbazar chief, Watts, and their sponsor-benefactors like the Seths, the French downplay their own attempts at influencing Siraj and his court. There is also a possible bias against Siraj that presumes the nawab was either illiterate or indolent, and paid the price for his rudeness when his scribes were actually doing the subtle bidding of other masters. This bias precludes the possibility of Siraj actually playing a balancing game similar to that of the French from early 1757 onward—only months into his reign—of being desperately worried, feeling quite cornered, and therefore playing all sides as the reality of opposition closed in on him.

Law's memoirs add to such colour.

Witness the letter written to the English Admiral Watson, by which it is pretended the Nawab authorized him to undertake the siege of Chandernagore. *The English memoir* [here he refers to the work of Luke Scrafton] confesses it was a surprise, and that the Secretary must have been bribed to write it in a way suitable to the views of Mr. Watts. The Nawab never read the letters which he ordered to be written; besides, the Moors never sign their names; the envelope being closed and well fastened, the Secretary asks the Nawab for his seal, and seals it in his presence. Often there is a counterfeit seal.

(According to Hill this also provides a convenient exit strategy to the nawab—in this case, Siraj. In case of an objection it can be interpreted as the scribe exceeding the instructions of the nawab; and it also leaves the correspondent—in this case, Watson—to interpret with expediency.)

Even the eunuchs stationed in Siraj's harem harboured hatred against the nawab and conspired against him, suggests such lore. With the wheels of inevitability greased by the Seths and destiny urged by the British, what would these near-future rulers of Bengal 'not expect to achieve by the union of all these forces,' asks Law, 'when guided by so skilful a man as Mr. Watts?'

Law remained convinced that the bankers had it in for the French—because they had in effect chosen the British as their instrument for Siraj's destruction. Law claims he had actually influenced the court enough for a detachment of the nawab's troops to be readied for a march to Chandannagar to counter the English advance. And although he thought of Rai Durlabh as undependable and somewhat of a coward he went to see him as he did his second-in-command Mir Madan—'a good officer,' in Law's words. This Frenchman at ground zero, as it were, claims that he promised Rai Durlabh 'a large sum if he succeeded in raising the siege of Chandernagore' and he also visited 'several of the chief officers, to whom I promised rewards proportionate to their rank'. But Law holds that his entreaties to Siraj to urgently provide troops met with words of caution from the nawab. "All is ready," replied the Nawab, "but before resorting to arms it is proper to try all possible means to avoid a rupture, and all the more so as the English have just promised to obey the orders I shall send them."' (The promise is evidently a reference to Clive's letter of 7 March 1756 in which he expressed a wish to attack Chandannagar and Clive's willingness to await word from Siraj before precipitating action.) Law insists this delay in aiding the French was the subtle work of the Seths.

While that is eminently logical, seen without the French lens it also suggests a move by a badly stung and nervous Siraj to calm Clive, and not tip his own hand too much towards the French. It could also be interpreted as a move to calm things down to the extent Clive wouldn't be driven to take Chandannagar and, therefore, clear the way for Siraj to ally with the only meaningful military opposition among European powers, a move that would, in one stroke, also prevent a relatively uncontested drive upriver towards Murshidabad. It could even be interpreted as a hedging of bets by a nawab who learnt his lesson too late even if he was unaware that Clive was determined to push on to take Chandannagar, ignoring and once again humiliating the highest authority of Bengal: a nawab who had inexplicably withdrawn when the going got tough in Calcutta. Besides, to actually send aid to the French openly would be like waving a red flag to Clive & Co., providing the merchant-marauders with a compelling reason to take the battle directly to Siraj's door.

Much of the run-up to Plassey is a matter of interpretation by diverse and sometimes conflicting sources and tellings—as is the character of Siraj. But to be fair, Law's accounts make for fascinating reading and offer great insight into the several layers of court and conspiracy from a person actively involved in Bengal's dynamics, and blessedly bereft of the grandstanding, self-congratulatory tone in British and British-sponsored accounts in the years after Plassey. Even Law's bias largely takes the tone of a particular perspective, not gratuitously damning except the hearsay instance of describing Siraj's blood sport as a prince. His is a compelling tale with its own parameters of logic: Law doesn't deny Siraj was in a tricky place even though he is always insistent that Siraj ought to take primary responsibility for that situation.

◆

Law also doesn't pass up any opportunity to trash talk the Seths, for him the key Machiavellians for British success in Bengal. Take this exchange with the Seths before the fall of the French settlement in Chandannagar—an exchange, he is careful to note, which was conducted with great politeness. 'I resolved to visit the bankers. They immediately commenced talking about our debts, and called my attention to the want of punctuality in our payments.'

Law turned around that deflection, insisting such matters weren't uppermost in his mind. Although if they insisted on discussing these, as a condition for supporting the French in Chandannagar, he said that 'concerned them as well as us with respect to those very debts for which they were asking payment and security'.

'I asked why they supported the English against us,' continues Law. 'They denied it, and, after much explanation, they promised to make any suggestions I wished to the Nawab. They added that they were quite sure the English would not attack us, and that I might remain tranquil.'

Law told them he knew of 'English' designs as well as they, and he saw 'no way of preventing them from attacking Chandernagore except by hastening the despatch of the reinforcements which the Nawab had promised, and that as they were disposed to serve me, I begged them to make the Nawab understand the same'.

The bankers, who Law thinks actually believed the British wouldn't attack Chandannagar, told him pretty much what Siraj told him, that the nawab wished no 'rupture' with the British. Law came away convinced the Seths wouldn't do anything to safeguard French interests in Bengal. He recounts the comments of the Seths' agent, Ranjit Rai—also an agent of the Company, and often referred to in correspondence and chronicles as Rungeet Roy—who in a jarring note mocked the French predicament in Bengal: 'You are a Frenchman; are you afraid of the English? If they attack you, defend yourselves! No one is ignorant of what your nation has done on the Madras Coast, and we are curious to see how you will come off in this business here.'

Revealing, even entertaining, as these recollections are, none surpass the Jagat Seth's admission about what amounts to the Plassey conspiracy. This happened, claims Law, during the same visit to the banker at which Law's request for assistance to the French was turned down, with a reminder of what was already owed by the French company to them. In Law's own words, the banker would never have revealed such a thing unless he felt confident that Law was powerless to do anything about it. Essentially, Siraj was a marked man:

The conversation having turned on Siraj-ud-daula, on the reasons he had given the Seths to fear him, and on his violent character, I said I understood clearly enough what they meant, and that they certainly wanted to set up another Nawab. The Seths, instead of denying this, contented themselves with saying in a low voice that this was a subject which should not be talked about. Omichand, the English agent was present. If the fact had been false, the Seths would certainly have denied it, and would have reproached me for talking in such a way. If they had even thought I intended to thwart them, they would also have denied it, but considering all that had happened...they imagined that we should be just as content as they were to see him deposed, provided only the English would leave us in peace. In fact, they did not as yet regard us as enemies.

Hill writes that, on the last count, Law was skilfully misdirected. Clive, he maintains, had 'already promised, or did so soon after', to simply give over all the property of the French to the Jagat Seth in lieu of what the French owed the bankers, after the conspiracy came good. (As we shall see, a post-Plassey compact gave the Seths leave to do just that.) Deluded or not, Law appears to have finally realized the depth of the matter, and the trouble the French clearly were in, let alone the nawab.

As a last-ditch gamble to cement Siraj's French connection, Law claims he took news of the conspiracy to the nawab the same evening. Siraj simply laughed it off: '...the poor young man began to laugh, not being able to imagine I could be so foolish as to indulge in such ideas.'

Law wrote it off to the young man not being a 'master of himself', alluding to a lack of firmness of character, indiscreet, sharing whatever struck him when in his harem, 'surrounded by his wives and servants'. Easily deceived.

There would be more of it, suggesting the die was truly cast for a showdown. As it turned out, Watts, chief of the English factory, came to the durbar that evening. Siraj pressed both Watts and Law on the point of neutrality, urging both to pledge peace. But Watts 'skilfully avoided' any such undertaking, Hill tells us, referring here to Law's memoir. Instead, the canny British factory chief suggested the nawab write to Admiral Watson about it. Law couldn't hold himself back at this point, telling Siraj the admiral would ignore his missive with disdain as he had his earlier ones.

Siraj erupted.

'"How?" said the Nawab, looking angrily at me instead of at Mr Watts: "who am I then?"

'All the members of his Court cried out together that his orders would certainly be attended to.'

◆

Admiral Watson and Colonel Clive attacked Chandannagar before the admiral's reply to Siraj arrived. Meanwhile, Siraj carried on playing his two-step. It isn't clear if it was with, or without, the gentle persuasion of the Seths. When Law rushed to Siraj on 15 March with news of the British attack on Chandannagar, there was a flurry of orders and countermanding of orders that seemed skewed towards English interests by the very action of Siraj seemingly being unwilling to take them on—especially at the slightest sign the British were winning.

Around midnight on 15 March, a eunuch of the nawab brought a message that the French had held off the English advance. Siraj ordered his troops to march but quickly countermanded the order when, later the following day, news arrived of the French retreating to their fort, a sign of an imminent siege, and a sign of possible French defeat. 'Every one cried out that the Fort must fall, and that it was mere folly to incense the English by sending down troops,' writes Hill.

Then news arrived the French were holding out. Rai Durlabh was ordered to advance. With news arriving of the fort falling—it was a false alarm—that order was rescinded.

All through the British siege of Chandannagar, there was controlled chaos in Murshidabad. 'Law was at his wits' end,' writes Hill. So was Siraj. The nawab's state of mind is evident from the contradictory decisions he made. From Siraj's point of view, while Chandannagar was a couple of weeks march away from Murshidabad it was still too close to the rampaging British. An alliance with the French might help but that would be of no use if and when Chandannagar fell. After that, there was only one significant fortress along the Hugli at Katwa, only a day's determind march to a point southwest of Plassey.

Although a little late to stave off the inevitability of defeat at Chandannagar and, subsequently, the inevitable British push towards Murshidabad—which would happen sooner than later—Law decided to take matters in hand. To get a heads-up on Clive and Watson's progress, 'he intercepted Mr Watts's letters,' Hill tells us. From these Law gathered that the 'English intended to march straight upon Murshidabad', although that presumed immediacy was eventually proven to be Company forces chasing upcountry all 'fugitives' from Chandannagar who managed to escape. At any rate he was able to prevail upon Siraj to send a hundred musketeers to bolster the several dozen troopers at the French factory in Qasimbazar. Law also pushed Siraj for permission to fortify the French factory with some earthworks.

Then matters descended to a farce. According to Law, Siraj made him destroy the earthworks, insisting that 'under the present circumstances he had himself to do many things contrary to his own wishes, that by refusing to obey I should draw the English upon him and upon us, that we could not defend ourselves and must therefore submit...'

Law claims that, seeing his situation as hopeless, he was 'ready to withdraw and to make over the Factory to him [Siraj], with which he could afterwards do as he liked, and for which I should hold him responsible'. When Law prepared to do just that, leaving with a few cartloads of munitions, provisions and 'small amount of money' of his own and that of some colleagues, one of Siraj's officers reported the matter to the nawab. Siraj 'absolutely forbade my leaving the Factory'.

And yet, Siraj wouldn't give in to the Company pressure to have Law surrender.

In this situation of increasing certainty of a British ascendancy, Law decided to leave, but insisted on 'passports' for safe passage, and some funds. On 8 April, he received the documents, with a suggestion he head to Phulbari near Patna for every assistance. On 10 April, he received orders to not leave, for reasons we shall discuss shortly.

◆

Meanwhile, Watts, Law's British counterpart and formidable adversary, was hardly idle in addition to his part in keeping the Plassey conspiracy in working order. The Company, Law understood, 'were steadily increasing their garrison at Cossimbazar by bringing up soldiers who pretended they were deserters and wished to pass over to the French. By this trick, indeed, many soldiers had passed through the Moorish camp without being stopped.' Law mentions that at this time he engaged a frequent visitor to the French factory and 'minor' confidante of the nawab, to convey matters of import to Siraj, such as Law's views on the Seths and the British, as well as British reinforcements at their factory in Qasimbazar.

Perhaps more disturbing to both Law and Siraj was news that the British were planning to move upriver, loaded with weapons and ammunition. When this minor confidante—a dalal, an agent—conveyed this intelligence from Law to the nawab, he asked Law to not go anywhere—that order of 10 April. (Law notes how he later discovered that agent had benefited as much from the British as he had from the French.)

As tension cycled up in this multilayered, multiplayer game of thrones and territories, the French factor received a summons from Siraj to be present at durbar on 13 April. Delayed by rain, Law left around 10 a.m. with instructions that, if he didn't return from court by 2 p.m. his colleagues should send forty troopers to ensure his safety. By the time Law reached the court it was noon. Siraj had ended his public interactions for a midday sojourn in his harem. Law was escorted to the hall of audience where he was provided a meal (he shares a quite French critique: '...they brought us a very bad dinner').

There was no sign of Siraj even at 5 p.m. Law managed to elicit an answer from an arzbegi, a person who received petitions for the nawab, as to the reasons for being summoned. He was told the nawab had been 'constantly receiving' complaints from the British about the boosted garrison at the French factory, and had therefore decided to summon both Law and Watts in the hope of rapprochement. The arzbegi had a word of encouragement for Law: 'He added that the Nawab was quite satisfied with my behaviour, and wished me much good.'

But Watts appeared to have the jump on him—kind words of the nawab notwithstanding—when Law was summoned for an audience in another hall. Siraj wasn't present. Watts was, along with some senior courtiers he doesn't name, 'an agent of the Seths'. After the usual preliminary pleasantries, a 'diwan' directly asked Law if he had anything to say to Watts. Law declined.

Watts had no such hesitation. 'The question is, sir,' Law recounts Watts addressing him in English, 'whether you are prepared to surrender your Factory to me and to go down to Calcutta with all your people. You will be well treated, and will be granted the same conditions as the gentlemen of Chandernagore. This is the Nawab's wish.'

Law emphatically declined, claimed his status and that of his colleagues as free men, and said if at all there was to be a surrender, he would leave the French factory in the care of Siraj. That didn't go down well with Watts. 'Mr. Watts, turning round to the Diwans, says excitedly, that it is impossible to do anything with me, and repeats to them word for word all that has passed between us.' The courtiers, including the arzbegi then took Law aside and 'begged' him to consider 'what I was doing in refusing Mr. Watts's propositions, and said that as the Nawab was determined to have a good understanding with the English, he would force me to accept them'. Law says he was adamant in sticking to his position that he would remain in Qasimbazar and resist the 'ambitious designs' of the British.

'"Well, well, what can you do?" the courtiers replied. "You are about a hundred Europeans; the Nawab has no need of you; you will certainly be forced to leave this place. It would be much better to accept the terms offered you by Mr. Watts."'

After about fifteen minutes or so of discussions with Watts, of which Law says he had no knowledge, the courtiers went to Siraj. Law remained where he was. In a few short minutes the arzbegi, the Seths' agent, some agents of the British and some officers of court returned and told Law that Siraj 'ordered' him to submit 'entirely to what Mr Watts demanded'. Law protested the order, even deeming it impossible, and demanded to see the nawab.

'"The Nawab," they said, "does not wish to see you."'

'I replied, "It was he who summoned me; I will not go away till I have seen him."'

Law's troops had by now arrived in Murshidabad, and not seeing him, advanced to the palace. The next conversation is telling, from the perspective of the Seths' heft and interest. 'The Arzbegi, not knowing what would be the result of this affair, and wishing to get out of the scrape and to throw the burden of it on to the Seths' agent, said to him, "Do you speak, then; this affair concerns you more than us."'

Law remained adamant, wishing to speak to no one but Siraj, so the court officials trooped off to convey the message. Siraj agreed to meet Law alone.

As with several sections of Law's memoirs, the following description is presented as evidence of just how much the British had already permeated Siraj's court and his mind since the retaking of Calcutta by Clive & Co., their subsequent sacking of Hugli and conquest of the French settlement of Chandannagar.

'I presented myself before the Nawab, who returned my salute in a kindly manner,' Law recalls. 'As soon as I was seated, he told me, in a shamefaced way, that I must either accept Mr. Watts's proposals, or must certainly leave his territories. Your nation is the cause, he said, of all the importunities I now suffer from the English. I do not wish to put the whole country in trouble for your sake. You are not strong enough to defend yourselves; you must give way. You ought to remember that when I had need of your assistance you always refused it'—a reference to the French Council and other factors refusing to throw in their lot with Siraj against the British as Clive and Watson advanced up the Hugli after retaking Calcutta. 'You ought not to expect assistance from me now.'

Law writes that Siraj, as he conveyed his decision, 'kept his eyes cast down, and that it was, as it were, against his will that he paid me this compliment'. In any event, Law maintains he told the nawab that he couldn't possibly accept Watts's proposal, that he would be 'dishonoured'.

As the nawab clearly didn't want him around he would head to Patna—after all the nawab himself had given him a 'passport'. There was general consternation at this suggestion from all but Siraj and Khwaja Wajid, and all but these two recommended a passage south and southwest towards Medinipur and Cuttack—and likely interdiction by the British. Law declined, and claims to have thrown the problem back to the nawab. 'Wishing to force him to speak, I asked if it was his intention to cause me to fall into the hands of my enemies? "No, no," replied the Nawab, "take what road you please, and may God conduct you." I stood up and thanked him, received the betel'—the betel leaf a sign of goodwill and, in this case, dismissal—'and went out.'

The drama wasn't over. Historians and chroniclers here quote the *Siyar* to offer an ironical clincher to the entire episode, a portrait of Siraj as a man who realizes he is quite adrift as nawab and at the mercy of whatever the future may bring, especially the conspiracy Law had cautioned him about. It's a deft, stagey foreshadowing of doom by a storyteller:

> ...but as he did not dare to keep him in his service for fear of offending the English. He told him that at present it was fit that he should depart; but that if anything new should happen he would send for him again.
>
> 'Send for me again?' answered Law. 'Rest assured, my Lord Nawab, that this is the last time we shall see each other. Remember my words: we shall never meet again. It is nearly impossible.'

♦

Law made preparations to leave Murshidabad and by the evening of 15 April had completed his arrangements. According to Orme, Siraj shot off an insurance-like letter to Clive on the same day: 'Mr. Law I have put out of the city, and have wrote expressly to my Naib at Patna'—Raja Ram Narain, the governor who would remain loyal to Siraj till the end—'to turn him and his attendants out of the bounds of his Subaship, and that he shall not suffer them to stay in any place within it.'

If it was done for form's sake, the nawab needn't have bothered. The British knew exactly what was going on. Siraj tried to placate Law on his departure with a parting gift of ten thousand rupees. Hill writes that the same way Clive found out about so much else of the communication between Siraj and the French—the intercepted correspondence we read a little earlier—he found out about this too through the good offices of Watts. Siraj wrote to Law in the second half of April: 'I send you Rs. 10,000 for your expenses. Remain quiet at Rajmahal. When Monsr. Busie, Bahadre, &c., comes on this side Cuttack, I will then send for you.'

Orme writes of the formidable and crafty Watts reporting to Clive about Law's flashy group, comprising a hundred Europeans, sixty 'Tellingees', Indian troops from the Andhra region at times also referred to as Telingas, thirty bullock wagons ('hackerys', reported Watts), and four elephants, which marched through Murshidabad in some style. Hill writes that Watts sent two spies after the French train, to 'seduce' their soldiers and sepoys.

Watts was so effective for the Company in general, and the conspiracy in particular, that Clive himself would praise him to the Court in London when the heat and dust of Plassey had settled. On 6 August 1757, he would write: 'I must here do that gentleman the justice to say his services at the Durbar have been very great, as well in promoting the ruin of the French, as in negotiating the treaty with Jaffer Ally Cawn.'

◆

Dogging the French were also messengers of the deeply conflicted Siraj, by now nearly psychotic with worry at losing a prospective ally and yet feeling the need to play along with the British who figuratively had him over a rack. Whenever the French party stopped for a while, such as at Bhagalpur on 2 May, around two-thirds of the way to Patna, Siraj sent word to keep going. When they picked up the pace, he sent word ordering them to slow down. It took Law nearly a month-and-a-half to make the distance of about 450 kilometres, his group meanwhile boosted by forty-five men from the ship *Saint-Contest* who had escaped the debacle at Chandannagar.

'To satisfy him we should have been always in motion and yet not advancing; this did not suit us,' writes Law. 'It was of the utmost importance to arrive at some place where I could find means for the equipment of my troop. We were destitute of everything.'

It was of some relief to Law that Siraj's deputy Ram Narain received them with courtesy in Patna. The Frenchman stationed himself there—if necessary he could, within a week or so, sail or march to Murshidabad.

◆

By now word of conspiracy against Siraj was common knowledge.

The Frenchman Renault would on 4 September, more than two months after Plassey, write to Dupleix from Chandannagar of his time in Calcutta as a British prisoner:

> Never was a conspiracy conducted as publicly and with such indiscretion as this was, both by the Moors and the English. Nothing else was talked about in all the English settlements, and whilst every place echoed with the noise of it, the Nawab, who had a number of spies, was ignorant of everything. Nothing can prove more clearly the general hatred which was felt towards him.

The British arrangement with Mir Jafar was already a done deal. Hill maintains the Calcutta Council had signed a treaty with Mir Jafar on 19 May, 'but Mr. Watts's first intimation of his readiness to join the English is, I believe, in a letter dated the 26th of April'. Law holds that Mir Jafar signed the Treaty early in June.

Here it is tempting to raise the flag of Siraj's impotence in the face of conspiracy as much as his supposed ignorance of conspiracy that Law mentions. Either way, Law offers ever more instances of the steady hobbling of Siraj.

Law sent a representative to seek an audience with Siraj, who found the nawab 'tranquil' as late as 8 June. His letter to Law on 10 June presents an undisturbed tone—less than two weeks from his defeat. That letter reached Law on 19 June, just four days before Plassey. Law protesting such delays to Raja Ram Narain, the conduit, were to little effect, for reasons we shall soon see. In any case it would all be too late.

BOOK III
THE BATTLE

14

CLIVE BEFORE PLASSEY

'What is there to fear, my child?'

How could events ever turn against Clive at Plassey? His victory was foreshadowed by Britannia herself.

The fort at Katwa, the last stronghold of Siraj's troops before Murshidabad—and not far from Plassey—was won. On 17 June, the day his forces had arrived at Patuli, a village along a loop of the Bhagirathi, Clive had ordered the newly-promoted Major Coote to take Katwa, about 19 kilometres to the northwest along the river. Coote set off with this troops on the 18th: 200 Europeans went by boat, which also carried a couple of pieces of artillery; the 500 sepoys marched. They reached the outskirts of Katwa late that night to news that Siraj's troops had withdrawn into the fort, and reinforcements of cavalry led by the nawab's flighty commander, Manikchand, were soon expected.

The latter proved to be smoke, but the former held their ground. A recce to the fort by Coote's forces was detected by the defenders, and they began a withering fire. Coote withdrew his forces to the town, on the opposite bank of the fort. Then Coote's field piece and howitzer couldn't be set up; some parts had gone missing. On the morning of 19 June, Coote sent a message under a flag of truce to the faujdar of Katwa, in turn cajoling—'we came as friends to assist them against the tyranny of the Nabob'—and threatening a give-no-quarter attack. The faujdar demurred—according to Coote—swearing fealty to Siraj. In the end Coote opted for a pincer attack after crossing the river, with sepoys moving up from the south, and the Europeans from the north. The defenders fled after a brief battle, leaving behind cannon and ammunition. Around two in the afternoon Clive joined Coote at Katwa Fort.

◆

The situation offered a perfect set piece for some unbridled fantasy as poetic license. With Plassey looming, the Company's officers and troops dreamed of glory at camp. Some looked forward to promotion, some 'painted temples of gold in their minds', others had through powers of imagination already slain Siraj, arrived at the treasury waving banners of victory, and looted it.

A little away from camp, Clive was seated under a tree in deep contemplation, his wide forehead a 'battlefield of bravery, repository of wisdom, his breast a doorway to Yama's realm of death...awash in compelling streams of doubt and courage... His eyes bright as diamonds, his stare still, penetrating, resolute... "Hāi," despaired the warrior. "I disregarded the council of war, the counsel of everyone, and waded into this sea of battle without once thinking of the future... If I sink, we will all sink—even Britain."'

That's when an apparition—a vision—arrived, 'an exquisite lady bathed in the light of a million Koh-i-Noors', dressed in 'Inglondiyō' fashion, and said:

...Ki bhoy bāchhnōni?
Inglondér rājlōkkhi āmi, shubhāgini,
...shunō birōmōni!
...porākrōmi putrér gōurobé
Āmi chirōgōurobini...

What is there to fear, my child? Hear me, o jewel among the brave, hear me as I am England's Lakshmi, her fortune!..I am ever so proud of my brave son...

...Tōmār chintāy āji tōlilō āshōn,
Āshinu prithibitole, tōmaré, bāchhōni!
Shunāité bhōbishhot bidhir likhon, -
Shunilé ullāshé tumi nāchibé ekhōni...

...Your initiative has unsettled the throne, and I have come down to earth to tell you, my child, of what Fate has scripted for you. And you shall dance with joy when you hear it...

...Jobōnér ōttāchār shōhité nā pāri
Hotōbhāggō Bongōbāshi—chirōporādhin—
Lōyéchhé āshroy tobō...

The unfortunate people of Bengal, long subjugated, and unable any longer to withstand the cruelties of the Jobōn, have sought shelter with you...

◆

That is fantasy in the second canto of 'Polāshir Juddhō' by Nabinchandra Sen, an epic poem published in 1875. It is a paean to Clive and Crown with criticism by a Bengali Hindu of the real and perceived depredations in the region of several centuries of Jobōn rule. Jobōn is derived from the Sanskrit yavana, literally barbarian or foreigner, and in classical Bengali often used for Muslim rulers. The assurance to Clive by the gorgeous and inspirational Britannia consumed fully eighteen stanzas of the canto. Bengali historians like Akshaykumar Maitreya severely criticized the poem about twenty years later when, the scholar Rosinka Chaudhuri tells us in an essay in *The Journal of Asian Studies*, Maitreya raised the question 'of the relationship of history to poetry and to truth'. Maitreya even wrote to the poet questioning the historical roots of the poem—even for 'imaginary' depravities of Siraj that we have already seen. In reply, Chaudhuri notes, 'an interlocutor (Sureshchandra Samajpati, the editor of *Sahitya*,) said on behalf of the poet, "Not a single line (ek line ō noy)... [Polāshir Juddhō] is poetry, not history—that is what he has permitted me to write you".'

But Maitreya stood his ground, in particular because many people wouldn't have the 'courage' to conclude that the poem written by 'a patriotic, erudite man of letters' was anything but history. There were other factors too that Maitreya thought needed debunking. As Chaudhuri relates (citing Nabinchandra's autobiographical work of 1908), within months of the poem's release, 'it was put up as a play by a group called the New Aryan Theatre, where the famous actor-director Girishchandra Ghosh is said to have first made a name for himself when he acted the part of Clive'. Chaudhuri adds: 'The matter was complicated by the fact that [the poem] had been published in a textbook version by Sanyal and Company of Calcutta, with a preface attached to it that vouched for it as "the history of Bengal" and attested to its suitability as a textbook for use in schools. In a footnote, Maitreya quotes from the preface to this "history" book edition: "Not only has a complete poem like this a merit of its own superior to that of mere compilation of fugitive pieces but as it is also the history of Bengal of the period in verse, the introduction of such a book into our schools will be doubly beneficial to the students and an encouragement to real talent and for the literature of Bengal."'

◆

There are numerous other creative preludes to the battle, but few of these use imagery alongside a dramatic mix of fact and fiction as effectively as the tableaus and plays presented in present-day Motijheel, a gilded playground of politics subtly riding on patriotism and history as entertainment.

The place is pure fantasy, after a government makeover in 2015 named it Prakriti Tirtha: a pilgrimage for nature. The 350-acre lake ebbs and fills with the dry season and the wet, decorated with clusters of water hyacinth and reeds. The entrance is through an arch of concrete and plaster, painted beige, somewhat resembling the stonework of the Arc de Triomphe in Paris but resembling far more an entrance to a pandal to view a display of Durga Puja in Kolkata. The entrance leads to a faux cannon and signs that lead to a 'food court'. Manicured lawns and lush beds of rose, dahlia, and gerbera embroider a history made kitschy. The place is managed by the Government of West Bengal. 'Motijheel, a journey back in time', is printed on the entry ticket of twenty rupees.

A large wall of text near the entrance proclaims Motijheel as the 'cradle of British Rule in India that stands witness to a remarkable turning point in Indian history'. It also claims a little breathlessly: 'Motijheel is sometimes compared to Magna Carta-famed historic Runnymede of London.'

Statues of Murshidabad's nawabs lurk behind neat hedgerows, artfully blackened bronze casts of Murshid Quli, Alivardi, and Siraj. Past luxurious accommodation and prominent signage that proclaims a global Bengal, 'Bisshō Bānglā', a pride-and-marketing slogan of the government of the day, is an afterthought in this place of fairground grandeur as a tourist destination: a son et lumière show of history as theatre.

Another twenty rupees permits entry to Motijheel's open air

theatre for the Plassey show.

It is nearly sunset on a breezy February evening. There are three rows of concrete slab seating. To the right of the audience an intricately, even beautifully, rendered tableau shows Siraj at the head of his army, seated on a caparisoned elephant. A troop of heralds and foot soldiers lead the kuch—march. More elephants carrying his generals follow, and a train of camel-borne troops, cavalry, and more foot soldiers. With flights of egrets returning home in a russet sky tinged with blue, it doesn't seem like a warlike palette, more like colours of romantic intent, of history deliberately made more dramatic and poignant with nature as co-conspirator, as the tableau is almost always viewed at the end of the day.

It's more sobering to the front. On a stage and seated in an arc are five still figures all painted glossy black. From the audience's perspective, Watts is on the extreme left, and to his right is Clive. As hostess, Ghaseti Begum is seated centre stage. To her right is Mir Jafar. Jagat Seth Madhab Rai, to Mir Jafar's right, is the last in this cast of conspirators that is historically correct, but not in terms of such a boardroom gathering and their conversation that mixes fact, fiction, and supposition. Squadrons of dive-bombing mosquitoes add a realistic touch. The show begins late, the audience meanwhile serenaded by a Bengali pop song with the opening lyrics urging decency in love: 'Dushtumi ār kōrōnā'—Don't be mischievous.

Then follows twenty-two minutes of passion play and pathos, designed to anger, sadden, and entertain. There is a brief prelude about how the paradise of Murshidabad is now as absent as the golden age of Bengal, its remains now attended by the sighs of Siraj carried by the breeze. After stating 'how a great storm arrived unnoticed across the oceans', the narrator cuts to the genesis of the conspiracy.

Ghaseti Begum demands retribution for the killing of her lover, Hussain Quli Khan, by Siraj. Mir Jafar complains about being ignored and losing his prestige. The Jagat Seth feels gravely insulted by Siraj's 'impossible' demand of him to raise thirty million rupees from European merchants—and for being slapped by Siraj at court. 'Chhee,' Ghaseti Begum scoffs. 'Such arrogance. Even khuda'—god— 'will never forgive such transgressions.'

Clive and Watts are upset with Siraj for a range of sins from not permitting the Company any additional fortifications and accusing them of unfair trade practices to attacking Calcutta and hurting British pride. The actors speak in a mix of archaic Bengali and English with stilted accents beloved of a particular species of Indian actor who employ it for nearly all characters from Shakespearean plays to, in this case, avaricious colonialists. Siraj is a nuisance, they announce. The begum agrees that Siraj must be removed, or else 'Bengal and all of us will suffer'.

'Begum Sahiba, don't you worry,' Clive assures her. 'We shall get that subahdar. We will finish him—uhāké āmrā shésh karibō.' He thunders: 'I will get that bloody Siraj. Uhāké chhāribō nā.' We won't spare him.

'But there's a problem with that outcome,' the begum cautions. 'Siraj is young, but he's intelligent.'

This caution is accepted, and the dialogue follows in a mix of Bengali and English onto the next phase of the conspiracy, the selection of the new nawab.

Clive: 'Why Mir Jafar-saab, you seem to be a great candidate...'

Mir Jafar: 'Nā-nā...'

'That would be unwise,' the Jagat Seth counsels, 'such a plum opportunity for enrichment may not come around again.'

Clive seconds that thought. 'We shall only take a small compensation for the East India Company... The rest, sir,' he gallantly offers, 'will belong to you to do as you please.'

Mir Jafar (in Bengali): 'Be careful... He has many faithful ears here, many faithful to his salt.'

Clive: 'Well, very soon uhādér āmrā namak harām banāi dibō, ha-ha-ha.'

Watts (in response to Clive's comment about converting the faithful into traitors against Siraj's 'salt'): 'The army is of quite a sizeable number, if I may say so...'

Clive concurs, but with a figurative nudge and wink—'...you know what I mean!'—lectures Watts about how numbers matter only when they come into play. With Mir Jafar, Rai Durlabh, and Yar Latif as Siraj's commanders that was unlikely to happen.

Watts: 'Correct, sir. But Mir Madan is still loyal to the nawab.'

Clive: 'What is one man against an army?'

♦

Reality was somewhat more infirm even with the Plassey conspiracy signed and sealed, because it wasn't yet delivered. For Clive, victories in Chandannagar and Katwa were no guarantee that everything that lay ahead would play out as planned. 'His bouts of activity were so furious,' writes Brendon, 'that they seem to have brought on attacks of nervous derangement, which he calmed with opium.'

Mir Jafar, the linchpin of the coup, remained a major concern. Not even a treaty with him, scripted about a month earlier, which formalized the conspiracy and a post-Siraj world—Mir Jafar would become nawab, and Clive & Co. and other co-conspirators would benefit—dispelled Clive's unease.

♦

The Company and Crown had put their names to the document. Clive had signed it. When Admiral Watson demurred, his signature was forged.

Watts, Clive's political weathervane in Murshidabad, had kept the colonel informed of every change of direction of breezes, every slackening and firming. The pieces started falling into place after the battle of Chandannagar, overriding correspondence of negotiation between Siraj and Watson and Clive. Mir Jafar, who made the initial overture to the British, remained at the centre of it. In the wings were Rai Durlabh and Yar Latif, who is believed by some to have begun the Plassey conspiracy by claiming the nawabship if it came through, but fell in with the plan to make Mir Jafar nawab when his claim was met tepidly. True to their mien, the Seths remained obliquely active, as did Ghaseti Begum with her long reach. And there was Umachand.

What followed was murky even by the standards of the day.

Alexander John Arbuthnot, a senior Raj-era Crown official, and one among several biographers of Clive and chroniclers of Plassey mechanics, repeats Clive's great distrust of Umachand—this distrust played an unsavoury cameo right till the conclusion of the Plassey conspiracy. There is no doubt that 'negotiations with Mir Jafar were principally conducted through the agency of the Hindu, Omichand,' Arbuthnot writes in his *Lord Clive: The Foundation of*

British Rule in India. But Umachand was considered by Clive to be little more than a petty blackmailer. As Arbuthnot puts it: '... having entered into solemn engagements to support the English cause, [Umachand] was accused of having threatened to divulge the conspiracy to Suraj ud Daulah, demanding thirty lakhs of rupees as the price of his silence.'

He correctly maintains that the 'story has been accepted by successive historians of British India, and until very recently by successive biographers of Clive'. In his opinion, Orme placed a weak qualifier of 'It is said' to attribute to the claim a judicious degree of hearsay. The Umachand theory is accepted by Mill, by his 'annotator', Wilson, Marshman, John Malcolm in *The Life of Robert, Lord Clive*, by Macaulay in his 'famous' essay on Clive, George Robert Gleig, and Charles Wilson in *English Men of Action*. Only Malleson among the Raj writers of Arbuthnot's era, questioned the claim. 'But Colonel Malleson does not question the fact that Omichand made an excessive demand, or that at a meeting of the Council, Clive denounced him as "the greatest villain upon earth"'.

Even with his apparent aid to the British after Siraj attacked Calcutta in June 1756, the Council had retained its suspicion about Umachand playing a double hand. The proceedings of a Council meeting that took place on 20 January 1757, less than three weeks after the retaking of Calcutta by Clive and Watson, actually considered penalizing the merchant:

> Omichand, his behaviour during the siege of Calcutta, his conduct since, and the universal notion that prevails of his having been aiding in the councils of our enemies, giving great room to suspect his having been directly or indirectly concerned in involving the Settlement in the late troubles...
>
> Agreed that all his houses, tenures, grounds and effects be for the present attached and sequestered, and that all his perishable effects be sold by our Agents, and the amount deposited in the Treasury till some determination is come to concerning Omichand.

Long explains that the attachment of Umachand's effects was waived, as the Council found it 'impossible to ascertain if he had been directly concerned in involving the Settlement in the troubles and disgrace we underwent.' Suspicion would return scant days later, as Siraj arrived for his disastrous second campaign at Calcutta, and camped at 'Omichand's Garden'.

In any event, Clive and the Calcutta's Council outmanoeuvred Umachand. The merchant insisted that a clause be inserted guaranteeing his payment, and the agreed amount. With the sanction of the Council, Clive had two treaties drawn up, one on white paper, the other on red paper. The draft treaty on white paper was the real one. It didn't contain any insertion guaranteeing payment to Umachand. The treaty on red paper, which he was shown, did. It isn't certain if agreements of the day were drawn up on red paper or red-hued parchment, but whatever the expedient eccentricity of it, Umachand was snared.

By several accounts, Admiral Watson declined to sign the 'red' treaty. It was only the latest in a series of disagreements between Watson and Clive, which, as we have seen, began as early as their departure from Madras and continued in Calcutta over the decision to attack the French. Among other disputes one was about the share of loot on campaigns. 'It was feared that the absence of Watson's signature would be noticed by Omichand,' writes Arbuthnot, 'and might therefore lead to the disclosure of the plot. Accordingly Watson's signature was attached to the red treaty by another person— by Clive, according to Macaulay, but if not by Clive, at all events under his orders.'

Malcolm defended this duplicity, Arbuthnot notes, on the 'strength of evidence subsequently' provided by Clive, and defended the matter as 'a pious and necessary fraud'. Indeed, Malcolm went as far as to suggest that the admiral, 'while refusing to affix his signature to the fictitious treaty, did not object to it being done on his behalf.' At any rate he did not resent the use which was made of his name; for before the expedition started for Plassey, and after having been made fully acquainted with what had taken place, he wrote to Clive in the following manner:

I am glad to hear that Mi'r Jafar's party increases. I hope everything will turn out in the expedition to your wishes, and that I may soon have to congratulate you on the success of it. I most heartily pray for your health and a speedy return crowned with laurels.

Such an argument isn't unwarranted. After all, Admiral Watson claimed his share of Plassey plunder. 'Clive to the last maintained that, looking to Omichand's misconduct, the artifice which had been resorted to was perfectly justifiable,' continues Arbuthnot, 'and that while he believed that Watson had authorised Mr Lushington to attach his signature to the fictitious treaty, he would, in the circumstances, have ordered Watson's name to be attached, whether he had consented or not.' Clive had once again gainfully employed the argument of the big picture.

The treaties, in red and white, were signed on 19 May. They were immediately sent to Mir Jafar for signature. His agreement on the genuine treaty was in any case required. His agreement to the deceitful one, a sub-conspiracy, would be required to make it appear genuine in Umachand's eyes.

Watts was on behalf of the Company the eyes and ears of the conspiracy in Murshidabad, leaving only in the last weeks before Siraj marched to Plassey. Kept under close watch by Siraj, he would escape by pretending to go on a hunt, and thereafter not return to his residence.

But he sealed the deal. Plassey lore has it that the last secret conference before the Battle of Plassey took place between Mir Jafar and Watts at the aspiring nawab's residence at Jafarganj—some ruins of which still stand. Watts, goes the lore, entered the house in a palki—palanquin—dressed as a pardanashin lady. Watts's act in a purdah would cap the aggregate of facts and legends of the conspiracy.

◆

Affixing signatures to a conspiracy was only the latest in a series of plays and ploys, as we have seen, that were designed to reclaim for Clive & Co. the redoubt of Calcutta, dominate if not destroy the French in Bengal and the entire east, and push northward to effect a coup against Siraj—the nawab who stood in the way of the business and bluster of John Company, and leaned dangerously towards the French. But getting Mir Jafar to sign a document was one thing, as Clive soon realized. Getting that key signatory to deliver on his commitment for the grand prize of Bengal was quite another. Mir Jafar was seemingly the shaman who controlled the endgame of Plassey. He frayed Clive's nerves. As we shall soon see, Mir Jafar's nerves weren't doing much better. Just days before the final push, Plassey remained a slippery precipice for both.

Clive had written to Mir Jafar every day since leaving Chandannagar, but in turn received only one reply, on 17 June, dated a day earlier. The message was ambiguous. 'In this Jaffier acknowledged his seeming reconciliation with the Nabob, and his oath not to assist the English against him,' writes Orme, 'but said, nevertheless, that the purport of his covenant with them must be carried into execution.' The ironical possibility of Mir Jafar's betrayal so rattled Clive at such a 'decisive' stage in his enterprise that he decided not to cross over to the eastern bank, to the 'island' of Qasimbazar. As we have seen, it was so called because of a vast and extreme horseshoe bend of the Bhagirathi. Plassey and the eventual battlefield lay to the south and southeast. Clive wasn't prepared to cross until he was on surer ground with Mir Jafar. Two more days passed in tense expectation.

Meanwhile, the rainy season arrived on 18 June, five days short of the battle at Plassey, and a day before Katwa fell to the Company. Orme tells us that it arrived with 'violence'.

In Bengal, the monsoon usually does. It arrives after a brief winter and spring. From mid-March the sun bakes and broils the land and its people. Then arrive the terrifying curtain-raiser storms as the warm and moist air of the southeast marries cooler, drier air from the northwest. That's how storms Bengalis call Kālbōishākhi— Nor'westers—are born. They bring violent thunderstorms and rain for an hour and more mixed in with winds that can gust at speeds of up to a hundred kilometres an hour. These storms presage a season from about mid-June, that makes and sometimes breaks Bengal, the region's life-giving, life-taking force of borshā, rain. Most of the annual rain is decanted in three months, and is sometimes accompanied by storms that sweep up from the Bay of Bengal. In the days of Plassey, the rainy season stopped most shipping on the seas and the mouths of Bengal's great rivers. Much of deltaic Bengal would be inundated, and its northern regions turned to slush. Bengal's rains have for centuries sustained the lives and livelihoods of millions and sustained entire empires. But they also retain the power to erase life by the hundreds, thousands, even hundreds of thousands.

Indeed, that day it rained so violently that the main body of Company troops camped in the plains around Katwa were compelled to strike their tents and seek shelter in town—'the heavy rains... prevented the men from lying' in the tents, noted Major Eyre Coote, the hero of Katwa, and a future hero of the Battle of Wandiwash in 1760, that decisively diminished French power in the subcontinent, and a future commander-in-chief of British troops in India.

For Clive it was a time of some despondency. On 19 June, he wrote from Katwa to the Select Committee at Fort William with a plea to reach out to all possible allies, even the Mughal emperor's vazir, Ghazi-ud-din Khan, as insurance, because he was assailed by doubt as to Mir Jafar's intention and ability to stand by the conspiracy. He also voiced the option of staying put at Katwa—he would in a couple of days articulate this to his officers at a council of war. In those tense days he didn't quite cut the picture of a resolute commander, hero, and saviour, but more of a man who had his career on the line:

Gentlemen,—The party I sent has taken Cutwa town and fort. Both are strong, notwithstanding which I feel the greatest anxiety at the little intelligence I receive from Meer Jaffeir, and if he is not treacherous, his sangfroid or want of strength will I fear overset the expedition. I am trying a last effort...to prevail upon him to march out and join us. I have appointed Plassey the place of rendezvous, and have told him at the same time without he gives me this or some other sufficient proof of the sincerity of his intentions, I will not cross the river. This I hope will meet with your approbation. I shall act with such caution as not to risque the loss of our forces, and whilst we have them, we may always have it in our power to bring about a revolution, should the present not succeed. They say there is a considerable quantity of grain in and about this place; if we can collect 8 or 10,000 maunds [about 300 to 375 tonnes] we may maintain our present situation during the Rains, which will greatly distress the Nabob, and either reduce him to terms which may be depended on, or give us time to bring in the Beirboin Rajah [the nawab of Birbhum], Marattas, or Gazoody Cawn. I

desire you will give me your sentiments freely how you think
I should act, if Meer Jaffeir can give us no assistance.

◆

Some news arrived on 20 June by way of one of Watts's messengers.
It was unclear in its import. Was Mir Jafar play-acting to bolster
the conspiracy, or selling it out? The messenger relayed news of a
meeting with Mir Jafar and his son Miran in their palace. The two
were questioning him when, suddenly, some people appeared in the
'private court', writes Orme. They were evidently Siraj's men because
as soon as they were seen 'Meirum [Miran] threatened to cut off his
head as a spy, and the heads of all the English, if they should dare
to cross the river into the island.'

Surer news arrived that evening: two letters from Mir Jafar, one
to his representative Umar Beg, who was in Clive's camp; the other to
Clive. They had been written a day earlier. The letter to Clive assured
him that Mir Jafar planned to leave Murshidabad on 19 June, the
same date as on the letter. His tent would be 'either on the left or the
right' of his army. And that he would then send more 'intelligence'
after he joined the body of the army. He had been unable to do so
earlier as he had been fearful of discovery; Siraj had posted guards
on all routes with the purpose of intercepting messengers. Mir Jafar
addressed Clive as Sabut Jang Bahadur, firm or daring in war, the
honorific he had gained from the nawab of Arcot:

> Health, &c., to Sabut Jung Bahadre, the day of the Eade. Your
> note from Colsannie is arrived. I have perused the contents.
> To-morrow the day of the Eade by the blessing of God I shall
> march. I shall have my tent fixed to the right or left of the army.
> I have hitherto been afraid to send you intelligence. After I am
> arrived in the army mutual intelligence will be easier, but here
> the Nabob has fixed chokeys [guards, checkpoints] on all the
> roads. Your letters come too open to me. I hope that till our
> affairs are publicly declared you will be very careful.

But even this wasn't of great assurance to Clive as Mir Jafar's letter
was cryptic, revealing neither any of his own plans of battle nor
suggesting any for Company troops. Clive was spooked into writing

a letter requesting support from the raja of Bardhaman, Tilak Chand, 'who was discontented with the Nabob'. Orme provides the reason Clive needed cavalry, of which he had little. He realized the danger of 'coming to action without horse'. The raja would be of great help even if he could quickly despatch a thousand cavalry.

He also wrote a letter on 20 June to the nawab Assad-uz-Zaman of Birbhum, a zamindari west of Murshidabad, as the nawab had evidently professed friendship to the Company. Again, there was a plea for cavalry:

> The letters you wrote to the Governor of Calcutta... I have well considered, and the strong friendship you expressed gives me great pleasure. By continued marches I have reached Cutwa, and the fort, which had a great force in it, by the blessing of God fell into my hands in a very short time. If you are firmly inclined to join me call God and your Prophet to witness your sincerity, and send 2 or 300 good horse to march day and night to join me in the time of battle, and I shall look upon your affairs as my own, and end them happily for you; and your country shall not be injured, nor shall any collector be put over you; and whatever may be the charge of the forces you send me I will make the Government pay you. My real meaning is that I will content you, if your people arrive in time. Send me an immediate answer.

At this point, Clive had no idea of when his forces would clash with that of Siraj—and even if they actually would, as subsequent correspondence indicates. All he could do was boost his forces by calling in every promise of friendship towards the Company, leveraging every animosity against Siraj. Even so, Clive couldn't be sure going by his experience in the Carnatic, about an alliance against the young nawab. Orme writes that Clive recollected 'that the princes of Indostan never join the standard which doubts of success, his anxieties increased by the dread of those imputations, to which he foresaw the present caution of his conduct would be exposed, if, after having engaged the public welfare in a project of such importance and risque, he should recede from the attempt in the very hour of event'.

♦

On edge, Clive called a war council with twenty officers on 21 June.
Clive had for some days mulled over several options:

One: Write to the Company's Council in Calcutta asking for
instructions.

Two: The army should immediately cross over to Qasimbazar
and 'risque' attacking Siraj.

And, three: They should stay put at Katwa for the duration of
the monsoons, living off the vast amounts of foodgrain they had
captured at the fort. ('Within the fort, and in several granaries
in the neighbourhood,' writes Orme, 'was found as much rice as
would sustain 10,000 men for a year.') Meanwhile, the ever-ready
Maratha marauders could perhaps be invited with their astonishingly
successful cavalry to join the British expedition. This would throw
against the nawab of Bengal a force of impressive numbers, expertise
and verve, especially if other 'country' powers and possible allies
like the zamindar of Bardhaman arrived.

Clive's thoughts about allying with the Marathas against Siraj
must have been triggered by the message he received from the
peshwa, Balaji Baji Rao, during his march northward along the Hugli.
He admitted as much in a letter he would write in less than a fortnight
to his colleagues in the Select Committee at Fort St George in Madras:

> I must acquaint you that some days before I left Chandernagore
> letters arrived from the Nanna [Nanasaheb, an honorific]
> desiring our friendship, for that he would engage to enter the
> Province with 150,000 Marattas and make good to us double
> of all the losses we had sustained; that as we were powerful in
> ships we might keep out the French by sea, and he would take
> care to do it by land.

Clive provided determined logic at this first and only council of war
he ever convened, noted Coote in his diligent journals—a record of
which is taken here from a biography of Coote by Col. H. C. Wylly:

> The Colonel informed the Council that he found he could not
> depend on Meer Jaffier for anything more than his standing
> neuter in case we came to an action with the Nabob; that

Monsieur Law with a body of French was then within three days march of joining the Nabob, whose army (by the best intelligence he could get) consisted of about 50,000 men; and that he called us together to desire our opinions, whether in those circumstances it would be prudent to come to immediate action with the Nabob, or fortify ourselves where we were and remain till the monsoon was over, and the Morattoes could be brought into the country to join us.

Then Clive being Clive decided to have his way, and break the protocol in a council of war of asking the most junior officer present to first present views. Instead he inverted the protocol and cast his vote first: Remain at Katwa, ride out the rains, wait for help. The company present followed the top-down order in opinion, and as it turned out, the majority took his cue. Coote noted the vote:

Lieutenant-Colonel Robert Clive, President: against an immediate action.

Majors
{ James Kilpatrick: against.
{ Archibald Grant: against.
{ Eyre Coote: for immediate action.

Captains
{ Frederick Gaupp: against.
{ Alexander Grant: for.
{ John Cudmore: against.
{ Thomas Rumbold: against.
{ Christian Fischer: against.
{ Charles Palmer: against.
{ Andrew Armstrong: for.
{ Grainger Muir: for.
{ M. le Beaume: against.
{ Robert Campbell: for.
{ Rudolph Waggoner: against.
{ John Corneille: against.

Richard Hater, lieutenant in the Navy, did not give his opinion because he thought he had not his proper seat in Council.

	{ Peter Casters: for.
Captain-Lieut.	{ Wm. Jennings: for.
	{ John Francis Paschoud: against.
	{ Molitore: against.

The 13-7 vote to remain consisted of officers largely drawn from the Madras army and the 39th Foot, the British infantry regiment to which Coote belonged. Coote's motion for immediate action was backed mostly by those from the Bengal army. Two officers from the Bombay army were evenly split. The artillery man, Jennings, voted for immediate action. (Gaupp and Waggoner—Wagner—were Swiss infantry men, and Paschoud, also Swiss, was an artilleryman.)

Coote, the first to dissent against Clive in the war council's descending order of opinion, wanted to push on, and offered compelling reasons:

...which were that, as we had hitherto met with nothing but success, which consequently had given great spirits to our men, I was of opinion that any delay might cast damp ['...a stop so near the enemy would naturally quell this ardour, which it would be difficult to restore', is Orme's more dramatic recall]; Secondly, that the arrival of Monsieur Law would not only strengthen the Nabob's army and add vigour to their councils [Orme: '... they would surround the English...'], but likewise weaken our force considerably, as the number of Frenchmen we had entered into our service after the capture of Chandernagore would undoubtedly desert to him upon every opportunity. Thirdly, that our distance from Calcutta was so great that all communication from thence would certainly be cut off, and therefore gave us no room to hope for supplies, and consequently that we must be soon reduced to the greatest distress. ['...cut off its communication with Calcutta, when distresses not yet foreseen might ruin it as effectually as the loss of a battle...,' noted Orme.] Therefore gave it as my opinion that we should come to an immediate action, or if that was thought entirely impracticable, that we should return to Calcutta, the consequence of which must be our own disgrace and the inevitable destruction of the Company's affairs.

General Sir Charles Monro, an unabashed empire man, veteran of the Second Boer War and World War I and, subsequently, commander-in-chief in India, lauded this pivotal dissenter in his introduction to Coote's biography, that the major 'seems to have won if not the affection at any rate the admiration of his superiors for his high military qualities; his courage and rare judgement are indicated in the opinions which he expressed at the Council of War assembled by Clive...'

◆

Clive didn't sit on his council victory—or 'sanction', as Orme describes it, as it in 'no wise alleviated the anxieties of Clive'. Immediately afterwards he went off by himself into the adjoining grove, 'where he remained near an hour in deep meditation'—and where he mythically encountered the vision of Britannia as imagined by the poet Nabinchandra—'which convinced him of the absurdity of stopping where he was; and acting now entirely from himself, he gave orders, on his return to his quarters, that the army should cross the river the next morning'.

Coote notes that momentous climbdown with a slight difference, and in his typically matter-of-fact manner:

> About an hour after we had broken up, the Colonel informed me that, notwithstanding the resolution of the Council of War, he intended to march the next morning, and accordingly gave orders for the Army to hold themselves in readiness, leaving a subaltern officer's command, together with all our sick, in the fort at Katwa.

There's another narrative, Clive's own, which reflects his confusion in a note on the council of war to Company 'nabobs' in Calcutta—a note negated by his own action to cross the river the following morning:

> Letter from Colonel Clive to Select Committee, Fort William, dated Cutwa, 21 June, 1757.
>
> Gentlemen,—Enclosed are copies of two letters received last night. I likewise transmit the sentiments of a Council of War held this day, whether or not it was proper without the assistance of some country Power to attack the Nabob. I wait

only for some encouragement from Meir Jaffeir to proceed, which must be the issue unless the Nabob makes very fair offers of accommodation.

I have the honour to be, &c. &c., Robert Clive.

Even so, in a letter to the Select Committee at Fort William dated the same day—probably written before the council of war—Clive harboured his ongoing misgivings and insecurities about the Company's oust-Siraj project, including the possibility of Mir Jafar staying neutral instead of publicly throwing in his lot with the British. To pursue Siraj with only the numbers at hand was a great risk, he added, and defeat of the enterprise was as likely as gaining advantage. Clive also sought the committee's counsel even though it would arrive too late to be of any use. He suggested again the possibility of reaching out to 'Gazoody Cawn'—Ghazi-ud-din Khan—and, as he presented to the council of war, of also pulling in the Marathas against Siraj. Clive even hints at détente with Siraj—which he would shortly hold out to Mir Jafar as a threat! At this point it seems Clive was as consumed with worry as Siraj was:

Letter from Colonel Clive to the Select Committee, Fort William, dated Cutwa, 21 June, 1757.

Gentlemen,—Since my last another letter has been delivered Meir Jaffeir and no answer returned in writing... I am really at a loss how to act at the present situation of our affairs, especially should I receive a confirmation by letter of Meir Jaffeir's resolution to stand neuter. The Nabob's forces at present are not said to exceed 8,000 men but a compliance with their demands [over pay] may easily encrease them. If we attack them it must be entrenched, and ourselves without any assistance. In this place a repulse must be fatal, on the contrary success may give the greatest advantage. The Nabob's apprehensions at present are great, and perhaps he may be glad to grant us an honorable Peace. The principle of fear may make him act much against his private inclination and I believe that has been the case ever since the capture of Chandernagore. There still remains another expedient of sending an embassy either to Gazoody Cawn or the Morattoes to invite them in. I beg you will let me have your sentiments how I ought to act at this critical juncture.

Whatever the Rashomon-like variations, major and minor, in records, recollections and living histories of Plassey, Clive did own up to one central reality, as Coote's biographer noted with some satisfaction: He gave in to the minority view of all-in war where, once committed, there would be no recourse to retreat without jeopardizing every recent military gain since the retaking of Calcutta in January 1757, jeopardizing the Company's very existence in Bengal.

Clive—by then elevated to Baron Clive of Plassey—would admit as much in 1773 to the Select Committee of the House of Commons that was investigating his conduct in India that, 'had he abided by the votes of the majority he would have caused the ruin of the East India Company'.

15

THE MARCH TO THE MANGO ORCHARD

'I am determined to risque everything on your account...'

There remain some grey areas as to what followed the next day, 22 June—Plassey Minus One. Here I have largely followed Orme's and Coote's narratives, and some observations in Reid's *The Battle of Plassey*. Coote's records maintain the army crossed the 'Baggiruttee' (also 'Bogrutty' in some tellings but really our history-entwined Bhagirathi) at 6 a.m.

By the fourth week of June, the Bhagirathi–Hugli is plump with rain and run-off even as far north from the Bay of Bengal as Plassey, Qasimbazar, and Murshidabad. Its alluvial banks, overgrown with grass and weed, is frail with the wet. The ground is damp, even sodden in places, skies overcast and sunny in turn transforming the region into a veritable greenhouse. The air is so heavy with moisture it can appear to slow even a determined bluebottle fly.

Clive's army marched for a little over 3 kilometres, before stopping to recover their energy and allow colleagues to catch up. They resumed their march at 4 p.m., not halting until they reached Laksha Bagh, the 'tope' or mango orchard at Plassey, a roughly rectangular area surrounded by an earthen bank, around midnight.

Reid describes Clive's deposition before the parliamentary Select Committee as 'surprisingly evasive'. Clive claimed Coote misunderstood him, and pointed 'to the fact that the army did not cross the river...until the evening of 22 June' and only after receiving a letter of assurance from Mir Jafar. Clive's journal, Reid notes, 'explicitly states the army crossed the river at 5 in the evening'.

Evasive or not, that day Clive was undoubtedly a person under great stress, perhaps feeling even a little ahead of himself at this point. It shows in the two letters he wrote to Mir Jafar on 22 June, one presumably sent before, and the second after receiving a message from Mir Jafar.

Clive's first letter, reproduced in Hills' *Bengal in 1756-1757*, is desperate—whining, threatening:

> I am determined to risque everything on your account, though you will not exert yourself. I shall be on the other side of the river this evening. If you will join me at Placis, I will march half way to meet you, then the whole Nabob's army will know I fight for you. Give me [leave] to call to your mind how much your own glory and safety depends upon it. Be assured if you do this you will be Subah of these Provinces, but if you cannot go even this length to assist us I call God to witness the fault is not mine, and I must desire your consent for concluding a Peace with the Nabob, and what has passed between us will never be known. What can I say more than that I am as desirous of your success and welfare as my own.

Orme's more detailed description of the movement also confirms the intervening letter from Mir Jafar, and that the reply from Clive contains another threat for a last-ditch détente with Siraj, but differs in the timing of the crossing.

Orme mentions that the sick among the company were first secured in the fort of Katwa. And then 'at sun-rise, on the 22d, the army began to pass: all were landed on the opposite shore by four in the afternoon, at which time another messenger arrived with a letter from Jaffier, which had likewise been dispatched on the 19th, but had taken bye-roads, and was delayed by other precautions. The purport was, "That the Nabob had halted at Muncarra [Mankara, by the present-day highway from Kolkata to Malda], a village six miles to the south of Cossimbuzar, and intended to entrench and wait the event at that place, where Jaffier proposed that the English should attack him [Siraj] by surprize, marching round by the inland part of the island."' The 'island' being the figurative description for a large tract of land nearly surrounded by an extreme loop of the Bhagirathi.

This is the translated text of the somewhat nervous letter from Mir Jafar to Clive, received on 22 June at 3 p.m.:

> I have received your letter advising the taking of Cutwa and was highly pleased. Sunday I marched from the city and reached Ammony Gunge and staid a day there to collect my people. The

Nabob marched to-day from Tarrackpore [Tarakpur] and has pitched his tent at Moncurra near the bridge. By the blessing of God to-morrow I shall march from hence Tuesday, and shall have my quarter to the left at a distance. The Nabob's intention is to have his intrenchment at Moncurra, therefore the sooner you march to fall on him the better before his design can take place. As yet you are now only designing, but it is not now proper to be indolent. When you come near I shall then be able to join you. If you could send two or three hundred good fighting men [along] the upper road towards Cossimbuzar, the Nabob's army would of themselves retreat. Then the battle will have no difficulty. When I am arrived near the army I will send you privately all the intelligence. Let me have previous notice of the time you intend to fight.

Clive wrote a quick message to Mir Jafar in reply—records show Clive's message being despatched at 6 p.m. It's also an indicator of his decision to finally cross the Bhagirathi:

Upon receiving your letter I am come to a resolution to proceed immediately to Placis. I am impatient for an answer to my letter by the trusty man.

Orme writes that 'Colonel Clive immediately sent back the messenger with this answer: That he should march to Plassy without delay, and would the next morning advance six miles farther to the village of Daudpoor; but if Meer Jaffier did not join him there, he would make peace with the Nabob.'

Here's the letter Orme refers to:

Whatever could be done by me I have done, I can do no more. If you will come to Daudpore I will march from Placis to meet you, but if you won't comply even with this, pardon me, I shall make it up with the Nabob.

But this reaching out by Clive to Mir Jafar one final time before the battle was, according to Hill, only sent around the time the nawab's forces began their march on 23 June, the day of the battle. Hill notes the message was sent through Amir Beg, the confidante of Mir Jafar— the 'trusty man'—who acted with kindness to British ladies during the siege of Calcutta by Siraj. Here's Hill's record: 'Message from Colonel Clive to Jafar Ali Khan, dated Placis, 23 June, 1757. Dispatched at 7 a.m.' Reid justifiably considers this as Hill 'hopelessly' confusing matters by erroneously recording the time of despatch as seven that morning, by which time the battle 'was well underway'.

It wasn't quite, as we shall see. But such discrepancy doesn't diminish Orme's description of the crossing and the tough march to Plassey:

> Accordingly the troops proceeded before sunset, conforming their march to the progress of the boats, which, as before, were towed against the stream; and having, by unceasing toil, advanced fifteen miles [or 24 kilometres in fading light and then dark, through soft and slushy tracks and fields, accompanied by rain] in eight hours, arrived at one in the morning at Plassy.

Coote's biographer also notes the slog: 'The march, though comparatively a short one, had been fatiguing, for rain had fallen continuously.'

Reid's conclusion as to varying timings of the march is on point, and he looks to Orme's account to streamline the flow of troops. It's most likely that the advance guard crossed on the 22nd morning to 'secure a bridgehead', and that Clive 'delayed bringing the main body over until he had heard from Mir Jafar later in the day'. An anonymous account reproduced by Hill notes that the last elements of the force reached Plassey only around 3 a.m. on 23 June, just hours before the battle.

◆

At first, it all appeared to be lost for the British.

When Clive and his troops arrived at Plassey, they were stunned to discover that Siraj's army had got there well before them, having decided to push on instead of staying a while at the village of Mankara—and even expecting a skirmish if not a battle there—as Mir Jafar's letter had suggested. Orme explains well the consternation and confusion in Clive's camp as well as Siraj's decision to press on from Mankara:

> The army immediately took possession of the adjoining grove,

when, to their great surprize, the continual sound of drums, clarions, and cymbals, which always accompany the night Watches of an Indian camp, convinced them that they were within a mile of the Nabob's army. His intention to remain at Muncarra, had arisen from a supposition that the English would advance immediately after they had taken Cutwah, and would arrive at Plassy before his own could get there; but as soon as he found that they were not so active, he continued his march, and arrived at the camp of Plassy twelve hours before them.

By all accounts they were there in force. 'On arrival at Plassey grove Clive received information that the Nawab's advance guard of 6,000 men was then within three miles' of the British camp, records Coote's biography. This number was already a thousand in excess of the total number of troops at Clive's command.

On Clive's orders the British force took precautions as best as they could. Coote writes that 'an advanced guard of 200 Europeans, 300 seapoys, and two pieces of cannon were posted at Plassey House'— the name given after the battle to Clive's field headquarters, a riverside hunting lodge of the nawab sequestered by the British. It lay a little to the northwest of the grove and was enclosed within a garden wall. Coote writes that 'several seapoy guards' were posted 'around the Grove'.

The grove would prove to be a superb location for the British force—the weather, and Clive's watchfulness would ensure it. The grove extended, Orme tells us, from the north to the south for about 800 yards (or a little over 730 metres) in length and 300 yards (nearly 275 metres) wide. The mango trees were planted in 'regular rows'. It was enclosed by a 'slight bank and ditch choked with coarse weeds and brambles'. At its top left, the northwest, the grove was just a dash over 45 metres from the Bhagirathi, and a short distance, as you've just read, from the 'hunting-house of the Nabob's'—as Orme puts it. The grove was angled away from the river at its southwest corner—just over 180 metres (200 yards) from the river.

It's difficult to better Orme's description of the lay of the land:

The river, a mile before it reaches this house, curves to the south-west nearly in the shape of an horse-shoe, including a peninsula about three miles in circumference, of which the neck, from the stream to the stream again, is not more than a quarter of a mile across. About 300 yards to the south of the peninsula, began an entrenchment, which Roydoolub [Rai Durlabh Ram] had thrown up to secure his camp: the southern face, fronting the grove of Plassy, extended nearly in a straight line, about 200 yards inland from the bank of the river; and then turning to the northeast by an obtuse angle, continued nearly in this direction about three miles [4.8 kilometres]. Within this entrenchment encamped the whole army, of which a part likewise occupied the peninsula. In the angle was raised a redoubt, on which cannon were mounted. About 300 yards to the east of this redoubt, but without the camp, was a hillock covered with trees; and 800 yards to the south of this hillock and the redoubt, was a small tank or pond; and 100 yards [a little over 90 metres] farther to the south was another, but much larger tank: both, as all such public reservoirs of water in Bengal, were surrounded by a large mound of earth at the distance of some yards from the margin of the water.

Just how close the nawab's troops were would become clear in the morning. The closest—southernmost—of these tanks would be used by French cannoneers to fire on Clive's troops. At daybreak, Coote himself would be positioned to the east of the hunting lodge and at the front of the grove.

That was still some hours away. As Clive's advance guard and camp sentinels kept watch, the remainder of the force, some arriving just three hours or so before daybreak, rested in the mango grove. But 'few' officers did, Orme writes, 'least of all' Clive who remained within the compound of Plassey House.

From all accounts there he fretted, weighing his options, wishing for assurances from any of the Plassey conspirators—key beneficiary Mir Jafar, notable beneficiary Rai Durlabh Ram and even Yar Latif, who, as we know, was briefly in the running as a candidate to replace Siraj.

At least one among the Plassey conspirators had already lined up to be counted: Rai Durlabh, the commander Siraj had sent on ahead as his vanguard. The *Siyar* tells it bluntly:

The Prince...sent part of his forces to Palassy, under the command of Radja Dullub-ram, with orders to prepare an intrenched camp, and everything necessary for defence and war. That Commander repaired thither, and in appearance, seemed busy in executing the orders he had received; but in fact he was only intent upon his own business; for he not only entered into a private agreement with the English, but added some articles to their treaty with Mir-djaafer-qhan, whilst at the same time he was daily gaining to his party some officers amongst the troops he commanded, under promise of doing for them something according to their own wishes.

That ploy would be exposed on the battlefield to Clive's advantage. Meanwhile, the restless, jittery colonel may even have mulled over the apparent folly of giving in to Coote's counsel. Suggests Reid: '...Clive might well have reflected that taking on heavy odds and trusting to pluck and European discipline to carry the day was one thing, but this was ridiculous.'

◆

What of the scenes and emotions in Siraj's camp?

Orme has a revealing though unsourced description that carries the fantastic tones of Nabinchandra's poem:

On the other hand, the despondency of the Nabob increased as the hour of danger approached. Sitting in his tent in the evening of his arrival at the camp, it chanced that his attendants quitted him one after another in order to say their usual prayers at sun-set, until they left him quite alone; when a common fellow, either through ignorance, or with an intention to steal, entered the tent unperceived, until he was discovered by the Nabob; who starting from the gloomy reflections in which he was absorbed, hastily recalled his attendants with this emphatic exclamation, 'Sure they see me dead.'

This could be dramatic, premonitory foreshadowing by a Company man, tempted to cut loose with an uncharacteristic flourish from his otherwise diligent record of 'military transactions'. But there is little doubt that matters had reached a desperate state with Siraj. His force looked overwhelming as a battle plan but did he really think he could pull off a victory at so late a stage after desperate parleys with Mir Jafar, or, as Orme suggests, did he see his plan for the charade it had already become? Siraj could have been as much on a knife's edge as Clive was, desperately hoping for the exact opposite of Clive's wishes as to aid in battle from Mir Jafar, Rai Durlabh, and Yar Latif.

Chronicles like the *Siyar* and *Riyazu-s-Salatin* spend remarkably less time on describing the battle at Plassey than even the one in which Siraj's forces defeated that of his cousin Shaukat Jang. *Riyazu-s-Salatin*, a relatively less rigorous work that was published seven years after the *Siyar*, devotes less than a page to it. The *Siyar*, less than five. It's possible they did not possess enough information about the battle. But it appears as if both acknowledged that the crowning glory of Clive & Co. was a general embarrassment and it was best to be done with it quickly, with more space accorded to reasons for Siraj's downfall: as both these Company-era chronicles note at length these were the flaws of his character, more than any other flaw or reason attributed to any other person or institution. Even so, both works provide interesting highlights and reflections.

Siraj was clearly troubled, although, as the *Riyazu-s-Salatin* notes, upon hearing of Clive's steady march upriver from Calcutta he had finally taken 'out the cotton of recklessness from the ear' to approach Mir Jafar, offering him 'flattery and endearment, and sending the Begam of Mahabat Jang [Alivardi's wife] to Mir Jafar to [open] the gates of apology for his past shortcomings'.

The nawab's overture of sending his grandmother, Sharf-un-Nisa, as peacemaker didn't work, and Mir Jafar did not listen to her, as he had no 'reliance on Siraju-d-Daulah's assurances and actions'. This last is low-handed hindsight, as Ghulam Husain Salim, a Company postmaster, would have had little chance to question Mir Jafar—as he would die in 1765, twenty-three years before the *Riyaz* was published in 1788. Besides, by the time of the begum's overture the Plassey conspiracy was well in motion, and Mir Jafar, a contender for the title of nawab, had little reason to wait on the man he fervently hoped to replace.

It's nevertheless a compelling tale, made more so by being among the few subcontinental texts from the eighteenth century to record those years of tectonic shift in Bengal.

Siraj was finally impelled to set out to meet the British force. The *Siyar* evokes the mood of a ruler with superior numbers marching to his doom on account of inferior management:

> The report being now spread that Colonel Clive had moved from Calcutta at the head of an army, this intelligence engaged that Prince to draw from his ears that cotton of sloth and neglect with which he had stuffed them. With visible reluctance of mind, and a heart big with grief and despondence, he quitted his palace of Mansur-gundj, and marched with those troops in which he reposed a confidence, that is, those belonging to Mir-meden, and to Radja Mohon-lal, and a few others, with which he arrived at Palassy.

There's also a fascinating description in the *Riyaz* in which Mir Madan, who would give his life for his young nawab and prove to be a pivot at Plassey, repeatedly urges Siraj to dispense with Mir Jafar—dispatch him, even—after Siraj had set off from Motijheel for the Plassey campaign:

> After this, when Siraju-d-daulah advanced from Chunahkhali [the village of Chunakhali, about halfway between Motijheel and Qasimbazar], the aforesaid Khan (Mir Jafar) also marching encamped at a distance of half a farsakh [about two miles] from the army of Siraju-d-daulah. Mir Madan, Superintendent of the Artillery, told Siraju-d-daulah that the English were coming at the instigation of Mir Muhammad Jafar, and that it was, therefore, expedient to finish first Mir Muhammad Jafar, and that after the latter was killed, the English would not have the daring to approach this side. In that the arrow of Fate cannot be parried by the shield of Effort, and in that God's decree had already been passed another way...
>
> To the advice of that wise sage, that light-hearted man (Siraju-d-daulah) was deaf.

This text even has the newly appointed diwan, Mohanlal, losing his temper with his master Siraj over this matter of miscalculating his hand with Mir Jafar and Rai Durlabh:

When next day, Siraju-d-daulah reached Daudpur, tidings came to the effect that the English had set fire to Katwah. At that time Mohanlal reproached Siraju-d-daulah, and said: 'You have ruined me, and rendered my children orphans. If you had not removed Mir Muhammad Jafar Khan and Dullab Ram from the Katwah outpost, things would not have taken this turn.'

◆

Then there is epic fiction with a sting in the tale for the British. The poet Nabinchandra has Siraj facing his demons alone in his lavish Plassey tent. Well, not quite alone: Seated on a golden throne, surrounded by beautiful women, a hundred or so, singing for the nawab's pleasure. A hundred or so of these beauties, half-naked, even danced for Siraj—'to fulfil the desires of this sinful nawab':

...Purāité pāpāshoktō nobābér mōn,
Nāché ordhōbiboshōnā shoték shundōri...

Go on, urges the poet, pour more wine in the cup of gold, pour—pour! Sacrifice yourself at the altar of desire. Drink, pour. Pour, drink. Let the dancing continue, let the banner of lust fly tonight. War can wait for morning.

But his doubts won't leave Siraj, neither will an eternity of regrets. 'I'm a fool,' he berates himself, 'to have kept Mir Jafar even after learning of his betrayal, mesmerized by his oath of fealty. I'm a fool to have been calmed by Clive's message of reassurance. Who knew the English were a race of liars? A race of such cunning? People who are with you in word, but against you in deed? That their assurances are a mirage? Where do I go now? What do I do?'

Then the nawab resolves, violently, to begin anew.

'If I somehow survive tomorrow,' he tells himself, 'I will give a fitting reply to Mir Jafar and all the other traitors, I shall kill them and their families. I shall defile their women in front of them, I shall cut down the wives and the children, and their blood shall enter the hearts of their fathers and husbands and quench the rebellion. Then it will be their turn. First the eyes...'

If. At least that much is true.

16

A GAME OF CHESS: CHOICE AND CHANCE

*'(They) began to cannonade so briskly
that it was advisable we should retire...'*

A battle begins differently for different people.

'It was on a Thursday, the fifth of Shevval, in the year 1170,' the *Siyar* heralds the battle with a flourish, 'and there the fire of battle and slaughter, that had been hitherto kept alive under a heap of embers, now blazed out into flames.'

'23rd June 1757', Coote's journal is dispassionate, like a captain's log.

'Soon after daybreak in the morning,'—another account, by an anonymous Company source, marks the time as 7 a.m.—'discovered the Nabob's Army marching in two lines towards Plassey grove, which we were in possession of as if they intended to surround us, upon which we formed the line a few paces without the grove...'

◆

Siraj's forces, arrayed to the north, northeast and southeast of the British force, soon presented an awesome sight, far larger than what Clive had been led to believe through various reports and interviews with people as he travelled along the Hugli–Bhagirathi. '50,000 foot, 18,000 horse, and 50 pieces of cannon,' Orme wrote of the controversial numbers with absence of drama even in the afterglow of Plassey, numbers as self-evident truth that could be seen for what Plassey could well have been as a conventional war: a rout of the British.

To the west of Clive's forces in and around the mango grove, was the Bhagirathi. To their south lay farmland and more groves. In an arc, from the northeast—a little distance away from the southern tank and the hillock—along a large plain that stretched just short of 5 kilometres all the way to the southeast of the grove, were arrayed the forces of Rai Durlabh, Yar Latif Khan, and Mir Jafar, in that order. This comprised the vast majority of the Bengal troops under the three compromised generals. In the gaps between these troop columns of cavalry and infantry commanded by 'Roydoolub', 'Latty' and 'Meer Jaffier', writes Orme, were placed clusters of artillery in two, three, and four 'pieces'.

Major Grant and his division faced this ultimately benign arc—Clive couldn't take chances with the battle yet to begin and the fate of his expedition in the hands of fellow conspirators.

The remainder of Siraj's troops were to the north of the grove. These were all under the command of Mir Madan—'Meer Murdeen' to Orme—and a son-in-law of Mohanlal ('Moonlol'). These troops totalled 5,000 cavalry and 7,000 foot soldiers. A majority of the infantry carried matchlock muskets, and the remainder were armed with pikes, swords, arrows, rockets. The cavalry, Orme notes, 'both men and horses', were from 'northern regions' and 'much stouter' than seen in the armies of the Coromandel region.

There is a suggestion by Orme that Siraj's forces hadn't much heart in the impending battle because in it they saw 'no prospect of plunder, as in the sacking of Calcutta, and much more danger'. They were also upset about arrears in pay, he mentions, a reason why they were reluctant to leave Murshidabad.

But not reluctant enough, evidently, to balk at marching upon the forces led by Clive, Sabut Jang, Firm in War. At least, the forces led by generals who hadn't sold out.

Ahead of this force was a train of cannon, mostly large 24- and 32-pounders—firing projectiles of that weight, about 11 kilograms and 14.5 kilograms. These massive guns weighing over 2.5 tonnes each were mounted on large wheeled platforms raised about 6 feet from the ground. These platforms were self-sufficient: they also carried shot, powder and other cannon accoutrements, besides, of course, the 'gunnels', or artillerymen. The platforms were pulled by between forty and fifty yoked white oxen 'of the largest size, bred in the country of Purnea' (and captured for posterity in an excellent 1923 lithograph by the American artist Richard Caton Woodwille Jr.). An elephant walked behind each platform, 'trained to assist at difficult tugs, by shoving with his forehead against the hinder part of the carriage'.

'The infantry and cavalry marched in many separate and compact bodies,' writes Orme. 'Forty vagabond Frenchmen under the command of one Sinfray [de St Frais, former secretary to the French Council in Chandannagar; these were the Frenchmen who had escaped the carnage and surrender at Chandannagar and signed up with Siraj], appeared at the larger tank, that nearest the grove, with four pieces of light cannon. Two larger pieces advanced and halted on a line with this tank, close to the bank of the river.'

Coote's telling is less descriptive and flashy, but as a primary source of the battle for Orme and other historians—indeed, nearly all chroniclers of Plassey—it's as priceless as Orme's for its brevity. To Orme's 'Forty vagabond Frenchmen' is Coote's 'body of about 40 Frenchmen'.

Now these Frenchmen, writes Coote, along with 'a large detachment of their army, commanded by Meer Murdan' formed what present-day American military jargon would call the 'forward edge of the battle area', and others call 'the front'. They occupied all prominent features overlooking British troops—the tank, the wooded hillock. 'The enemy took possession of the adjacent eminences with their cannon, which appeared to be irregularly supported by their horse and foot... [and] lodged themselves within the banks of a tank, distant from us about 200 yards...'

Directly ahead of Coote's detachment lay the British forward edge.

Clive was responsible for that positioning, writes Orme. When the colonel viewed 'the enemy's array from the top of the hunting-house' he was somewhat stunned—'surprized at their numbers, as well as the splendor and confidence of their array...' Awed as he was, Clive was concerned about being perceived as overawed '...judging, that if his own troops remained in the grove, the enemy would impute the caution to fear, and grow bolder...' So, Clive decided to position a number of troops in a line in front of the 'hunting-house', which faced the nearest tank—where the French cannon and cannoneers, soon to prove impressively feisty, were positioned.

Coote, with typical understatement, describes the British forces, European and Indian, at his position as well as that of his colleagues, and even refers to himself in the third person:

...our army consisting of 750 men in battalion (including 100 Topasses), which was told off into four divisions; the 1st division was commanded by Major Kilpatrick, the 2nd by Major Grant, the 3rd by Major Coote, and the 4th by Captain Gaupp. We had besides 150 of the Train, including 50 sailors, 8 pieces of cannon, 6-pounders, and one Hobit [most likely a howitzer—haubits in the three Scandinavian languages, and haubitze in German; besides, Orme mentions 'two howitz'], with 2,100 Sepoys who were formed on the right and left.

Coote had to his left a division led by Captain Gaupp, which was close to the hunting lodge, and to Coote's right was Major Killpatrick with his own division, in a line which extended beyond the boundary of the grove into the large Plassey field. Three cannons each were positioned at both ends of this line, as were a division each of sepoys. 'The other two field-pieces and the howitzes,' notes Orme, 'were advanced 200 yards in front of the left division of Sepoys, and posted behind two brick-kilns' which fortuitously provided some cover from the opposition's bombardment. This British position was the nearest to the nawab's forces.

Major Gaunt, as we've already seen, was on the east side facing the arc of the conspirators. Orme notes that this position was relatively safe from the surprise of a flanking attack (seen in purely military terms, and discounting the complicity of the conspirator-generals) on account that the 'distance of the enemy in this quarter, prevented any danger of their falling upon the flank before whatsoever troops were ordered could fall back, and range along the east side of the grove.'

Clive kept watch from the rooftop of Siraj's hunting lodge.

Siraj waited inside his tent at the back of his formation, to the north of the impending action, shielded by the bulk of troops loyal to him.

The chess pieces were in place.

◆

Major Coote and Lieutenant Colonel Clive wouldn't know this for some days, but by a coincidence the Select Committee that met at Fort William on the day of the battle at Plassey endorsed Coote's view at the council of war in Katwa, that for Clive & Co. it would have to be now or never. In his letters to the Select Committee written before the council of war Clive offered the same options he would offer his officers.

The Committee were also going by information received from Clive several days earlier in the form of three letters that showed just how rapidly things were moving. A letter dated the 18th mentions the possibility of capturing Katwa Fort, as that would be of advantage on the march towards Murshidabad. The letter dated 19th records Clive sending an advance force to capture the town and fort—200 Europeans and 500 sepoys. Clive also sent word that the kiladar, commander of the fort, had accepted his overtures ('...in answer to a letter wrote him has promised to be our friend; that his intelligence of the smallness of the Nabob's forces is confirmed,' is how the Committee acknowledged it.) Clive's letter of the 20th declared that Katwa had fallen to British forces.

The Committee came directly to the business of war after considering all three of Clive's letters, openly acknowledged the business-like conspiracy for regime-change, and agreed to rapidly push ahead—provided all the pieces were in place. It was the Select Committee's very own council of war, attended by Roger Drake, Charles Manningham, and Richard Becher.

The Committee acknowledged Clive's concern about Mir Jafar's loyalty to the Company in particular, especially an account of Siraj having already set off from Murshidabad along with the general in his train, and Clive's concern that 'his opinion of the scituation of Meir Jaffeir's affairs being less favorable than had been represented to us,' as the Committee noted, and, 'if he [Mir Jafar] is not treacherous, his cautiousness from our want of strength will (he fears) overset the expedition...'

But none of these concerns outweighed the need for quick action:

The Committee...were of opinion that the Colonel's apprehensions were not well grounded...but if contrary to our expectations no further advice has come from Meir Jaffeir yet we presume no thoughts can be entertained of making a fresh treaty with the Nabob, nor do we think it could be depended on if made...it would be best to put the issue of our affairs on a decisive engagement as the only alternative we know of after engaging so far as we have done in the present undertaking, delay being fatal to our affairs as we shall daily diminish in our numbers while the Nabob will be able to increase his army by calling in forces from all quarters...

The Committee decided to formally endorse war, but with a caveat that all the conspirators had to be on board or the risks would be unacceptable:

> At the same time it must be remembered when we engaged in the confederacy to change the Government in favour of Meir Jaffeir we were informed that Roydolub, Jugget-seat and others had likewise entered into it: we think therefore that we should not act of ourselves only, unless we find no assistance can be expected from them, in which case we must conclude the whole is united against us.

The Select Committee wouldn't know it for some days, but they got their wish.

◆

The first shot was fired at 8 a.m.

It came from Siraj's forces grouped on the tank, and drew first blood. Orme writes that 'it killed one, and wounded another of the grenadier company, which was posted on the right of the battalion.'

An anonymous but 'endorsed' account in Hill's *Bengal* recorded six days after the battle, claims that opening shot came as a surprise— because, according to the intelligence received 'the enemy' had 'no cannon with them'. Strange as this may appear, as the British were fully aware of Siraj's arsenal, the illusion was dispelled with that shot soon after Clive's troops had formed up in front of the grove: 'We were scarcely drawn up in this manner, when a 24lb. shott from their camp, bounding along, and carrying off the arm of one of the King's granadiers, convinced us that their cannon was come up.'

This acted as a signal, and the rest of Siraj's artillery on their mobile stages opened up, raining shot on Clive's force—in a 'continual fire', Orme notes. The two small cannon by the brick kilns retaliated along with other British artillery but they fell short of the nawab's heavy artillery. The shots did kill and injure many in Siraj's infantry and artillery, but 'ten for one killed [of the British], was no advantage in such a disparity of numbers'. Because, even though more than two-thirds of Siraj's force wouldn't pitch in, it was still a ratio of 3:1 for Siraj's active forces against Clive's, besides a clear superiority with artillery. It showed. Although 'most' of the shot had flown high above the British force, at the end of the first half an hour of such bombardment ten European soldiers and twenty Company sepoys lay dead.

Clive had seen enough. He gave orders for the troops to pull back and behind the embankment of the grove. '[They] began to cannonade so briskly that it was advisable we should retire into the grove,' recalled Coote, 'where we formed behind the ditch that surrounded it, our left being covered by Plassey house which was close to the river side.'

This little retreat energized Siraj's loyal commanders. Their heavy cannon were nudged closer to the grove by the great teams of bullocks—the anonymous account describes the scene: '...their whole front was almost covered with the bullocks that drew them.'

The intensity of fire increased. To little effect, as it happened. '...their shot only struck the trees,' Orme tells us, 'for the troops were ordered to sit down, whilst the field-pieces alone answered the enemy's cannon from behind the bank. Explosions of powder were frequently observed amongst their artillery.' Siraj's forces had decided to wait it out, working the equation of attrition, wearing out the British with cannon, instead of charging with cavalry and infantry and being susceptible to fire from entrenched, protected British positions at the grove.

◆

At 11 a.m. Clive consulted his officers, and decided to adopt the tactics he had used during the retaking of Calcutta from Siraj. British forces would 'maintain the cannonade', limited but consistent, through the day, as most of his troops lay in the shelter of the grove. Then, at midnight, they would 'attack the Nabob's camp'. (Coote offers a perspective different than Orme's. He writes of a consultation around noon: 'In this situation we cannonaded each other till 12 o'clock, when the Colonel came from Plassey house and called the captains together in order to hold a council of war, but, changing his mind, returned without holding one.' Either way, it shows things were somewhat chaotic in the British camp.)

That's when the weather intervened—it would have happened soon after Clive's abortive council of war that Coote mentions. Even after knowing the lay of the land and the weather at that time of the year, Siraj's fighting generals and cannoneers had made a fatal error. They discounted the monsoon. Clive had gained an advantage with the retreat into the grove: his forces were outnumbered and outgunned, but they had cover from rain, their stock of gunpowder kept mostly dry through that cover, and also from the caution of covering the powder.

'About noon a very heavy shower covered the plain, and very soon damaged the enemy's powder so much, that their fire slackened continually,' Orme continues, 'but the English ammunition served on.' The anonymous account dated 29 June in Qasimbazar (and included in Hill's volumes) endorses this: 'About 12 a heavy shower of rain came on, we had some apprehension that the enemy would take advantage of this opportunity, and make a push with their horse, but our guns continued to play very briskly, prevented any such motion. The enemy's guns during the rain which lasted half an hour did not fire a shott.'

All through this the forces of Mir Jafar, Yar Latif, and Rai Durlabh stayed where they were with their generals, calculating bystanders, watchful, not interfering. It isn't difficult to visualize how the situation might have both Siraj and Clive on edge, mulling over the similar questions but with opposite implications. Would they join the battle? If so, on whose side? Why weren't they joining the battle? Had they double-crossed—from Clive's perspective?

'All this while Mirdjaafer-qhan, the author of all these evils and troubles, contented himself with standing at a distance with the troops under his command, exactly like one who had come only to see the engagement,' the *Siyar* employs an uncharacteristically sympathetic tone towards Siraj at this point, 'although his sole aim was to effect Seradj-ed-doulah's downfall.'

Clive remained greatly concerned, but there was one consolation, such as it was. If the conspirators weren't visibly with Clive, at least they were visibly not against him either.

Siraj, of course, remained concerned with good reason, and with his suspicions yet again confirmed after four hours of battle. If three of his key commanders had not moved from their position across the right flank of Clive's troops, from where they could have swept in after softening up the British with artillery and rolled over the grove through sheer numbers, they were definitely against Siraj. (Orme, unsurprisingly, has a pejorative take on Siraj who, like many rulers, remained in the background, and had his generals execute the battle, that 'the Nabob had remained in his tent out of the reach of danger, continually flattered by his attendants and officers, of whom one half were traitors, with assurances of victory'. There is little indication of such flattery, only of a desperate nawab leaving the battle to his loyalist generals.)

The cannonading between both forces continued, but with a difference. Seeing the efficacy of their cannon diminish, Mir Madan and Mohanlal with their troops moved gradually towards the grove. Focused cannon fire from the grove continued to pick off their troops but this hardly proved a deterrent: they knew they had superior numbers even if they had relatively inferior weaponry—matchlocks and ammunition pouches a generation behind that of the British forces, and cannon that, even though larger, couldn't match the rapid fire of British cannon. And they still had the handful of Frenchmen on their side, trained in artillery in a manner similar to the British.

◆

As Siraj's troops advanced, Clive grew tense. The *Siyar* describes his state of mind: Clive, committed to the battle, and concerned with this advance and with Mir Jafar and his colleagues still not stirring, whether on account of 'his sangfroid or want of strength', as he had written to Calcutta just four days earlier.

> It is reported that the Colonel, at sight of this [advance] severely reprimanded some agent, who was then near his person, and said, 'that his master had promised and pledged himself, that the troops, as well as the Commanders, were totally alienated from Seradj-ed-doulah; and that as soon as some engagement should take place, they would do his business effectually.' As much as I

can see, added the Colonel, the very reverse of all that is taking place. The agent answered, that 'those that were now pressing upon him, were those corps that were attached to Seradj-ed-doulah; and that whenever these should be vanquished, the Colonel would not fail to see tokens of what he (the agent) had promised.

Essentially, Clive was left to deal with the situation as best as he could. And he surely would, the *Siyar* pronounced with retrospective finality and flourish. 'But as the nation of Hat-wearers have no equals in the art of firing their artillery and musquetry with both order and rapidity, there commenced such an incessant rain of balls and bullets, and such a hot endless firing, that the spectators themselves were amazed and confounded,'—the *Siyar* does too much credit too early to Clive's forces—'and those in the battle had their hearing deafened by the continual thunder, and their eye-sight dimmed by the endless flashing of the execution'.

There is little indication in that descriptive opus of just how hard-pressed the British forces were even with most of Siraj's army out of the equation, before rain intervened.

And a fateful shot.

17

THE ENDGAME

'...take care of the conservation of my honour and life'

Well-known colonial-era paintings of Plassey are dramatic and detailed in their rendition. But not one depicts the field as slushy, the soldiers on all sides—Siraj's, Clive's and the non-combatant conspirator generals'—sodden with rain, the active soldiers dishevelled, touched by mud or dirt, uniforms a little faded with use and the privations of earlier marches and skirmishes, or even awry with the battle at hand, their general appearance unkempt.

In the paintings, their uniforms are as bright as the day the fabric would have been dyed and as pristine as the day tailors were done with them. You have the red frock coats and white wigs of the British officers, the red coats of the rank and file made of broadcloth. Or you have the 39th Foot in coats with green lapels and green cuffs alongside the usual conical or broad-brimmed hats, white cotton breeches and black shoes. Artillerymen in blue coats. Company sepoys in their turbans, single-breasted tunics with crossed bandoliers and a mix of white breeches and curious hemmed shorts in that tropical weather. The nawab's troops, with commanders in fancy turbans and necklaces of pearl, ornate tunics, and pantaloons of choicest fabric; the soldiers and artillerymen in plainer tunics, coloured or white, and a mix of white tightly wound dhotis or loose pantaloons and tight pyjamas—churidar—and leather sandals.

The weapons are spotless. The matchlocks of the British forces and the Company sepoys, and the less sophisticated ones of the barkandāz among the Bengal forces. The sabres of Clive's troops—though most would rely on bayonets fixed to the end of their muskets—and the talwars or curved swords of their opponents. Cannon are menacingly black, but almost too prettily glossy to fire the abomination of cannonballs that were the mainstay of the brief battle.

Only some faces and eyes register emotions of life and death, but even that, as if self-consciously. Nobody bleeds. A couple of paintings depict Clive, Napoleon-like, observing the battle from the roof of the hunting lodge. One even incongruously has Clive on a white charger leading a pack of sepoys and, behind them, a line of caparisoned war elephants. In the imagination of Empire, Plassey comes to us immaculately as if insecurity, conspiracy, transfer of power and acquisition of empire needed to be seen to be spotless.

◆

A cannon ball hit Mir Madan.

Some accounts mention the ball hit him on his thigh ('...carried away one of his thighs,' the *Siyar* observes). Others note a hit with a shell splinter. One account mentions grapeshot. At any rate Mir Madan was mortally wounded, and was quickly brought by some troopers to Siraj's tent, where he died in front of his nawab.

It's difficult to disagree with Hill's assertion in *Three Frenchmen* of the impact of Mir Madan's passing: '...though it cannot be said that his death caused the loss of the battle, it is certain that it put an end to all chance of the [English] victory being contested.' Because, by all accounts, Siraj unravelled at that point, the months of tension finally proving to be too much.

A resolute ruler would perhaps have stepped up, pushed aside emotion, and taken the battle fully into Clive's camp—although there is no saying whether, after dark, when the day's battle ceased, Siraj would have survived an ambush on his camp that Clive had reportedly planned, or survived whatever machinations Mir Jafar and his colleagues were plotting. Instead, the twenty-four-year-old nawab opted for desperation.

'The misfortune disturbed him to excess,' Orme writes, 'he immediately sent for Meer Jaffier; and as soon as he entered the tent, flung his turban on the ground, saying, "Jaffier, that turban you must defend."'

The scene is more detailed in *Siyar*, and well worth the read for dramatic effect—and import, even after making an allowance for exaggeration:

He sent for Mir-djaafer-qhan, and patiently waited till the other should be pleased to come. But that General having shewn a disinclination from such an interview, repeated messages and pressing solicitations became necessary to put him in motion.

At last he came, accompanied by his son, Miren, alias Mir-mahmed-sadyc-qhan [Mir Muhammad Sadiq Khan], by Qhadem-hassen-qhan [Khadim Hussain Khan], and by a numerous body of his friends and followers, well-armed. Seradj-ed-doulah spoke to him in the humblest strain, and at last descended to the lowest supplications; he even took his turbant from off his head, (at least this was the report) and placed it before the General; to whom he addressed these very words: 'I now repent of what I have done; and availing myself of those ties of consanguinity which subsist between us, as well as of those rights which my grandfather, Aaly-verdy-qhan, has doubtless acquired upon your gratitude, I look up to you, as to the only representative of that venerable personage; and hope therefore, that, forgetting my past trespasses, you shall henceforward behave as becomes a Seyd, a man united in blood to me, and a man of sentiments, who conserves a grateful remembrance of all the benefits he has received from my family. I recommend myself to you; take care of the conservation of my honour and life.

This affecting speech had no effect on Mir-djaafer-qhan, who finding that the occasion for which he had been looking out this long while, was now at hand, thought only of availing himself of it; so far was he from forgetting what indeed he ought to have forgotten. Treason having already taken possession of his heart, he coldly answered, 'that the day was now drawing to its end; and that there remained no time for an attack. Send a counter order to the troops that are advancing,' said he, 'recall those engaged; and to-morrow, with the blessing of God, I will join all the troops together, and provide for the engagement.'

Seradjed-doulah observed, that they might be attacked by the enemy in the night. This also the General took upon himself to provide against, and he promised that the enemy would not form a night attack.

A short while later, Orme recounts, 'as the terrors of the Nabob increased continually', it was Rai Durlabh's turn to offer counsel: order a retreat, return to Murshidabad. His advice 'prevailed'.

◆

Some British historians question the accuracy of depictions of the episode in Siraj's tent. Reid, who largely confines himself to Company chronicles and British sources for his book on Plassey, writes: 'How far later accounts of their meeting (if it ever took place) are to be trusted cannot be determined, although Orme followed the general's [Mir Jafar's] own account...'

Reid has a point because this tale rests almost entirely on Mir Jafar's assertion, but something like this conversation, purported or otherwise, may have taken place, because orders to cease and desist soon went out to Mohanlal who was at the time engaged in attacking British forces. According to this telling, Mohanlal was appalled as he was pressing home an advantage. Again, there isn't any significant corroboration of the event except in the *Siyar*:

> By this time Mohon-lal, who had advanced with Mir-meden, was closely engaged with the enemy; his cannon was served with effect [to the extent possible, by the Frenchmen and Siraj's own artillerymen]; and his infantry having availed themselves of some covers and other grounds, were pouring a quantity of bullets in the enemy's ranks. It was at this moment he received the order of falling back, and of retreating. He answered: 'That this was not a time to retreat; that the action was so far advanced, that whatever might happen, would happen now; and that should he turn his head, to march back to camp, his people would disperse', and perhaps abandon themselves to an open 'flight'. Seradj-ed-doulah, on this answer, turned towards Mirdjaafer-qhan, and the latter coldly answered: 'That the advice he had proposed was the best in his power; and that as to the rest His Highness was the master of taking his own resolutions.' Seradj-ed-doulah intimidated by his General's coldness, and overcome by his own fears and apprehensions, renounced his own natural sense, and submitted to Mir-djaafer-qhan's pleasure; he sent repeated orders, with pressing messages, to Mohon-lal; who at last obeyed, and retreated from the post to which he had advanced.

The battle began to unravel for Siraj.

The loyalist sections of his army began to retreat upon this fight-another-day order. Major Coote records it—and a sense of wonder escapes his stiff-upper-lip recall of the sight: 'The cannonading continued on both sides till about 2 o'clock, when we could perceive the enemy retiring into their lines...'

The cannonade stopped, Orme continues, Siraj's army was 'perceived yoking the trains of oxen to their artillery, and as soon as these were in motion, their whole army turned and proceeded slowly towards the camp'. They—the artillerymen and their platforms, cavalry, infantry—went all the way back to the southern tank, and beyond, with the bewildered French artillerymen still continuing their work and offering covering fire to retreating troops. The section of the army that began the morning with vigour was now mostly leaderless, and, with Mohanlal given orders to pull back, confused. The greater part of Siraj's army in the arc to the northeast and southeast of the grove, far from centre of the battle—the conspirators' forces—gradually began to withdraw. One anonymous account I've also used to recreate a particular scene of the battle expresses a sense of surprise and some bewilderment in the British camp: 'The enemy whether from the smartness of the fire from our guns, or some of their chiefs being killed, or what other motive, begun at this time to retire, and withdraw their cannon within their entrenchments.'

It was time for the British counterattack. Major Killpatrick sensed the confusion, sensed the moment—'The opportunity of attacking them was too great to be neglected,' notes the anonymous account— and set off from the grove towards the tank closest to them, the southern tank, with two companies of the battalion, and two pieces of British light artillery. He sent information of 'his intention, and the reason of it, to his commander', writes Orme.

Clive was resting in the hunting lodge when he was alerted to the major's actions. 'Some say he was asleep,' recounts Orme, 'which is not improbable, considering how little rest he had had for so many hours before [as we have seen, one painting of the battle shows Clive on the roof of the lodge, keeping an eye on the battle; one account has him going indoors to change out of his sodden clothes]; but this is no imputation either against his courage or conduct.' (John Walsh, a Company writer who became Clive's private secretary would, through a note published in 1763 in Britain, term the matter of Clive being asleep at the time a 'malignant' insinuation. He maintains Clive had just come indoors to change his clothes and left hurriedly when he heard news of Killpatrick's intention.)

Clive ran to Killpatrick's detachment, and 'reprimanded' the major for giving chase without his orders.

Clive ordered Killpatrick back to the grove to bring reinforcements. ('Here the Colonel joined him and sent to the grove for another detachment, upon which I marched out and joined him with my division,' Coote narrates.) Clive then headed out with the detachment towards the tank. They managed to drive back the doughty Frenchmen who were now bereft of support from Siraj's army, from the tank, but they were far from neutralized. 'Sinfray,' Orme writes '...retreated to the redoubt of the intrenchment, where he planted his field-pieces ready to act again.'

The battle was as yet far from won for Clive. Even with co-conspirators ranged against Siraj, Clive & Co. would have to fight their way out of Plassey for the riches of Bengal.

First, came a scare.

Coote and his colleagues were on their way to join Clive, who was by then pinned down at the tank by fire from the French party and the nawab's troopers firing matchlocks—the barkandāz hadn't given up. Although Siraj's army had lost its commander of artillery, Mir Madan, and would soon lose to British fire a captain of artillery, Nauwe Singh Hazari, a commander of the musketeers, Bahadur Ali Khan, son-in-law of the dejected Mohanlal, was still rallying the troops, covering their withdrawal. Just as the body of British troops headed out in support of their commander ('During the warmest part of the action,' as Clive noted a day later), the inactive part of Siraj's army to the southeast of the grove, the division commanded by Mir Jafar, came uncomfortably close, and 'halted, faced, and advanced towards the northeast angle,' relates Orme, closer to the battle, and the route of the British moving to aid Clive. 'Their signals not being understood, it was supposed that they intended to fall upon the baggage and boats at the grove, whilst the English army were engaged at the tank.'

Three platoons of the line and a 'field-piece', continues Orme, were 'detached' to oppose them, 'under the command of Captain Grant and Lieutenant Rumbold; and Mr. John Johnstone, a volunteer, managed the field-piece, the fire of which soon stopped the approach of the supposed enemy'. Coote provides more detail as to what transpired after 'some shot' were fired at this army: '...a messenger arrived with a letter to the Colonel from Meer Jaffier, acquainting him that he—Meer Jaffier—commanded that body, and requesting an interview with him that night or the next morning.'

This is in all likelihood the letter from Mir Jafar that is recorded as Clive receiving at 5 p.m.:

> Your note is arrived. I was in the Nabob's presence on this plain, and observed that everybody was intimidated. He sent for me and flung his turband off before me, and...made me write on the side of the Koran so that I cannot come over to you. By the blessing of God you have the better of the day. Meer Murdun was wounded by a ball and is since dead. Buxshee [Nauwe Singh] Hazarry is killed, and ten or fifteen horsemen are killed and wounded. Roydullubrum, Luttee Codair Cawn, and myself are moved from the right to the left. Make a great and sudden discharge and they will run away and we shall do our part. The Colonel, the Rajah [Durlabh], Cawn, and myself, we four men, must absolutely consult together on the proper measures to be taken.
>
> We will certainly finish the matter; the bildars and beldears (gunmen and pioneers) have acted according to their agreement. I swear by my Prophet that the above is fact. Attack him at 3 in the morning; they will run away, and then will be my opportunity.
>
> The forces want to return to the City. Attack him in the night by all means. We three shall be to the left of the Nabob. Coja Haddee will remain firm to the Nabob. If you come you may have an opportunity of seizing [him]. We three are ready for your service and will see you by and by... The commanders of the foot and of the swordmen have left the intrenchments, leaving the guns there. I have mentioned but a small part of

the loss that the part of the army commanded by Meer Murdun has sustained. Had you taken that opportunity to advance with your army there had been nothing more to do. It grieves me that I was then at a distance. Your man was present while the above passed. Coddum Hossein, Meerun, Meer Cassim, Luttee Cawn, and Raja Dulubrum all send their salam to the Colonel and the rest of the gentlemen.

◆

But all this lay ahead. Clive was still engaged, without realizing the way had been made clear. The fighting became more intense at the narrow front. The French and the matchlock-wielders wouldn't quit. They fired at the British from every available defensive position.

'The Colonel then sent the King's Grenadiers and a Grenadier Company of Sepoys to lodge themselves behind a bank that was close upon the enemy's lines, from whence they kept up a continual fire with their small arms,' recalls Coote, 'as we likewise did from four pieces of cannon from the tank.' These field pieces were on the earthen mound that bordered the tank. This height provided a vantage from which to pour cannon shot into Siraj's camp.

This had the effect of provoking several of the nawab's troops out of their defensive position. They prepared to attack. Some artillerymen too were drawn back into battle. Orme writes that Clive realized the risk and repositioned a number of his forces.

> Colonel Clive advanced nearer, and [positioned] half his troops and artillery at the lesser tank, and the other half at a rising ground about 200 yards to the left of it. From these stations the cannonade was renewed with more efficacy than before, and killed many of the oxen which were drawing the artillery, which threw all the trains that were approaching into disorder.

The French contingent held on in the face of this onslaught, and retaliated. The Frenchmen with de St Frais 'plied their field-pieces from the redoubt; and matchlocks from the intrenchments, from ditches, hollows, and every hole or shelter, as also from the bushes on the hillock east of the redoubt, kept up a constant although irregular fire, whilst the cavalry advanced several times threatening to charge sword in hand, but were always stopped and repulsed by the quick firing of the English field-pieces'.

Clive's forces were suffering. They appeared to have been fought to a standstill for about two hours as the two sides continued this battle of attrition and will. Orme writes that around this time, 4 p.m. or so, Clive and his colleagues noticed that the inactive troops to their east seemed to moving away from the battlefield but not with Siraj's army. This finally convinced Clive of Mir Jafar's word—that there would not now be any risk of his intervention on the side of Siraj.

The colonel decided to make a determined push to break through Siraj's defences. He directed one body of troops, both European and Indian—sepoys—to attack the French positions still being commanded by the indefatigable de St Frais at the second—northern—tank. Another similar body of troops was sent to a rise to its east, the hillock, where Clive expected an ambush. He had the major component of his army remain in the centre, ready to support either position, and push through if it could.

The thrusts worked. The hillock was won without a shot fired or received. And matters finally proved too much for the small French band. They withdrew, leaving behind their cannon. Clive described the moment in a letter written from Daudpur to the Select Committee in Calcutta the following day:

> ...the French, making a stand at a breastwork that was part of the fortification of their old camp, put some courage into their troops again, and drew up within their old camp and in front of the Grove, and their musquetry supported by their horse took possession of a bank within musquet shot of the Tank, from thence and from their old camp they kept a continual fire on us, and made many attempts to bring their cannon on, but we kept so brisk a fire that they could not get their coolies and oxen to advance. At about 4 the grenadiers and seapoys stormed both these places; at the same time their ammunition blew up...

◆

Resistance turned into rout. Mohanlal had been pulled back by Siraj. The French had abandoned their position. Manikchand, the skittish defender of Calcutta, too retreated. Further demoralizing the nawab's army was the sight of the masses of the armies of Rai Durlabh, Yar Latif, and Mir Jafar withdrawing from the battle. The loyalist troops fled.

'This retreat of Mohon-lal's made a full impression on his troops,' the *Siyar* takes us one final time to this bizarre battle.

> The sight of their General's retreat damped their courage; and having at the same time spied some parties which were flying (for they were of the complot), they disbanded likewise, and taking example from his neighbour; and as the flight now had lost all its shame, whole bodies fled although no one pursued...

This panicked Siraj, who had reportedly agreed to withdraw so he could fight the British another day. Along with the withdrawal of his three non-combatant generals, he had by then heard of, and thereafter seen—how, even after his desperate plea, Mir Jafar hadn't moved a finger to aid him in battle, completely and with utter finality exposing the conspiracy. Siraj now witnessed a wholesale flight of his troops with the unnerving sight of nobody pursuing them. But, of course, there would soon be: Clive's forces had to be chasing up this grand retreat.

> Seradj-ed-doulah informed of the desertion of his troops, was amazed; and fearing not only the English he had in his front, but chiefly the domestic enemies he had about his person, he lost all firmness of mind. Confounded by that general abandonment, he joined the runaways himself...

He mounted a camel, relates Orme, 'and fled at the utmost pace of the animal, accompanied by about 2,000 horsemen'.

When Clive's forces entered the camp at 5 p.m., they found it empty except for tents, artillery, baggage, and stores. Reid quotes John Corneille, a captain, as saying that, besides the heavy cannon that seemed so menacing before the thundershower of the morning, were 'more than a hundred oxen yolked to them, others dismounted, and all in the utmost confusion'.

Clive realized he had won a victory when the note Mir Jafar had sent him earlier in the afternoon finally managed to catch up with the colonel. Another note to him from Mir Jafar arrived shortly:

...I congratulate you on executing your design. Mirza Aumar Beg or Mr. Watts or Coja Petrus, send one of them to me. I am here on the banks of the lake agreeable to your desire.

Clive replied quickly, requesting Mir Jafar to meet him in Daudpur the following morning. But first there was still work to be done that day. Siraj's forces had to be pursued to ensure they wouldn't rally at any point. And Clive had to urge on his forces, without any cavalry, to give chase on foot—and pass up on any loot the nawab's abandoned camp had for them. Clive cajoled the English soldiers, bribed them.

'The English soldiers being told that they should receive a donation of money, received the orders to march on to Daudpore with acclamations, nor shewed any desire to stop for the plunder which lay spread around them,' Orme notes. 'They halted, however, until the commissaries had taken possession of as many oxen as sufficed for all the artillery [42 cannon, according to the anonymous Company account in *Bengal in 1756-1757*] and carriages of the army: their own being much inferior to the Nabob's.'

Major Coote, who led the pursuit into Siraj's camp, now led the pursuit after the nawab's retreating soldiers—'which we continued,' he recalls in his journal, 'till it was dark'. They halted at Daudpur, which, as we've seen, was about 10 kilometres north of the field at Plassey. Eventually, 'the rest of the army under the command of Major Kilpatrick joined us...'

It was 8 p.m.

And, just like that, the Battle of Plassey was over.

◆

For an engagement that would help found an empire, the large opposing numbers—even accounting for the numbers the Plassey conspirators managed to keep away from battle—it was a remarkably economical victory.

'A General Return of Sepoys Killed and Wounded' filed by a Major John Fraser, 'major of the brigade', counts sixteen killed and thirty-six wounded. Of these, the 'Coast Establishment' or the Madras Battalion had among them three dead and nineteen wounded; the

'Bengal Establishment' or the Bengal Battalion recorded thirteen dead, twenty wounded.

For the Europeans, the General Return recorded the first battalion, a mix of King's troops, Bengal troops and artillerymen, as having eleven wounded and two missing personnel. The second battalion, which comprised troops from Bombay and Madras alongside artillerymen, had four killed, nine wounded, and two missing. Of these, artillerymen took the brunt of casualties, with three dead and five wounded—probably on account of the fierce engagement at the southern tank. Altogether, twenty-eight killed, wounded or missing. (Orme notes a lower number: '...about 20 were killed and wounded...')

Clive thought the endeavour well worth the price in lives, in particular the economy in European lives. In his detailed update for the Select Committee in Fort St George in Madras, written in Murshidabad and dated 2 July, he would note: 'On our side there were twenty-two killed and fifty wounded and those chiefly blacks.'

(This wasn't the only indignity heaped on sepoys, upwardly mobile mercenaries in the context of the day. Law, the Frenchman, is particularly harsh in his description of Indian sepoys, but quite on point seeing as how, apart from rare events like the Revolt of 1857—'native' soldiers would generally stand with Company and Crown for their conquest of the subcontinent. 'In fact it may be said that the sepoy is a singular animal, especially until he has had time to acquire a proper sense of discipline,' Law notes. 'As soon as he has received his red jacket and his gun he thinks he is a different man. He looks upon himself as a European, and having a very high estimation of this qualification, he thinks he has the right to despise all the country people, whom he treats as Kaffirs and wretched negroes, though he is often just as black as they are...')

Going by the anonymous Company account, Mir Jafar later estimated 500 dead among Siraj's forces, with no estimates of the wounded. Clive's letter of 24 June to the Select Committee in Calcutta notes: '...the loss of the enemy I conceive to be about 500 men.' (A letter sent a night earlier, also from Daudpur, noted that 'five hundred horse are killed'—a reference to cavalrymen—'and three elephants'. Other estimates, including in some encyclopaedias, record

1,500 dead, with no estimates of wounded. Reid surmises that, at best, it's an estimate, exact losses are 'unknown'.)

◆

'Unknown' isn't such a bad description either for the battle.

Just how touch-and-go it was for Clive & Co. is demonstrated by Clive's somewhat outraged letter to the Select Committee in Calcutta on 26 June, a sign of frayed nerves even three days after his greatest victory:

> Gentlemen,—I have received a letter from Mr. Drake in answer to my letters to the Committee, which is very unusual on such important occasions and I cannot help thinking that had the expedition miscarried you would have laid the whole blame upon me.

(Even with his stupendous military success in Bengal in the few months since his arrival, Clive's uneasy relationship with Company folk and British gentlemen in general would continue for several years. He was evidently foul-mouthed. Reverend Long noted one such instance: 'The limited community of Calcutta, having little to distract their attention, had ample leisure to indulge a quarrelsome disposition, and little restraint was placed upon language even in high quarters; thus Mr. Grey, a Civilian dismissed from Malda, writes to Lord Clive officially: "Your language is more calculated for the meridian of Billingsgate or Grub Street than for the Records of the Hon'ble. Board".')

A day later, on 27 June, Clive would again write to the Select Committee in Calcutta, in response to their deliberations of 23 June about which we read a little earlier. Clive permitted his outrage free reign:

> Gentlemen,—I have received your letter of the 23rd instant, the contents of which are so indefinite and contradictory that I can put no other construction on it, than an intent to clear yourselves at my expense, had the expedition miscarried. It puts me in mind of the famous answer of the Delphic oracle to Pyrrhus, Aio te [Aeacide] Romanos vincere posse.

I say, Pyrrhus, that you the Romans can conquer.

It was masterfully ambiguous. It could mean: You, Pyrrhus, can conquer the Romans. It could also mean: Pyrrhus, the Romans can conquer you.

18

THE LOST NAWAB

'On your arrival to-morrow Surajah Dowlat
will be either taken or killed'

Siraj rode hard. He arrived in Murshidabad, a capital which already
had a foretelling of doom—with some cavalrymen having returned
far earlier than the nawab. The *Siyar* mentions that Siraj reached
Murshidabad the following morning at 8 a.m. after travelling through
the night. But Orme mentions he reached 'before the midnight after
the battle'. And Dutch sources—for instance, a letter dated 24 June
to the Dutch Committee at Hugli from the Dutch deputy resident
at Kalikapur at the time, George Lodewijk Vernet—note that Siraj
reached Murshidabad sometime later. Vernet, who between 1763–69
would be the director for Bengal for the Dutch Company, and like
other Dutch in the region kept a hawk's eye on developments in the
region, reported: 'The Nawab arrived with his defeated hordes, after
a hurried and disorderly flight, at Moorshedabad about midnight.'
Siraj went straight to Heerajheel, his palace in Mansurganj.

He quickly realized that bereft of power he was now a pariah.
The *Siyar* relates how he ordered his principal commanders to engage
their troops for his safety, 'until he might take breath, and resolve on
what he was to do next', but they all left for their own homes. This
was even true of Muhammad Iraj Khan, his father-in-law, the *Siyar*
claims, despite Siraj attempting the turban manoeuvre with him:

> In vain did the Prince lay his turbant [*sic*] at his feet, and intreat
> him for God's sake to remain with him, and to assemble some
> troops about his palace, that he might stay with safety, if staying
> should become proper; or depart with some decency, should
> flight become necessary.' Mirza Iraj made polite excuses to
> decline, and went his way.

Although he had been abandoned by his troops and his court, Siraj 'resolved to retain some people at least about his person; and he ordered that whoever had any demand upon the treasury, should be immediately satisfied. Numbers immediately thronged into it, some [like many soldiers] for their arrears, and some for advances to help themselves out. Some others likewise, under a variety of pretences, crowded into it, and received as much as they pretended to; for orders had been given to reject no man; so that during the whole night the treasury was full of people, who took money on every pretence they could devise, and carried it home.'

Orme's version of that night of Siraj's distress and melancholia is more methodical and logical, beginning with the distressed nawab's arrival and that of some 'principal officers' who reached Murshidabad around the time Siraj did:

> These he assembled in council. Some advised him to deliver himself up to the English, which he imputed to treachery; others proposed, that he should encourage the army by the offer of great rewards, and appear again at their head in the morning. This he seemed to approve, and, having ordered an immediate distribution of three months pay to the troops, dismissed the council, and retired into the seraglio, where, left to his own reflections and his women, his terrors returned.

Both accounts have a common conclusion: by the morning few besides his harem remained with Siraj.

◆

Both accounts differ as to the timing of what happened next, but not the intent. Orme writes that on the 24th morning, Siraj 'sent away his women, with 50 elephants laden with their furniture and necessaries, and with them a great part of his own jewels, and some gold rupees...' (A letter from Mir Jafar that Clive received on 25 June offers more details: '...Mohun Loll he has dispatched to Purneah with his women and many treasures. I hope in God to take them all.')

Siraj planned to follow at night, a plan he shared only with the eunuch 'who governed his seraglio'—one among a scarce handful he could trust. The *Siyar* has him leaving 'in the dead of the night', at about three in the morning on 25 June, driven to 'desperate resolution' after a day without 'a single friend to unbosom his mind with'. Siraj escaped with his wife and principal consort, Lutf-un-Nisa, and some 'favourites' with 'as much gold, and as many as jewels' as possible. He escaped towards Bhagwangola, about 20 kilometres northeast of Murshidabad, hoping to escape by boat on the Ganga–Padma.

This village, in which a garrison was stationed during the reign of Alivardi to secure a supply line from the Ganga, is where Siraj began his 'flight northwards' after Plassey, writes O'Malley. At the time the great river, here known as Padma, flowed by the village; in the present-day the main channel of the river has moved about 10 kilometres to the east of the village. This place associated with Bengal's doom by Indian nationalist historians and Islamist historians was in the 1820s celebrated by Reginald Heber, the Oxbridge educated poet-bishop of Calcutta:

> If thou wert by my side, my love,
> How fast would evening fail,
> In green Bengala's palmy grove,
> Listening the nightingale.

Orme's recall of post-Plassey developments is anchored by greater chronological proximity to events, and access to Company archives that drive historians to his accounts and Company records more frequently than to writers of the *Siyar* and *Riyazu-s-Salatin*—who, to be fair, didn't have access to such records or even extensive Bengal Court records, and often went by hearsay. (For instance, the scholar Joel Bordeaux describes Salim as having 'no privileged access to the nawabi government, but he was a diligent amateur historian and his work—a history of Bengal from the first Turkic conquests in the thirteenth century through the early 1770s—set the standard for studies of the "Muslim Period" in Bengal.') And, certainly, Orme's work is more objective than those like Holwell, and Macaulay—who lionized Clive & Co.

Besides a very visible abandonment by his soldiers and commanders in Murshidabad, for Siraj the inevitability of departure may have been triggered by the arrival of Mir Jafar in Murshidabad on the evening of the 24th, even though, as Orme surmises, he did not immediately move against Siraj. It's possible Mir Jafar's hesitation was prompted by the need to gauge the popular mood in Murshidabad: pro-Siraj, or anti-Siraj—if not specifically pro-Mir Jafar.

In any case it spurred Siraj into further flight. 'Having disguised himself in a mean dress,' Orme tells us, 'he went secretly at ten o'clock at night out of a window, carrying a casket of his most valuable jewels, and attended only by his favourite concubine and the eunuch.'

Orme may have been an hour off the mark:

Letter from Jafar Ali Khan, to Colonel Clive, dated 25 June, 1757, at 8 a.m.

About 11 at night he fled: at 12 I was advised of it. I have sent people after him. By the blessing of God he will be taken. Wherever you are continue. When I write you, proceed.

Later that day, at 6 p.m., Clive received another update from Mir Jafar, which suggests Siraj may have remained in his palace for a few hours longer, having misled both Mir Jafar and, in his chronicling, Orme:

By Rungeet Roy I sent you word that his fortune was changed, and he has run away, but he is at his house...I hope on receipt of this you will oblige me by advancing with your army... On your arrival to-morrow Surajah Dowlat will be either taken or killed. Arrive soon. Do not delay.

◆

For Mir Jafar, 24 June was a grand day, a prelude to a grander day. He made good with Clive, and there was little the colonel, however aggrieved he might have been with Mir Jafar's non-conduct of the war, could do about it. Mir Jafar that day was imagined for posterity in regal tones—though, of course, not as regally as his key British co-conspirator.

Francis Hayman captured that moment of transference of power from Siraj to Mir Jafar. Actually, it portrayed the greater reality: John Company's arrival as the supreme power in Bengal.

It's a compact oil-on-canvas for the statement it made, at 50 inches wide and 39-and-a-half inches tall. The painting now at London's National Portrait Gallery was completed around 1760, five years before the Company's formal endorsement as the diwan of Bengal. A later work may have been much larger, matching the ego of a South Asian empire well on the make, but even by 1760 the impact of the British victory at Plassey was abundantly clear: it was the year Mir Jafar would be replaced as nawab by another Company-blessed candidate, his son-in-law Mir Qasim. Clive was by then a bona fide hero, above the parliamentary reproach that would visit him in a little over a decade. Hayman presciently portrayed that commanding mood—even though he or an archivist evidently mistook Mir Jafar's kingdom: at the lower left corner of the painting is a scrawl, 'Clive with the Nawab of Arcott'.

Clive is near the centre of the portrait, resplendent in red frock coat with green lapels and cuffs, lace trimming at the sleeves, knee-length black boots over red breeches, on his bewigged head a broad-brimmed black tricorn hat, his plump face benign but firm, torso effecting a polite bow, his left arm outstretched as a welcome and query towards Mir Jafar, who is towards the right of the portrait, but not as centred as Clive. Between them, nearly dead centre, is a large flag of Britain, the standard held up by a soldier on a small platform, and assisted by another; at their feet lies a green-and-white flag, presumably of Siraj and the Bengal forces. A rearing, richly caparisoned chocolate horse is to Clive's left—a king's horse, or that of a general.

Mir Jafar, for all his elaborate golden silks—a flowing, ankle-length angrakha—golden shoes, double-stringed necklace of jewels and pearls, jewelled turban, is portrayed by Hayman as bent at the waist, his posture lower than that of Clive, arms extended, palms out in a gesture of explanation and the overall body language of a supplicant. Some interpret the body language as apology as much as gratitude. After all at Plassey didn't Mir Jafar wait, not only to withdraw from Siraj, but to see how Siraj's forces fared without him? What might have happened if the gunpowder had remained dry and the massive cannon pulverized the Company's forces? Would he have switched sides and played yet another role, faithful only to himself, as he so effortlessly did since before the accession of Siraj?

Behind Mir Jafar stands his son, Miran, wearing pink silks and a somewhat stunned expression on his boyish face. At their feet lies a dead Bengal infantryman. They are placed against a backdrop of a blue sky of gold-flecked clouds, and Mir Jafar's transport, a disproportionately large elephant that wouldn't look out of place as mûmakil in J. R. R. Tolkien's Middle Earth moral fantasies, looking askance at the tableau. A few soldiers and courtiers from both sides are peripheral accoutrements.

Clive punctiliously followed form, setting aside his continuing unease at Mir Jafar's neutrality at Plassey, and awareness that the war to depose Siraj and place a Company-approved puppet in Murshidabad was still far from over. 'I congratulate you on the victory, which is yours not mine,' Clive, still at Daudpur, had a note delivered by Luke Scrafton to Mir Jafar on 24 June. 'I should be glad if you would join me with the utmost expedition. We propose marching to-morrow to compleat the conquest that God has blessed us with, and I hope to have the honour of proclaiming you Nabob. Mr. Scrafton will congratulate you on my part. From him you will know how much I am yours.'

But was Mir Jafar unequivocally Clive's? Orme evocatively recalls the background that ultimately led to the 'Rule, Britannia!' set piece, as it were, by Hayman:

In the morning. Colonel Clive deputed Mr. Scrafton and Omarbeg to conduct Meer Jaffier to Daudpore, who received them with reserve, and an air of anxiety, as if he apprehended that the English resented his conduct, in not having joined them, conformably to his promises; he, however, immediately proceeded with them to Daudpore, accompanied by his son, Meirum, and his usual retinue.

On entering the English camp, he alighted from his elephant, and the guard drew out, and rested their arms, to receive him with the usual honours. Not knowing the meaning of this compliment, he darted back, as if he thought it a preparation to his destruction; but Colonel Clive advancing hastily, embraced, and saluted him Nabob of Bengal, Behar, and Orixa, which removed his fears.

They conferred about an hour, he making some apologies, and the Colonel no reproaches; but advised him to proceed immediately to the city, and not to suffer Surajah Dowlah to escape, nor his treasures to be plundered.

Now that the main political aspect of the conspiracy was largely complete, the financial aspect of the conspiracy had to be safeguarded. Mir Jafar left for Murshidabad.

◆

Siraj left for Bhagwangola. From there he embarked on a boat with the intention to rendezvous with the never-say-die Frenchman, Law, whom he had sent away from Qasimbazar. As we have seen, it was a reluctant banishment brought on by Siraj's need to not further aggravate the British. The plan appears to have been to link up with Law and then make their way to Patna where the governor, Ram Narain, remained an ally of Siraj.

Again, there is more than one version of the manner of his escape. Orme writes that Siraj and his immediate family got 'undiscovered' into a boat his faithful harem-eunuch had 'prepared at the wharf of the palace' and that 'it immediately rowed away to the northward'. The Bhagirathi winds its way west of Bhagwangola on its journey north to meet the main channel of the Ganga. As we have seen, Tabatabayi, the author of the *Siyar*, leans towards the certainty that Siraj went overland towards Bhagwangola to then take the boat to Rajmahal. Tabatabayi offers an interesting what-if insight that appears to have been gleaned from palace-talk. He maintains that, had Siraj kept to his initial instinct of travelling overland to Rajmahal—taking a left instead of taking a right to the riverine port of Bhagwangola, he may yet have turned around the fiasco at Plassey. He could have regrouped, persisted and reached out once again to commanders who had remained loyal to him until he reached Murshidabad from Plassey, perhaps some may yet have joined him 'through personal attachment, and many more by a principle of avarice and ambition'. In some hours, by this tactic, and through the radiating effect of such commanders in turn reaching out to men loyal to them, Siraj could have gathered to his side several thousands.

Seeing such numbers nobody would dare stop him—let alone interdict him. 'It is even probable that his retinue would have swelled at every stage, and that he would have found himself at last at the head of a respectable force. But what man has had it in his power to withstand his own destiny; and how is it possible to parry the decrees of an impending fate?'

Meanwhile, fortune favoured the conspiratorial. Clive's army had reached the outskirts of Murshidabad around noon. Clive was cautious. He didn't wish to take a chance and walk into a capital city roiled with confusion and intrigue, at a cost to his own person and that of his army. Clive sent along a group of hundred sepoys with the quick-thinking Watts and John Walsh. Orme writes that Watts and Walsh arrived in Murshidabad around 3 p.m., and then sought a meeting with Mir Jafar. Soon after, more of the general's troops were despatched to pursue Siraj.

Perhaps far more than the fact and fiction around Siraj's removing himself from Murshidabad, the arrival of Watts and the British force signalled to citizens of Bengal's capital that the power shift was real. 'Their visit convinced the inhabitants whom they were to look up to as their future lord,' Orme writes with some exaggeration, as the English domination at this point was far from complete—let alone assured.

A crucial next step for the conspirators was to visibly fill the power vacuum Siraj's loss at Plassey and departure from Murshidabad had created. Siraj would need to be completely neutralized. Mir Jafar would need to be formally proclaimed nawab. He would need to be placed on the masnad of Bengal, Bihar, and Orissa. Be acknowledged. Receive nazar as homage. It had to happen as soon as possible.

Mir Jafar proclaimed himself nawab, and had it announced across Murshidabad. It wasn't a formal appointment endorsed by a higher political power, just a prudent act on his part. He then despatched his son-in-law, Mir Qasim, with a posse after Siraj, and sent orders to his own brother, Mir Daud, the faujdar of Rajmahal, to do everything in his power to capture Siraj.

That to Mir Jafar and others appeared to be just a matter of time. As Siraj continued his flight, by the forenoon on 25 June Mohanlal and his band, which included some members of Siraj's family, were captured. Mir Jafar would write to Clive the next day:

I have had the honour of your note advising me you was on your march, and that you would stay at Moidapore [Maidapur]. Mohun Loll and his son are now brought back here prisoners.

Twenty-five hackeries and some elephants belonging to his beteri (retenue) are also taken. Narrain Sing and all the other hircarahs are arrived. I have dispatched part of my army in pursuit of Surajah Dowlat whose fortune has now changed. With God's assistance they will soon bring him back prisoner. Of this you need make no doubt.

It was then time to address the remaining order of business in the Battle of Plassey: business.

19

THE UNEVEN DISTRIBUTION OF WEALTH

'...he appears to pride himself in shuffling and tricking...'

When it comes to wealth and its distribution matters can be uneven.
It was no different with Plassey plunder. Some sought to enhance
gain, while others apparently sought to diminish it in order to hide
true gain. Plassey's Rashomon effect continued here too.

The *Siyar's* translator insists what transpired next is true, and
offers as proof the assertion that both the author and he were, by
1758, in the 'Company's service, as Linguists to Colonel Clive', and
as his camp followers. In that capacity, they 'remember to have heard
from the mouth of Mr. John Walsh', as to what was found when Walsh,
accompanied by among others, Watts, the diwan Ramchand, and
'Labekishun, the Moonshy or Persian Secretary'—who subsequently
became the very wealthy Raja Nabakrishna, of whom more shortly—
entered Siraj's treasury.

This hearsay account mentions that they found in it 'one hundred
and seventy-six lacs [17.6 million rupees] in silver, two and thirty
lacs [3.2 million] in gold, two chests of gold ingots, four of jewels
set, and two lesser ones of loose stones and gems...'

It wouldn't nearly be enough for what Orme politely terms
'the restitution'—which several Indian nationalist and post-colonial
historians suggest was just the beginning of the looting of Bengal
and India. 'Donations' to the squadron, the army, and the Select
Committee, amounted to '22,000,000 of Secca rupees, equal to
2,750,000 pounds'. Besides, there were other promised 'donations',
Orme admitted, which have since Plassey 'been the foundation of
several fortunes, although not then publicly avowed'.

Rai Durlabh, who had concluded the terms of the agreement with
the Company, held that there was actually a lot less in the treasury
(than mentioned in the *Siyar*): not more than 14 million rupees.

On 26 June, Watts took a hard line at Rai Durlabh's accounting of what was found in the treasury and insisted that the Company's dues under the agreement be met. That day Clive's army was halted at Maidapur. On a day of typical monsoon downpour, after attending Mir Jafar's durbar, and during a meeting with the yet-to-be formalized nawab and his right-hand man, Rai Durlabh, Watts pressed hard for the deal to be honoured. If necessary, he demanded, Jagat Seth Madhab Rai and his family could advance the amount of the shortfall which, as bankers to the nawab, they could surely recoup. Rai Durlabh declined, insisting that the Seths were in no position to offer tens of millions of rupees to straightaway fulfil the terms of the agreement.

That evening Watts and Walsh shot off an angry note to Clive:

> Sir,—We waited on the Nabob this morning and went through the ceremony of his Durbar for full two hours, when he and Roy Dulup retired with us, but instead of Juggat Seat's advancing the money, Roy Dulup with his whole stock of Gentue [Hindu] rhetoric endeavoured to persuade us that the Treasurer had been examined, and it appeared there could not be above a crore and 40 lack [*sic*] in the Treasury, and added that Juggat Seat could not advance crores of rupees; we were not acquainted with facts sufficiently to contest the matter well with Roy Dulup, but desired we might talk with Moonloll and carry him to visit Saabat Jung, which with some difficulty, on Roy Dulup's part, was consented to. When we asked Roy Dulup at what time he and Monickchund proposed setting out for camp, he answered till this affair was settled he could not think of going. In short he appears to pride himself in shuffling and tricking, and we are persuaded, whilst he is Minister, our affairs will meet with all the interruption that Gentue cunning can raise.
>
> We should be glad you would interrogate Omichund and let us know his sentiments of the Nabob's wealth. He told Mr. Watts he knew all the places where the treasures were hoarded; for hoards there are and many by the information we have had. He would certainly be a necessary person here, if he was not always so full of taking care of himself...
>
> We are, Sir, &c. &c., William Watts, John Walsh.

◆

As to 'hoards there are and many', there are several versions.

The *Siyar*'s translator claims that what Watts and others walked into was merely the 'outer treasury'. The English were hoodwinked, he maintains, lending credence to Watts's suspicion of more, to uncover which he had wished to bring the captured Mohanlal to Clive—in his letter referred to as Sabat Jang—for interrogation. But that wasn't to be—and here we return to the main translation— because Mohanlal, the 'Prime Minister, whom his master had raised so high that he touched the firmament with his forehead' and so, 'acquired and hoarded up an immense capital in hatred and envy' was placed in Rai Durlabh's custody after his capture in Murshidabad. The *Siyar* speculates that Rai Durlabh used the opportunity to grab Mohanlal's wealth and properties, and, for the sake of convenience, 'the man's life was made away with'. Haji Mustapha offers some additional gossip about Mohanlal's demise. 'It was reported a year after that Mir-djaafer-qhan had sent some Satellites of his with orders to cudgel him to death,' he writes. 'Others say that Radja Durlubh-ram got him poisoned, to free himself from the necessity of surrendering a prisoner of that consequence.'

The *Siyar* quite uncharacteristically sneers at the predicament of Clive & Co. in their pursuit of wealth and return on investment for the conspiracy and the battles from Calcutta to Plassey:

> ...those renowned English, who look down with contempt
> on the intellects and abilities of the Bengalees, and yet are
> perpetually bubbled and duped by them, did not know anything
> of the inner treasury, said to contain eight corors [80 million
> rupees], and which, pursuant to a custom well-known in India,
> and which is ordinary even to private men, was kept in the
> Zenana, or women's apartments.

This inner treasury would never be found, the *Siyar* maintains, because it was 'made away with' by Mir Jafar, his trusted aide and communicator Amir (or Omar) Beg, and the clerk-agents Ramchand and Nabakrishna—'whose silence was purchased by a share in the contents, or who, it was said, made away with the Colonel's share'. The *Siyar*'s gossipy translator points out that when Ramchand died ten years after Plassey, a man who earned sixty rupees a month in

1758 left an estate worth 7.3 million rupees in 'cash and bills', 'four hundred large water-pots, eighty of which were of gold, and the rest of silver', 1.8 million rupees worth of property, and jewels and jewellery worth two million rupees. Another estimate by a Company employee downsized this estate of around twelve million rupees to eight million, but even this, maintains the *Siyar*, couldn't possibly have been earned by Ramchand in his subsequent appointment as diwan to Henry Vansittart, who was governor of Bengal between 1759–64. Vansittart himself left Bengal with a fortune of no more than a million rupees after years as a man who was made 'omnipotent' by a 'revolution which put every thing in their power', so Ramchand must have made off with some Plassey treasure.

The same accusation is placed at the doors of 'Labekishun'— Nabakrishna—also a Company employee at sixty rupees a month who is said to have spent 900,000 rupees at his mother's funeral.

By way of example, the accusation extends also to Munni Begum, the dancing girl who became Mir Jafar's favourite consort and greatly influential second wife. She would, after the death of her besotted husband, deal with Clive & Co. to secure for her sons the masnad at Murshidabad:

> ...and by the immense fortune which Menni-begum, the favourite consort of Mir-djaafer-qhan's, is known to be possessed of to this day [Munni Begum died in 1813, aged ninety-three, a lady of abundant means]. This fortune, which is computed by corors, could not be made anywhere, but at that precise occasion; for her husband is known to have lived and died poor, distressed, and enormously indebted; so much so, that his troops more than once endangered his life for their pay, and at last conspired against him with Mir-cassem, his son-in-law.

Such tantalizing detail, albeit at best circumstantial, easily carried over from that century to the next as it became established word of mouth. A passage from the mid-nineteenth century history of Bengal, *Tarikh-i-Mansuri*, written by Saiyid Ali Khan Bilgrami and named after his friend and patron, the nawab Syed Mansur Ali Khan Bahadur—a descendant of Mir Jafar also known as Feradun Jah—was translated by the German orientalist and Persian language specialist,

Heinrich Blochmann, for an 1867 issue of *The Journal of the Asiatic Society*. It repeats the funerary expenses for Nabakrishna's mother to raise a red flag:

> It is also well known that besides this treasure there existed another in the Harem, which fact Mir Mahomed Jafar concealed from Colonel Clive, at the instigation of the Dewan and Clive's Moonshee. The value of the gold and silver articles and of the jewels found there was not less than 80 millions of rupees. The whole was divided among Mir Jafar, Ram Chand, Amir Beg and Nobokissen. This transaction is indeed very probable, as Ram Chand left a fortune of 12½ millions of rupees at his death, ten years later, whilst Nobokissen could afford to pay 9,00,000 rupees on the occasion of the death of his mother. Yet both men were in receipt of only 60 rupees per month at the time of the division.

◆

Until now we have largely concerned ourselves with major players in the events leading up to the battle, the battle itself, and its aftermath, but it is important to take note of characters like Canto Babu and even Nabakrishna Deb.

Canto Babu was another person besides Nabakrishna who attracted the attention and trust of young Hastings and played his own part in events around Plassey. Also referred to as Cantoo Baboo and relatively less often as Kanta Babu, the polite form of address in Bengali for Krishna Kanta Nandy, he is recognized as founder of the 'Cossimbazar Raj' of titled gentry that took wing in the post-Plassey years of mercantilist euphoria. O'Malley notes that Nandy's father was a small shopkeeper selling silk, betel nut, and kites ('his skill in flying kites, we are solemnly told by the family chronicler, earned for him the name of Khalifa, i.e, "the expert."') Now this kite flyer evidently rooted in reality joined the Qasimbazar factory as an apprentice 'and in due time was brought on the establishment as a clerk, in which capacity he came into contact with Warren Hastings'.

As we've seen, young Hastings first arrived in Murshidabad in 1753. Three years later, the 'obscure young clerk' made his mark with the future governor general. 'When the Cossimbazar factory was captured by Siraj-ud-daula, Warren Hastings was sent a prisoner to Murshidabad, but managed to make his escape, with the help, it is said, of Kanta Babu.' O'Malley relates the popular story that Nandy first concealed Hastings in his house and later managed to have him 'taken down the river in a boat'. A grateful Hastings provided him a 'memorandum' that he was later to produce as proof of his identity. The story extends to the time Hastings 'rose to power'. Several Cantoo Baboo impersonators were exposed by Hastings when, 'at length, Kanta Babu himself appeared and produced the memorandum, whereupon Hastings gave him an appointment as his Banyan'. And thereafter the former flyer and seller of kites amassed a fortune as ijaradar or revenue farmer, 'directly or indirectly,' writes O'Malley, '...of several highly productive zamindaris'. It hadn't hurt that, along the way, Nandy had also been minder to Francis Sykes, who was also a resident at Murshidabad, enriching him as he enriched himself.

And with these two famous charges Nandy, like his artful and better-known colleague, Nabakrishna, had arrived as a part of what the historian Ronald Edward Robinson describes (here I refer to a foreword by Peter James Marshall in a biography of Nandy) as 'collaborating and mediating elites' who helped build the foundation of European imperialism.

◆

Nabakrishna Deb would go from being a translator and record-keeper for a young Hastings and a surging Clive, to Maharaja Nabakrishna Deb Bahadur; his houses in Kolkata's Shōbhabājār (also Shovabazar) area are still resplendent despite creeping decrepitude all these years after his death in 1797. Nabakrishna opted early on for the side that would ensure a generous measure of fine ghee on his golden plateful of fragrant steamed rice, as it were. Some chroniclers describe him as a glorified messenger in the Plassey conspiracy, others as a supreme wheeler-dealer, and some others, as we have just seen, as a handsome beneficiary of Siraj's fabled secret treasury that Clive & Co. never got their hands on.

Nabakrishna was a Company man through and through. A 1901 publication, *Memoirs of Maharaja Nubkissen Bahadur*, a family-sponsored hagiography written by the Middle Temple barrister and advocate at Calcutta High Court, N. N. Ghose, actually strives to cement that truth, besides enhancing Nabakrishna's role in Plassey and diminishing his role in the sharing of Plassey loot. He proudly asserts that 'ordinary' Britons were generally ignorant of people of their own kind who worked for empire, so they would naturally be ignorant of the quiet and 'unambitious' work put in by those of 'another complexion and denizens of another clime, who furnished the ideas and suggested the steps that led to the establishment of England's great empire in the east.'

Rarely have claims of collaboration and establishing the roots of colonialism been so lyrically composed and embroidered upon. If the British knew so little of the achievements of Clive and Hastings, Ghose lamented, 'what can they know of the counsels of Nubkissen—the plans he made, the information he gave, the protection he rendered, the dangers he braved or warned against, the light he threw on the designs of Mahomedan rulers, the intricacies he unravelled, the peace he maintained, the possibilities of empire that he saw and revealed to a body of merchants, bold and adventurous no doubt, but apparently not yet alive to the grandeur of the prospect before them?'

To embellish the biography, the author quotes Harry Verelst, the governor of Bengal from 1767 to 1769, as Nabakrishna being the 'native Hindu who was extremely zealous in the English cause during the troubles preceding Meer Jaffer's elevation to the Subahdaree'. And also, that when war broke out with Mir Qasim, the nawab who turned against the Company's interests after being manoeuvred into the nawabship when Mir Jafar was deemed as unworthy by the Company, Nabakrishna stood with his English masters until Mir Qasim 'was driven out of the Provinces'.

It appears as if Nabakrishna was born to the cause. The uncertain year of his birth is assumed by Ghose to be 1732, the year in which his future benefactor, Hastings, 'saw the light'—the very year Clive, another of Nabakrishna's masters and benefactors, was already 'a rowdy boy of seven at Hope Hall'.

The barrister-hagiographer, Ghose, exults:

> If Nubkissen was actually born at Govindpore there is a fitness
> in the decree of destiny that reared a bulwark of England's

empire in the east on the very soil that received the child that was eventually to help in laying the foundations of that empire. What a discovery it would be that would identify the place of Nubkissen's birth as the very spot where the corner-stone of the Fort was laid!

Such Plassey genealogy would place Hastings and him at eighteen in 1750, the year Nabakrishna came into the employ of one of the minor stars of Plassey and the future governor general of the Bengal Presidency and Company dominions in the subcontinent. From complete obscurity—and yet, some initiative at having learnt the language of the Bengal and Mughal courts—he was appointed Persian tutor to Hastings, who arrived as a cadet Company-wallah. Nabakrishna's career, which would in a few short years propel him to the position of a prominent 'banian'—a baniya, in this usage, 'native' or Indian agent and assistant to a European—had begun. (Marshall, a historian with a decades-long association with King's College, London, and an acknowledged expert on empire and Company, writes that a banian was much more: 'A banian was the personal factotum of his European "master". He managed his household, kept his accounts, provided both the capital and local knowledge for his commercial transactions, and in general was his link with the Indian world.') Such a pairing wasn't unusual. Europeans looked out for useful Indians, a matter of convenience recorded by both formal histories and apocrypha.

◆

After six years as tutor to Hastings, Nabakrishna was appointed 'moonshee'—or munshi, secretary—to John Company. The account of that appointment, going by the assertions of *Nubkissen*, marks the beginning of Nabakrishna's participation in the early machinations against Siraj.

The story begins right after the tensions precipitated by the flight of Krishna Ballabh to Calcutta to seek refuge with Drake (as we have seen, there is a version that claims the Calcutta Council granted him refuge as Drake was absent from Calcutta at the time). A somewhat panicked Drake sought assurances against Siraj, which the incarcerated Raj Ballabh, the refugee's father, provided. And, as by several accounts he was already arrested by Siraj, such an assurance could arrive only if provided on his behalf by conspirators in Murshidabad. It was in the shape of a letter by 'Ministers and Sirdars of the Nabob, or at least several of them', and written in Persian. The messenger who brought it had a curious message for Drake: that a letter containing 'important secrets' shouldn't be 'placed in the hands of a Mahomedan', but a 'Hindu'. So, Drake ignored 'Tajuddin', a Company munshi, and sent people to look for a 'Hindu Moonshee'. Nabakrishna, by virtue of the law of 'accidents' that often aid the 'making of great men', happened to be in the Burrabazar area north of Fort William when one of Drake's men came by him, and off they went to Drake. Nabakrishna read and explained the letter, and also scripted the Company's reply.

'Nabakissen came forward in Clive's time'—here Reverend Long's 1868 pamphlet, *Peeps Into Social Life in Calcutta a Century Ago*—is taken as endorsement by this remarkable munshi's biographer.

> Living in an obscure village...near Diamond Harbour, he supplied the English refugees there with provisions in spite of the prohibition of the Nabob and he brought them valuable information relating to the Nabob's movements.

And he is said to have done more. As Siraj arrived for his second expedition to take Calcutta, as we have seen, he camped in Umachand's garden. 'Colonel Clive deputed Nubkissen and an Engineer to obtain information in regard to the particulars of the Nabob's encampment under the pretence of making proposals of peace and offering presents to the Nabob,' the munshi's biographer notes of his foray to the place also known as Halsibag. 'They brought with them a detailed account of the situation.' Ergo: Nabakrishna directly contributed to Clive's eventual surprise dawn attack on Siraj and the nawab's eventual retreat—and set off a domino effect that ended with Plassey. Why would Nabakrishna's descendants lie about such things, his hagiographer notes, by 'investing' the founder of the family's grand run of success with 'the functions of a spy'?

The biography finally comes to the point of Nabakrishna's wealth, taking great pains to indicate that Nabakrishna came by his wealth legally, and not by deceit—indeed, deceiving even the crafty Clive.

Ghose, the biographer of Nabakrishna, quotes what he claims is a fantastic account of hidden treasures that Clive never laid his hands on.

Nubkissen claims that the canny munshi benefited from 'donations' to which he was 'entitled' quite like his 'masters', and he also employs as defence John Malcolm who, in his worshipful work, *The Life of Robert, Lord Clive* dismisses the claims of great treasures altogether:

> The treasures of Serajuddowlah had been greatly over estimated by Mr. Watts, who states in one letter that they were computed to amount to 40,000,000 sterling, a sum so extravagantly beyond what the revenues of the country could have enabled Allaverdy Khan, or his successor, to amass, that it is quite extraordinary how such a belief could have been entertained.

An account by G. B. Malleson, who also wrote a biography of Clive (*Rulers of India: Lord Clive*), too is quoted as defence. As is the logic that it is inconceivable Mir Jafar would 'conceal from Clive' such treasure but share it with others, and that he had 'something to gain by pleasing Clive; he could have had no reason to please Nubkissen or Ram Chand...' While it is logically possible to dispute this assertion—Mir Jafar could easily have offered a portion of this hidden treasure to a few in order to keep Clive & Co. from gaining more reparation, reward, and personal loot—the matter of this and other hidden treasure remain a matter of dispute.

◆

Stories of mysterious treasure abound to this day. Visitors to a mosque of that era, which is on the way to the Motijheel tourist area, are shown a low structure of brick and mortar to the left of the mosque and its small graveyard. The several-rooms-length structure is solid. In places brickwork seems gouged out: local guides take pains to explain that within this structure may lie part of Motijheel's and Murshidabad's fabled treasures; the missing masonry was the result of the damage caused by cannonballs the British used to blow the place apart to search for treasure, and failed. (The mosque remains the only structure standing in Nawazish's grand complex. His grave lies by the mosque. It provides his title 'Sahamatjang', or Shahmat

Jang, the conqueror of kings—there's a chess term in Persian, Shah Mat! for checkmate. The grave of his adopted son, and Siraj's brother, Ikram-ud-daulah, is by his side. Nearby are graves of Ikram's tutor and nurse.)

Even in 1914, when O'Malley published his history and observations on Murshidabad, the adjacent solid structure, 65 feet long, 23 feet wide, and 12 feet high was as 'moss grown' as it is today, and was associated with legends of treasure and ill-fortune for those hunting for it. 'No one, however,' writes O'Malley, 'dares to break into it, for it is said that some labourers who were employed in opening it died of spitting blood as soon as they started work.'

What is indisputable is that Nabakrishna came into great wealth and pomp. Indeed, in late 1757, he hosted Clive for an at-home of considerable lavishness. Nabakrishna hosted a Durga Puja in 1757 as thanksgiving for the victory at Plassey. Clive attended the celebrations to worship Mā Durga, the evil-slaying super-goddess—mohādébi—beloved of the Bengali. In 'Goddesss Encounters: Mughals, Monsters and the Goddess in Bengal', the historian Kumkum Chatterjee notes that Clive sent over 'a number of goats to be sacrificed to the devi'. Nabakrishna's puja evidently became quite the event in the social calendar of the 'sahib', an occasion for carousing with alcohol and meat at a time of some abstinence for worshippers.

♦

Anyway, to quote the author of *Riyazu-s-Salatin*:

What was I saying? and to what have I digressed?
Where lay the horse? and where have I galloped away?

The pujas to celebrate Plassey were still several months away. Meanwhile, Clive was clearly impatient that a conquest had been effected and yet not been monetized as agreed. Also the new government had not yet been stabilized, without which the purpose of the Plassey conspiracy would be lost. The angry note dated 26 June from Watts and Walsh about Siraj's presumably overestimated treasury, and Rai Durlabh's resistance to their suggestions of making good any shortfall, prompted Clive—then at Qasimbazar—to send his own irritated note dated 27 June to the Select Committee at Fort

William. It was part of the same note in which, as we've seen, he rebuked the Committee, quoting the Oracle of Delphi:

> The chicanery and villany of Roy Dulub obliges me to go tomorrow to the City to prevent the ill consequence that attends the great power lodged in his hands, so prejudicial both to the Nabob and the Company, as also to hasten the execution of the treaty, to which he would otherwise be a great obstacle, as he pretends the whole ballance in the Treasury is but one crore and forty lack of rupees. I shall see the Nabob and Juggut Seat to-morrow [for which he planned on marching to Murshidabad later in the day on 27th], and consult with them on what measures to be taken to get Serajah Dowlat into his hands, and to fix the government on a solid foundation.

◆

As it happened, Clive did not march to Murshidabad as he had threatened to, but stayed put in Qasimbazar, where the entire body of his army had joined him by the 28th. Major Coote reported that the King's troops and Bengal troops were quartered in the premises of the English factory, the Madras and Bombay troops quartered in the French factory.

There was a perceived threat to Clive's life—or so Watts communicated. In the Byzantine and Machiavellian world in which Clive & Co. were fully vested, Rai Durlabh had now identified Clive as an impediment. So had Miran (and possibly Mir Qasim, who must have returned from giving chase to Siraj). The information was conveyed to Watts by the Jagat Seth through his trusted agent Ranjit Rai, whom we first encountered during the siege of Calcutta.

Letter from Messrs, Watts and Walsh to Colonel Clive, dated 27 June, 1757. 1 p.m.:

Rungeet Roy is despatched to us by Juggatseat to desire that you will not come into town this afternoon for treachery is intended you. A consultation was held last night between Meerum, Roydulup and Cossim Hussain Cawn about cutting you off at your visit to the Nabob. You may return on pretence of illness if you are on the road, but it will be necessary to write of it. Juggatseat will then visit you to-morrow morning. He begs you will not mention a syllable of this intelligence as you value his life. The Nabob's jewels and treasures have been taken and privately sent to Goodagurry. [Godagiri in present-day Rajshahi district of Bangladesh, to the northeast from Bhagwangola across the Ganga–Padma. It isn't clear if that was intelligence on Siraj's treasures the deposed nawab sent off before his own flight, or it was a hoard removed by the new rulers for safekeeping.] What we hear further we will either write to you or tell you by word of mouth.

Clive spent all day of 28 June in Qasimbazar waiting for matters to cool down in the post-Plassey power circle of Murshidabad. It isn't clear how that happened. Did the Jagat Seth creatively let slip that Clive was now wise to this new conspiracy, which panicked the plotters? Did Watts pass on word on the lines of if-it-can-happen-to-Siraj-it-can-happen-to-you? But the threat of assassination diminished quickly enough for Clive to prepare to march to Murshidabad the following day. ('...his apprehensions were removed,' writes Orme, 'but by what intelligence we do not know'.)

Clive's apprehensions may have lessened, but he would take no chances. Coote's journal entry of 29 June reads: 'A detachment of 100 of the King's troops with 300 sepoys under the command of Major Grant (was) ordered as a guard to the Commander-in-Chief to go with him to Muxadavad.' The concern appears to have quickly escalated. His journal entry on 30 June read:

> The detachment ordered yesterday, reinforced by the Company's Grenadiers, 200 sepoys and two field pieces, escorted Colonel Clive to Muxadavad, the whole army ordered in readiness to march at a moment's warning.

◆

News of the victory at Plassey and subsequent messages from Clive reached Fort William within three days or so by fastest messenger. It took a further three days, so between six and seven days round-trip, before responses from Calcutta reached Clive. It was, of course, speedy as compared to the time taken for news and orders to reach Madras from Calcutta, or London—battles were lost, as at Calcutta in 1756, or won, like Plassey, before redundant advisories arrived from Company headquarters in London. As we have seen, the battle at Plassey was over by the time the letter the Select Committee in Calcutta wrote on 23 June reached Clive asking for an ultimate showdown with Siraj.

Now congratulations and suggestions poured in with the usual delay—and would, as usual, be overtaken by events. A letter signed by Admiral Watson and his colleague Admiral Charles Pocock—here representing the Crown interests—and the Company (Roger Drake Junior, Charles Manningham, Richard Becher) dated 29 June lavished praise on behalf of 'His Britannic Majesty' and the Company on Clive and his party's 'rapid success'. They recognized the 'extraordinary importance' of this 'revolution' not only to the Company 'but to the British nation in general'.

But form had yet to follow function. The power vacuum had to be filled with pomp and spectacle.

The gentlemen of Crown and Company wrote:

> Although in your last letter Jaffier Ally Khan is stiled Nabob, yet we have not ventured on that authority to make any public rejoicings for him as Subah of these Provinces. We should be glad therefore to be informed in your next letter if he has been proclaimed in form, and is in possession of the government. This will add very much to our satisfaction, and give us a proper opening to address him as the Subah, proclaim him such in our town, and salute his accession.

Indeed, the ships *Kent* and *Tyger*, and Fort William, had already fired '21 guns' in celebrations that very day at noon, Drake wrote to Clive in a separate note. 'When we are certainly informed that Meer Jaffeir is proclaimed we shall make a whole day of rejoicing.' (And, meanwhile, as Clive was close to the court at Murshidabad, could the colonel please send him a nice draft of a letter in Persian for Mir Jafar, as Drake had 'bad Persian writers here'?)

◆

Clive did the honours. On the morning of 29 June, he entered Murshidabad in state. He was finally in the city he would describe as being 'as extensive, populous and rich as the city of London, with this difference, that there are individuals in the first possessing infinitely greater property than in the last city'. The next sentence, as recorded in *The Imperial Gazetteer of India*, is perhaps more telling and rather less quoted, and fully sums up both his surprise at the Plassey conspiracy coming through, and the reality of Bengal politics of the day. 'The inhabitants, if inclined to destroy the Europeans, might have done so with sticks and stones.'

Clive and his entourage were watchful as they made their way to the Murad Bag palace. The complex with its gardens was deemed spacious and appropriate for his party. Miran called on Clive here, all traces of conspiracy absent, and together they went, Clive's guard accompanying him, to nearby Heerajheel Palace, till a week earlier Siraj's home and court.

Clive would write to the Select Committee the following day of what transpired. His tone was dry—for all the import and emotion, it was now time for business:

> Gentlemen... In the afternoon I waited on Jaffeir Ally Cawn, being escorted to him by his son. As I found he declined taking his seat on the musnud, I handed him to it.

The *Siyar* and Orme amply fill in the mood.

'The day of his being proclaimed, he invited the Colonel and the principal English, as well as the principal Grandees of his Court, and the principal Commanders of his troops,' the *Siyar*'s translator elaborates as if there was no pressure at all from the British on Mir Jafar to get it over with.

> A magnificent Mesned, or throne, was spread at the north end of the hall ['in which Surajah Dowlah used to appear in public,' writes Orme], where it remained empty for a time, notwithstanding the Colonel's intreaties [Mir Jafar 'seemed desirous to avoid the Musnud']. At last the victorious Commander got up ['perceiving' this hesitation], took Mir-djaaferqhan by the hand, carried him to the Mesned, made him sit in it, kept him down with the arm ['made obeisance

to him, as Nabob of the provinces, in the usual forms'], and then presented his Nezer ['presented a plate with gold rupees; he then, by an interpreter, exhorted the great men to be joyful that fortune had given them so good a prince, in exchange for such a tyrant as Surajah Dowlah']. This was followed by the Nezers and homages of the English, and of all present ['they likewise paid homage, and presented gold']; and a Royal salute announced the proclamation to the whole city.

So began the first reign of the general who wouldn't fight: Shujah-ul-mulk Hashim-ud-daulah Mir Jafar Ali Khan Bahadur Mahabat Jang. Valorous Hero of the Country and Sword of the Empire, the high and valiant Jafar Ali who is a Formidable Horror in War and Majestic in Battles. The last honorific was Alivardi's too, as we've seen: he was often referred to only as Mahabat Jang. Mir Jafar, the first of the Najafi line of Murshidabad nawabs, named after his father, Sayyid Ahmad Najafi—also known as Mirza Mirak—a line that the family's creative genealogy traced all the way to the Prophet Muhammad through one of his daughters, Fatimah.

Mir Miran, his son, was hailed as Shahamat Jang. Valorous in War. Mir Qasim, his son-in-law, as Haibat Jang, Who Causes Awe and Panic in War.

The new nawab ordered a new seal of office to be struck, and ordered medals of gold, 'broad and thin, the language and characters are Persian', commemorating his victory in Plassey. He would use for these his favourite title, Mahabat Jang, which he also took care to inscribe on his seals. The Mughal emperor, Alamgir II, who was placed on the throne by the powerful vazir, Imad-ul-Mulk, precedes Mahabat Jang's name on the medals in nominal show of form. Clive's name follows Mir Jafar's.

There was no ambiguity in several less flashy medals struck in Britain to celebrate Plassey. The quirkily named Society for Promoting Arts and Commerce issued a medal in 1758, depicting Lady Victory delicately holding a trophy and a sheaf of palm leaves, seated daintily side-saddle on a diminutive elephant—the elephant for long the symbol of imperial power in India. The letters crowning Lady Victory are sharp: VICTORY AT PLASSY CLIVE COMMANDER.

The obverse shows an imperious, straight-backed Clive wearing a

Roman tunic. In his left hand he lightly holds a staff surmounted by a lion. With his right he hands a slightly bowed and clearly supplicating Mir Jafar a staff surmounted with the image of a fish. Between them is a cornucopia, a map of the world, and a rudder. Below them is a telling claim: A Soubah Given to Bengal. Along the rim of the medal, surrounding the figures, is an even more telling claim: INJURIES ATTONED PRIVILEGES AUGMENTED TERRITORY ACQUIRED.

To be clear, Mir Jafar's coronation was authorized by Clive, not the increasingly impotent Mughal emperor. Clive would write to the Select Committee in Calcutta that the new nawab was 'fully confirmed and proclaimed Subah of the three Provinces'. Clive, the colonel, was now Clive, the kingmaker. And his employers had begun their journey to being employers of the nawabs of Bengal, only the first step in a rapid, astonishing run that would, in fifty years, bring the Company control of the Carnatic, Awadh, Mysore, and the Mughal seat in Delhi.

Clive had made that power shift abundantly clear in a declaration—the exhortation Orme mentions—to Mir Jafar and his court right after Clive led the new nawab to the masnad. His letter of the following day would explain it to the Select Committee. Clive's words at court presented elegant lies, peerless double-talk, and misdirection—even inviting God to the conspiracy—artful hypocrisy, and outright threat, all mixed in with the kernel of truth about Siraj's desperate effort to ally with the French:

> I only attempted to convince them, that it was not the maxims of the English to war against the Government, but that Surajah Dowlat not only would not fulfil the treaty he had entered into with us, but was taking measures by calling in the French to destroy us; but it had pleased God to overthrow him, and that as the present Nabob was a brave and good man, the country might expect to be quiet and happy under him; that for our parts we should not anyways interfere in the affairs of the Government, but leave that wholly to the Nabob; that as long as his affairs required it, we were ready to keep the field, after which we should return to Calcutta and attend solely to commerce, which was our proper sphere and our whole aim in these parts.

The necessary fuss over, it was time for unfinished business.

When Clive returned to Murad Bag after his proxy's coronation, Jagat Seth Madhab Rai visited him. They had 'a good deal of conversation', Clive wrote of the meeting. It was only natural, he clarified to the Select Committee, as the Jagat Seth 'is a person of the greatest property and influence in the three subahs, and of no inconsiderable weight at the Mogul's Court', he would be the 'properest person' to resolve issues.

Mir Jafar visited Clive the following day, on the morning of 30 June. He repeated what Rai Durlabh, now his first minister, had told Watts, that there simply wasn't enough in the treasury to meet obligations to Clive & Co. ('...that as the money in the Treasury fell short of his expectations, and was not sufficient to satisfie his obligations to us,' Clive wrote, 'and leave him wherewithal for his necessary expences...')

Clive suggested the Seths as mediators. Mir Jafar agreed. In any case, Clive would note, the proposal of the Seths as mediators 'was too agreeable to me to decline, for as I had sufficient reason to think great sums had been secreted and made away with by his Ministers, it would have been both a difficult and invidious task for me to have sifted into this affair'. Clive evidently decided to recover whatever he could as best as he could.

Mir Jafar and he immediately set off for the House of Jagat Seth. It was an indication of the still-great influence of the bankers that the new nawab, and the person who would soon be the most powerful man in Bengal, would defer to Jagat Seth Madhab Rai and his cousin, Maharaja Swaroop Chand, 'in order to extinguish as soon as possible this brand of contention'. Watts, Scrafton, Miran, and Rai Durlabh accompanied them.

So did Umachand, over whose deception Clive and Admiral Watson had bickered: the morality or immorality of duping a fellow conspirator as a means to an end, and ironically, to pay him back for his own greed. Even now, the man who signed the decoy treaty of red paper thought he was held in high esteem by Clive. That thought must have been deflated somewhat when, upon arrival at the Seths', Umachand was not invited for the conference to the 'carpet'—

the traditional floor seating for conferences at the Seths. He placed himself a little distance away.

Orme presents the drama.

> The treaties, as written in Persic and English, were read, explained, and acknowledged. After much conversation, Roydoolub insisting always on the scantiness of the treasury, it was agreed that [Clive wrote: 'Juggut Seat after a long but friendly debate settle the point as follows'] one half of the money stipulations should be paid immediately; two thirds of this half in coin, and one third in jewels, plate, and effects ['jewels, plate and goods', Clive noted], at a valuation; but that the other half should be discharged in three years at three equal payments: Roydoolub was allowed a commission of five in the hundred on the sums for restitution, which amounted to 17,700,000 rupees, and this was one of the gratuities which had been held out to Omichund.

At 5 per cent, the commission for Rai Durlabh ensuring the amount of reparation reached the Company and its officials, worked out to 885,000 rupees. (Clive justified this commission to the Select Committee citing reasons of realpolitik: 'As it was absolutely necessary to satisfy Roy Dulub, who is the principal Minister, and through whose hands our affairs must pass, I thought it not improper to admit him to a commission of 5 per cent...')

There was a lot more business conducted and soon sealed in treaty. Mir Jafar would honour the previous grants of the Mughal emperor that permitted the Company duty free movement of its goods, and reaffirm the treaty the Company had signed with Siraj— the Treaty of Alinagar in February 1757. In addition there was 'an alliance offensive and defensive against all enemies, Europeans or country,' Clive would write in a few days to the Select Committee in Madras, 'the delivery of the French and their property into our hands and a perpetual exclusion of them from these provinces; a tract of land extending between the lake [Salt Lake] and [Hugli] river from Calcutta to Culpee [Kulpi, south of Diamond Harbour, and across the Hugli from the present-day port and industrial city of Haldia—a vast tract of the South 24 Parganas] to be given to the Company, also one crore of rupees 50 lack [15 million] to the European sufferers at the loss of Calcutta, twenty lack [2 million] to the blacks, seven [700,000] to the Armenians, and fifty [5 million] to the army and navy.'

These were all to be fulfilled within a month from Mir Jafar's 'accession to the Subahship'. That meant: by the end of July 1757.

The author of the *Siyar* suggests that Mir Jafar threw in an exceptional deal-sweetener for Clive, his key benefactor—and the chronicler was clearly disappointed by it. 'As to those men who style themselves Mussulmen, and have laid their hands upon the properties and honour of other people, their actions are no better than so many suggestions of the Demon of Concupiscence, and so many illusions of the Devil, their prototype and master...' he fumed in righteous outrage. The *Siyar*'s translator echoed the tone of moral outrage about this 'bribe'—apparently offered by Mir Jafar to Clive: '...ten handsome women out of his seraglio, that is, out of Seradj-ed-döulah's seraglio, although he was himself a Seyd, or a descendant of the Prophet's, and, like all the Mussulmen Princes of India, had assumed the surname of Ghazi or champion fighting against infidels.' It isn't clear whether Clive accepted this gift or if the first among 'nabobs' viewed it as a conflict of interest.

As a part of several clarifications that followed as corollaries to the deal that had been struck, a kind of profitable Pax Bengala as it were, Clive wrote to the 'Nanna'—Nanasaheb, the Peshwa—that 'Jaffir Ally Cawn is in peaceful possession of the kingdom, and will duly pay him the chout' (chauth) according to the deal signed by Alivardi.

For his labours Clive did rather well. 'Of this sum Clive himself received £234,000 or nearly Rs 19 lakh—a "gigantic" sum for those days,' writes Irfan Habib. 'He also gave to himself a jagir near Calcutta', he continues, which yielded £30,000 or about Rs 250,000 a year. His colleagues in Calcutta's Council received up to £80,000 or about Rs 650,000 each out of the 'plundered treasury'. (Hill notes in his *Bengal in 1756-1757* that Clive calculated that £4.5 million sterling were paid in compensation to those who had been ruined by the loss of Calcutta, to private persons and to the Company', besides land grants the Company received. 'In one of his letters he wrote that every subaltern would be £3,000 the richer for the Revolution.') 'Indeed,' adds Habib, 'it seemed after 1757 the Company's own monetary gains were trifling compared to those of its officials in India.'

Clive would validate his personal profit in a letter he wrote on 6 August to the Court in London: 'The Nabob's generosity has enabled me to live with satisfaction in England...' He said he would much rather leave Bengal, as the 'frequent attacks I have here of a nervous disorder make me very desirous of an opportunity of changing this climate.' The only thing keeping him back in Bengal, Clive assured the gentlemen in London, was 'solely a desire of seeing your affairs, important as they now are, firmly established...'

Meanwhile, as the deal-making continued in Murshidabad, Siraj was still on the run.

♦

As the conference ended, Clive and Scrafton made their way to an expectant Umachand, and at Clive's go-ahead, Orme resumes, Scrafton told him in the 'Indostan language': 'Omichund, the red paper is a trick; you are to have nothing.'

The declaration hit Umachand 'like a blast of sulphur', we learn. He fainted, and would have fallen to the ground if an attendant of his hadn't caught him. He was carried to his palanquin and then escorted to his Murshidabad residence. He remained there in 'stupid melancholy', and soon began to show 'some symptoms of insanity'.

A few days later, the broken merchant-conspirator would visit Clive, and the solicitous colonel advised him to 'make a pilgrimage to some pagoda', writes Orme. Umachand did, visiting a major temple near Malda, 'and returned insane, his mind every day more and more approaching to idiotism'.

(Clive would in some weeks justify his actions in a letter dated 6 August to the Court I have referred to earlier: 'Omichund had merited well while acting in concert with Mr. Watts, but I had reason to think his intriguing disposition was carrying him too far in the pursuit of his private interest, therefore recommended to him a visit of devotion to Malda.' He would add an odd afterthought, although how he could any longer expect Umachand's trust was a stretch: 'He is a person capable of rendering you great services while properly restrained, therefore not to be wholly discarded.')

The aged merchant, delirious and delusional, evidently became something of a male version of Miss Havisham, waiting for lost grandeur to return, always dressed in opulent garments and the costliest jewels. 'In this state of imbecility,' Orme relates, 'he died about a year and a half after the shock of his disappointment.' Orme injects an oddly sympathetic tone at this point, maintaining that, as Umachand's 'tales and artifices' misled Siraj from trusting news from his core of faithful aides who brought news of Mir Jafar's treachery, Umachand should at least have been paid the two million rupees he expected and then left alone to enjoy the conspirators' fee in 'oblivion and contempt'.

The expendable Umachand was for several months a candidate for collateral damage, too eager and too venal for even this motley crowd of eager and transparently corrupt power players. For the conspirators, there were matters bigger than him to be dealt with. The meeting that publicly sealed his fate and gave away, according to Orme, his share to Rai Durlabh, had also decided on other matters.

Clive writes that the 'Juggut Seat', who usually presented his house's position as being entirely altruistic in diplomatic endeavours and for resolving disputes of all sorts, finally made a pitch for restitution, 'that he had been a sufferer of seven lack by the French, and as he was joining in measures for their extirpation, it was probable he should never be paid...' Clive agreed, and suggested—in the same breath urging the Select Committee to acquiesce—that the Jagat Seth could take whatever he might find at any French 'out- Settlements and aurungs'. A shortfall, he suggested, could be 'made good' by John Company in case the Jagat Seth was unable to recover an equivalent amount from the French.

This suggestion greatly pleased Madhab Rai, who then offered a slew of services to cement the new regime. Clive noted that the banker offered his 'best services' to the Company, that would have Mir Jafar 'confirmed' from Delhi, 'represent our transactions in the fairest light, and procure for us any phirmaund we may have occasion for'.

The banker had a final piece of advice for the new nawab: reinstate to their former positions all officers of Alivardi replaced by his grandson Siraj.

There was more. 'It was agreed that letters should be wrote by the Nabob and myself to the Naib of Patna [Ram Narain, who still remained loyal to Siraj] with offers of friendship, and desiring him to deliver up Surajah Dowlat or drive him out of the Province, as we understood he had taken his route that way.'

But even Clive with his newly plump status, and all his machinations and veiled threats couldn't push the process beyond its natural pecuniary speed for Mir Jafar's formal confirmation as nawab by the Mughal court. On 23 December 1757, Clive would in exasperation write in a letter to the Court in London, as we learn from Long's records: 'The Nawab's confirmation is not yet procured at Delhi, nor can I tell when it will, the difficulty is in the price.'

◆

Extract from a letter from Colonel Clive to Admiral Watson, dated 30 June 1757.

Surajah Dowlet was taken by one of the Nabob's jemidars and suffered to escape for a bribe of 30,000 gold mohurs. As all his treasures have been taken from him I don't think he can do much harm. Ram Narain, the Nabob of Patna, is confirmed and will scarcely risque his place for a man who has not wherewith to bribe him.

◆

Letter from Colonel Clive to Select Committee, Fort William, dated Muxadabad, late at night, 30 June 1757.

Gentlemen,—I wrote you a letter this evening since which I have received a note from the Nabob informing me that Surajah Dowlat is taken and that he has dispatched his son to secure him. I congratulate you on this happy news.

20

A PROBLEM THAT NOBODY WANTS

'Enough,—that is enough—I am done for...'

Mir Qasim and Mir Daud, the son-in-law and brother of the new nawab, took Siraj into custody in Rajmahal. Miran was on his way. In a letter to the Select Committee at Fort St George, Clive would gloat that Siraj was 'in a distressed condition with hardly cloaths to his back, such is the misery he has been reduced to by his injuries to the English and by a general course of folly and wickedness throughout the short time he has reigned'.

Although many would—and have—contested Clive's justification, from most accounts Siraj's past had caught up with him yet again in the strangest possible manner. Orme writes that Siraj's boatmen were exhausted by their run up the Ganga. They stopped on the evening of 29 June to spend the night in the vicinity of Rajmahal, which some Company correspondence and records refer to as Rajahmaul—also known as Akbarnagar for some time. Siraj and Lutf-un-Nisa took shelter in a deserted garden.

The *Siyar* presents a more dramatic, and different, sequence of events for 'this unfortunate Prince, already overtaken by the claws of destiny'. The plan upon arriving on the shore facing Rajmahal was for a quick stop, just long enough to cook and eat some khichri, as his party—wife, daughter, and other 'women'—hadn't eaten for three days.

The *Siyar* says that a fakir, Shah Dana—most accounts refer to him as Dana Shah—lived in the neighbourhood (*Riyazu-s-Salatin* largely follows the *Siyar*'s version, and refers to the fakir as Dan Shah Pirzada). 'This man, whom probably he had either disobliged or oppressed in the days of his full power, rejoiced at this fair opportunity of glutting his resentment, and of enjoying a revenge.' Orme writes it was because Siraj had ordered the fakir's ears to be cut off at the time of his campaign against his cousin Shaukat Jang about thirteen months earlier that he was betrayed. Orme doesn't offer a reason for Siraj's order to punish the fakir. Hill quotes from *History of the Rise and Progress of the Bengal Army* by Captain Arthur Broome, to mention Siraj also had the fakir's nose cut off—'...a fakier, named Dana Shah, whose nose and ears he had ordered to be cut off thirteen months before, when on his march against the Nawaub of Purneah.'

The fakir now welcomed Siraj, helped prepare food and, meanwhile, surreptitiously sent word by boat to Mir Daud and his search party in the bastion of Rajmahal that the fugitive former nawab was with him.

(As we have seen, the *Siyar* is sometimes drier without the footnotes of its translator, Haji Mustapha. The Frenchman doesn't disappoint with his input about the capture, throwing in a clue that gave Siraj away to the fakir, and even offers an orientalist comment on khichri, the dish the fakir prepared for Siraj and his party, as literally an arresting digression: 'Kichri is a mess of pulse and rice boiled together, but so, however, as that all the grains should remain asunder. It is the usual food of the poorest people in rice-countries, although there is a way of rendering it acceptable to great folks, by frying it in butter first, and then boiling the same with spices, &c.')

According to the *Siyar*, the Fakir at first did not recognize the prince taking him to be one of those many travellers that daily pass that way; 'but on casting his eyes on the very rich slippers of his guest'—this detail is repeated by numerous later-day historians and chroniclers—'he put questions to the boat-men, who soon gave him full information'.

Orme mentions that the fakir identified Siraj at the 'break of day'—which would suggest it was the morning of 30 June—before sending word to Mir Daud, who in turn told the troops sent from Murshidabad by his brother Mir Jafar. The news was carried by riders to Murshidabad.

Both Orme and the *Siyar* agree that Mir Daud and his guards arrived swiftly to arrest Siraj. *Riyazu-s-Salatin*'s version is that Daud's 'spies' arrived to bring Siraj to 'Akbarnagar' from where Daud's guards and Mir Qasim ecorted Siraj to Murshidabad.

The lost nawab pleaded for mercy, but that 'only served to render him an object of taunt and reproach to a set of men, to whom, but a few days before, he might have disdained to speak,' the *Siyar* observes, 'every one of them he intreated to obtain a pension for him, and a corner of ground, where he might live forgotten; but no one heard him'.

Siraj's party didn't fare any better, according to this telling—and it is one not mentioned by others, whether for lack of information, or accuracy, or embarrassment, isn't clear. Mir Qasim, like his peers no slouch when it came to appropriation, pressured Lutf-un-Nisa— 'partly by threats, and partly by promises'—to disclose the location of her 'casket of jewels...the value of which could not be computed but by lacs', and took it. Mir Daud took the cue and similarly assaulted the 'other ladies', and took what he could. This triggered a general loot of Siraj's remaining possessions.

'Every one was only intent on the opportunity now before him.' The *Siyar* even offers a moralistic verse, translated with the touch of France that Haji Mustapha's adoptive land clearly hadn't erased:

> Be this my advice to thee, if thou wilt but hear me;
> If thou hast planted thorns, thou canst not expect to reap jonquils.

Orme is less fussy, never a sentimental word about reaping daffodils or any other flora:

> They hurried him back to Muxadavad with the eager diligence of men who knew the value of their prize; and to recommend themselves still more to their employers, treated him with every kind of insolence and indignity compatible with the preservation of his life.

◆

Even the capture of Siraj was touch and go. Just a few hours may have meant the difference between capture and escape. As Clive would write to the Court in London on 26 July 1757:

> Monsr. Law and his party came down as far as Rajmahaul to Suraja Dowla's assistance, and were within three hours march of him when he was taken; as soon as they heard of his misfortune, they returned by forced marches and passed Patna.

◆

And there lies a story, we learn from Hill's *Three Frenchmen in Bengal*. As Law discovered later, after Plassey was done but not quite dusted, 'The Faujdar of Rajmehal used to stop all his [Siraj's] messengers and detain them as long as he thought fit.' This was unsurprising: as we have seen, the commander of Rajmahal who would play a role in Siraj's capture was Mir Jafar's brother Mir Daud. A letter from Siraj requesting Law to return to Murshidabad was sent on 13 June, but didn't reach Law until the 22nd, just a day before Plassey.

The letters of Law to Siraj evidently never reached Siraj. The Frenchman started out for Murshidabad 'at the first rumour of danger', as Hill conveys Law's words, but by the time he reached Rajmahal on 1 July, Siraj had already been taken prisoner and was well on his way to Murshidabad. 'All was over,' as the *Siyar* puts it.

Law wondered later, injecting his observation with a leavening of realpolitik, whether saving a Siraj on the run would have at all been worthwhile. 'In saving Siraj-ud-daula we should have scored a great success, but possibly he would have been saved for a short time only,' Law observed.

> He would have found enemies and traitors wherever he might have presented himself in the countries supposed to be subject to him. No one would have acknowledged him. Forced by Mir Jafar and the English to flee to a foreign country, he would have been a burden to us rather than an assistance.

He concluded his observation with a damning statement about politics in the subcontinent though it could easily be applied anywhere in the world: 'In India no one knows what it is to stand by an unfortunate man.' Siraj would have likely been looted of whatever remained with him, the same fate as would in a few short years befall a future nawab of Bengal, Mir Qasim, during his flight westward to Awadh, and on to Delhi.

Besides, Law maintains, Siraj's character may have again rendered him utterly without a 'real' friend.

Law's own journeys would be that of a fugitive. He was on the run from the new nawab, Mir Jafar, whom Law describes as 'a very intelligent man', an impression gained from their interaction in Murshidabad when Law was desperately scouring for support to allay the siege of Chandannagar—a time, in March 1757, when to Law, Mir Jafar appeared to be a man who hadn't fully absorbed the plan to see himself as Siraj's successor ('He had not then taken up the idea of making himself Nawab')—or perhaps it was just that Mir Jafar masked his emotions well, as the Plassey conspiracy was at the time well underway.

Law was by then also on the run from the British. Clive had sent Major Coote with a detachment to capture Law and his group. Orme refers to Clive's correspondence to offer a letter written by Clive on 9 July in Murshidabad, urging Law to surrender as the Frenchman headed towards Patna from Rajmahal. Clive's tone is of a man in full command, having just crowned a new nawab in epic fashion:

> As the country people are now all become your enemies, and orders are gone everywhere to intercept your passage, and I myself have sent parties in quest of you, and orders are gone to Ramnarain, the Naib of Patna, to seize you if you pursue that road, you must be sensible if you fall into their hands you cannot expect to find them a generous enemy. If, therefore, you have any regard for the men under your command, I would recommend you to treat with us, from whom you may expect the most favourable terms in my power to grant.

As it turned out, Ram Narain aided Law. The Frenchman and most of his band finally made it to the territory of Awadh by early September, thinking himself safe in the territory of the nawab Shuja-ud-Daulah, a friend of Siraj who didn't want to tangle with the British when Siraj was alive but whom Law, a die-hard adventurer, hoped to encourage to invade a post-Siraj Bengal. Law would spend the next four years in northern India, keeping up his entreaties with everyone from the Mughal crown prince, Ali Gauhar (later the emperor, Shah Alam II), and the dominant Marathas, to local chieftains in the Bundelkhand region. An expedition sponsored by the prince was defeated by Bengal's forces and that of the British in early 1759. Law would in 1761 surrender to British troops in Siwan in Bihar after fierce battle. By his own words Law was treated, then and later, with honour and dignity by his arch foes, the British.

For its part, the *Siyar* describes Law's surrender to a 'Major Carnac' in typically florid fashion. It quotes the major's purported request to Law:

> You have done everything that could be expected from a brave man; and your name shall be undoubtedly transmitted to posterity by the pen of history; now loosen your sword from your loins, come amongst us, and abandon all thoughts of contending with the English.

Law would be honoured by France upon reaching home in 1762, made Chevalier of the Royal and Military Order of St. Louis, a colonel of infantry, commandant of the French Nation in the East Indies. But Clive's implacable dominance, and great confusion over events in Bengal leading up to Plassey, were of little comfort to Law during his four years on the run, which included desperate machinations against the British in the imperial capital Delhi. Indeed, in Delhi there appeared to be lack of understanding of the full measure of what Clive & Co. had wrought, and their place alongside other key Plassey conspirators. Law himself evocatively sums up the mood of the time, a confounding mix, a complete khichri (or kedgeree, a soon-to-be Anglo-Indian favourite), of perception and reality that continue to engage historians to this day:

> I felt sure that, after the revolution in Bengal, they would be the only subject of conversation in the capital. The Revolution had made much noise, but it was ascribed entirely to the Seths and to Rai Durlabh Ram. Clive's name was well known. He was, they said, a great captain whom the Seths had brought from very far at a great expense, to deliver Bengal from the tyranny of Siraj-ud-daula, as Salabat Jang had engaged M. Bussy to keep the Marathas in order. Many of the principal persons even asked me what country he came from. Others, mixing up all Europeans together, thought that I was a deputy from Clive. It was useless for me to say we were enemies, that it was the English who had done everything in Bengal, that it was they who governed and not Jafar Ali Khan, who was only Nawab in name. No one would believe me. In fact, how could one persuade people who had never seen a race of men different from their own, that a

body of two or three thousand Europeans at the most was able to dictate the law in a country as large as Bengal?

◆

To return to Siraj, the deposed nawab was brought back to Murshidabad on 2 July.

There was some discussion about keeping him imprisoned, even exiling him, but in the end, a live Siraj presented a festering sore, a dead Siraj cauterized that sore. It was strictly business.

A day earlier, the Company party had already begun the process of emptying the treasury along the lines brokered by the Jagat Seth. Clive fully expected to despatch by 4 July 'under a proper guard' the first tranche of the funds, 7.5 million rupees, to be distributed, as we have read, in pre-determined proportion, to the Company, the navy, the army, 'private Europeans', and 'blacks'. There would be numerous boats, as Clive expected each boat to carry 100,000 rupees worth of coin in a large chest, 'nailed down and sealed'. He had sent on a request to Admiral Watson to send some 'boats' up the Hugli to Nadia to 'escort the treasure' downstream to Calcutta, as Clive would be unable to spare his entire force. Murshidabad and its new nawab—and the Company's interests—remained to be secured. Orme too writes of this treasure run, with more specific detail than Clive had, including more treasure chests, seven, to every boat: 'At length, after a variety of discussions and equivocations, the committee by the 6th of July received, in coined silver, 7,271,666 rupees. This treasure was packed up in 700 chests, and laden in 100 boats...'

These made a grand spectacle on their journey south to Calcutta. Scrafton takes us to that time in his *Reflections*:

> As soon as they entered the great river [the Hugli] they were joined by the boats of the squadron, and all together formed a fleet of three hundred boats, with music playing, drums beating, and colours flying, and exhibited to the French and Dutch, by whose settlements they passed, a scene far different from what they had beheld the year before, when the Nabob's fleet and army passed them, with the captive English, and all the wealth and plunder of Calcutta.

On the day Siraj was brought back to Murshidabad, Clive had already written to his colleagues in Fort William and the two admirals that Siraj was expected to reach the city that very evening, and he expected the deposed nawab to be treated by Mir Jafar with every courtesy the situation permitted. '...the Nabob who is a humane, generous and honest Prince,' Clive wrote, 'intends only to confine him and to allow him all the indulgence which a prison can admit of.'

But there is another letter he wrote, dated 2 July, to the Select Committee at Fort St George in Madras. The letter appears to have been completed only late at night, perhaps even the early morning of the 3rd. The postscript suggested a far more rapid action against Siraj:

> P.S.—Surajah Dowla arrived in the city the 2nd at night and was immediately dispatched having created some commotions in the army by the letters he wrote on the road to the several jemidars.

He then drove the event home in another letter dated 4 July to his colleagues in Calcutta:

> Gentlemen,—Surajah Dowlat is no more. The Nabob would have spared him, but his son Miran and the great men thought his death necessary for the peace of the country, as on his approach to the city, the jemidars grew mutinous. He was publickly buried at Cooshe Baug [Khosh Bagh, the garden of joy] yesterday morning.

According to Clive's unsentimental and business-like accounts, Siraj was killed on the night of 2 July and buried at Khosh Bagh the following day to prevent restlessness, even mutiny, among his former troops. There are versions as to what exactly transpired in the interim, and, as ever, Orme and the *Siyar* provide a mix of detail and drama that later chroniclers have drawn on for every manner of interpretation.

Orme echoes Clive about the timing of the killing of Siraj, writing that the former nawab was brought on 2 July, 'about midnight, as a common felon, into the presence of Meer Jaffier, in the very palace which a few days before had been the seat of his own residence and despotic authority'. Mir Jafar is portrayed as a compassionate man now that the business of conspiracy was done: 'It is said that Jaffier seemed to be moved with compassion; and well he might, for he owed all his former fortunes to the generosity and favour of Allaverdy, who died in firm reliance, that Jaffier would repay his bounties by attachment and fidelity to this his darling adoption'— here Orme makes a remarkable assertion—'who, himself, to Jaffier at least, was no criminal'. Siraj then prostrated himself in front of Mir Jafar and with 'excessive tremor and tears' implored for his life to be spared. He was then escorted by soldiers to a 'distant chamber, one of the vilest of the palace', while Mir Jafar consulted courtiers and officials who were present at the time, either to pay their respects or transact business, to decide on what ought to be done about Siraj.

There were three options: imprisonment in Murshidabad, exile or imprisonment in exile, and death.

A group swayed by the fâit accompli of Plassey put aside their earlier disposition of fear or dislike towards Siraj. Some were drawn to his grandfather Alivardi's memory, and others sought to prevent Mir Jafar's reign beginning with 'despotic acts of bloodshed'. This group suggested that Siraj be permitted to live. They 'wished to preserve Surajah Dowlah,' Orme recalls, 'either as a rebuke to themselves, or as a restraint upon Jaffier; all these proposed a strict, but mild imprisonment.'

Mir Jafar's son, Miran, 'a youth not seventeen, fierce, barbarous, and in his nature cruel as Surajah Dowlah himself', strongly opposed this.

(The *Siyar* is far more brutal about Miran's character, making him out to be a regular Caligula. 'This son of [Mir Jafar's] was not only equal to his father, but he went beyond him by some degrees in every thing, whether we consider his manners and dress, or his riveted inclination to oppress and torment; he was also still more expeditious and quick-minded in character of slaughtering people, and in committing murders, having a peculiar knack at such matters, and looking upon every infamous or atrocious deed as an act of prudence and foresight.' Basically, that there wasn't a compassionate bone in this effeminate boy-man's body.)

Miran wished instant death for Siraj citing reasons Clive noted in his letters. So did a group of courtiers. They were driven, Orme writes, by the 'risques of revolt and revolution' that Mir Jafar's administration would remain exposed to as long as Siraj lived. He would need to be quickly killed, rid of as a problem nobody wanted.

Mir Jafar didn't offer an opinion.

Miran took that as a cue, and advised his father to rest while he took care of the prisoner. 'Jaffier, pretending to understand these words as if they meant no violence,' concluded the late-night mini-durbar, and retired to his 'apartments'. (This suggests Siraj was incarcerated in Heerajheel Palace. Some versions mention Siraj was imprisoned in Mir Jafar's own palace in Jafarganj—sometimes colloquially called Jafraganj. The *Siyar* insists the new nawab, after moving into Siraj's old home, had given over his old home to Miran, a favourite son born to him from Shah Khanum, half-sister to Alivardi.)

Soon after, Miran instructed a confidante, Muhammadi Beg, also known as Lal Muhammad, with the 'fatal mandate which they received with the ruthless alacrity of ruffians who murder for reward'—presumably, a species unlike those who go to war for reward. Anyhow, when Miran arrived at Siraj's cell with his associates, Siraj, realizing what was about to happen, lost composure, and the 'instant terrors of death threw him into a strong agony of bitter lamentation'. Siraj recovered shortly to request that he be permitted to offer prayers, after washing his hands and feet in the Mussalman fashion.

It quickly turned brutal. The executioners impatient to perform their work, hastily threw a pot of water that was nearby on Siraj's head. The *Siyar* offers a variation: 'The Prince having so far recollected himself as to wish to purify himself according to law (for such a purification, and also another, together with two short prayers are of obligation on any man going to the charge, or to death) was refused; upon which he asked some water to quench a violent thirst; and this also having been refused, he submitted to his fate.'

The servant then struck with his 'poignard', Orme writes, and after the dagger had done its work, the others finished the 'massacre' with swords.

◆

Even more than Orme's evocative recounting, the *Siyar* offers drama worthy of theatre that survives today as folk history, and eschews timing—such as describing Siraj's arrival to Murshidabad as a captive at night, as day—for mood. The *Siyar* milks pathos for Siraj, a man it repeatedly diminished and damned earlier in its narrative, now even bizarrely offering comment on Siraj's handsomeness, and turns the lens of disgust on Miran:

> Such was the man, who first heard of Seradj-ed-doulah's arrival; for his father was then fast asleep at noon-day.

Mir Jafar wasn't just taking a nap, he was sleeping off a dose of bhang which had steadily increased in intensity since he became nawab a few days earlier.

> The dose now being taken on the chair of command, and on the Mesned of dominion, had operated in a twofold manner: he lay dead to every thing; nor was any man daring enough to awake him.

But there was no need to interrupt his sleep. Miran had taken charge, moving swiftly to have Siraj—'that unfortunate prince'—killed.

> He immediately ordered him into confinement, near his own apartment, and proposed to a large company of his friends, then present, to go directly, and dispatch that Unfortunate. This was peremptorily refused by them all, to a man, not one of them choosing to sully his hands with so ugly an action; and some even complained of the proposal. At last, one Mahmedy-beg [Muhammadi Beg] accepted the commission, which so many had rejected with indignation. This man, who had been bred in the house of Seradj-ed-doulah's father, and in that of Aaly-verdy-qhan's consort; who had made his fortune by marrying an orphan virgin, in whose education that unfortunate grandmother had taken pleasure; this was the man who undertook the murder; this was the man who accepted the horrid commission; and two or three hours after the fugitive's arrival, he set out to dispatch him. Seradj-ed-doulah had no sooner cast his eyes upon that miscreant, than he asked, whether he was not come to kill him? And the other having answered in the affirmative, the unfortunate Prince, on this confession, despaired of his life. He

humbled himself before the Author of all mercies, asked pardon for his past conduct, and then turning to his murderer, 'They are not then (broke he with a passionate tone of voice), they are not satisfied with my being ready to retire into some corner there to end my days upon a pension; (here he paused awhile, and, as if recollecting something, he added)—No—they are not,—and I must die—to atone for Hoeséin-culi-qhan's murder.' He had no time to say more; for at these words the butcher smote him repeatedly with his sabre; and some strokes falling upon that beauteous face of his, so renowned all over Bengal for its regularity and sweetness, the Prince sunk on the ground, but with these words in his mouth: 'Enough,—that is enough—I am done for—and Hosséin-culi-qhan's death is revenged.' On uttering these words, he fell on his face, returned his soul to its Maker, and emerged out of this valley of miseries, by wading through his own blood. His body was hacked to pieces, by strokes without number...

When Mir Jafar finally woke up and was apprised of matters, he quickly sent a message to Miran recommending 'vigilance and watchfulness over the deposed Prince'. Miran merely laughed as he received the message. He even taunted his father in front of his familiars and bystanders as a person already out of touch with reality.

Pray Gentlemen, (added he) is not my father a curious man with his message? And indeed as a son to Aaly-verdy-qhan's sister, how could I prove dilatory in so important a matter?

◆

The following morning, Siraj's mangled corpse was placed on the back of an elephant and carried through the thoroughfares and busy lanes of Murshidabad. It was the ultimate show of his defeat.

The drama didn't end there, we learn from the *Siyar* in a melodramatic aside that British chroniclers ignore as apocryphal, and several informal historians and pamphleteers among South Asian chroniclers highlight as the closing of a tragic but karmic loop. At one point on the macabre journey the mahout, for reasons of his own, brought the elephant to a stop right at the door of Hussain Quli Khan, the nobleman Siraj had killed a couple of years earlier. Here, 'some drops of blood were seen to drop from the mangled body, and they fell on the very spot where that nobleman had been murdered...' The *Siyar* then offers a lament in the robes of a moral lesson:

> See, and take warning, ye that have eyes,
> It was in this manner the wind shifted, and the face of things changed...
> You shall carry no more with you, than what you have enjoyed, or bestowed.—
> Do good to-day, since the field is yours, and you have the power of it
> Make haste; for the next year, the field will pass to another tenant.

Siraj's death and departure continued to receive dramatic denouement with myth and hearsay presented as judicious fact, even by great personalities of the Company-sponsored New Bengal such as the rationalist and emancipator Ishwar Chandra Vidyasagar, whose criticism of Siraj we have read earlier in this book. Ishwar Chandra, too, repeated the moment of the mahout's halting the elephant and Siraj's blood spilling from his corpse, whereupon 'everybody noticed' that it was the exact spot where eighteen months earlier Siraj had taken the life of Hussain Quli and where his 'innocent blood' was spilled.

As much as when he was alive, in defeat and death too Siraj made a great story.

◆

The single-elephant power-cortège then reached the house of his mother, Amina Begum. Here the *Siyar* makes a somewhat bizarre assertion that, as she was a 'Princess accustomed to live immured, knew nothing of the revolution.' It's difficult to believe as the conspiracy had been stewing for several months, and was nearly an open secret at the top echelons of Murshidabad society of which Amina Begum had been an active part for several decades. At best, it's likely she was unaware of the exact circumstance of her son's brief incarceration and death. But the *Siyar* is nothing if not an emotional script of impressive scale, in this case the conveyor of a mother's love, a mother who 'lost her mind' at the sight of her son's body:

> She only inquired what was the cause of the confused noise and cries she heard today without her walls. On being informed of the matter, the unfortunate Princess, unable to contain herself, forgot at once her sex, veil and slippers, and running out of the house, like one distracted, she threw herself on the body, which she covered with her kisses, and sat disconsolate, striking repeatedly her face and breasts. This spectacle greatly affected the bystanders.

At this point, a treacherous noble saw the effect the spectacle had on bystanders, and sent servants to forcibly remove Amina Begum and other ladies of the household and neighbourhood from their source of lament.

Then it was time to inter Siraj near the grave of his grandfather.

21

APRÈS-PLASSEY

'...the importance of your possessions now in Bengal...'

Kolkata, perhaps more than any other place besides Murshidabad, and certainly, Plassey, offers Plassey markers. Take this modest-sized patch in the central business district.

The vast General Post Office complex, the entrance to which is through a gate on the southern side, opens up into a series of adjacent buildings around a courtyard that doubles as a parking lot. Two of the buildings are linked by a walkway. Entry is restricted but a polite request is usually all it takes. As you walk towards the Mail Department, a building to the left carries a modest description of the past: 'The brass lines laid in the floor of this building mark the outlines of that portion of the arcade of Old Fort William which was dismantled in 1920.' The third edition of the Old Fort William, as it were, the second edition being damaged during Siraj's overpowering attack in 1756. A building to the right contains 'brass lines' set in stone on the ground floor, which mark, as another sign describes, the 'position and extent of the South Curtain [the defensive wall] of the old fort'.

The Black Hole of Calcutta to the north is now absent. There's a row of grimy toilets and a community kitchen near where it used to be.

On the way to St John's Church, where the replica of Holwell's memorial to victims of the Black Hole now rests, are living testimonies to empire, and enduring ironies. The main local office of Hongkong & Shanghai Banking Corp., is located at 31 B. B. D. Bag, the first-name initials of three Bengali revolutionaries, Benoy Bose, Badal Gupta, and Dinesh Gupta, young men who perished as a consequence of their assassination in 1930 of a senior colonial inspector-general of prisons in Calcutta with a reputation of brutality towards political prisoners. But Hongkong House, a couple of minutes' brisk walk from the vicinity of the Black Hole, also proclaims the colonial place name on a polished brass plaque: Dalhousie Square, after James Broun-Ramsay, a governor-general of the Company's possessions in India.

Across the road is 1, Council House Street, which takes its name from the Company's administrative nerve centre here in the late eighteenth century. It's a vast, cavernous three-storey building from 1911 that houses several offices of the Government of India, from the director general of commercial audit and the coal controller to the central statistical office and the department of official languages. Above the arch at the entrance is a claim on behalf of King George V, 'Emperor of India':

GEORGIVS REX
IMPERATOR
MCMXI

In a remarkable and perhaps deliberate irony, just a block away, Waterloo Street in the area known as Bow Barracks is today the grimy, crowded, unheralded, and renamed Nawab Siraj-ud-Daula Sarani.

Both George and Siraj can thank Clive & Co. for their lot.

◆

It isn't difficult to understand the general adulation of eighteenth- and nineteenth-century Britons for Clive, let alone some twentieth and twenty-first century ones. He created for himself, the Company, and Britain vast wealth amidst chaos.

Here was a man with a sharp eye to the future, whatever John Company hagiographists may claim about a motley group of London-based merchants not having any desire for control, let alone empire, in a corner of Asia. But Clive did, even if in the beginning it was just a portion of Bengal to the east and south of Calcutta. Bengal's nawab was now the Company's plaything, and Clive a puppetmaster who saw beyond the crossroads. As early as 26 July 1757, Clive would write to the Court in London:

> I persuade myself the importance of your possessions now in Bengal will determine you to send out, not only a large and early supply of Troops and good Officers, but of capable young gentlemen for the Civil branches of your business.

Much of post-Plassey deals came through for the Company, including the vast tracts of land. In the same letter, Clive would advise London about the value of lands to the east and south of Calcutta in terms of revenue:

> It is impossible as yet to form a judgment how much the granted lands will produce [for] you, as the Europeans are quite ignorant of the extent of the country between the river and lake; but in order to give you some idea of the value, I will venture to estimate it at ten lacs per annum. An Officer on the part of the Nabob is already despatched to Calcutta to begin the survey in company with one of ours.

Reverend Long adds that the Company moved immediately to ensure revenue arrived from these lands, to offset any delay in receiving 'ready money from the Durbar'. The Company insisted on, and received, permission from Mir Jafar to write to the zamindars of thirty-eight villages near Calcutta, 'demanding of them the terms they wanted for ceding the zemindary and possession of the 38 villages mentioned in the Government Phirmaund'. The survey, particularly of the 'Salt Water or Great Lake', large parts of it built over and under great ecological threat in the present day, was part of this process.

William Watts, who opted to continue as chief at Qasimbazar, and Clive, who stayed on in Murshidabad for some time to run affairs of state and Company at court, ensured the momentum was maintained—the historian T. G. Percival Spear succinctly describes Mir Jafar's first tenure as nawab, as 'Clive's first government'.

There was a strategic aspect, too, to secure Calcutta and its environs for the Company. As a Council meeting on 1 August 1757 in Calcutta noted:

> That other boats might be sent into Culpee River, and if the design is executed by experienced men, an exact and useful survey may be made which will enable us to settle beneficial boundaries; for if the lake, as is conjectured, has its rise adjacent to Culpee, our territory will then be nearly surrounded by water, and by a communication from Bagh Bazar to Kissnapore on the borders of the Lake, Calcutta may be effectually secured from any country enemy.

A plan of the area would also be sent to the Court in London. (Reclamation of the Salt Lakes would begin several decades later, and a company formed for the purpose.)

The matter was perceived as being of such urgency that the Company requested help from Admiral Watson and the Crown fleet under his command—yet another example of government and business working as an extension of the other. The admiral would reply to the Select Committee on 3 August 1757, one of his last acts of correspondence before his death from a fever thirteen days later in Calcutta, where he was buried (his tomb is at St John's Church):

> ...It appears to me to be a work requiring so much care and exactness, that I know of none in the squadron capable of it, and if there were I am very certain such a performance would require much more time than I shall continue here. But if upon an enquiry in the squadron you find any one who will answer your purpose and is willing to remain in India, I will give orders for his being discharged.

At this time Clive of India, the man who could make an opportunity out of adversity, could do little wrong, the exact opposite of Siraj, the callow nawab who would turn victory into headlong defeat, and for so many could do little that was right.

As if to underscore that axiom, a karmic sanad, as it were, would arrive in January 1758, erasing another vestige of Siraj. On the 10th of that month Company officials in Calcutta would write to London: 'We have the pleasure to inform your Honors that the word "Alinagore" is, by our present sunnud, to be omitted in the impression on our siccas, an indulgence we could not obtain from Suraja Dowla.'

◆

For all the flurry of activity in Bengal, acknowledgement from London of the importance of Clive's victory would take a while—not merely on account of the time taken to complete the circle of communication, but evidently a lack of full understanding of local dynamics, and Plassey's true import for the Company.

For instance, there's a fascinating story around the creation of the 'Company' town of Berhampore that illustrates how the Court of Directors appeared to not have realized just how much more of a military and political venture their business venture in Bengal had become. In Long's *Selections from Unpublished Records* we read that in October 1757, Capt. J. Brohier, a Company employee, wrote to Drake and the Council at Fort William that the Qasimbazar factory was inoperable on account of the 'principal part of the Factory house at that place having been burnt down by the Moors', and that it would be more practical and more financially reasonable to build a new military facility in 'Berhampore plain at the south end of Cossimbazar' than expand the facility in Qasimbazar. Although that enclave regained its commercial importance—including a restored factory—its political clout 'was transferred to the Agent at the Court of the Nawab, who lived in Motijhil', O'Malley writes; and so, the plan emerged to create a well-fortified cantonment about 3 kilometres further south.

Brohier suggested that in Berhampore a 'pentagone may be erected, and by removing a few huts and levelling some hedges have an esplanade of seven hundred yards around it'.

In January 1758, Drake and his colleagues in Calcutta passed the suggestion on to directors in London with a superscription that such a place made eminent sense to keep watch over and influence the post-Siraj court at Murshidabad. Besides, Mir Jafar had already granted 400 bighas (about 130 acres) for the project.

With the typical time lag of more than a year for a round trip for communication, the directors replied in March 1759 (in July the same year the Company's resident in Murshidabad, Warren Hastings would inter his first wife, Mary, and their infant daughter, Elizabeth, at the old Residency Cemetery at Qasimbazar):

> We cannot avoid remarking that you seem so thoroughly possessed with military ideas as to forget your employers are merchants, and trade their principal object; and were we to adopt your several plans for fortifying, half our capital would be buried in stone walls.

This time around the Council of Calcutta was hesitant unlike the pre-Plassey instance of being swayed by Clive to attack up the

Hugli and take the battle to Siraj in Plassey, instead of waiting for London's affirmation to decide strategy and tactics after learning of the declaration of the Seven Years War in Europe. But that its representation in Bengal had a keener sense of things—including their conflation of battle with business—was only realized by Company brass in London after Mir Qasim, who would for a short while become nawab after Mir Jafar, attempted to shake off Company control in 1763 and place its entire Bengal project in jeopardy. Berhampore, the present-day district headquarters of Murshidabad, got its factory and fort.

Long writes that there was also some justifiable nervousness about the new fort in Calcutta:

> Its building was watched with intense interest by the authorities, as Calcutta was utterly defenceless until it was ready... It is very singular that the French never sent an expedition against Bengal, had they done so between 1758 and 1767, nothing could have saved Calcutta... [And, perhaps, this work might well have been written in French instead of English.]

Long's concern about the vulnerability of Calcutta wasn't only on account of the French. There was also the matter of vulnerability on account of the new Fort William being held back by Captain Brohier, the officer-engineer behind the Berhampore Fort. Brohier added to the 'extraordinary delay arising from the consummate villainy and fraud connected with carrying on the works', which is supposed to have 'nearly' driven 'Clive to despair'. As it happened, Brohier escaped to Ceylon, having embezzled the Company's money. 'The Company,' writes Long, 'were cheated in bricks, in wood, in coolies, in every possible way.'

Even with this temporary vulnerability of the British, perhaps the French didn't have the necessary momentum to deal with Bengal in the wake of Plassey, which was further blunted by the conclusion of the Seven Years War in 1763. They preferred instead to focus on protecting what they could in southern India—a project that didn't go so well either, with loss of influence in the Carnatic and Northern Circars, and with Pondicherry overrun by the British.

The English Company pushed limits where it could, both from

a position of relative weakness to, certainly, a position of relative strength—as was evident in their post-Plassey attitude towards the French in Bengal (even with the détente with the French in Europe). The historian Sailendra Nath Sen refers to an interesting development in his book *Chandernagore: From Bondage to Freedom 1900-1955*. While the British used their concern over possible war with France— the Seven Years War, as it turned out—to upgrade their fortifications in Bengal and, thereby, add to Siraj's ire against them, they had no hesitation demanding from the French compliance identical to that Siraj had asked of all Europeans.

The British captured Chandannagar in March 1757. The Treaty of Paris, signed between the two powers in 1763, which formally ended the Seven Years War, restored French possessions in India but they were 'restored without any fortifications'. These included Pondicherry, which would fall to the British in January 1761. There would be another war, another treaty, this time in Versailles, in 1783; and another restoration of French possessions with caveats. Sen quotes the arrangement: the French agreed 'not to erect fortifications, or to keep troops, in any part of the Subah of Bengal'.

It didn't end there. Jean-Baptiste Chevalier, a post-Plassey French governor of Chandannagar, 'who had caused a deep ditch to be dug around Chandernagore, was forced to have it filled up by an English engineer aided by 800 sepoys,' writes Sen. The prosperity of the town had meanwhile suffered 'immeasurably' with Fort d'Orleans 'in ruins, and the population dwindling from 60,000 in 1757 to 24,000 in 1765'.

And yet the French in their India venture persisted like the merchants and governments of every other European nation, and took what was given. The French traded in Bengal principally for silk, cotton goods, opium, and saltpetre—'sinews of the commercial operation of the French company'. Even in their reduced circumstances, business in Bengal was good. The raison d'être for the gold rush in Bengal, which led to Plassey in the first place, was articulated by Law in his memoirs: 'Everybody knows that Bengal is the principal place for the commerce of the company; it is even the only place which can procure sufficient profit to cover our expenses in India.'

If even the French were willing to persist in India from their few remaining toeholds, it isn't difficult to see why for John Company the emerging business horizon in the subcontinent would appear to be limitless. Certainly, Clive saw that horizon.

◆

There would be several steps yet to be taken before the British became the supreme power in the region, but it nevertheless arrived with great speed. The Company would gain near-complete dominance over the subcontinent within a hundred years of Plassey. The first significant steps to dominance would arrive less than a decade after Plassey, nearly all in Bengal, and marked by tumult.

We've read earlier as to how Mir Jafar, pushed to deliver dues and reparations to the Company, conspired with the Dutch to shake off the British, only to have the Dutch comprehensively lose the Battle of Chinsurah in November 1759. For all purposes that set in motion wheels to replace Mir Jafar with a Company cipher. For some time that replacement appeared to be Miran, Mir Jafar's eldest son—and his weakness. The prospect wasn't pleasing to the Company. Henry Beveridge provides an account of it in his essay, 'Warren Hastings in Lower Bengal', in which he sources Clive's biographer, John Malcolm, to offer some correspondence as evidence.

On 17 August that year, Hastings wrote to Clive to remain in Bengal, as matters weren't quite settled; Clive was already considering a return to Britain, citing exhaustion. On 21 September, a time when Mir Jafar's dalliance with the Dutch had become clear, Clive wrote trenchantly about Mir Jafar, Miran, and a shark or two already testing the waters at court:

> Mir Jafar's days of folly are without number and he had long before this slept with his fathers if the dread of our power and resentment had not been his only security. Sooner or later, I am persuaded, the worthless young dog will attempt his father's overthrow. How often have I advised the old fool from putting too much power in the hands of his nearest relative. Tell him from me Raja Ballabh is an aspiring ambitious villain; and if he does not get him removed from his son's presence, he will push him into some unnatural and violent resolution.

Clive 'considered it safe', writes Hill, to visit Britain in early 1760. He left Calcutta on 8 February. Clive evidently felt that whatever the churn in Bengal and its vicinity, it was within the Company's ability to handle it. This included such intrigue that brought the forces of the Mughal prince, Ali Gauhar, and his allies, including the indefatigable Frenchman Law, to challenge Bengal and Company forces. The challengers remained checked though not yet completely defeated in Bihar as Clive departed.

Miran was removed from Bengal's chessboard by a freak accident at that very battlefield. There would be much tumult after Clive left, of course. Miran, said to be a great lover of parrots—arguably the only civilizing aspect of that bloodthirsty boy-man—and considered by many as a shoo-in for the Company's second pliant nawab of Bengal, died while on campaign in Bihar, early in the morning of 3 July 1760. The journal of Archibald Swinton, an army officer who had campaigned with Clive at the beginning of the year, noted: 'This day was rendered remarkable by the death of the young Nabob, who was struck dead by lightning as he lay in his tent, between twelve and one in the morning.'

An explanatory note observes: 'All his attendants in the tent were also killed, and his followers much discouraged by this bad omen.'

The incident devastated Mir Jafar, and cleared the path for Mir Qasim to be appointed nawab later in the year.

It was a somewhat tortuous period even by the standards of Bengal's recent history. It appears from Beveridge's reading of matters that 'Black Hole' Holwell, who took temporary charge as governor of Fort William after Clive's departure (a run that would last six months until August, when Henry Vansittart assumed that office), put the squeeze on Mir Jafar for funds—'poor old Mir Jaffir was tyrannised over', is how Beveridge puts it. There's a letter to the nawab from May 1760 in which Holwell asks for funds ('I am obliged to press your obtaining at least one lac rupees') and is especially miffed at the Seths for refusing him a loan of '10 or 15 lacs'. Holwell writes again two days later, on 8 May: '...a time may come when they (the Setts) may stand in need of the Company's protection in which case they may be assured they shall be left to Satan to be buffeted.' Mir Jafar also began to be blamed for the death of some key officials and that of Alivardi's wife, Sharf-un-Nisa, and daughter, Ghaseti Begum, among other female members of the house of Alivardi and Siraj—matters that until then had been evidently been glossed over in the throes of the two year-long après-Plassey celebrations and acquisitions.

The upshot was that the momentum of those opposed to his rule became insurmountable for Mir Jafar, and he made way for Mir Qasim that October—but not before the canny Rai Durlabh made an abortive play for becoming nawab. Beveridge writes that Hastings, then the Company resident in Murshidabad, wrote a letter comparing the 'merits of the two men, giving the decided preference to Mir Kassim'. It was at first proposed that Mir Qasim could become the diwan, or 'deputy nawab', but the abdication was forced when Mir Jafar disagreed with that arrangement. True to Company practice, there was a treaty to mark it all, signed and sealed by Mir Qasim. 'The first treaty with Mir Kassim was on 27th September 1760,' writes Beveridge, 'and the deposition took place the following month.'

Matters didn't go well for Mir Qasim either. He was made to pay £2,00,000 as tribute to the Company officials in Calcutta for the privilege of becoming nawab, and that was merely the fee for his appointment. The Company soon insisted on preferential trade. Matters snowballed into dispute. Mir Qasim was deposed in 1763 when he demanded British soldiers leave Bengal in exchange for trading and tax concessions. Mir Jafar was restored as nawab on 7 July 1763, and in exchange for that favour paid out another fortune to the Company: £230,356 or over 1.85 million rupees.

Mir Qasim's ejection and his compact with allies with a mind to reclaim the masnad led to the Battle of Buxar on 21 October 1764, another landmark that enhanced the Company's reputation. Mir Qasim allied with Shuja-ud-daulah, the nawab of Awadh, and the Mughal emperor Shah Alam II—who had earlier attempted to force his hand as a contender in Bihar and Bengal as the prince Ali Gauhar (he had escaped the Marathas and travelled eastward, hoping to recoup his fortunes). The emperor who was crowned in early October while on the run from the capital, accompanied by his army of mercenaries was practically living under the shelter of nominal liege lords like the nawab of Awadh. Shah Alam II, quite like Mir Qasim, saw an assault on the subah of Bengal and Bihar as his ticket to power. And, therefore, ran headlong into the Company's interests which were set on controlling the very region.

The combined army of the farcical emperor fought Company forces led by Major Hector Munro at Buxar, on the southern bank of the Ganga (today a district headquarters town a five-hour drive west of Patna). Better disciplined Company forces, this time fighting an enemy at a ratio of about 1:4, and without the aid of conspiracy, won again in a hours-long battle that saw its uncoordinated opponents—who included Law and a band of about 200 Frenchmen—flee in disarray. Shah Alam II who would subsequently, as a Maratha- and British-controlled emperor, have little influence beyond Delhi and its suburbs, was compelled to sue for peace. He was also compelled by the Company to issue a farman recognizing Mir Jafar's return to the masnad of Bengal. The victory at Buxar directly contributed to extending Company and Crown influence over Bihar, Awadh and the Gangetic plains further to the west, and enormously enhanced their prestige and martial reputation. Here was a nation that had defeated in battle the Mughal emperor, farcical as his power was. This battle topped the Company's capture of the French subcontinental headquarters of Pondicherry in January 1761 after a four-month siege, and conclusively winning control of the Northern Circars from the French that year.

◆

Mir Qasim retreated after the debacle at Buxar, among other burdens carrying with him the reputation of a butcher for his gratuitous killing of 150 Company employees in Patna during his run westward from Murshidabad.

He also killed the Seths. Mir Qasim had compelled Jagat Seth Madhab Rai and Maharaja Swaroop Chand to accompany him upon his flight from Murshidabad. They were hostages, quite literally, useful bargaining chips. But an increasingly cornered Mir Qasim had them killed instead—which some Bengali nationalist chroniclers view as a sting of karma that visited nearly all Plassey conspirators. Long's compilation of Company records viewed the event more clinically, 'Attached to the English, they paid the penalty for it in being flung like dogs from the bastions of Monghyr fort into the raging Ganges by Kasim Ali.'

And Mir Qasim? Disenchanted, disavowed by the now frantic and fearful Shuja-ud-daulah of Awadh, robbed, Mir Qasim would make his way to Delhi, where he lived unheralded, and would die a pauper years later in 1777.

He was buried, as lore has it, in his only possession of note, a shawl.

◆

These events of great import occurred without Clive's presence in India, but it didn't diminish his stature back home. In terms of optics in London, opportunism fed by the combination of mercantile imperative and martial application that Clive displayed with Plassey, was a rage. Already an overachiever at thirty-five, Clive arrived home a hero. William Pitt 'The Elder', who would become prime minister of Britain, described him as a 'heaven-born general'. In 1761, Clive contested, and won, elections as a member of parliament from Shrewsbury. In 1762, he received an Irish peerage, and became the first Baron Clive of Plassey. Two years later he received a knighthood.

The threat of events that ultimately led to Buxar, and weaknesses and chaos in Bengal's post-Plassey administration which had by then become glaringly obvious, led the Company to insist their celebrated general-merchant return to Bengal. Lord Clive arrived in Calcutta in May 1765, as both governor of the Company's possessions and interests in India, and commander of its forces.

Clive saw a changed political landscape. Mir Qasim was lost, and Buxar won. Mir Jafar had died in January that year while Clive was in transit. Mir Jafar's second run as nawab wasn't much of a rule, at least for historians like Jadunath Sarkar. 'Sunk in gross sensual pleasures and weakened by his addiction to opium and the hemp drug (bhang), he had not even the energy of Alivardi, who was twenty years older in age,' writes Sarkar. He was for Sarkar a wretched creature as unworthy of the throne of Bengal as Siraj: 'In his last years, in the ignominious repose of the throne of Bengal, as "Lord Clive's jack-ass", he developed leprosy—a loathsome end to a loathsome life.'

(Whatever his life may have been, a grateful Mir Jafar, made nawab twice over by Clive & Co., left a gift of 500,000 rupees for Clive, whom he once called the 'light' of his eyes. Clive, who prudently mixed his politics with gestures which endeared him to certain groups, used this inheritance to push for a pension fund for Company employees in 1770. The result of an 'agreement' between Clive and the Company, it was called the Lord Clive Fund and, as an article notes at the UK National Archives, after his death was referred to as the Military (Late Lord Clive) Fund. It benefited invalided and retired officers and soldiers in the service of the East India Company's army and their widows, and even chaplains attached to this army and their widows, as detailed in a 'vade-mecum' for Company chaplains in Bengal. This latter group answered to the Church of England and its Indian offshoots in spiritual matters but Company rules for everything else, from posting to pay and, as earmarked by the Fund, pension.)

As we have seen, Miran's death had preceded his father's. Upon Clive's return he found the young nawab Nazam-ud-daulah, the second son of Mir Jafar, was now on the masnad. The privilege of this 'confirmation' by the Company had cost the fifteen-year-old nawab £140,000, to be shared among the Council in Calcutta.

The same year, in a mark of acquiescence—although it appeared more like obeisance—by the Mughal court, the East India Company received the diwani of Bengal, Bihar, and Orissa from Emperor Shah Alam II, the same itinerant royal who was defeated at the Battle of Buxar. A pliant Shah Alam II signed the Treaty of Allahabad with Clive on 16 August 1765, which awarded the diwani, and among other things, reiterated the permit of duty-free trade for the Company, and allowed the Company to intercede militarily in the affairs of Awadh. The Company now presided over the revenue administration of eastern India, and, as it controlled the court in Murshidabad, it became the true power in the East. As its chief representative, Clive was now without question a 'nabob'.

The future was made more evident in early May 1766, a scant nine years after Plassey, when Clive held the first 'English Punya', as the civil servant O'Malley describes it in his fine district gazetteer on Murshidabad. Punya was the annual collection and settlement of revenues, that year conducted with Nazam-ud-daulah, 'sitting on the masnad with Clive, as Diwan, on his right hand'. (Young Nazam-ud-daulah appears to have contracted a fever right after the punya ceremony at a celebration in honour of Clive, and died on 8 May 1766.)

In 1767, O'Malley tells us, punya was held here 'with even greater pomp' by the new governor of Bengal, Harry Verelst, 'in conjunction' with the new nawab of Bengal, Saif-ud-daulah, another of Mir Jafar's sons who was appointed nawab after the death of his brother, and after another fortune as fees passed into the hands of the Council at Calcutta.

And then Clive of India was finally done with India. He returned to Britain in 1767 for a life of politics, peerage, and lasting fame and infamy. At an inquiry in 1773 in the British Parliament's House of Commons, over accusations of maladministration and massive personal enrichment bordering on corruption, Clive would exclaim to the chair of the committee: 'By god, Mr. Chairman, at this moment I stand astonished at my own moderation.' Clive was, perhaps unsurprisingly, acquitted, but he had little time thereafter to enjoy his circumstances. 'With his already shaken health, the strain on his melancholic temperament was too great,' writes Spear, '...he died by his own hand at his house in London.'

That was in 1774. Calcutta had become the capital of British India a year earlier. Clive's legacy was already twenty years into its two-hundred-year gallop, which ended only with India and Pakistan's independence from colonial rule in 1947. Burma (now Myanmar) shook off the colonial yoke the following year. (Ceylon, later Sri Lanka, which was administered from 1795 by its own British governor, also became independent in 1948.) The triumph at Plassey, overpowering the French in both Bengal and southern India, the emphatic defeat of the Mughal figurehead in Buxar, and the granting of the diwani, revenue collection of Bengal and Bihar, placed the British at the head of a subcontinental power surge of a magnitude unseen since the rise of the Marathas in the second half of the seventeenth century. As stunning as all this was, what followed in the years of British domination from 1857 onwards—when the sepoy revolt ended Company rule and announced the formal arrival of the British Raj —was perhaps even more stunning in speed and colonial scope.

◆

Before 1857, the British approach to gaining control had two main planks. One, as is well-recorded, was the application of force and aggressive diplomacy to subdue subcontinental powers and gain control of territories through treaty. This could either be an outright takeover of the territory, or through a treaty that owed allegiance to the Company in the name of the Crown. The second was to put in place an orientalist machinery for administrative and intellectual dominion.

The two streams were symbiotic. Warren Hastings, the callow but ambitious clerk for whom the circumstances of Plassey proved to be a trial by fire, was appointed the first governor general of the presidency of Fort William in 1773, an upgrade from the station of governor that Clive was appointed to in 1765, with control over all Company possessions in India and their growth. In a tenure of less than twelve years, Hastings had overseen the establishment of a Supreme Court that answered only to Company law, tried to streamline revenue collection after the nightmare that was the Bengal famine (of which more shortly), taken the battle to the Marathas, the kingdom of Mysore, and the Pathans in Rohilkhand—expanding its footprint in the west, beyond Bombay, and the south, beyond Madras and the Northern Circars the Company already controlled, while bringing it ever closer to Delhi. Much of eastern India was a done deal. In 1772, the control of Bengal formally ended for the nawabs of Bengal. Until then the nawabs technically had administrative control while the Company controlled revenue collection as diwan. By ending this dual system of government and shifting administration to Calcutta, John Company became the undisputed power in the former subah of the Mughals.

By the 1790s, John Company had ratcheted up its activities and this dynasty of shareholders and mercantile soldiers would, in the next two decades, acquire the heft of territory, revenue, and frightful respect at a rate unseen since the run of the Mughal emperor Akbar who ruled for nearly fifty years until 1605. Hastings's successor as governor general, Charles Cornwallis, entirely upended the existing land revenue system in Bengal and Bihar, and created a new class of zamindars—the template would soon spread across Company-controlled territories in northern India—by implementing the

Permanent Settlement in 1793. The arrangement fixed revenue for zamindars to pay the Company, an attempt to assure both landlord and leaseholders predictable income and streamline revenue. A civil service for India, flagged in a post-Plassey memo by Clive, was born at this time. (The East India Company College at Hailey, to train writers and future administrators, a process that would after 1857 morph into the Imperial Civil Service—and, eventually, the Indian Civil Service—would be established in 1806.)

From 1793 to 1798, John Shore as Cornwallis's successor oversaw the political acquisition of two prestigious kingdoms—Travancore and Jaipur. Ceylon was wrested from the Dutch. (Meanwhile, the British were already looking beyond eastern India. As early as October 1757, word arrived to the Council in Calcutta that a treaty with the 'Burmah King' had provided 'a full and free grant to the Hon'ble Company and their successors of the Island Negraise [today, the island of Hainggyi Kyun in the Irawaddy delta], together with a tract or spot of ground for a Factory...' British settlers would be attacked and massacred by locals in 1759, but that was more a beginner's blip. In a little over eighty years, with the subcontinent mostly in the bag, the Company with the active oversight of the Crown government would begin its rule over Burma.)

The warlike years of 1798 to 1805, when Richard Wellesley as governor general was almost Clive-like in his application of force and guile, were notable for a winning a conclusive war against Mysore's Tipu Sultan in 1799, which finally won control of the territory for the Company and erased the vestige of French military consultancy in that region. Wellesley also oversaw the extension a year earlier of the very corporate-minded mergers and acquisitions strategy, with the introduction of what came to be called the Subsidiary Alliance by which rulers in the subcontinent were allowed to retain key privileges in return for allegiance to Company and Crown. In 1803, with much of the territory of Awadh already under their control, British armies won a landmark victory against the Marathas in Delhi. For all practical purposes, the British took over control of symbolic Mughal rule from the Marathas.

Now orientalism began to keep pace with militarism. The orientalist redoubt at Fort William came into existence in 1800. The

College of Fort William became a hub for scholarship, and although it was premised on the need for rulers to better understand the ruled it did spawn a treasure trove in translations of texts from across South Asia and elsewhere; it became a repository for old manuscripts, and a centre for languages: Sanskrit, Bengali, Arabic, Persian, and even Mandarin—China, the next great leap for the Company—were taught there by Indian, British, and Far Eastern scholars. Also in 1800, the Baptist Mission was established by William Carey in Srirampur along the western bank of the Hugli, across from what would come to be called Barrackpore—as self-evident an etymology as any. This signalled the beginning of an organized proselytization that would transform the religious map in great swathes of the subcontinent, and also eventually facilitate the genesis of the 'mission school' and 'mission college', from which would eventually emerge many of the educated middle class and elites of Bengal, and of British India.

Such transformation would be speeded up after Thomas Babington Macaulay wrote his far-reaching blueprint for the Brown Sahib: the 'Minute on Education' on 2 February 1835, his views presented to the Committee of Public Instruction endorsed by the governor general at the time, William Cavendish-Bentinck.

...English is better worth knowing than Sanscrit or Arabic, that the natives are desirous to be taught English, and are not desirous to be taught Sanscrit or Arabic that neither as the languages of law nor as the languages of religion have the Sanscrit and Arabic any peculiar claim to our encouragement, that it is possible to make natives of this country thoroughly good English scholars, and that to this end our efforts ought to be directed.

We must at present do our best to form a class who may be interpreters between us and the millions whom we govern a class of persons Indian in blood and colour, but English in tastes, in opinions, in morals and in intellect. To that class we may leave it to refine the vernacular dialects of the country, to enrich those dialects with terms of science borrowed from the Western nomenclature, and to render them by degrees fit vehicles for conveying knowledge to the great mass of the population.

By the time 1857 came around, the mutinies and numerous skirmishes in northern and central India exposed the fault lines in the subcontinent and the Company's own weaknesses through grand overreach; such overreach nevertheless allowed the British government to seamlessly take over the running of India, Myanmar, and Ceylon from the Company. In the Company's liquidation in 1858 would be born Britain's formal Indian empire. It was a gigantic empire that the government took charge of, an empire won through deceit, overwhelming fire power, effective battlefield tactics, ruthlessness, and Indian complicity and alliances. It included the territories of the nizam of Hyderabad, the Marathas, all Rajputana, central and southern India (Mysore, Travancore among the acquisitions) and Assam. The kingdom of Nepal had ceded vast territory. The Indian empire, and its structured subsidizing of the British economy, British industry and several British war efforts, instead of merely attending to the Company's balance sheets and the enriching of several of its key shareholders and executives, had begun.

◆

There is a generally less-regarded legacy of Clive & Co. that ravaged Bengal the same year Clive initiated the pension fund named after him: famine.

We have seen how, after Plassey, Mir Jafar agreed to pay the equivalent of £3.4 million to the British East India Company and its officials, officers, and soldiers as reparation and a service charge, if you will. When Mir Jafar proved unsuitable for their purpose, the Company appointed Mir Qasim in his place. Besides his confirmation fee, he had also handed over to the Company direct revenue control over several districts, including Medinipur (or Midnapore) and Bardhaman (or Burdwan) in Bengal's west, and Chottōgram (Chittagong) in the east. In turn the Company auctioned revenue collection to the highest bidder. This would become the norm after the Company was made diwan in 1765.

This dismantled the revenue collection system of over a thousand zamindars in a range of small to big, established by Murshid Quli as nawab, and later bolstered by Alivardi. 'Let them grow rich,' Alivardi is said to have advised Siraj of Bengal's farmers, textile workers, and traders who formed the backbone of the economy, the zamindari system, and the nawab's treasury, 'and the state will grow rich also'. As Madhusree Mukerjee notes in her study of Bengal's famine, *Churchill's Secret War: The British Empire and the Ravaging of India During World War II*, that advice was remodelled to generate maximum revenue using any device at hand. 'Thus numberless harpies were let loose to plunder,' observed a future governor of Bengal, Harry Verelst, 'whom the spoil of a miserable people enabled to complete their first year's payment.' Such sentiment was rare.

Just over a decade after Plassey, the Company ran Bengal's revenue collection, giving the shaky Mughal emperor in Delhi an annual sum while the Company's profits were eight to ten times that amount—soon, even more. Such revenues paid for purchasing local goods, staunching the Company's and Britain's revenue drain of the previous centuries. We learn that Bengal exported £6,311,250 worth of goods and products during 1766–68, and imported a tenth of that. The exports were financed by Bengal's revenues the Company now controlled.

'Bengal was bled white,' Brendon notes with chilling simplicity. 'Indian revenues (which perhaps amounted to a billion pounds sterling between Plassey and Waterloo [1757 to 1815]) spelled the redemption of Britain, said the Earl of Chatham. They were kind of a "gift from heaven"'—here Brendon refers to P. J. Marshall's *Problems of Empire: Britain and India 1757-1813*.

The rains failed in 1769–70. Crop failure loomed. In *Murshidabad*, O'Malley writes (quoting a work by the civil servant George Campbell, who was lieutenant governor of Bengal in 1871–74) that red flags had already been raised about the impending disaster by the Company's own, including Richard Becher, British resident at the Murshidabad court. 'The first allusion to the impending distress was made in August 1769 when Mr. Becher reported "the alarming want of rain which has prevailed throughout all the upper parts of Bengal, both the last and this season, and particularly the latter, to a degree which has not been known in the memory of the oldest man." On 26 August he added, "There is great reason to apprehend that in all the districts to the northward of Nadia the crops of rice will be very short indeed. Since the season for rain began, they have hardly had any; and if God does not soon bless this country with plentiful showers, the most fatal consequences will ensue—not only a reduction in the revenues, but a scene of misery and distress that is a constant attendant on famine."'

As it happened, traders and speculators purchased as much rice as possible—Indian and British traders alike—setting a cold, calculating, mercantile template that would repeatedly visit Bengal. British 'bullies, cheats and swindlers continued to prey on the carcass of Bengal. Some profiteered in hoarded grain...' as Brendon quotes from R. K. Ray's study, 'Colonial Penetration and the Initial Resistance: The Mughal Ruling Class, the English East India Company and the Struggle for Bengal 1756-1800'.

And, instead of shoring up resources for the local population, Company officials shipped grain wherever else in its subcontinental domains it was required. William Wilson Hunter, an Indian Civil Service officer who in 1871 became the first director general of statistics to the government of India, in his *The Annals of Rural Bengal* provides a recollection from India Office Records that is as chilling as any horror in Belgian Congo—or the horrific Bengal famine of 1943 that Britain's war-time prime minister Winston Churchill helped on its way, for that matter:

> All through the stifling summer of 1770 the people went on dying. The husbandmen sold their cattle; they sold their implements of agriculture; they devoured their seed grain; they sold their sons and daughters; till at length no buyer of children could be found; they ate the leaves of trees and the grass of the field; and in June 1770 the resident [Becher] at the Durbar [Murshidabad] affirmed that the living were feeding on the dead. Day and night a torrent of famished and disease-stricken wretches poured into the great cities...even the dogs and jackals, the public scavengers of the East, became unable to accomplish their revolting work...

He also refers to a few lines of eyewitness poetry written by John Shore, a Company employee who arrived in Kolkata during the famine—and would after two decades become governor general of Bengal:

Still fresh in memory's eye the scene I view,
The shrivelled limbs, sunk eyes, and lifeless hue;
Still hear the mother's shrieks and infant's moans,
Cries of despair and agonizing moans.
In wild confusion dead and dying lie;—
Hark to the jackal's yell and vulture's cry,
The dog's fell howl, as midst the glare of day
They riot unmolested on their prey!

It came to be known in Bengali lore as Chhiāttōrér monnōntōr, as it began in the year 1176 of the Bengali calendar—1176 Bongābdō; chhiāttōr is seventy-six.

Ten million died in Bengal. A third of the population. With typical exactitude, W. W. Hunter writes of it in his *Famine Aspects of Bengal Districts* as: 'Five in every 16 were officially admitted to have perished'. Mukerjee notes that the Company's directors would later complain about the 'disappointing' revenue from some districts even as overall revenue collection was, quite amazingly, maintained at the previous year's level. Warren Hastings, the future governor general, maintained it was on account of collections being 'violently kept up to its former standard'. Meanwhile, 'only £9,000 was expended on relief by Government,' Hunter informs us. According to the *Imperial Gazetteer of India*, nearly a third of the population of what eventually came to be Murshidabad district was 'carried away' by the famine of 1770.

◆

Time isn't exactly still in Murshidabad and its neighbourhood. History lives on in monuments and museums and minds. Showcased, celebrated, even lamented with ceremonial fury in this playground of the nawabs of Bengal, Bihar, and Orissa.

In Roshni Bagh, right across the Bhagirathi from Hazarduari Palace, and not far from the Magic Moment Dance Club, is a sign of how far the Marathas came. There's a temple to Eklingaji Mahadev— Shiva—with prayers and inscription in Nagari script carved on black stone. This is how we learn it was constructed by Ranganath Pandit from 'Maharashtra', a name that came to the western region in the early centuries of the Common Era, and was in use when the Marathas raided Bengal right up to Murshidabad. Locals today ensure the temple remains active, the black basalt Shivalinga worshipped.

Murshidabad lost some importance in 1772, when Warren Hastings transferred the supreme, civil, and criminal courts from Murshidabad to Calcutta—but after three years the criminal court (nizamat adalat) was re-transferred to Murshidabad. That was a brief reprieve. In 1790, the criminal court and the revenue and civil administration offices of Bengal moved to Calcutta. The Murshidabad Mint, the recognized emblem of metropolitan supremacy, was abolished in 1799. Murshidabad became little more than the home of the nawabs.

The Hazarduari Palace, the palace of a thousand doorways, now a well-attended museum and marker for tourists and historians alike, is a trove of symbols that mark the passing of Bengal's power from a string of progressively toothless nawabs to the British. The construction of the palace itself, along a road named after Siraj in a modern-day rush of nationalistic reclamation, took till 1836 to complete, opening for habitation the year after. It was designed by Duncan McLeod, then a colonel with Bengal Engineers, who was 'directed' by the Company to go ahead with the building that would subsequently be described by Emma Roberts in her *Scenes and Characteristics of Hindostan, with Sketches of Anglo-Indian Society* as 'a fine building, in the European style, of dazzling whiteness, and rising in glittering splendour, amid stately groves of flourishing trees'. A biography of McLeod notes that it was constructed 'to promote the health, comfort, and respectability' of the nawab Humayun Jah and his family.

It evidently did, with several halls and 114 rooms of private chambers and relatively public spaces, and a grand durbar hall for audiences. The *Imperial Gazetteer of India* published in 1908 noted with some awe:

> The palace is 425 feet long, 200 feet wide, and 80 feet high. The ground floor is of stone, the first floor of marble, and the second floor of wood. The banqueting hall is 191 feet long and 55 feet wide. In the centre of the building is a dome, from which hangs a superb chandelier of 110 branches. The palace contains many rare old pictures, costly jewellery, china, and arms.

Humayun Jah lived on a generous allowance fixed by the Company, though this had vastly diminished by 1908. The *Imperial Gazetteer* noted: 'The residences of the Nawab Bahadur and the members of the Nizamat family are a series of one-storeyed buildings, devoid of beauty and unsafe to live in.' But some of their baubles and treasures have come down to the present day.

Besides portraits of various nawabs, and their Indian and Asian luxuries, empire and European accoutrements from the time of post-Plassey nawabs adorn Hazarduari's walls and floors. An oil from the Mysore wars. An ivory palki of Zeb-un-Nisa Begum, a daughter of the Mughal emperor Aurangzeb isn't too far from a rendition of William Shakespeare 'reviving' *Macbeth* at the court of Queen Elizabeth. A 1905 book, *The Musnud of Murshidabad (1704–1904)*, lists a Rembrandt and Raphael and works of several other European masters that are absent from view, as is the 'dazzling whiteness' of the building now in various shades of yellow depending on how many stretches of the wall have faded and been repainted. The 'stately' grove of trees is absent; instead you might find the sometimes stately march of the Hazarduari Morning Walkers Association, mostly middle-aged, pot-bellied men in matching maroon or brown tracksuits. But there remain numerous arresting displays of importance and overlordship.

There are documents with the tones of polite formality that accompany statecraft and protocol in relatively benign times—benign in the sense Bengal, Bihar, and Orissa were in Britain's bag by way of the Company and politically underwritten by the British government. Take, for instance, a khat or official letter to Sayyid Mubarak Ali Khan Bahadur Firoz Jung in September 1770 in which Company officials would discuss with the nawab the administrative affairs of the nizamat or governorship of the state. When Sayyid Ahmad Ali Khan Bahadur Mahabat Jung, better known as Walah Jah, became nawab nazim of the provinces of Bengal, Bihar, and Orissa after the death of his elder brother, more commonly known as Nawab Ali Jah, he formally did so only after an ishtihar nama—proclamation—was issued by the governor general of the Presidency of Fort William, Francis Rawdon-Hastings, the Earl of Moira, on 18 August 1821.

William Bentinck, the first governor general of India (he was for five years till 1833 the last governor of the Presidency of Fort William before re-designation to this grander title reflecting the increasingly grander ambition of the Company and Crown), addressed a letter dated 24 February 1835 to Nawab Humayun Jah with a gentlemanly 'My Honoured and valued Friend' to announce his retirement from public service in India and to introduce his successor, Charles Metcalfe. The letter merely indulged a callow titular nawab not much younger than Siraj was when the latter ran afoul of the Company.

In a few short years the benevolence of the Company added a layer of benevolence of the King. Few things underscore it better than a massive oil of William Henry in the Hazarduari Palace in Murshidabad, a gift to his contemporary. A brass plaque records it: 'This Gift of His Majesty King William the Fourth' to 'His Highness The Nawaub Nazim Behadoor Hamaon Jah Feroze Jung of Moorshedabad in the East Indies.'

Humayun Jah, as we have seen, was the nawab of Bengal, Bihar, and Orissa only in name. Mubarak Ali Khan who died at twenty-eight may have had as his title of office, Shuja-ul-Mulk Humayun Jah (the Courageous Ruler of the Land, the Auspicious One), nominally blessed by the Mughal emperor Akbar Shah II, but that emperor was himself under the protection of Company and Crown. It was hardly surprising, therefore, that young Mubarak Ali extended his honorifics as a Knight Grand Cross of the Royal Hanoverian Guelphic Order with Insignia which he was awarded by William IV in 1837. That he was the first non-European to be conferred this honour hardly diluted the chain of command and control.

In 1880, the nawab of Bengal became merely the nawab of Murshidabad, the first of whom was Ali Kadir, or Syed Hassan Ali Mirza Khan Bahadur. The House of Murshidabad even got itself a coat of arms in the European style, with a lion on the left and a unicorn on the right with a crown on top, with the house motto in Latin: Nil Desperandum.

Do Not Despair.

◆

The famed bankers to Bengal's nawabs never returned to the heights they had once scaled after the killing by Mir Qasim of Jagat Seth Madhab Rai and his cousin, Maharaja Swaroop Chand. The Seths' sons tried to 'rally in business', Hill notes, 'and we find in 1764 the English Government borrowing 5 lacs from them'. This relationship continued for a while even as the Company steadily whittled away the Seths' hold in a clinical way.

The Company's remarkable post-Plassey financial position ensured there was no need to import bullion—but the Seths still clung to their advantage. 'In 1758, the Council at Calcutta complained, in a letter to the [Mughal] Court, that their mint [which had been established the previous year, after Plassey] was of little use to them, partly because no bullion was arriving from Europe, but more especially because the commend of specie possessed by the Seths of Murshidabad was used to force down the exchange value of their sikkas,' O'Malley writes. (And yet, in 1759, Clive 'entertained Jaggat Set for four days at a cost of Re. 17,374,' we learn in Hill's compilation of records. '...among the presents are 1 otto box set with diamonds Rs. 3,222, 8 tweezer cases at Rs. 55 each. Rs. 500 was given to servants.')

As we have seen, the Company managed to swing things in their favour in 1760 as among their conditions for installing Mir Qasim over Mir Jafar was the demand for a parwana awarding 'full privileges to the Calcutta mint'. 'From this date the mint of Murshidabad began to decline, and, indeed, was soon abolished,' writes O'Malley, triggering a visible slide in the fortunes and vast influence of the Seths as the Company's and Britain's fortunes began their spectacular upward arc.

Bizarrely, even as the Seths had their prized monopoly, the mint, taken away, in 1768 the Court of Directors, directing the debts due by the Government to the Seths to be paid, remarked: 'that family, who have suffered so much in our cause, are particularly entitled to our protection'.

Developments would sully that act of condescending charity. Abhik Ray, an expert in the history of banking in India, in his essay, 'Two Centuries of Apex Banking: The State Bank of India and the Evolution of Modern Banking in India', notes the evolving situation.

Soon, however, the European merchants formed agency houses and took upon themselves the business of banking in addition to their commercial and trading activities. Apart from their inability to make use of the indigenous banking system for long, the European merchants also needed a safe place to deposit the capital they had steadily been accumulating. The agency houses accepted deposits, lent money to merchants, shipowners, ship managers, planters and governments, and generally helped finance external trade. In 1770, the first western-style bank, The Bank of Hindostan, was set up in Calcutta by Alexander & Co., one of the leading agency houses of Bengal.

Meanwhile, as we have seen, the Seths' meaningful hold over the mint that remained in Murshidabad diminished. In 1796, all provincial mints were abolished by the Presidency government, but the Murshidabad mint still managed to claw a few years' respite. It was not till 1799 that—O'Malley notes—'the Collector of Murshidabad despatched the mint utensils to the Presidency, and disposed of the buildings used as the mint office by public auction'.

And with that the last traces of the glory days of the Seths, partners in the joint venture of Plassey, were gone, the principle of nothing-personal-it's-just-business turned against them by those who had played the game much better. John Company, the horse that won, unseated the Seths. It is somewhat ironical to read the end of a poem dedicated by a family priest to Seth Manik Chand's principal wife after her death:

Wealth is acquired by charity;
Conduct is the source of happiness;
Religious austerities destroy Karma;
Virtuous thoughts attain salvation.

It is perhaps even more ironical to visit a complex known as the House of Jagat Seth in the Mahimapur locality. This lies to the north of the palace complex of Hazarduari, past Jafarganj or Jafraganj as it is sometimes called, past the tomb of Azim-un-Nisa Begum—she of liver-eating lore. Nothing remains of the former grand palace of the Jagat Seths. Today's 'House' is a complex of former offices of the banking family, a modest two-storey house by a narrow lane, garbage strewn by its entrance. There's another bungalow-like building of a single storey, and a well-maintained temple. Plaster figurines of half-naked ladies are everywhere, on rooftops, adorning defunct fountains, welcoming visitors near the gate. On display are lavish furniture and dining-table accoutrements, some muslin, paintings, some weapons, a few coins. The pièce de résistance is a tunnel—'Hidden Tunnel Founded by Jagat Seth', proclaim signs near the entrance, alongside 'Underground Secret Chamber of Jagat Seth', which now houses family bric-à-brac.

For an Indian, it costs fifteen rupees to visit. A foreigner pays a hundred.

◆

At Khosh Bagh as elsewhere in this region of tombs and tense history, guides offer a folksy meld of hearsay history and recorded history. This Garden of Joy was laid out in 1740, to which Murshidabad's nobility are said to have sailed in elaborate and graceful boats called mōyurpōnkhi, the prow the shape of a peacock's head, the stern a fantail. Today it's just a modest, well-tended garden with a number of unobtrusive, curiously clustered tombs of some of late-medieval Bengal's most powerful people: some of whom loved each other; or fought each other to the death; or conspired against, or betrayed, Siraj.

The first cluster of graves, with no signs to mark them belongs to Sharf-un-Nisa, the wife to whom Alivardi was devoted ('Shirājér didimā,' a guide might tell you in a folksy manner, Siraj's granny). Nearby lies her eldest daughter, Ghaseti Begum—Mehr-un-Nisa. This aunt of Siraj ('Shirājér māshi') was among those who urged Siraj's cousin, the nawab of Purnea, Shaukat Jang, to rebel against her nephew, and would shortly ally with Clive & Co. By her side lies her younger sister, Amina Begum, the mother of Siraj ('Shirājér mā').

In a far corner, by a wall, is a cluster of seventeen graves: Siraj's relatives who, so goes the story, were poisoned by Miran at a dinner he had invited them to, killing off any remnant of opposition to the rule of his father. Across from them, to the left of the compound, is the grave of the fakir, Dana Shah, who outed Siraj in Rajmahal during his desperate escape. It's believed the fakir received a reward of a thousand rupees for this act of revenge. The fakir himself was subsequently killed.

Just before the entrance to the main colonial-era building, all wooden beams and roof of plain plaster, that protects Siraj's grave and that of several others, family and foe, is the grave of his confidante,

Ghulam Hussein. A Plassey myth maintains he swapped his clothes with Siraj and helped him to escape, but in the end, as we have seen, Siraj's shoes gave him away to the grudge-bearing fakir. By either side of the confidante lie two eunuchs who guarded the harem. Apparently Miran ordered their deaths too.

◆

Siraj's grave is a plain one, with a small headstone of white marble. On most days, visitors will find a few roses, or some marigold and jasmine placed on his grave. In the local present-day apocryphal telling, Siraj's main killer, Muhammadi Beg, comes off quite brutally. 'He killed Siraj, cut him into four pieces, then sewed him up and placed him on an elephant that transported his remains around Murshidabad.' That's the version you may hear from a tribe of attendant guide-storytellers who spout ready history at about a rupee a minute.

At the foot of Siraj's grave is the grave of his devoted wife, Lutf-un-Nisa. To her right is the grave of Aliya, Siraj's sometime lover, the dancer who was sister to his trusted diwan, Mohanlal. The dancer Siraj is supposed to have walled up, according to a tale related by the *Siyar*.

Apocrypha credits Miran with more murder. After Siraj's death, his mother, aunt, principal wife Lutf-un-Nisa, and first-born daughter, Zohra, were sent away to Dhaka and kept under guard at the Jinjira Palace, used by several Bengal nobles as a residence, across the Buri Ganga River. On the pretext of an outing they were drowned on the orders of Miran. It isn't clear how the sisters died, but Lutf-un-Nisa, who again apocrypha credits being asked for her hand in marriage by both Miran and Mir Jafar, was permitted to return to Murshidabad in 1765. The Company provided a pension for her and Zohra. Lutf-un-Nisa is said to have tended to Siraj's grave every day until her death in 1790.

The cluster of graves to the left of Siraj is led by that of Alivardi. At his feet is the grave of Zohra. To Alivardi's left lies Shaukat Jang, the nawab of Purnea appointed by him, and incited by Murshidabad's finest, including Mir Jafar and Ghaseti Begum, to rebel unsuccessfully against his cousin Siraj. As it turned out, Shaukat Jang's death would predate Siraj's by a year or so. Shaukat's wife, Moti Begum, is interred by his side.

Across the Bhagirathi, to the north of Hazarduari, the palace of Mir Jafar in Jafarganj has a forlorn look. A ruined archway—often called Namak Haram Deori, the Traitor's Gate—leads to a walled compound that contains a building and a prayer hall that is usually barred to all except family faithful. A closed iron gate is the only entrance.

The grave of Mir Jafar a few steps along the road is a ticketed affair, and the ticket has on the obverse a plea in Bengali. 'Except Miran, Mir Qasim, this cemetery contains the graves of all Nawab Nazims,' declares the collective of caretakers which describes itself simply as 'four guards and Munshi'. Miran's favourite parrots, too, are said to be buried here. As with other cemeteries and historical sites in Murshidabad, guides offer a magical mystery tour for twenty rupees—thirty, if a visitor is generous. 'We have taken care of this cemetery for long years but it is a matter of regret that the monthly allowance of eleven rupees provided for upkeep in the era of the Nawabs [nobābi āmōl, in Bengali], continues to this day. It is difficult to sustain a livelihood with this amount so, to save our lives, we are compelled to request five rupees from you and for that we give our thanks.'

And so, one comes upon the uneasy resting place of 'Shujaul Mulk Hosamuddowla Nawab Meer Mohamed Jafer Khan Bahadur Mahabat Jang Nawab Nazim of Bengal' as the inscription in English proclaims below the one in Farsi. Clive's sometime favourite 'Jaffier Cawn' is today an unkempt memory that feeds rich imaginations and poor relatives.

In an article published in *India Today* magazine in early 1994, a descendant of Mir Jafar, Syed Mohammed Reza Ali Khan, described how he used to lose his temper when, as a child, he would see tourists spit on his ancestor's grave. Khan, whom the article described as a teacher of Urdu at a local school, and part-time historian, complained of his family being 'victims of an historical injustice'. To clear the name of Mir Jafar, he said, he had for twenty years scoured libraries in Calcutta, Dhaka, Murshidabad, and Patna to gather evidence of innocence. At any rate, innocence according to the practices of the age—employing the same metric that defenders of Clive & Co. use: 'It is unjust to judge a person of the 18th century in the light of the 20th century.' Didn't Alivardi depose and kill Sarfaraz Khan, his 'master', for the masnad? Khan asks. And, in any case there was no concept of nationhood—in terms of India as we know it today—in those times.

Khan could be echoing the words of Jadunath Sarkar, although in his book the character of Mir Jafar, or Ja'far Ali, as Sarkar refers to him, is dealt with as brutally and with a veneer of sarcasm. Sarkar maintains that Siraj's usurper cannot be hidden behind the prophylactic of merely acting as the brutal times demanded, even though he had only done what Alivardi had to his own benefactor's family. 'If Alivardi could kill his benefactor Shuja-ud-din's heir and seize the throne, Ja'far Ali had the same moral right to kill Alivardi (or his heir) and take the throne; that was his argument.'

Mir Jafar was a 'pious and honest man,' Khan is quoted as saying in the article. 'According to him,' the article notes, 'Mir Jafar had been put under house arrest by the young upstart nawab.' His ancestor had no choice, pleads Khan. 'It was a question of life and death for him and he opted for life by siding with Siraj's enemies.'

EPILOGUE

'Where Clive's blade was reddened by the blood of Bengal!'

Among all the morbid memories and mysteries, Plassey lives.

To the south of the Plassey memorial, an obelisk with a simple inscription in capital letters on its base—Battle Field of Plassey, 23 June 1757—is an inspection bungalow built in 1908. The compound is large, with a dozen or so mango trees alongside other species. The bungalow has been made gaudy and grotty in the present day, far from the well-maintained place I first visited as a child, in the early 1970s. A clay model of the battlefield, with an oxbow loop of the Bhagirathi to its west, rows of British tents and green-brown clumps of mango trees, and tiny clay figurines depicting Company troops and that of Siraj, lie dusty and broken. The figurines are absent. A package-insert advertising Nadia's Bhai-Bhai Bakery—Brotherhood Bakery—lies on the tableau. An amateur acrylic-on-canvas painting of the battle, with British troops massed on the lower left corner, and the nawab's towards the right, is placed on the ground against a speckled wall damp with moisture and covered with busy strings of cobweb.

While history is made destitute here, outside there is the celebration of defeat, of a scripted martyrdom, of leveraged nationalism, that make for more astute politics and a sense of loss that is also at once a sense of belonging, of reclaiming a nervous past as emphatic present and a robust future. Plassey is on this 23rd day of June a moment of magical realism.

I had arrived by the Bhagirathi Express from Murshidabad early that morning, just after seven, the clammy chill of dawn long past. Visitors to Polāshi-Palāsi-Plassey station (train stations in India generally use trilingual signs, the regional—here, Bengali—Hindi and English) are greeted with a large mosaic of the battle outside the first-class waiting room on platform 1. This Plassey totem depicts a phase of the battle, fought about 2 kilometres northwest of the station, decidedly going the Company's way. A cannon of the nawab's forces is perched atop its ox-drawn carriage, Company soldiers and sipahis, sepoys to the Anglo, use sword and bayonet to skewer Siraj's soldiers. An impressionistic Union Jack unfurls over the battlefield. By its side, a likeness of Siraj faces Plassey's commemorative obelisk, a monument to both victory and defeat. Below is a blurb of an emotional, somewhat confusing post-colonial verdict, courtesy of Indian Railways:

> ...Nawab's soldiers were bribed by British to throw away their weapons and surrender prematurely. Siraj was captured and brutally murdered. Thus by promoting treason and forgery the English force established their Supremacy and the gruesome days of British Rule began.

By eight in the morning, the battle and battlefield are in full commemoration-mode. It's a bizarre memory recall, a mix-and-match of all manner of anti-colonial markers. A few steps away from a vendor selling the region's lush guavas with a sprinkling of rock salt and red chilli powder, volunteers hand out leaflets in Bengali that announce the imminent centenary in 2019 of the Jallianwala Bagh Massacre, that took place in Amritsar on 13 April 1919. The leaflet also encourages commemoration of the November 1945 killing of 5,000 prisoners of the Indian National Army or Azad Hind Fauj—literally, Free India Army; and a clutch of other instances of 'martyrdom'. Manik Samajdar, secretary of the grandly titled Bangladesh Bharat Pakistan People's Forum, extols the virtue of patriotism and peoples' struggles. He also hands out leaflets that urge India to leave the 'colonial' embrace of the Commonwealth, International Monetary Fund, and World Trade Organization. On a ramshackle stage festooned with the saffron-white-green of the Indian flag a young girl sings a plaintive song with lurid operative words:

> Chhurir tolé/ prān hārālén Shirāj. Siraj lost his life/ to a knife.

In front of the stage is a banner, proclaiming a stanza of poetry in classical Bengali:

> Kāndāri! Tobō shommukhé ōi Polāshir prāntōr,
> Bānglār khooné lāl hō'lō jéthā Clibhe-ér khonjōr!
> Ōi Gongāye dubiyāchhé hāye Bhārōtér dibākor!
> Udibé shé rōbi āmādéri khooné rāngiyā punōrbār!

Captain! The battlefield of Plassey lies before you,
Where Clive's blade was reddened by the blood of Bengal!
The sun of India set on that stream of the Ganga!
And it shall rise again, awash in our blood!

In front of the stage is a little sea of seated karatekas, wearing well-used and starched gi, many with Azad Hind Karate, Free India Karate, the name of a local dojo, screen-printed on the back. They practise the Ashihara style, a derivative of the resolutely combative Kyokushin school. A chubby young karateka collapses into his mother's arms in the sapping heat of the morning while his peers snigger, only to be silenced by older colleagues, men and women, who wear fierce expressions. They will soon perform an exhibition of drills with suitably blood-curdling kiai shouts to honour Siraj but, meanwhile, senior instructor Somnath Ghosh speaks to me of his dreams of two Bengals, West Bengal and Bangladesh, reuniting to become Golden Bengal ('Dui Bāṅglā ek hoyé shōnār Bāṅglā...')

We face the stage, adjacent to a bust of Siraj on a pedestal, inaugurated on 23 June 2007, placed just outside the enclosure that contains the obelisk. His likeness is freshly painted golden, adorned with fresh garland of marigold. A banner is placed by his side on the wall of the enclosure. 'I'tikaf', it proclaims, using Arabic in Bengali script. Unity. 'Ittemad'. Faith. 'Qurbani'. Sacrifice. Ancient guards in two-toned blue uniforms holding staffs stand by the bust and the entrance. A milestone helpfully announces: 'Monument: 0 K.M'. At a tiny tea shop, Kohinoor Russian Circus advertises three daily shows at Plassey's Mira Math Para Ground.

After a few minutes, the karatekas head out on a slim track through fields of pāt (jute) and potōl (pointed gourd), fodder-greens to make silage for cattle feed, some pumpkin, and a few mango trees at the edges. There are vast mango orchards in Murshidabad, Berhampore, and Qasimbazar, but not here, around the old battlefield. We arrive at another memorial about 300 metres away. Three small obelisks this time. A marble inscription on the red brick base announces three heroes of the Bengal army in Plassey:

Here fell Bakshi Mir Madan, Chief of Artillery; Bahadur Ali Khan, Commander of Musketeers; Nauwe Singh Hazari, Captain of Artillery of Nawab Siraj-ud-daula at the head of the charge ordered by Mir Madan at 2 P.M. on June 23, 1757 in the Battle of Plassey.

The memorial was constructed by the Nadia District Citizens' Council over 1972–73, to mark the twenty-fifth anniversary of India's independence. Garlands of rajanigandha, tuberose, their white a mark of mourning in many parts of the subcontinent, have been placed in front of the obelisks. Clumps of red hibiscus and marigold added by worshippers bring more ceremonial colour. A massively built karateka sporting a black belt offers his colleagues, numbering more than a hundred, jasmine blossoms that every adult and child gently throws at the memorials; they then fold their hands in respect, eyes closed, smoke from incense sticks making a few cough. A banner by the side proclaims that Subhas Chandra Bose, popularly known as Netaji, who allied with Axis Powers in an attempt to rid India of the British, 'did not die in an aircraft crash' in Formosa —Taiwan—in 1945, and lived to be variously guised as a Buddhist monk, a diplomat in Tashkent in 1966 at peace talks between India and Pakistan. 'Who is the man behind the mask?' the banner queries of a smudged face photographed at the funeral of Jawaharlal Nehru, India's first prime minister and political competitor to Bose.

Remembrance and respect done, the line of mourners snakes back to the Plassey memorial and their golden Siraj, the lead karateka waving a large Indian flag. A lady emcee had earlier led a chorus of Vande Mataram, 'I praise thee, O Mother,' a poem by Bengali literary legend Bankim Chandra Chattterjee long-transformed into patriotic overture, the first two stanzas officially India's 'national song'. She now wraps up proceedings: '...we will not allow Mir Madan, Mohanlal and Siraj's contribution to the Independence movement to ever fade...'

Then it's all over for another year.

ACKNOWLEDGEMENTS

This begins with David Davidar, publisher of Aleph Book Company, and Aienla Ozukum, publishing director. They have shepherded my travels with Aleph that began some years ago with a biography, *The Bengalis: A Portrait of a Community*, and led seamlessly to this work on Plassey. My work, fiction as well as non-fiction, is deeply rooted in history, but perhaps none more so than *The Bengalis*. For David, Aienla, and I, it was a short step from that work to total immersion in Plassey, an episode that greatly changed and defined the Bengalis, and a vast region in South Asia, besides indelibly changing Britain and, alas, strengthening the coda of colonialism.

History is my amor prima—first love—no matter the form it touches: pure history, historical fiction, cinema, documentary, theatre, poetry. For me it remained just ahead of literature through school, for which I credit my teacher in my senior years at Mayo College, Ajmer, Vijay Kumar Mathu. VKM, as we called him (there's a nickname too, but let that pass), brought history alive for us. I subsequently read history at St Stephen's College, University of Delhi. My professors, Upinder Singh, David Baker, Sumit Guha, P. S. Dwivedi, and Mohammad Amin helped to keep alive that interest in an arc from ancient to medieval to the modern histories of India, East Asia, and Europe. Their craft perhaps reflected more in my subsequent work than some of my grades. I have leaped at opportunities to write about and edit matters related to history during a three-decade career as a journalist and commentator. *Plassey*, then, is a sort of homecoming.

This book would not have been possible without Samuel Charles Hill (1857–1926), an indefatigable colonial civil servant and record keeper like many of his ilk, who with his outstanding *Bengal in 1756–1757* series and *Three Frenchmen in Bengal* presents a priceless collection of Plassey documentation, correspondence, information, and recollection. The Reverend James Long (1814–87), like Hill, provides another such repository with his *Unpublished Records* of Britain's Home and Foreign offices (Long observes that records in the

Bengal Office do not 'commence' until after 1770) and are primarily taken from twice-weekly 'Consultations of Government', despatches from Bengal to the Company's Court of Directors, the Court's letters to Bengal, and translations from the Persian of the President in Council's 'Country Correspondence' with 'Native powers'. The military historian and Company chronicler Robert Orme (1728–1801) knew Robert Clive in his pre-Plassey avatar, in Madras, and his magisterial *Military Transactions* completes this Plassey trinity, as it were. As we have seen, Orme's meticulous and sometimes racy accounts of battles match the best narratives of any war by twentieth and twenty-first century military historians.

The Indian Civil Service officer L. S. S. O'Malley (1874–1941) wrote an account of Murshidabad district as part of the 'Bengal District Gazetteers' series, in 1914. It was approached with typical administrative thoroughness that was the hallmark of officers who replaced John Company: intricate detail with occasional orientalist overlay. *Murshidabad* makes for fascinating reading.

Plassey hunters likewise benefit from the work of Ghulam Hussain Khan Tabatabayi, whose *Siyar-ul-Mutaqherin* remains an eighteenth-century pillar-work of Plassey, alongside the less voluminous *Riyazu-s-Salatin* of Ghulam Husain Salim. As a contemporary accompaniment there is *Muzaffarnama* by Karam Ali. These Persian works come to us in various translations. Although these are often spurned by Western historians and chroniclers except to cherry-pick theory-friendly aspects, mainly on account of their occasional flights of fancy, among a handful of subcontinental accounts of the Plassey period it's also difficult to ignore them. The three-volume *Siyar*, which translates as 'Review of Modern Times', richly details characters, politics and court intrigues. It is sometimes an impediment—where does fact end and fiction begin? What is reasonable and what is biased? —but to me, never unwelcome.

It is difficult to ignore the value of such works. It wasn't always easy for chroniclers and compilers to get to records. As Long writes of his pursuit:

> Scanty nature of the early Records is a great barrier; white ants, damp, the pilfering of ill-paid dufteries [daftaris, or clerks] and the borrowing without returning, have reduced the number

considerably... The great hurricane and inundation of 1737 must have destroyed many Records; but the capture of Calcutta in 1756 swept nearly all away; even the Account Books and Government Bonds in the hurry of flight were left behind, and the Court of Directors were, in consequence, for years in great difficulties how to balance their accounts.'

But Long does note that Siraj 'returned some of the later ones [records]'.

Among modern historians and chroniclers, I would like to offer my sincere thanks to several over and above acknowledgement in the bibliography and narrative—that also acknowledge the fine works of other historians and chroniclers. Irfan Habib and his 'A People's History of India' series firmly grounds matters made lofty. Piers Brendon's engaging *The Decline and Fall of the British Empire* provides dry wit alongside great insights. John Keay's formidable general histories on India and the English East India Company are excellent for overview—in particular *India* and *The Honourable Company*—as is Nitish Sengupta's *Land of Two Rivers*. Madhusree Mukerjee's path-breaking *Churchill's Secret War: The British Empire and the Ravaging of India During World War II* provides excellent insight into the Bengal famines.

There is my spirit-brother in Plassey, as it were, Stuart Reid, and his *The Battle of Plassey 1757: The Victory That Won an Empire* that was invaluable to compare technical details and trains of thought. Reid's compact military history arrived when I was already deep into researching this book, and beginning to write it. Like so many before us, he and I both source several pillar-works of Plassey, like those of Hill, Orme, and Long, and reference the eyewitness field journals of Eyre Coote and John Corneille about events near and at Plassey, and observations of the physician Edward Ives.

While some of Reid's and my citations and excerpts are similar—the reason is obvious: they best illustrate the mechanics of Plassey and the day of battle—my purpose for this book has always been to go beyond military aspects and nitty-gritty and provide a wider context, bring alive dramatis personae in the riveting theatre that Plassey also was. For that reason, I have accessed works beyond the immediate scope of military history, and beyond a few British and Western sources, which Reid limits himself to for the purpose of his work. It's understandable: there is a lamentable absence of contemporary Indian works of similar detail. Literature in Bengal hadn't yet moved beyond religious epic-poetry and hagiography; and historiography and an institutional appreciation of preserving records would, ironically, require the orientalist policy-push of the early nineteenth century! Our approach is also different: archival material is provided as appendices which form the bulk of Reid's book. In this work all archival material is woven into the narrative.

There are others I must acknowledge. Dr Carmen Brandt of the South Asia department at Bonn University who made several suggestions for simplifying Bengali in Roman script for this book. Maya Roy-Chakravarti, at the time an undergraduate student of liberal arts at Ashoka University, facilitated my research. Muhit Hassan Digonta, a young writer in Dhaka, took care to update me about Plassey-related publications in Bangladesh when he heard of my pursuit. Dr Antara Datta and Dr Saumya Gupta of the University of Delhi, and Dr Ravikant of Delhi's Centre for the Study of Developing Societies read an early draft of the book. Their encouragement and suggestions carry this work. Bena Sareen, Aleph's Creative Director, designed an excellent cover for Plassey. And Isha Banerji, Assistant Editor at Aleph, was the diligent force behind the photo insert.

Soma and Sankar Roy Chowdhury opened their Kolkata home to me, a place of comfortable transit during several research forays in the city, and between travels along the Hugli–Bhagirathi, literally Bengal's river sutra. Margaret Mascarenhas offered her quaint and lovely village home in Goa: my sanctuary to read, to write.

Muito obrigado. Dhōnnōbad. Thank you all so very much.

BIBLIOGRAPHY

BOOKS

Ahmad, Saiyid Amin, *The Black Hole of Calcutta*, Patna: The United Press Ltd, 1935.

Allah, Munshi Salim, *A Narrative of Transactions in Bengal during the Soobahdaries of Azeem us Shan, Jaffer Khan, Shuja Khan, Sirafraz Khan and Alyvyrdy Khan*, translated by Francis Gladwin, Calcutta: Stuart and Cooper, 1788.

Arbuthnot, Alexander John Sir, *Lord Clive: The Foundation of British Rule in India*, New York: Longmans, Green & Co., 1899.

Axon, Ernest, *The Family of Bayley of Manchester and Hope*, Manchester: Printed for the author, 1894.

Bandopadhyay, Sekhar, *From Plassey to Partition and After: A History of Modern India*, 2nd Edition, Kolkata: Orient BlackSwan, 2009, 2015.

Barbosa, Duarte, *The Book of Duarte Barbosa: An account of the Countries Bordering on the Indian Ocean and their Inhabitants, written by Duarte Barbosa, and Completed about the Year 1518 A.D., Vol. II*, translated by Mansel Longworth Dames, London: Hakluyt Society, 1921.

Baruah, Caroline Dutta and Jean Deloche, trans., *Adventures of Jean-Baptiste Chevalier in Eastern India: 1752-1765 (Les aventures de Jean-Baptiste Chevalier dans l'Inde orientale, 1752-1765)*, Guwahati: LBS Publications, 2008.

Biddāshāgōr, Isshorchondrō, *Bānglār Itihāsh, Ditiyō Khondō (*Iswar Chandra Vidyasagara, *The History of Bengal: From the Accession of Seerajooddowla to the Close of the Administration of Lord William Bentinck, Vol. 2)*, Calcutta: The Sanskrit Press, 1862.

Biswas, Oneil, *Calcutta and Calcuttans: From Dihi to Megalopolis*, Calcutta: Firma KLM Private Limited, 1992.

Bhattacharya, Sukumar, *The East India Company and the Economy of Bengal From 1704 to 1740* (Thesis approved for the degree of Doctor of Philosophy of the University of London, July 1953), London: Luzac & Company Ltd., 1954, Calcutta: Firma K. L. Mukhopadhyay, 1969 (repr).

Brendon, Piers, *The Decline and Fall of the British Empire 1781-1997*, London: Vintage Books, 2008.

Bryant, G. J., *The Emergence of British Power in India, 1600-1784: A Grand Strategic Interpretation*, Suffolk: Boydell & Brewer, 2013.

Busteed, Henry Elmsley, *Echoes from Old Calcutta: Being Chiefly Reminiscences of the Days of Warren Hastings, Francis and Impey*, Thacker, Calcutta: Spink & Co., 3rd edn, 1897, 4th edn, 1908.

Campbell Swinton, A. C. and J. L., *Concerning Swinton Family Records and Portraits at Kimmerghame*, Edinburgh: John Lindsay, 1908.

Carshore, Joseph James, *Bengal Chaplain's Vade-Mecum: Or A Collection of Extracts from Various Sources; Which Will Guide a Chaplain in the Performance of the Duties of His Office, and Also be of Use to Him in Other Respects*, Lahore: The Chronicle Press, 1857.

Chakravarti, Sudeep, *The Bengalis: A Portrait of a Community*, New Delhi: Aleph Book Company, 2017.

Chaudhuri, K. N., *The Trading World of Asia and the English East India Company: 1660-1760*, London and New York: Cambridge University Press, 1978.

Chaudhuri, Nirad C., *Clive of India: A Political and Psychological Essay*, London: Barrie & Jenkins, 1975.

Chaudhury, Sushil; Kéram Kévonian, eds., *Les Arméniens dans le commerce asiatique au début de l'ère moderne*, Paris: Éditions de la Maison des sciences de l'homme, 2007; New edition available at <http://books.openedition.org/editionsmsh/11283>.

Choudhury, Sushil, *Nobābi Āmōlé Murshidābād*, Kolkata: Ananda Publishers, 2004, 2015 (repr).

————, *Polāshir Ojānā Kāhini*, Kolkata: Ananda Publishers, 2004, 2016 (repr).

Datta, Kalikinkar, *Alivardi and his Times*, Calcutta: Calcutta University Press, 1939.

Farooqui, Amar, *The Establishment of British Rule (1757-1813): A People's History of India, No. 23*, New Delhi: Aligarh Historians Society and Tulika Books, 2014.

Firminger, Walter Kelly, ed., *Affairs of the East India Company (Being the Fifth Report from the Select Committee of the House of Commons 28th July 1812, Vol. 1)*, Calcutta: R. Cambray & Co., 1917 (repr).

Feldman, Gerald D. and Peter Hertner, eds., *Finance and Modernization: A Transnational and Transcontinental Perspective*, Farnham: Ashgate Publishing Limited, 2008.

Foster, William, *The English Factories in India 1618-1621: A Calendar of Documents in the India Office, British Museum and Public Record Office*, Published Under the Patronage of His Majesty's Secretary of State for India in Council, Oxford: The Clarendon Press, 1906.

Ghose, N. N., *Memoirs of Maharaja Nubkissen Bahadur*, Calcutta: K. B. Basu, 1901. (Courtesy: University of California)

Ghosh, Jamini Mohan, *Magh Raiders in Bengal*, Calcutta: Bookland Private Limited, 1960.

Goldsack, The Rev. William, *A Mussalmani Bengali-English Dictionary, 1923*, New Delhi: Gyan Publishing House, 2007 (republished).

Habib Irfan, *Indian Economy Under Early British Rule: A People's History of India No. 25*, 2nd edn, New Delhi: Aligarh Historians Society and Tulika Books, 2014.

Hamilton, Walter, *Geographical, Statistical, and Historical Description of Hindostan and the Adjacent Countries, Vol. 1*, London: John Murray, 1820.

Hill, S. C., *Bengal in 1756-1757 (Vols. I, II, III): A Selection of Public and Private Papers Dealing with the Affairs of the British in Bengal During the Reign of Siraj-uddaulah*, Indian Records Series, Published for the Government of India, London: John Murray, 1905.

————, *List of Europeans and Others in the English Factories in Bengal at the time of the Siege of Calcutta in the Year 1756, With an Appendix Containing Lists of European Sufferers*, Calcutta: Office of the Superintendent of Government Printing, India, 1902.

————, *Three Frenchmen in Bengal Or, The Commercial Ruin of the French Settlements in 1757*, London: Longmans, Green, and Company, 1903.

Holwell, J. Z., *Interesting Historical Events Relative to the Provinces of Bengal, and the Empire of Indostan, With a Seasonable Hint and Perswasive to the Honourable The Court of Directors of the East India Company, as also the Mythology and Cosmogony, Fasts and Festivals of the Gentoos, Followers of the Shastah, and a Dissertation on the Metempsychosis, commonly, though erroneously, called the Pythagoeran Doctrine, Vol. 1*, 2nd edn, London: T. Becket and P.A. De Hondt, 1766; Vol. 2, 1765.

Hunter, W. W., *Famine Aspects of Bengal Districts*, London: Trübner & Co., 1874.

————, *The Annals of Rural Bengal*, 2nd edn, New York: Leypoldt and Holt, 1868.

Huq, Muhammad Lutful, *Bāngāli Poltōn*, Dhaka: Prōthōma Prōkāshon, 2012.

Hussain, Iqbal, 'Hindu Shrines and Practices as Described by a Central Asian Traveller in the First Half of the Seventeenth Century,' in *Medieval India 1: Researches in the History of India 1200-1750*, edited by Irfan Habib, Centre of Advanced Study in History: Aligarh Muslim University, 1992 and New Delhi: Oxford University Press, 1999.

Keay, John, *India: A History: From the Earliest Civilisations to the Boom of the Twenty-first Century*, London: HarperPress, 2010.

————, *The Honourable Company: A History of The English East India Company*, London: HarperCollins Publishers, 1991, 1993 (repr).

Khan, Syed Ghulam Hussain (also Sayyid Ghulam Hussain Tabatabayi and Seid Gholam Hossein), *The Sëir Mutaqherin* (Also *Siyar ul Mutaqherin*), *Or Review Of Modern Times: Being An History of India, from the year 1118, to the year 1194, of the Hedjrah. Containing, in General, the Reigns of the Seven Last Emperors of Hindostan, and, in Particular, An Account of the English Wars in Bengal; With A Circumstantial Detail of the Rise and Fall of the Families of Seradj-Ed-Dowlah and Shudjah-Ed-Dowlah, the Last Sovereigns of Bengal and Owd. to Which the Author Has Added a Critical Examination of the English Government and Policy in those Countries, as Far Down as the Year 1783, Vol. I – IV*, translated by Haji Mustapha (or Nota-manus), Calcutta: R. Cambray & Co., (Reprinted by T. D. Chatterjee) Calcutta: Valmiki Press, 1902.

Krishna, Bal, *Commercial Relations Between India and England (1601 to 1757)*, London: George Routledge & Sons Ltd, 1924.

Long, Rev. James, *Unpublished Records of Government For the Years 1748 to 1767 Inclusive, Relating Mainly to the Social Condition of Bengal With a Map of Calcutta in 1784, 1867*, edited by Mahadevaprasad Saha, with Foreword, Notes and a Bio-Bibliographical Sketch of J. Long, Firma K.L. Mukhopadhyay, Kolkata, 1973). Also *Unpublished Records of Government For the Years 1748 to 1767 Inclusive, Relating Mainly to the Social Condition of Bengal With a Map of Calcutta in 1784, Vol. 1*, Calcutta: Office of the Superintendent of Government Printing, 1869.

Little, J. H., *The House of Jagat Seth* (With an Introduction by Mukhopadhyay, Subodh Kumar), Kolkata: K. P. Bagchi & Company, 2016 (first published in *Bengal Past and Present*, 1920–21).

Majumdar, Purna Chandra, *The Musnud of Murshidabad (1704–1904): Being a Synopsis of the History of Murshidabad for the Last Two Centuries to Which are Appended Notes of Places and Objects of Interest at Murshidabad*, Omraoganj, Murshidabad: Saroda Ray, 1905.

Malleson, Colonel G. B., *The Decisive Battles of India From 1746 to 1849 Inclusive*, 4th edn, London: Reeves and Turner, 1914.

Manucci, Niccolao, *Storia do Mogor (or Mogul India, 1653-1708)*, translated by William Irvine, *The Indian Texts Series-I*, edited under the supervision of the Royal Asiatic Society, London: John Murray, (for the Government of India), 1907.

Mason, Philip, *The Men Who Ruled India*, Indian subcontinent edn, New Delhi: Rupa Publications, 2016.

Maulik, Debabrata, *Mughal's Murshidabad Connection: A Socio-political Insight*, Chennai: Notion Press, 2017.

McLane, John R., *Land and Local Kingship in Eighteenth-Century Bengal*, Cambridge South Asian Series 55, Cambridge: Cambridge University Press, 2002 (repr).

Mehrotra, Arvind Krishna, ed., *The Last Bungalow: Writings on Allahabad*, New Delhi: Penguin Books, 2006.

Mõitréyõ, Okkhoykumār (Maitreya, Akshaykumar), *Meer Kāshim*, 1906, Kolkata:

Puthipatra, 2004, 2013 (republished).

———, *Shirājuddōulāh*, 1897, Kolkata: Dey's Publishing, 2015 (republished).

Moxham, Roy, *The Theft of India: The European Conquests of India 1498-1765*, Noida: HarperCollins Publishers, 2016.

Mukerjee, Madhusree, *Churchill's Secret War: The British Empire and the Ravaging of India During World War II*, New York: Basic Books, 2010.

Mukhopadhyay, Subhas Chandra, *British Residents at the Darbar of Bengal Nawabs At Murshidabad (1757-1772)*, Delhi: Gian Publishing House, 1988.

Nandy, Somendra Chandra, *Bondōr Kāshimbājār*, Kolkata: Bōngiyō Nāttōshongshod Prōkashōni, 1978.

———, *Life and Times of Cantoo Baboo (Krisna Kanta Nandy), The Banian of Warren Hastings, Vol. 1: The Early Career of Cantoo Baboo (1742-1772) and His Trade in Salt and Silk*, Calcutta: Allied Publishers Private Limited, 1978.

Neill, Stephen, *A History of Christianity in India 1707-1858*, Delhi: Cambridge University Press, 2002.

O'Malley, Lewis Sydney Stewart, *Bengal District Gazetteers: Murshidabad*, Calcutta: The Bengal Secretariat Book Depot, 1914.

———, *Bengal District Gazetteers: Santal Parganas*, Calcutta: The Bengal Secretariat Book Depot, 1910.

Orme, Robert, *A History of the Military Transactions of the British Nation in Indostan, From the Year MDCCXLV to Which is Prefixed a Dissertation on the Establishments Made by Mahomedan Conquerors in Indostan, Vol. 1*, 4th edn, F. Wingrave, London, 1763; Reprinted by Pharoah and Co., Madras, 1861; *Vol. 2 Section The First* (new edn), F. Wingrave, 1803; *Vol. 2 Section The Second* (new edn), F. Wingrave, 1803.

Ray, Nikhilnath, *Murshidābād Kāhini* [*The Story of Murshidabad*], 1897, Calcutta: Calcutta University, 1950 (republished as an abridged edition); Kolkata: Puthipatra, 1999, 2017 (republished unabridged).

Reid, Stuart, *The Battle of Plassey 1757: The Victory That Won an Empire*, Yorkshire: Frontline Books, 2017.

Rennel, James, *Memoir of a Map of Hindoostan; or the Mogul Empire: With an Introduction, Illustrative of the Geography and Present Division of that Country: And a Map of the Countries Situated Between the Head of the Indus, and the Caspian Sea*, London: George Nicol and W. Richardson, 1788.

Roberts, Emma, *Scenes and Characteristics of Hindostan, with Sketches of Anglo-Indian Society Vol. 1*, London: W. H. Allen And Co., 1835; 2nd edn, 1837.

Russell, Bertrand, *Freedom and Organisation 1814-1914*, London: George Allen & Unwin Ltd, 1934; in Brendon, Piers, *The Decline and Fall of the British Empire 1781-1997*, London: Vintage Books, 2008.

Rutherford, Alex, *Fortune's Soldier*, Gurugram: Hachette India, 2018.

Salim, Ghulam Husain, *Riyazu-s-Salatin, A History of Bengal*, Trans. Salam, Maulavi Abdus, Fasc. I-IV, Calcutta: The Asiatic Society, 1902–04.

Sarkar, Jadunath, ed., *The History of Bengal, Volume II: Muslim Period*, Dhaka: The University of Dacca, 1943.

Sen, Sailendra Nath, *Chandernagore: From Bondage to Freedom 1900-1955*, Delhi: Primus Books, 2012.

Sengupta, Nitish, *Land of Two Rivers: A History of Bengal from the Mahabharata to Mujib,* Gurugram: Penguin Books, 2011.

Smedly, Edward, The Rev., Rose, Hugh James, The Rev., Rose, Henry John, The Rev, eds.,

Encyclopædia Metropolitana, Or, Universal Dictionary of Knowledge on an Original Plan: Comprising the Twofold Advantage of a Philosophical and an Alphabetical Arrangement, With Appropriate Engravings, Volume XV, B. Fellowes, F. and J. Rivington, et al, London: Oxford, Cambridge, 1845.

Stewart, Charles, *The History of Bengal from the First Mohammedan Invasion Until the Virtual Conquest of that Country by the English A.D. 1757*, London: Black, Parry and Co., 1813.

Timberg, Thomas A, *The Marwaris: From Jagat Seth to the Birlas*, Gurugram: Penguin Global, 2014.

The Imperial Gazetteer of India Vol. XVIII, Moram to Nayāgarh, (new edn), Published Under the Authority of His Majesty's Secretary of State for India in Council, Oxford: The Clarendon Press, 1908.

Van Schendel, Willem, *A History of Bangladesh*, Cambridge: Cambridge University Press, 2009.

Wilson, C. R., *The Early Annals of the English in Bengal, Being the Bengal Public Consultations for the First Half of the Eighteenth Century*, Vol. 1, London: W. Thacker & Co. and Calcutta: Thacker, Spink & Co., 1895; Vol. 2, W. Thacker & Co., and Thacker, Spink & Co., 1900; Vol. 3 (Prepared for publication by Firminger, Walter Kelly, Archdeacon of Calcutta), Thacker Spink & Co., 1917.

——— (ed.), *Old Fort William in Bengal*, Vol. 1, Published for the Government of India, London: John Murray, 1906.

Wilson, Jon, *India Conquered: Britain's Raj and the Chaos of Empire*, London: Simon & Schuster, 2016.

Wylly, Col. H. C., *A Life of Lieutenant-General Sir Eyre Coote, K. B.*, Oxford: The Clarendon Press, 1922.

Yule, Col. Henry, Burnell, A. C., *Hobson-Jobson: A Glossary of Colloquial Anglo-Indian Words and Phrases, and of Kindred Terms, Etymological, Historical, Geographical and Discursive*, new edn, edited by William Crooke, London: John Murray, 1903.

Zaidi, A. M., *From Syed to the Emergence of Jinnah, Evolution of Muslim Political Thought in India, Vol. 1.*, New Delhi, 1975 <at http://dspace.wbpublibnet.gov.in>.

Zakariah, Abul Kalam Muhammad, *Nobāb Shirāj-ud-Daulā*, Dhaka: Prōthōma Prōkāshon, 2015.

ARTICLES, ESSAYS & OTHER SOURCES

Banerjee, Ruben, 'Descendant of Mir Jafar fights to erase stamp of treachery from family name,' *India Today*, 31 January 1994.

Barry, J. Grene, 'Plassey.' *The Journal of the Royal Society of Antiquaries of Ireland*, Vol. 4, No. 2, 1914.

Beveridge, Henry, 'Old Place in Murshidabad,' *Calcutta Review*, April 1892.

———, 'Warren Hastings in Lower Bengal,' *Calcutta Review*, Vol. LXV, 1877.

Bordeaux, Joel, 'The Mythic King: Raja Krishnacandra and Early Modern Bengal,' Submitted in partial fulfillment of the Requirements for the degree of Doctor of Philosophy in the Graduate School of Arts and Sciences, Columbia University, 2015.

'Burdwan (Zamindari)', <http://members.iinet.net.au/~royalty/ips/b/burdwan.html>, at World of Royalty.

Chatterjee, Kumkum, 'Goddess encounters: Mughals, Monsters and the Goddess in

Bengal,' *Modern Asian Studies*, Vol. 47, No. 5, September 2013.

Chaudhuri, Rosinka, 'History in Poetry: Nabinchandra Sen's "Palashir Yuddha" and the Question of Truth,' *The Journal of Asian Studies*, Vol. 66, No. 4, pp. 897-918, Association for Asian Studies, November 2007.

Chaudhuri, Susil, 'Saltpetre Trade and Industry in Bengal Subah, 1650-1720,' *Proceedings of the Indian History Congress*, Vol. 34, Indian History Congress, 1973.

Crawford, D. G., 'William Hamilton and the Embassy to Delhi,' *The Indian Medical Gazette*, Calcutta, January 1907.

Dalrymple, William, 'The East India Company: The original corporate raiders,' *The Guardian*, 4 March 2015.

Dé Prōdeep, (dir.) *Nobāb Shirājuddoulā*, (movie), Joy Films, 1989.

Dugar, Prodip Chand, 'Marwaris,' Banglapedia <http://en.banglapedia.org/index.php?title=Marwaris>.

'Duncan McLeod,' Grace's Guide to British Industrial History, <at gracesguide.co.uk> 25 November 2016.

Guha, Ranajit, 'A Conquest Foretold,' *Social Text*, No. 54, 1998, pp. 85–99.

Hill, S. C., 'The Old Sepoy Officer,' in *The English Historical Review*, Vol. 28, No. 110, pp. 260–91, Oxford University Press, April, 1913.

Islam, Riazul, '*Murshid Qulī Khān and His Times* by Abdul Karim; *Alivardi and His Times* by K. K. Datta,' *The Journal of the Royal Asiatic Society of Great Britain and Ireland*, No. 3/4, 1965.

'Job Charnock not Kolkata's founder: Expert committee,' PTI, 31 January 2003.

'Lord Clive Fund,' National Archives, United Kingdom, available at <discovery.nationalarcives.gov.uk>.

Macaulay, Thomas Babington, 'Lord Clive,' *Critical and Historical Essays contributed to the Edinburgh Review*, 5th edn, 3 vols., London: Longman, Brown, Green, and Longmans, Vol. 3, 1948, available at <http://oll.libertyfund.org/title/365 >.

———, 'Minute by the Hon'ble T. B. Macaulay, 2 February 1835', *Bureau of Education. Selections from Educational Records, Part I (1781-1839)*, Calcutta: Sharp, H. Ed. Superintendent, Government Printing, 1920 (repr); Delhi: National Archives of India, 1965, pp. 107–17.

Mahmud, Jamil, 'The Women in Siraj ud-Daulah's Life,' *The Daily Star*, 4 October 2012.

Makepeace, Margaret, 'Robert Clive arrives in India,' *blogs.bl.uk*, 31 May 2016.

Ranson, Jonathan, 'Instructions for Sailing Round the Reef at Point Palmiras, into Balasore Road and Over the Bar, *Oriental Navigator*, 1794, Mystic Seaport Museum <research.mysticseaport.org/item/l022689/l022689-c093/> (and the Andrew W. Mellon Foundation).

Ray, Balai, 'Evolution of the High Court at Calcutta and some Reminiscences', *The High Court at Calcutta Sesquicentennial Souvenir*, 2013. <www.calcuttahighcourt.nic.in>.

Ray, R. K. 'Colonial Penetration and the Initial Resistance: The Mughal Ruling Class, the English East India Company and the Struggle for Bengal 1756-1800,' *Indian Historical Review XII*, 1986 (in Brendon, Piers, *The Decline and Fall of the British Empire 1781-1997*, Vintage Books, London, 2008).

'Robert Clive and Mir Jafar after the Battle of Plassey,' (Painting by Francis Hayman, c. 1760), National Portrait Gallery, London.

Sengupta, Sachin, *Shirājuddoulā: Nāttō Utshob* [play], Saregama Ltd and Sony DADC, 2012.

Sharma, Dishya, 'Pune recalls Shivaji cutting off Shaista Khan's fingers.' *The Indian Express*

(Pune edition), 19 April 2013.

'The Battle of Plassey,' The Keep Military Museum, Home of the Regiments of Devon and Dorset <keepmilitarymuseum.org>.

Whitehead, R. B. 'Mīr Ja'far's Plassey Medal,' *The Numismatic Chronicle and Journal of the Royal Numismatic Society*, Vol. 15, No. 58, 1935.

RESOURCES

Archaeological Survey of India, Kolkata Circle

Banglapedia (*en.banglapedia.org*)

books.google.co.in

British Library (& *bl.uk*)

columbia.edu

Digital Library of India (*dli.ernet.in*)

Encyclopaedia Britannica (& *britannica.com*)

Google Earth (*google.com/earth*)

Jewish Virtual Library (*jewishvirtuallibrary.org/calcutta*)

journals.cambridge.org

JSTOR (*jstor.org*)

National Army Museum, London (*collection.nam.ac.uk*)

National Library of India, Kolkata

Project Gutenberg (*gutenberg.org*)

rijksmuseum.nl/en

The Asiatic Society, Kolkata

satsig.net

smithsonian.com

West Bengal Public Library Network (*wbpublibnet.gov.in*) and its Digital Archive of Rare Books (*http://dspace.wbpublibnet.gov.in:8080/jspui/*)

INDEX

England Trading to the East Indies, 17